# Attacks on the Press in 2011

*A Worldwide Survey by the Committee to Protect Journalists*

Committee to Protect Journalists
330 Seventh Avenue, 11th Fl.
New York, NY 10001

Twitter: @pressfreedom
Facebook: @committeetoprotectjournalists

(212) 465-1004
www.cpj.org
info@cpj.org

Founded in 1981, the Committee to Protect Journalists responds to attacks on the press worldwide. CPJ documents hundreds of cases every year and takes action on behalf of journalists and news organizations without regard to political ideology. To maintain its independence, CPJ accepts no government funding. CPJ is funded entirely by private contributions from individuals, foundations, and corporations.

Thomson Reuters, Agence France-Presse, and The Associated Press provided news and photo services for *Attacks on the Press in 2011.*

Editorial Director: Bill Sweeney
Senior Editor: Elana Beiser
Deputy Editors: Kamal Singh Masuta, Shazdeh Omari
Designer: John Emerson
Chief Copy Editor: Lew Serviss
Copy Editor: Lisa Flam
Proofreader: Naomi Serviss

COVER PHOTO:
Journalists run for cover during a bombing raid in Ras Lanuf, Libya. (Reuters/Paul Conroy)

*Attacks on the Press in 2011:*
*A Worldwide Survey by the Committee to Protect Journalists*

ISBN: 978-0-944823-31-6

# Board of Directors

# Attacks on the Press in 2011

## Asia

## Europe and Central Asia

## Middle East and North Africa

## Journalists Killed

## Journalists in Prison

# Preface

*By Sandra Mims Rowe*

Blogger Rami Nakhle leaned across the table toward a cluster of U.S. technology leaders. "People are tortured to death because their Facebook account is hacked. You can make a difference between life and death," he told the Silicon Valley executives and computer engineers representing Facebook, Google, and other companies.

Nakhle explained how he and his friends had been using the companies' software to smuggle video footage and news out of Syria to reporters across the world. Then he described the security bugs that enabled the authorities to track and torture them.

This was one of many dramatic moments during a September conference CPJ convened in San Francisco to connect the technology community with the journalists who risk their lives to report from some of the most restricted countries in the world. These journalists find themselves empowered by the digital explosion at the same time they are endangered by technological changes, both designed and unintended, that expose them to repressive forces.

"They are brave enough," Nakhle said of the journalists. "They know why they are taking these risks. With a small investment in their security, you can save many lives," he told the group.

Technology has democratized news publishing, and it has rattled regimes that equate survival with control of all aspects of society, especially the flow of information. Video footage of repression from Burma to Syria to Egypt dramatically illustrates the benefits of Internet platforms and social media. Only a few years ago, much of this footage could not have been recorded easily and would never have been allowed out of a restricted country. Yet the Arab uprisings of 2011 also demonstrate the urgent need for providers and users of digital tools to fully understand the dangers of deploying them in repressive nations.

As the threats to online journalists grow in scope and frequency, they also underscore CPJ's mandate to be a truly global organization. More journalists need CPJ's help than ever before. Because many of these online journalists are freelancers or work for small, local news outlets, they do not have the resources of large institutions behind them. They often lack the experience and training they need to minimize risk. Today, about half of the journalists imprisoned worldwide work primarily online.

Authoritarian states can, and do, buy communications surveillance and filtering equipment from Western manufacturers. While such equipment may have been intended for law enforcement to combat terrorism or organized crime, its uses have spread well beyond that. In much of the world, the enemies of free speech are monitoring journalists and bloggers, filtering online content, and attacking news websites.

During the popular uprising in Syria, authorities dragooned Internet experts into working for the regime. The government-aligned hacking group known as the Syrian Electronic Army targeted critical press outlets and sought to undermine online reporting deemed harmful to authorities. Supplementing the old-fashioned beatings used to secure the names of colleagues and sources from journalists, the digital "army" has employed the phishing of Facebook pages to dupe people into providing passwords and identities.

*From a crane high above a protest, journalists film crowds in the Yemeni city of Taiz. (Reuters/Khaled Abdullah)*

In November, just days after CPJ awarded its International Press Freedom Award to the founder of the Mexican weekly *Ríodoce*, Javier Valdez Cárdenas, the publication's website was forced offline by a denial-of-service attack. *Ríodoce* is one of the few publications in the region to report on drug trafficking. Even clearer was the message sent by the murderers of Mexican journalist María Elisabeth Macías Castro, whose mutilated body was accompanied by a computer keyboard and a cardboard placard stating her online pseudonym and threatening others who use social media to report the news. Macías' murder in September was the first case documented by CPJ worldwide in which a journalist was killed in direct relation to reporting done on social media.

CPJ is recruiting the people and acquiring the knowledge to defend online journalists. In 2010, CPJ hired Danny O'Brien as its first Internet advocacy coordinator. O'Brien, based in San Francisco, organized the September meeting between journalists and Silicon Valley technologists. The conference was the first in what will become many efforts by CPJ to act as a bridge between Silicon Valley and the journalists who depend on their products—not only to get the news out, but also to protect them and their sources from physical harm.

While the Internet has provided the equivalent of a printing press to millions of people across the world, it has also broadened the power to shutter those presses. Technology is allowing journalists to slip the chains of censorship, but that newfound freedom will be fleeting if not defended. CPJ is leading the way.

*Sandra Mims Rowe is chairman of the Committee to Protect Journalists.*

Global Issues

# Global Issues

PHOTO CREDITS

*Section break: A Libyan rebel shouts at a cameraman during the battle for Tripoli in August. (AFP/Patrick Baz)*

*Page 5: Police in Santiago seize a photographer during an anti-government demonstration. (Reuters/Carlos Vera)*

*Pages 11, 13, 15, & 17: CPJ awardees Umar Cheema, Mansoor al-Jamri, Javier Arturo Valdez Cárdenas, and Natalya Radina. (Photos by Jonathan Stephanoff, Reuters, and Roberto Benal)*

*Page 21: Thai website editor Chiranuch Premchaiporn faces criminal charges. (AFP/ Pornchai Kittiwongsakul)*

*Page 27: CBS correspondent Lara Logan moments before she was assaulted in Tahrir Square. (Reuters/CBS)*

*Page 33: Former Ukrainian President Leonid Kuchma arrives at the prosecutor's office after being charged in the murder of journalist Georgy Gongadze. (Reuters/Gleb Garanich)*

*Page 41: At a demonstration in Kabul, a photo of the slain Afghan journalist Ajmal Naqshbandi. (AP/Musadeq Sadeq)*

*Page 47: A journalist crouches behind a cement block during clashes between Israeli forces and Palestinian protesters in the West Bank. (Reuters/Mohamad Torokman)*

# The Next Information Revolution: Abolishing Censorship

## By Joel Simon

The most important battles of the Arab Spring were fought on the streets, but there was also a fierce battle over control of information. In Egypt, the government unplugged the Internet, shut down satellite channels, and orchestrated attacks on foreign correspondents. None of it worked. Protesters were able to keep channels of communication open to win sympathy and support for their cause, highlight the Egyptian government's record of abuse and corruption, and ensure there would be witnesses to any violence against them. The global visibility of the protests raised the cost of government repression to the point where it became unsustainable.

That new information platforms such as Twitter and Facebook helped journalists and other citizens break Hosni Mubarak's information blockade has been the source of legitimate excitement. But despite the triumphs of the Arab Spring, censorship is alive and well. In fact, some of the biggest stories of 2011 might have gone uncovered or under-covered because of effective censorship. These include rural unrest in China; the power struggle in Iran; the relationship between militants, Al-Qaeda, and the Pakistani intelligence service; political instability in Ethiopia; and the bloody battles between rival drug cartels in Mexico.

Journalists who sought to cover these and other stories faced violence and repression. In Pakistan, investigative reporter Saleem Shahzad was abducted and murdered in May after he exposed links between the country's intelligence services and Al-Qaeda. In Nuevo Laredo, Mexico, drug traffickers kidnapped, murdered, and decapitated journalist María Elizabeth Macías Castro after she tried to use social media as an end-run around their violence-imposed censorship. In Addis Ababa, Ethiopia, several journalists, including two Swedes, were jailed on terrorism charges in retaliation for their coverage of separatist and opposition groups.

Indeed, the lesson repressive governments and other enemies of press freedom may have taken from the Arab Spring is that maintaining a viable censorship regime is even more urgent in the Information Age. After all, once control of information slips from their hands, it is difficult to retain power. The Syrian government's ability to control domestic media and keep international reporters out of the country gave it a huge advantage in quelling protests. Social media networks made it impossible to fully suppress information, but what emerged from Syria was fragmented and did not penetrate the global consciousness to the same degree as what emanated from Egypt.

Thus the battle against censorship goes on. Technology is a fundamental tool in the struggle, but new and innovative political strategies must also be employed. While repressive governments have long sought to control critical information, the cost of censorship is much higher today because of the globalized nature of our existence. In China, for example, when authorities suppress information about food safety, they are not censoring news solely within their national borders. Because China exports so many manufactured foods, its leaders are effectively censoring news of interest and concern to people throughout the world.

## The cost of censorship is higher now because of our globalized existence.

Even as trade and new systems of communication turn us into global citizens, the information we need to ensure accountability often stops at national borders. Without adequate information, global citizens are essentially disempowered. "Whenever there is censorship anywhere, there is censorship everywhere," Columbia University President Lee C. Bollinger noted at a March 2011 event marking CPJ's 30th anniversary.

In a functioning democracy, few restraints are placed on the press because an informed public debate is needed to ensure accountability. Conversely, every totalitarian system is based on control and manipulation of information, which allows leaders to govern without oversight. Globally, the current situation more closely resembles a totalitarian society without a legal framework to ensure that information circulates freely across borders.

Journalists and other front-line news-gatherers operate in a legal void. While the right of people everywhere to "seek and receive information through any media and regardless of frontiers" is enshrined in Article 19 of the Universal Declaration of Human Rights and other international legal instruments, the reality is that there are few effective legal mechanisms to fight censorship on an international level.

What can be done to combat censorship in the Information Age? The key is to mobilize the many constituencies that have a stake in ensuring the free flow of information—civil society and advocacy groups, businesses, governments, and inter-governmental organizations—and build a global coalition against censorship.

While the ability to seek and receive information is an individual human right, there is a collective interest in ensuring that information flows freely. After all, an attack on an Egyptian, Pakistani, or Mexican journalist inhibits the ability of people around the world to receive the information that journalist would have provided. Advocacy groups with a global agenda, notably human rights and environmental organizations, have a powerful interest in promoting global press freedom even if it is not part of their explicit mandates. For example, combating global warming will depend in large measure on China's policies, which, because of official censorship, are often shrouded in secrecy. Human rights organizations such as Human Rights Watch, meanwhile, are hiring former journalists to provide real-time reporting from the front lines.

"We recognize the skills that journalists bring to human rights documentation—a knowledge of issues, countries, and institutions; the ability to gather information quickly; and a sense of how to tell the story," said Iain Levine, program director of Human Rights Watch. Human rights researchers are, in fact, filling a gap left by international media organizations that have cut back on foreign staff.

For many reasons, the global business community has a clear stake in

ensuring that information flows freely. With operations and supply chains spread throughout the world, navigating political unrest, environmental disaster, and other disruptions is crucial—and it cannot be done effectively when key information is censored. Financial services companies that manage global portfolios operate with the same considerations.

.................................................

*In an information economy, censorship constitutes a restraint on trade.*

.................................................

More broadly, in an information economy, it could be argued that censorship itself is a restraint on trade. For example, China's insistence that Google censor its search results undermined the company's business model. And Isaac Mao, a Chinese entrepreneur and blogger, notes that Chinese online censorship may be starting to disrupt the global Internet.

"China set up the Great Firewall at the gateway to the world to block people's free access to overseas websites," Mao said. But recent research has uncovered a global impact, including instances in which Internet users from Chile to California were routed through servers inside China—and were thus caught in the country's censorship web. "People living in New York City who try to study Chinese would hit the wall when websites include some 'sensitive words,'" Mao explained.

A paper published by Google on its public policy blog in late 2010 called on the international community to "take action to ensure the free flow of information online" and noted that "direct government blockage of an Internet service is tantamount to a customs official stopping all goods from a particular country at the border."

Trade experts say it would be extremely difficult to incorporate anti-censorship requirements into existing trade agreements. But some connections are being drawn already. In October 2011, the U.S. ambassador to the World Trade Organization wrote to his Chinese counterpart requesting information about China's Internet policies and noting that "some companies based outside of China have faced challenges offering their services to Chinese customers when their websites are blocked by China's national firewall." In response, the Chinese expressed willingness to engage in dialogue with companies but pointedly noted: "We oppose using Internet freedom as an excuse to interfere in other countries' internal affairs."

The Chinese reaction points to a significant challenge: the international perception that Internet freedom is a Trojan horse used by the United States to undermine political adversaries. In January 2010, U.S. Secretary of State Hillary Rodham Clinton spoke at the Newseum in Washington and laid out a U.S. government policy to promote Internet freedom around the world. "We stand for a single Internet where all of humanity has equal access to knowledge and ideas," Clinton said.

The speech—and the policy—were well-received by defenders of human rights and freedom of expression. But as Evgeny Morozov argued in his recent book, *The Net Delusion: The Dark Side of Internet Freedom*, Clinton's speech reinforced the notion in the minds of many global leaders that Internet freedom is nothing more than an instrument of U.S. foreign policy.

*A perception that online freedom is an instrument of U.S. foreign policy.*

In an era in which U.S. motivations are widely mistrusted, Pakistani journalist Najam Sethi noted, a multilateral approach to press freedom is more likely to have a positive impact. After the murder of Saleem Shahzad, for example, U.S. Adm. Mike Mullen, the recently retired chairman of the Joint Chiefs of Staff, told journalists in Washington that the Pakistani government had "sanctioned the killing."

"In normal times, it would have been a good thing," Sethi said of the U.S. condemnation. "But because it touched on the national security situation in Pakistan, it confused people and played into the nationalist narrative. There is confusion in the minds of people in Pakistan every time the U.S. tries to help."

What is needed therefore is a broad global coalition against censorship that brings together governments, the business community, civil society organizations, and the media. These powerful constituencies must unite in support of freedom of information, pressing international organizations, including intergovernmental groups such as the Organization of American States and the Council of Europe, as well as the United Nations, to create a legal framework to ensure that press freedom and freedom of information are respected in practice. Human rights and press freedom organizations should look for opportunities to adjudicate press freedom cases at the international level in order to build a body of global precedent.

In fact, Article 13 of the Inter-American Convention on Human Rights explicitly prohibits prior censorship, a ban reaffirmed in a 2001 decision by the Costa Rica–based Inter-American Court, which ruled that Chile had violated the convention by banning the Martin Scorsese film, "The Last Temptation of Christ."

Catalina Botero, the OAS special rapporteur for freedom of expression, argues that threats and violent attacks by individuals constitute a form of "indirect censorship" and therefore also violate Article 13. She acknowledged, however, that it's more difficult to make that argument in a global context. "The explicit prohibition on censorship in Article 13 does not exist in the European Convention of Human Rights or the Universal Declaration of Human Rights," Botero said.

On a political front, the leaders of international organizations must become outspoken advocates for freedom of expression, seeking to isolate and pressure the countries that actively inhibit the flow of information across borders. The role of special rapporteurs within the international system needs to be strengthened as well. Frank LaRue, the U.N. special rapporteur for freedom of expression and opinion, released a report in June that called online access a fundamental right that governments should restrict only in the most limited of circumstances. But the secretary-general and other U.N. leaders, while broadly supporting Internet freedom in their public comments, have not embraced LaRue's findings or advocated for their implementation.

## Building a global coalition of government, business, civil society, and media.

The Internet and new information technologies have made the process of gathering and disseminating news highly diffuse. This new system has some widely recognized advantages. It democratizes the information-gathering process, allowing participation by more people with differing perspectives. It opens the media not only to "citizen journalists" but also to advocacy and civil society organizations. The sheer volume of people participating in this process challenges authoritarian models of censorship based on hierarchies of control.

Andy Carvin, the self-described "social media guy" at NPR who used Twitter to report on the Arab uprisings, notes that "bloggers and citizen journalists" are now part of the media mix in the Arab world. Syrian authorities, while able to keep the mainstream media out of the country, were not able to completely suppress the news as a result.

"If their goal has been to prevent the outside world from knowing what's going on, I don't think Syria has been very successful," Carvin said. "While they often throttle Internet access so we lose contact for a while, eventually it's restored."

But there are also considerable weaknesses in this new system. Free-lancers, bloggers, and citizen journalists like those reporting on Syria work with few resources and little or no institutional support. They are far more vulnerable to government repression. New technologies cut both ways, and autocratic governments are increasingly developing systems to monitor and control online speech that are both effective and hard to detect.

....................................................

*A fundamental principle: Censorship anywhere affects people everywhere.*

....................................................

Just as global citizens have a stake in ensuring that information flows freely, powerful forces—criminal organizations, militant groups, repressive governments—have enormous interest in controlling the news. Censorship within national borders disrupts the flow of information around the world. A global coalition against censorship needs to unite behind a simple idea: Censorship anywhere affects people everywhere. It can and should be abolished.

*Joel Simon is executive director of the Committee to Protect Journalists. He led a CPJ mission to Pakistan in 2011.*

# The Calculus of Risk: Awardees Work Despite Perils

*By Kristin Jones*

Natalya Radina had been in a Minsk jail for several weeks when the guards escorted her from her cell and offered her a deal. She had been sleeping on the bare wood floor of a room without a toilet, alone and without any contact with the outside world. For the first week, her head hurt from a beating administered during her arrest. Blood seeped from her ears.

The jail was run by the Belarusian security service, known as the KGB, and Radina was accused of organizing mass disorder through *Charter 97*, a pro-opposition news website she edited. She faced five years in prison, the guards told her. They made oblique threats to her "health as a woman."

Then they offered her a way out. Tell us about Andrei Sannikov, they said.

It was January 2011. In the past month, hundreds of people had landed in detention facilities like this one. They were protesters who called foul on a December 2010 election that gave authoritarian leader Aleksandr Lukashenko 80 percent of the vote. They were journalists like Radina, whose website provided one of the few sources of independent information in the country. And they were opposition candidates like Sannikov, who had campaigned against the president and was a co-founder of *Charter 97.*

The offer, and what led up to it, was surely intended to break Radina, to extract from her what was needed. It did the opposite. "It was a very difficult decision," Radina said. "But I realized I cannot live with the thought that I am a traitor. I just made the decision that I'm not going to betray my friends, and I'm not going to betray my supporters."

"I felt more peaceful about the realization that I could stay in jail for five years," she said. "I realized I was stronger than" the jailers.

Radina was one of four journalists worldwide who were honored with CPJ's International Press Freedom Award in 2011. The three others are from Mexico, Bahrain, and Pakistan, and their experiences as journalists in far-flung corners of the globe are varied. But they share this: When men came to destroy the printing press, throw grenades at the office, or abduct, torture, interrogate, or threaten them, they resisted. They kept doing what they do.

*Why do they keep reporting?*
*It baffles the logic of oppression.*

It is a mystery that baffles the logic of oppression: When journalists are faced with the threat of imprisonment, violent attack, or worse, why do they keep reporting the news? A journalist, unlike a soldier, can walk away from a dangerous job without being court-martialed. A reporter in trouble can request a less risky assignment, or just quit. Many do. When life, freedom, or health is at stake, this is in many ways the most reasonable decision. But some stay.

Each of the 2011 awardees gave different reasons for doing what they do. But all of them said they felt an obligation, for reasons that were often as much personal as political. In negotiating a brutal calculus of risk, they considered their families, their countries, their heroes. Two of them described feeling at the lowest moments as if they were facing a test of character. One described his work as an act of hope. For all of them, it came down to the fundamentals of their beliefs.

It's hard to imagine a more turbulent place than Pakistan, where Umar Cheema began reporting the news a decade ago. The nation has played host to churning territorial disputes, Islamist militants, the U.S. war on terror, the fallout from a military coup, the assassination of a former prime minister, and devastating natural disasters.

"Pakistan has been in crisis for a decade now, and Pakistani society is being reordered from this crisis," said Cheema, who reports for *The News*, an English-language daily. The media has

an essential role, he believes, in determining the results of his nation's upheaval. For his part, he has covered corruption in national politics, military affairs, and the vast and tangled net cast by intelligence agencies.

Since 2001, 37 journalists have been killed in Pakistan for their work, according to CPJ research. Most of them covered politics or war. Most of them were murdered, like Daniel Pearl, who was kidnapped by militants in Karachi in 2002; Hayatullah Khan, who disappeared in 2005 after reporting an apparent U.S. missile attack in North Waziristan; and Saleem Shahzad, an online reporter whose body was found with signs of torture south of Islamabad in May 2011. He had received threats from intelligence officials.

*One should have a reason to live, Cheema says. His is to speak up.*

In September 2010, as he returned home late from dinner with friends in Islamabad, Cheema was pulled over by uniformed police. They didn't bring him to a police station, Cheema said, and they weren't really police. Instead, they tortured and abused him, shaved his head, mustache, and eyebrows, forced him into humiliating positions, and captured it on video. They also interrogated him about his reporting on the government.

Seven hours later, his captors left Cheema and his car about 100 miles (160 kilometers) from Islamabad. Don't talk, they had warned him, or we will post those videos online. You won't get away the next time. We will go after your editor, too.

As he started up the engine, Cheema had a choice to make. "I asked myself, what should I do? Can I live in this state of fear for my whole life?" he said. He thought about his family; he had a 2-year-old son, and his wife was pregnant. He also had international connections and a master's degree from the London School of Economics. He could easily leave Pakistan. Or he could stay. "I thought about the worst consequences," Cheema said. "The worst would be that I was killed."

For many, the choice would have been obvious, and it wouldn't have been the one Cheema made. He drove directly to his editor's house in Islamabad, still wearing his torn shirt and blood-soaked pants. Together they made a plan to publicize the abduction and torture immediately. He went back to work.

"I never thought I could do what I did. But sometimes, you realize you are being tested," Cheema said. "When I was heading home and I was in the process of deciding whether I should speak up or not, I was trying to put myself into the shoes of strong people, in the shoes of great people. How would they have reacted had they been in my place? Their decision would be to speak up."

His captors never identified themselves and left no trace of evidence. Cheema and other local journalists believe he was abducted by the Inter-Services Intelligence Directorate (ISI), the Pakistani security agency. Now, his professional life is constrained, as is his personal life. He lives and works under what he calls a "self-imposed house arrest." He tries not to leave the house alone, and if he's not home before sunset, his family worries. Even so, there's nothing he would do differently. "One should have some reason to live," Cheema said. "I have a reason to live, and the reason is I have to speak up. I have to remain truthful. I have to say what I have to say as a journalist."

Like Cheema, Bahraini editor Mansoor al-Jamri had other, more comfortable paths he could have taken. In fact, he was happily living one of these other lives, as an engineer in London in 2001, when he received a visit from the emir of Bahrain, now its king.

The emir had an unusual request. Bahrain was embarking on a process of reform, he said, and was inviting former opponents to participate. Al-Jamri was a known critic of Bahrain's government, and a frequent guest on international news outlets such as the BBC. His father was a prominent figure in Bahrain's political opposition as well as a Shiite spiritual leader. Would al-Jamri return to Bahrain?

He jumped at it. Turning down an offer to join the cabinet, he requested the emir's permission to launch a newspaper. "I thought I would be able to influence the political process in a way that preserves my independence," al-Jamri said.

Ten years later, the editor became a victim of his own success. At its peak, the newspaper he co-founded and edited, *Al-Wasat*, reached an estimated readership of 45,000 in a nation with a population of only around 1.2 million. Enjoying the king's apparent blessing, the paper became a trailblazer, continually pushing the line of acceptable reporting on touchy subjects like land grabs, environmental destruction, and political opposition.

"He has shown that journalism has a role in advancing human rights," said Abdulla al-Dirazi, head of the Bahrain Human Rights Society. Most newspapers, following the example, became more professional, he said. "Ultimately, this has created enemies."

The collapse was swift and unexpected.

Swept up in the Arab Spring, protesters crowded into the center of Bahrain's capital, Manama, to demand greater freedom and equality for the country's oppressed Shiite majority. *Al-Wasat* covered the protests. The newspaper staff continued to report the news from home even after its printing press was destroyed on March 15, at the start of a violent government crackdown. There were arrests, disappearances, beatings to report.

*A Bahraini newspaper editor pushes boundaries and becomes a target.*

On April 2, al-Jamri's friends called him and told him to turn on the television. *Al-Wasat* was the topic of a three-hour program on an official media channel, and it was being accused of spreading false news. That night, al-Jamri began to plan for the worst. He made arrangements with friends to take care of his children should he disappear into military custody, as others had. The next day, he and two colleagues were given a choice: Quit or the newspaper would be shut down. Al-Jamri, along with the paper's managing editor and local news director, stepped down.

The move might have saved the paper and its roughly 200 employees. It did not save al-Jamri and his colleagues from being criminally charged with spreading false news. Much worse was the fate of Karim Fakhrawi. A co-founder of the newspaper, as well as a board member and investor, Fakhrawi died in state custody on April 12 amid allegations of mistreatment.

Al-Jamri speaks with the ease and authority of a person who has spent his life in front of a camera. But when the subject turns to Fakhrawi, his voice falters and he sounds bewildered. "He was a good man, a very generous man," he said. "He gave lots of money to the poor. He was my exact age, 49 years old. I don't know why they targeted him. It's really crazy. So many people were targeted."

The editor second-guesses his choices. "On March 15, I should have taken the message," he said. "Now in hindsight, if I had stopped publishing, I had an excuse that the printing press was shut down."

Criminal charges still hang over his head. His own investigation showed that the government had planted the false reports his paper was accused of spreading; CPJ research supports this. At worst, he could face jail time; at best, he's expecting a heavy fine. But when martial law was lifted, al-Jamri returned to his role as editor-in-chief at *Al-Wasat*.

Why didn't he just leave? "In a way, it's a matter of dignity. I gave up my engineering profession, which was a very good one—I loved it—and came to take on a role in accordance with my goals in life, to promote democracy and human rights," al-Jamri said. "If I didn't stand up for my principles at this time, I'll always feel very low about myself, as a very cheap person," he said. "If they want me to disappear, they'll have to work harder."

Repressive governments can be predictable. Radina knows what her KGB captors were after. Al-Jamri knows there is a line between what the kingdom sees as tolerable dissent and dangerous treason. Even Cheema could see the footprint of the ISI in the shadowy violence that tried to crush him.

But in Sinaloa, Mexico, where drug cartels run their trade and their battles in homes and on the streets, the rules of survival can seem unknowable.

At dawn one day in September 2009, a grenade tore through the offices of *Riodoce*, a newspaper that Javier Arturo Valdez Cárdenas co-founded in 2003. Nobody was in the office at the time, and Valdez and his colleagues filed a report with the police. No investigation was done, and those responsible for the attack went unpunished and unidentified.

"We don't discount anybody," Valdez said. *Riodoce* reports aggressively on crime and corruption in Sinaloa, a key corridor in the drug trade, where violence and lawlessness are rampant. The reach of the drug cartels there is deep and wide, and extends into police stations and politicians' offices. The assault on *Riodoce* followed the pattern of other attacks on journalists in this region, CPJ research shows, where accountability is slippery and alliances are complex.

More than 40 journalists have been killed or have disappeared in Mexico since President Felipe Calderón Hinojosa took office in 2006, according to CPJ research. At least 13 were murdered in direct reprisal for their reporting on crime and corruption. Impunity is systematic; murders go uninvestigated and unpunished. With no guidelines to tell journalists what they need to do to stay alive, crippling self-censorship has become a rule.

Valdez is unwilling to be quiet. He has written books on crime and the drug trade, and its devastating impact on daily life. Just imagine growing up here, he said. "It makes me very sad that the young people are living in this environment of war," Valdez said. "They are assuming the language of war, as if these deaths are natural."

*Valdez says he is not closing his newspaper. It's an act of hope, no?*

He worries about his own children whenever they don't pick up the phone. Valdez knows that the stakes of his work can be life and death—not just for him but for his sources and the people he's reporting on. Journalism under these circumstances requires an astoundingly complex set of calculations. Valdez takes into account the city, who the boss is, whether he minds publicity, which organization he works for. Sometimes, something as simple as a car accident can be loaded with invisible risk; the names of the victims might be sensitive, the license plate numbers unrepeatable.

One decision is easy, Valdez said. He's not closing up shop anytime soon. "For this to happen, it would have to be something very strong. To turn off the light and walk to the corner, to close *Ríodoce*, it would be the day when there's nothing more that can be done," he said. That day hasn't come yet. "It's an act of hope, no?" Valdez said. "I would like that more people reflect on what's happening, that people reading the stories can be critical. And that they change this."

Radina was released from jail in late January 2011, pending trial. A condition of her release was that she leave Minsk and relocate to the western town of Kobrin. She was ordered to keep in touch at all times with the local police; her passport was confiscated and she was barred from speaking about her case. These were conditions she found intolerable, so Radina fled to Russia, which shares an open border with Belarus.

"To be away from my country is almost unbearable to me," Radina said.

"The understanding that you love your country doesn't hit you as strong until you know for a fact that you cannot go back."

In exile, she has lived the life of a fugitive. In Russia, she sensed the footsteps of the KGB at her back. From there, she flew to Amsterdam, and a friend drove her to Lithuania, where she was living at year's end.

She has just one possession of importance, she said. Friends in Belarus gave it to her before she left the country. It's small and light, and it wards off any regrets about the path she has taken.

"I have a computer. And that makes it possible to work."

She's still the editor of *Charter 97.*

*Kristin Jones is an independent investigative reporter. In 2011, she was part of a team that won a Robert F. Kennedy Journalism Award for "Seeking Justice for Campus Rapes," a collaboration between NPR and the Center for Public Integrity. Jones was CPJ's senior Asia research associate until 2007. She was the lead author of the CPJ special report,* Falling Short, *which documented press freedom abuses in China ahead of the 2008 Olympic Games.*

# Using Internet 'Crime' Laws, Authorities Ensnare Journalists

*By Danny O'Brien*

Chiranuch Premchaiporn, editor of *Prachatai*, is the model of a modern independent news website manager. From her office in downtown Bangkok, she guides a team of online journalists conducting investigative reports on the lesser-reported sides of Thai society: labor disputes, fraud in distant rural areas, and corruption. In these politically sensitive times, she has a challenging job. The website has to cautiously navigate the proprieties of reporting without favor on Thailand's dominant political factions, the Red and Yellow shirts.

But instead of concentrating on editing her news site, she spends weeks at a time in Bangkok's criminal courts, facing a government prosecution that has involved multiple arrests and a three-year-long trial. Chiranuch was first arrested in March 2009, when the *Prachatai* offices were raided by police and her laptop was seized. When I spoke with her in October 2011 (CPJ provided expert testimony on Internet law to the court), she had just heard that the decision in her case would be delayed another five months due to Bangkok's flooding. Even though a guilty judgment could lead to a sentence of up to 50 years in jail, she was impatient for the case to be concluded. "It is a distraction," she said. "I've tried not to involve the *Prachatai* team, but I'm always preparing for the trial and can't make long-term plans."

Chiranuch is being prosecuted under Thailand's strict *lèse majesté* laws against public criticism of the monarchy—but the charge lies not in the disloyalty of her own words, or those of her team at *Prachatai*. Instead, the language of a handful of visitors to her website who wrote comments on the site's discussion board led to her arrest on criminal charges.

The law she is accused of breaking is the Computer Crime Act, which was introduced ostensibly to combat cybercriminals. The act was the first piece of legislation introduced by military coup leaders when they restored the legislature in 2007. It has already proven to be a dangerously wide-ranging addition to the original *lèse majesté* laws, as well as a powerful tool to censor websites. "The military government considered the Internet so dangerous, one of its first orders was for censorship," said author C.J. Hinke, who heads the local pressure group Freedom Against Censorship Thailand. "Their original draft of the Computer Crime Act included the death penalty for computer crimes."

Laws like the Computer Crime Act, originally presented as targeting hackers and those who commit fraud, are being applied to reporters and news websites around the world. And in many cases, from Angola to Saudi Arabia, governments are using claims of online disorder as a cover to introduce far more repressive laws that unashamedly target journalists and the right to free expression.

................................................

*Laws said to target hackers and fraudsters are being applied to reporters.*

................................................

When Tunisian blogger Slim Amamou was detained in the dying days of Zine El Abidine Ben Ali's dictatorship, his interrogators said he would not be charged for his reporting online, but for hacking. "The case against me was of cybercriminality," he told CPJ. "I was accused of harming technical infrastructure." In fact, in some of his last posts before his detention, the independent blogger was reporting original research on the Tunisian authorities' own Internet fraud: creating fake Facebook and Google home pages to steal passwords from Internet users sharing video of the Tunisian protests. If not for the collapse of the Ben Ali government a few days later, Amamou could have spent up to 10 years in jail. But he was never charged. Just five days after his release from detention, and four days after the fall of Ben Ali, he was appointed secretary of state for sport and youth in the new government.

Allegations that reporters from the now-defunct *News of the World* in the United Kingdom illegally accessed private voicemails demonstrate that journalists must be bound by legitimate anti-hacking laws. But some country's cybercrime laws are constructed so broadly that normal journalistic activity online can be deemed illegal.

On April 1, 2011, Angola's National Assembly voted on a "Law to Combat Crime in the Area of Information and Communication Technologies and of Information Company Services." As well as including standard cybercrime provisions to combat unlawful access to computers and the distribution of child pornography, the bill included a blanket prohibition on the online posting or sharing of photos, recordings, or videos without the consent of those appearing within them. Another section would criminalize anyone who forwards a message with intent to "disturb the peace and tranquility or the personal, family, or sexual life of another person"; another would allow police to search homes without warrants when seizing data such as computer hard drives, cell phones, and digital video equipment. Violations of these sections could lead to prison sentences of 12 to 14 years—more than six times the term applied to online pornography distribution.

"The initial draft of the bill, submitted to the president by the Ministry of Telecommunications and Information Technology, contained none of this," said Rafael Marques de Morais, an Angolan journalist who reports on corruption in the country. "It was the presidency of José Eduardo dos Santos who added these provisions before presenting the law to the assembly." Marques points out that the additions coincided with the success of uprisings in Tunisia and Egypt, and were intended to criminalize the

......................................................

*In Angola, a cybercrime law becomes a means to suppress dissent.*

......................................................

online reporting of news and images that mobilized popular movements in the Arab world. Human Rights Watch explicitly views the bill as intended to extend dos Santos' strategy of restricting traditional media. The Angolan government and its allies had previously harassed or aggressively purchased independent voices such as the two leading weekly newspapers, *Semanário Angolense* and *A Capital*. The shrinking of Angola's independent print voices forced many writers and readers to switch to distributing and reading news online, Marques says. After protests by local media and human rights groups, the proposed law's passage stalled in the legislature, but Marques expects it to reappear by spring 2012.

Cybercrime laws are intended to extend existing penal codes to the online world, but they can easily be broadened to criminalize the standard practices of online journalists: running commentary boards or writing about third parties online without permission. The apparently benign—or at least, neutral—extension of existing media regulations to the Internet poses the same risks. On January 1, 2011, Saudi Arabia's Ministry of Culture and Information announced its "E-Publishing" regulations, which widened the country's news media registration laws to the Internet.

Saudi authorities have significant powers over traditional media outlets, including the right to appoint and fire senior editors at will. After the emergence over the past few years of a vibrant, but unregulated, online news sector, including popular local publications such as *Burnews* and *Hasanews*, authorities set about introducing the same controls on the Internet. The larger news sites initially welcomed the regulations, said Saudi blogger Ahmed al-Omran, explaining that they believed "official registration would provide them with legitimacy, which would help with access and reassure advertisers." However, the regulations also required government registration and official approval of editors for any organization or individual conducting "electronic journalism" as well as websites "displaying audio and visual material."

The authorities have stated that bloggers are exempt from compulsory registration, while leaving the distinction between bloggers and electronic journalists undefined. For instance, two video-bloggers, Feras Bughnah and Hosam al-Deraiwish, were detained for two weeks in October for their piece documenting poverty in Riyadh, which they posted to YouTube. The charges they faced were unclear, but one source to whom al-Omran spoke suggested that the detention was due to the video being aired by an opposition TV channel hosted outside of Saudi Arabia. With one broadcast, Bughnah and al-Deraiwish were transformed from bloggers recording the world around them to "electronic journalists."

Elsewhere, arbitrary registration requirements have been used as a pretext to block news sites. In November, Sri Lanka's government announced that any news site publishing "any content relating to Sri Lanka" was required to register. A day after the announcement, Sri Lankan Internet service providers began blocking some of the most prominent news sites, including the *Sri Lanka Mirror* and *Sri Lanka Guardian*.

Imprecision in new Internet laws frequently ensnares news sites. In India, "Intermediary Guidelines" introduced in May require any system hosting material deemed blasphemous, inciting hatred, being ethnically objectionable, infringing patents, or threatening unity to remove the content within 36 hours or face prosecution. The conditions are undefined and "so vague that it is open to arbitrary interpretation," Sunil Abraham of the Bangalore-based Center for Internet and Society told *The Washington Post*. The process for deeming content objectionable is simply a complainant's sending a registered letter or digitally signed email to the hosting service. As a consequence, any online article in India may be removed from view by a single complaint.

The Intermediary Guidelines did not pass through the Indian parliamentary process; they were presented by the New Delhi government as technical amendments to the country's Information Technology Act. They took effect shortly after introduction, despite complaints from press and Internet freedom groups, as well as from Internet companies such as Google India.

........................................

## *Regulators and companies wield vast power to remove online material.*

........................................

Because the Internet is still governed in most countries by information technology ministries and regulatory organizations rather than through directly elected institutions, provisions can frequently be introduced by regulators or companies with no consideration of press freedom issues. In September, VeriSign, the corporate administrator of the .com domain, requested permission from the global Internet regulatory body ICANN to enforce the "denial, cancellation, or transfer of any [domain name] registration" in response to "any applicable court orders, laws, government rules or requirements, requests of law enforcement or other governmental or quasi-governmental agency, or any dispute resolution process." As with the Indian provision, this permission would grant governments and agencies the ability to remove entire .com websites without due process. A single request to remove a domain would expunge a news site overnight. VeriSign withdrew the request following complaints, but the proposal demonstrates how much power some companies can have to censor across the entire global Internet at the request of states or regulators. The company gave no reason for the withdrawal.

The rise of cybercrime has also led to an opportunity for introducing seemingly benign transnational agreements that could be used to silence dissident voices. In September, a proposal for an "international code of conduct for information security" was presented at the United Nations. Its supporters were China, Russia, Tajikistan, and Uzbekistan, and the code of conduct included language "to cooperate ... in curbing the dissemination of information that incites terrorism, secessionism, or extremism, or that undermines other countries' political, economic, and social stability, as well as their spiritual and cultural environment." All four countries have an unenviable record in restricting journalists' freedom of expression under similar tenets. Terrorism, separatism, and extremism are classed as the "Three Evils" by China and its neighbors, and are used to target minority journalists such as Gheyret Niyaz, manager of the *Uighurbiz* website, who is serving 15 years in prison for "endangering state security."

Internet laws and regulations need not penalize press freedom. Accidentally broad laws can be re-drafted, and rules can be written to protect freedom of expression.

In 2009, Brazil began work on its *Marco Civil da Internet,* an attempt to introduce "rights and duties" for the use of the Internet in Brazil. Over the next two years, the bill was debated, not just in the country's legislature, but online, with the government of Brazil creating dedicated sites to allow individuals to comment and suggest amendments. In the original draft of the bill, as in Indian proposals, complainants could have critical articles online removed by simply requesting the action; journalists would have to apply to a court to restore their work. After criticism by CPJ and many others during the consultation, the proposal was reversed: critics will now need to obtain a court order to remove content.

................................................................

*China quickly picks up on Cameron's language of censorship and control.*

................................................................

The *Marco Civil* was being debated by the Brazilian legislature in late year. While its passage was not guaranteed, it shows what can be done if nations want to ensure that new laws do not interfere with one of the most powerful and liberating capabilities of the Internet: to act as a tool of free expression and press freedom. Those rights of free expression have to be built into the laws from the start; Internet journalists, experts, and users need to be consulted; and the rules should carefully and slowly evolve.

Sadly, politicians around the world are often more tempted to make sweeping proposals to combat whatever Internet-related problem has hit the headlines that day. The week after riots broke out in several areas of London, British Prime Minister David Cameron announced he would investigate ways to control or block communications online, and TV channels were forced to hand over raw footage of the riots to authorities.

While Cameron backed down from his threats to proceed with new legislation, the language of censorship and seizure was quickly picked up by others. "We may wonder why Western leaders, on the one hand, tend to indiscriminately accuse other nations of monitoring, but on the other take for granted their steps to monitor and control the Internet," China's state-run press agency, Xinhua, said. "For the benefit of the general public, proper Web monitoring is legitimate and necessary."

The year online has been, in some ways, a disturbing one for authoritarian and democratic governments alike. Political leaders and corporations blamed our increasingly connected world for uprisings, riots, and widespread hacking attacks. But without due care—and pressure from those most concerned with free expression—laws concerned with Internet security can quickly turn into weapons against journalists and the freedom of the new, digital media.

*Danny O'Brien, CPJ's San Francisco-based Internet advocacy coordinator, has worked globally as a journalist and activist covering technology and digital rights. In October 2011, he provided expert testimony in the trial of Thai online editor Chiranuch Premchaiporn.*

# More Discussion but Few Changes on Sexual Violence

*By Lauren Wolfe*

When word went around that a mob had sexually assaulted CBS correspondent and CPJ board member Lara Logan in Cairo's Tahrir Square in February 2011, the media jumped on the specifics: Why was the press release about her assault so precise? Why did it say the attack was "brutal" and "sexual"? What people didn't know was that Logan was more than satisfied with CBS' wording, and relieved that the information was finally public. Waiting a few days, she recently told CPJ, was painful. She was ready to speak immediately, to let the world know that her sexual assault was an attack not just on her body but also on the press, and that she would not only survive it but continue her work, unbroken.

"Your silence is like denial," Logan said, adding that CBS had delayed the news release to allow her to physically recover a little and fly to the United States. She said that she never considered concealing what had happened from her viewers and that she could not have asked for more from her employer. "The single most important thing a company can do is stand behind a journalist," she said. "If my boss had questioned what I was wearing, that would have broken me."

Logan's assault was not entirely unusual—CPJ uncovered a number of serious sexual assaults or rapes of journalists in its June report "The Silencing Crime"—but her disclosure and her employer's supportive response were. Since that attack, awareness and sensitivity to sexual violence against journalists have increased in the news industry, with managers in particular expressing a desire to provide help to reporters and photographers on assignment, a CPJ follow-up survey has found. Still, for the most part, the profession lacks training programs that address the risks in a meaningful way.

Of more than 50 local and international journalists CPJ interviewed for "The Silencing Crime," more than a dozen said they had experienced rape or other violent sexual assault, such as digital penetration or sodomy with an object. The majority of international correspondents reported having been repeatedly groped while working. But most of the journalists told CPJ that they had chosen not to tell their editors or go public about the sexual assaults, and of the few who did speak up, all but one said they had been met with censure, such as being pulled from an assignment or being told to remain quiet.

"I think it's difficult for us to talk about this stuff because we don't want to look like we're weak, or whiners," *ProPublica* reporter Kim Barker told CPJ in May. "The tendency of bosses is to want someone who knows what to do and doesn't need hand-holding."

..................................................

*For many, a reluctance to speak out for fear of being seen as weak.*

..................................................

Logan told CPJ that she had experienced sexual violence in the course of her reporting before—in one instance, a man had violently grabbed her breasts in Afghanistan—but the extreme nature of the 2011 attack led her to speak out.

With the lack of communication between journalists who don't disclose sexual assaults and newsroom leaders who do not ask directly about a delicate or taboo subject, both sides have been in the dark about what to do next. But since Logan spoke out, and since *New York Times* photographer Lynsey Addario went public about her own sexual assault in Libya in March, some journalists, particularly editors who directly manage reporters and photographers, say they are interested in opening up the conversation or trying new approaches.

Jamie Wellford, *Newsweek*'s photo editor, works with at least a dozen journalists around the world who are often on dangerous assignments. He said he believed that "most people would be pretty forward about telling me" if they had been sexually assaulted. After a lengthy conversation with CPJ, Wellford said he realized that he had never asked his photographers directly whether they had ever been sexually assaulted but that he was ready to do so now because there would be great value in having the information.

"It's extremely important when you put people in a world of chaos and disorder that they speak about their experience," he said. "It's important to know so you can orient yourself how to put your people in the field. It's so chaotic out there."

MaryAnne Golon, a photo editor at *Time* magazine for 24 years until she left as director of photography in 2008, told CPJ that, having been close to many of her photographers over the years, she understands why journalists keep sexual assault a secret in their professional lives.

"I'm like their den mother," said Golon. "I'm the one who sets up the sat phone. I had a firsthand notion of what they had to go through in the field." Female journalists have told Golon about several "horrific experiences" in places such as Kuwait and Israel, she said. She recalled urging one journalist who was particularly traumatized after being groped to tell her editors what had happened. "I said, 'This needs to get publicized.' She said, 'It won't be by me.' People are afraid of what it does to their own reputation rather than seeing the bigger picture."

Golon, like Wellford, said there should be more open discussion of sexual assault. "What could happen, and what should happen, is particularly wealthy, big media organizations should be required to give these people training," Golon said. "It should include that kind of sexual assault training. They should understand that this is a real possibility. There are steps that need to be taken when they come back. News outlets don't even want to talk about [post-traumatic stress disorder] much less sexual assault."

Prashant Rao, Baghdad bureau chief for Agence France-Presse, told CPJ that he felt unsure of what he should do if one of his journalists was sexually assaulted. "Particular training on this would of course be useful, because, I must confess, I have little to no idea how I would handle such instances or advise colleagues on how to avoid/prevent them," Rao wrote in an email.

CPJ's informal survey of international news organizations found only limited efforts to implement training that specifically addresses sexual assault. Only NBC said it was moving ahead with designing a specific curriculum. (Local news outlets, meanwhile, face additional challenges in addressing sexual assault, with intense cultural barriers in many countries keeping reporters from disclosing rapes or attacks.)

Since May, when NBC's vice president for worldwide newsgathering, David Verdi, told CPJ that the network would implement training on how to prevent and deal with sexual assault, the network has created and run a pilot course in conjunction with a consulting social worker who works with the military on post-traumatic stress.

....................................................

*Journalists in the field, says Logan, must count on managers for support.*

....................................................

"We felt there was a hole in that training, and we needed to fill that hole," said Tracey Leaf, director of human resources for NBC Universal and NBC News, who described the process of creating a course as "very challenging" because there is no model from which to draw. "Right now I feel like I'm shooting arrows into the dark, to be honest," Leaf said. It's not like creating a training session on finance for your staff, she said. "We didn't have a buy-off-the-shelf for this one." NBC's training includes safety tips and discussion of how to identify post-traumatic stress disorder, Leaf said, as well as medical advice and tools. Rape kits that include the morning-after pill and a pricey HIV blocker will be prescribed to any journalist who requests them.

As for the fear that disclosure of sexual assault will result in being pulled off a story, Leaf said that at NBC's pilot training, Verdi told the journalists: "Your assignment would never be compromised because of this. We want to help you, but we would never stop you from going into the field again because of it."

But training alone would not have prevented what happened to Logan, said Jeff Fager, chairman of CBS News and executive producer of Logan's program, "60 Minutes." He likened her attack to being hit by a tsunami, saying that she was "lucky to be alive." Though Logan and her crew were accompanied by a security specialist on the night of the attack—the crew had been roughed up a week earlier—the situation demanded greater support, Fager said. "We will never, ever, send a reporter into a situation like that again without significant security. And if we do not think we can provide enough security to feel safe? Then we will not cover the story."

When attacks do occur, Logan said, journalists in the field should be able to count on their managers for support. "They need to know they're not going to be questioned, they're not going to be blamed, they're not going to be discriminated against," she said. "They have to know that. You're talking about something very bare here. You're talking about something completely vulnerable."

*Lauren Wolfe is the director of Women Under Siege, a project on sexualized violence and conflict at the Women's Media Center. While CPJ's senior editor, she wrote the CPJ report, "The Silencing Crime: Sexual Violence and Journalists." Previously, she was a researcher on two New York Times books on the 9/11 attacks.*

# As Impunity Pledges Offer Hope, Focus Turns to Action

*By Elisabeth Witchel*

At the presidential residence Los Pinos, Mexico's Felipe Calderón Hinojosa expressed regret for the growing death toll among journalists. "It pains me," he told a CPJ delegation in 2010, "that Mexico is seen as one of the most dangerous places for the profession." At his office in Islamabad, Pakistani President Asif Ali Zardari accepted responsibility for unchecked, anti-press violence. "The protection of journalists is in my mandate," he told CPJ representatives in 2011. At Malacañang Palace in Manila, senior Justice Department officials laid out plans to win convictions in dozens of journalist murders, a commitment later reiterated by President Benigno Aquino III. And at the headquarters of Russia's national investigations agency, top officials opened their files and agreed to restart several cold journalist murder cases.

Since 2009, heads of state and senior officials in many of the world's most dangerous nations for the press have lined up to acknowledge the scourge of impunity and promised in meetings with CPJ to take action. Their promises are still largely unfulfilled, but high-level recognition of the issue has provided a foundation for what advocates expect will be a long campaign against impunity.

The official attitude has not always been this way. Philippine President Gloria Macapagal-Arroyo once derided CPJ's research as "exaggerated," while Russian officials long refused to discuss any details of their work on journalist murders. But several years of intensive advocacy by numerous press freedom groups, human rights bodies, and journalists around the world have pushed the issue of deadly anti-press violence higher on the international agenda. In September, UNESCO convened a two-day meeting of U.N. agencies and representatives of member states to develop a long-term plan to promote the safety of journalists and end impunity. A draft of the plan offers little to hold nations accountable, but it would establish emergency response programs and place the issue of impunity onto the wider U.N. development agenda.

"We have hope," said Nadezhda Azhgikhina, executive secretary of the Russian Union of Journalists, who said the campaigning has influenced her government's decisions for the better. Russia's impunity rate, while still exceedingly high, has inched downward in the past two years. "And even more," she said, "beatings are taken more seriously. People are ready to demand justice."

This public pressure yielded some notable progress in 2011. In Russia, two people were convicted in the 2009 double murder of reporter Anastasiya Baburova and human rights lawyer Stanislav Markelov. In Ukraine, authorities brought a high-ranking ex-Interior Ministry official to trial on charges of strangling and beheading online journalist Georgy Gongadze in 2000. In the United States, grassroots pressure pushed authorities to bring to trial and convict the masterminds behind the killing of Oakland editor Chauncey Bailey. With prosecutors bringing several successful cases over the past six years, Brazil's record of impunity has shown signs of improvement. And in Colombia, a recent conviction and a drop in lethal violence have nudged the country's impunity rate downward.

*Optimism set against cold reality: Hundreds of murders are unsolved.*

Yet press advocates can muster only the most guarded optimism given this cold reality: More than 500 journalist murders—most of them far lower in profile than that of Bailey or Gongadze—remain unsolved worldwide over the past two decades. CPJ research shows the impunity rate across the world remains stubbornly high, hovering just below 90 percent, and largely unchanged over the past five years.

Roland Bless, principal adviser to the media freedom representative of the Organization for Security and Co-operation in Europe, said advocacy has led to improvements in nations throughout his region. But he added: "I can only hope this raised awareness will translate into realities on the ground for media professionals, but I would not be too optimistic on these issues.

"It seems to be a battle of many years."

For an idea of how the battle will unfold, look to several key cases and countries.

When Aquino took office in the Philippines in 2010, he pledged to stop the killings of journalists and to end a decades-old culture of impunity. His ability to deliver is being severely tested by the trial of dozens of suspects in the November 23, 2009, massacre in Maguindanao province. More than 30 media workers were among the 57 people killed in a horrific, politically motivated ambush. Government prosecutors, law enforcement authorities, and judicial officials have come under increasing criticism for what many see as the sluggish, unfocused handling of the case. More than two years have passed and the courts are still hearing bail arguments. Of 195 total suspects, only 70 had been arraigned by late 2011 and at least 100 were still at large. For many international observers, whether the Philippines can successfully prosecute the perpetrators of this large-scale atrocity will be a lasting measure of the nation's commitment to the rule of law and effective government.

*An international event to ensure the work continues and hope is not lost.*

Groups in the Philippines have also criticized the government for neglecting its promises of systemic reform. The witness protection program is still chronically short of resources, forensics expertise remains sorely lacking, and Philippine court rules are still routinely abused by defendants seeking to delay prosecutions. In the Maguindanao case, defense lawyers have filed a stream of motions, many of them duplicative, that challenge the very foundation of the prosecution, from the validity of arrest warrants to the standing of the trial judge.

"I feel dismayed by the slow trial. Suspects are still at large, and what we really want, and what we pray for, is their capture," said Mary Grace Morales, whose husband and sister, both journalists, were murdered in the Maguindanao ambush. Dozens of free expression organizations worldwide tried to make sure that international attention to the case did not wane. On the second anniversary of the massacre, CPJ and the other groups held the first International Day to End Impunity to highlight the Maguindanao slayings and other unsolved journalist murders.

In Russia, advocates are looking at recent developments with wary but hopeful eyes. Not only did prosecutors win a conviction in the Baburova slaying, investigators reported progress in the 2006 murder of Anna Politkovskaya, which is seen as a test of Russia's will to prosecute sensitive cases involving powerful figures. A new investigation led in 2011 to the arrests of two suspects and charges against a third in the killing. Among those in custody is a former high-level police officer accused of helping to organize the killing.

But prosecutors failed before in the Politkovskaya murder, bringing a sloppily prepared case to trial that ended in the 2008 acquittals of three men charged as accomplices. Even now, the masterminds of the crime have yet to be identified. Sergey Sokolov, deputy editor of *Novaya Gazeta*, Politkovskaya's paper, told a Council of Europe forum that the Russian criminal justice system has been incapable thus far of holding politically connected people accountable for crimes. "One way or another, these are people connected to power, which in turn means that they are connected to big money and criminality," he said. And that, Sokolov added, has meant a free pass in the criminal justice system.

In Ukraine, 11 years after the murder of Georgy Gongadze, prosecutors opened a trial in July against former Interior Ministry Gen. Aleksei Pukach on charges that he carried out the horrific crime. Three other Interior Ministry officers had been convicted earlier on conspiracy charges related to the murder. In a potentially ground-breaking move, prosecutors also indicted former President Leonid Kuchma in March on abuse-of-office charges in connection with the plot.

But the case against Kuchma fell apart before the year was out. After Ukraine's Constitutional Court tossed out a key audiotape said to implicate the ex-president, a trial court dismissed the charges in December. And advocates were less than sanguine about prospects in the Pukach trial, which was being conducted entirely in private. The presiding panel of judges sealed the proceedings after finding that the evidence against Pukach—a former chief of the Interior Ministry's surveillance department—includes

state secrets. The judges did not address why they closed the entire trial, rather than only portions of the proceedings. The trial was pending in late year.

Gongadze's widow, Myroslava, has waged a relentless decade-long campaign to secure justice in her husband's murder. While deeply skeptical of Ukrainian authorities, Gongadze said the new proceedings had provided "a new opportunity to pursue justice in this case. ... Is the prosecutor's office professional and able enough to investigate? That is the question."

...............................................

*Pressure from an international court makes a difference in Gongadze's case.*

...............................................

Gongadze said the outside pressure offered by international courts had made a difference in her husband's case. Years ago, when it seemed clear Ukrainian authorities would not prosecute the killers on their own initiative, Gongadze brought a case before the European Court of Human Rights, the Council of Europe's adjudication body. The court's mandate allows it to review alleged violations of human rights in member states when all domestic avenues have been exhausted. In 2005, the court found that Ukraine had violated several articles of the European Convention on Human Rights—notably in failing to protect the journalist's life or investigate his death—and ordered that it pay damages of 100,000 euros (about US$118,000 at the time).

"I was struggling for a way to push the government to stay invested," Gongadze said. "The attention of the international community was very important—crucial. At the same time, it was not enough to speak about the case. You needed a judicial mechanism to find justice."

A perceived weakness of the European Court and other similar, regional courts is the inability to directly enforce decisions against recalcitrant states. When the Media Foundation of West Africa filed a case against the Gambia with the Court of Justice of the Economic Community of West African States concerning "Chief" Ebrimah Manneh, a journalist who disappeared in state custody, no government representatives bothered to attend the proceedings. The court ruled against the Gambia in 2008 and ordered damages for Manneh's family, but the ruling was ignored by the nation's leaders. Nevertheless, Media Foundation Director Kwame Karikari said he believes the case, along with regional and international advocacy, has played a role in deterring new attacks against journalists in West Africa.

Gongadze said the bully pulpit of the regional courts should not be underestimated. "In my 11 years, what had the most effect was the

European Court of Human Rights. I was able to appeal to the court and for a few years it kept the Ukrainian government alert. They had to respond to questions by the court," she said.

"What it offers is a definitive judgment," says Bill Bowring, a human rights attorney and co-founder of the European Human Rights Advocacy Centre, which specializes in bringing cases to the court. In 2011, the center filed a petition to open a case on behalf of the mother of Russian journalist Maksim Maksimov, who disappeared in 2004 and was ruled dead in 2006. The submission asks the court to rule whether Russia has fostered a climate of impunity in cases of anti-press violence, which could set an important precedent in other unsolved cases. In September 2010, the European Court ruled that Turkey had failed to protect the life and free-expression rights of Armenian-Turkish journalist Hrant Dink, who was assassinated in 2007 even though he had notified authorities of a series of death threats. The Turkish government has since set up a special commission to oversee the prosecution, although domestic efforts are still heavily criticized for focusing on low-level conspirators.

In the Americas, the Inter-American Court of Human Rights has rarely been used as direct recourse for justice; instead, regional journalists under threat tend to seek immediate responses to security risks, according to Michael Camilleri, a human rights specialist for the Inter-American Commission on Human Rights. "They come to the system typically over protection matters," said Camilleri, who works in the office of the special rapporteur for free expression. The court can rule that a member country is obliged to take protective action, while the commission can undertake country visits in cases of great concern.

National journalist security programs in the region have had mixed results. Under Colombia's protection program, a committee of government officials and civil society representatives meets regularly to assess the security needs of journalists under threat. In some cases, the government assigns direct protection such as security guards, while in other cases it supports tactics such as relocation. The program is often cited for helping to reduce anti-press violence, although critics say it has doubled as a surveillance tool for the Colombian government. Still, said Camilleri, "there are elements that are useful to other countries in thinking about how a serious protection program can be put in place, particularly in terms of the scale of government investment needed."

In November 2010, Mexico announced the creation of its own protection program based on Colombia's model. But in its first full year, the Mexican program was limited and ineffectual, a CPJ analysis found. Just eight journalists were offered protection, and most of them told CPJ that the services were of little value. "The budget commitments are not there to do it on the scale that is needed," Camilleri said of Mexico's program. "The government understands that it needs to do something and has reiterated to the rapporteurship its willingness to move forward. But journalists continue to be killed while the program struggles to get off the ground." Brazil's security program, created in 2004, has been similarly criticized for insufficient funding and administration.

Brazil in many ways reflects both the challenges and opportunities of the worldwide anti-impunity effort. A persistently dangerous place for the press—19 journalists have been killed in reprisal for their work in the past two decades—Brazil has had recent success in prosecuting journalist murders. Nationally, the profession is well-organized and vocal in pushing for arrests and prosecutions in anti-press attacks.

"Every case of menace or murder of journalists is immediately denounced by a large group of people demanding this crime be punished. Such 'noise' leads authorities to do their job in a more effective way," said Clarinha Glock, a Brazilian investigative reporter who works for the Inter American Press Association's Impunity Project.

................................................

## *Brazil reflects the challenges and opportunities in the global impunity fight.*

................................................

Brazil remains a deadly place for the press, particularly in the northeast provincial areas. At least one Brazilian journalist was murdered in direct relation to his work in 2011, and four others were slain in unclear circumstances. "You have to consider that Brazil is a large country," Glock said. "The effect of pressure from journalists in São Paulo is different when the crime is in the countryside of the northeast states, which are very, very far from the main newspapers and tend to be forgotten and not punished as they should be."

In the last six years, however, perpetrators have been sentenced in at least five journalist slayings, and authorities have won convictions against masterminds in at least two cases, a significant achievement compared with other violent countries where senior figures are rarely prosecuted. In 2009, for example, a Brazilian court sentenced a military police sergeant for plotting the murder of reporter Luiz Carlos Barbon Filho, who had exposed corruption in police ranks.

Brazilians cite the case of television reporter Tim Lopes, who was tortured and beheaded in 2002, as a turning point in the impunity effort there. Journalists came together to form the Association of Brazilian Investigative Journalists, or ABRAJI, to complete Lopes' work and pursue justice in his slaying. Glock said the association has galvanized Brazil's news media. "ABRAJI has improved a natural net of communication," she said. "They have a great capacity to unite and spread information about impunity, laws, how to obtain accurate information, how to work ethically."

Similarly, in the United States, colleagues banded together to thwart impunity. After the 2007 Bailey murder in Oakland, Bay Area journalists created the Chauncey Bailey Project to finish his reporting and shed light on his killing.

Thomas Peele, a reporter who worked on the project, recalled that the gunman confessed shortly after he shot Bailey, but police seemed uninterested in pursuing any other suspects. "It was pretty clear from the beginning that this was not a solo act by the gunman," Peele said. "Some time went by and we began to see no evidence that police were investigating beyond the initial confession."

The Bailey Project did its own investigative work and reported regularly through multiple media outlets about evidence the police had failed to pursue. "We published—a lot," said Peele. "There was incriminating video, cell phone records, a bunch of things that the police were not following up." Evidence exposed by the Bailey Project led to the arrest, trial and, in 2011, convictions of two additional suspects, including the man who ordered the killing. Both are in prison for life without parole.

There is one thread that runs through the successes, however qualified they may be: unceasing pressure, attention, and action by advocates, family, and colleagues. "We were rather relentless," Peele said. "We pursued the story until something happened."

*Elisabeth Witchel is the U.K.-based consultant for CPJ's Global Campaign Against Impunity. Witchel launched CPJ's campaign in 2006.*

# In Afghanistan, International Coverage Relies on Local Links

*By Monica Campbell*

In a decade of NATO-led war in Afghanistan, it was one of the highest-profile attacks. On the afternoon of September 13, Taliban insurgents in a high-rise building fired rockets and bullets at the U.S. Embassy and the headquarters of NATO's International Security Assistance Force, or ISAF, both in Kabul's heavily fortressed "green zone." Within seconds, U.S. Embassy personnel bolted for bunkers and passers-by fled the area.

Sangar Rahimi of *The New York Times* rushed to the scene. As he took notes during the blitz, many things worried him, from whizzing rockets to nervous Afghan police. "I'm not sure what scared me most—the rockets or the panicked cops with their fingers on the trigger," Rahimi said.

Throughout the war, foreign media have relied on Afghan colleagues—commonly known as fixers, although many are now seasoned journalists in their own right—to assist with things like arranging interviews and interpreting. Most crucial, these Afghans guide international correspondents' coverage of the country's evolving and complex war, helping determine whether a story is feasible or deadly.

If you happened to visit Kabul before 2001, you would have found Rahimi as a budding doctor. Following a path similar to those of many Afghans working with foreign media, Rahimi had graduated from Kabul Medical University but, with few job prospects, found himself offering English-language services to foreign journalists. The work meant a decent income that his medical degree would not have provided during wartime. And over the years, Rahimi and fellow Afghans earned increasing journalistic recognition, including bylines and greater responsibilities within their news organizations.

Bonds between these Afghans and their foreign counterparts have grown strong after sharing close calls at insurgent checkpoints, enduring threats from warlords, and surviving brushes with roadside bombs. "They are comrades, colleagues, and journalists," said Jonathan Landay, a senior

McClatchy national security correspondent who has reported on and off from Afghanistan since 1985. "You trust them with your life. If they say to me, 'Look, this place is not safe and we need to leave,' I drop everything and go." And to be clear, Landay added: "It's not a one-sided affair. These are smart, educated people. They do not take on jobs without knowing the risks."

Still, with the partnerships come unsettled questions. While Afghan journalists, typically young and ambitious, perform much of the same work as foreign correspondents, they run greater risks. They cannot leave the country at will. Western troops can mistake them for insurgents. In great swaths of Afghanistan, their association with foreigners leaves them marked as infidels and spies. Some have paid the ultimate price for their work. Among the dead: Sultan Munadi, who was shot in 2009 during a British-led rescue mission that freed his colleague, *New York Times* correspondent Stephen Farrell, from Taliban captivity. There was also 24-year-old reporter Ajmal Naqshbandi, who was abducted by the Taliban with Italian journalist Daniele Mastrogiacomo in 2007. Mastrogiacomo was released; Naqshbandi was beheaded after the Afghan government refused Taliban demands to release imprisoned insurgents.

"We've lost many friends," said Farouq Samim, who worked for years in Afghanistan for *The Chicago Tribune* and Al-Jazeera. Afghan journalists say that economic pressures—their income often makes them their family's breadwinner—can compel them to accept risky assignments they would otherwise refuse. "I've seen young Afghans who felt pushed to go to places they should avoid, to meet people who were simply too dangerous," Samim said.

There are also the inherent dangers of war reporting. On July 28, U.S. forces killed Ahmad Omaid Khpalwak, a 25-year-old Afghan working for the BBC in the eastern city of Tarin Kot. About noon that day, suicide bombers attacked the government complex, which included news offices where Khpalwak filed stories. As Khpalwak fled, U.S. forces shot him, mistaking him for a suicide bomber about to detonate his explosives. Twenty-one journalists have been killed in Afghanistan since the conflict began in October 2001, CPJ research shows.

Over the years, Rahimi, 30, has moved up the hierarchy of local journalists. Also in the established go-to club is 26-year-old Habib Zahori, who has worked with *New Yorker* staff writers and contributed to the McClatchy news service and *The Washington Post*. The two journalists earn a Western-sized salary and are increasingly reporting stories under their own byline, leveraging years of shadowing foreign correspondents. "A lot of these guys are just incredible, courageous journalists, pushing the levels of safety to get a story," said Tim McGirk, a former *Time* bureau chief who has reported on Afghanistan since 1990.

But because of his work, Rahimi can't go home. For the past two years, his family's village in Laghman province, which neighbors Kabul, has been off-limits. Rahimi believes it was his reporting on the 2009 assassination of a high-ranking intelligence official in Laghman province by a Taliban suicide bomber that got him labeled as a "traitor and bad Muslim." While reporting the story with Farrell of the *Times*, he went to the hospital to see civilians also wounded by the suicide bombing. Fellow villagers spotted Rahimi with Farrell. "They said, 'Hey, what are you doing here with that foreigner?'" Rahimi tried to distance himself, saying that he was a doctor and was there to treat the wounded. "They knew I was lying," Rahimi said. "I was standing there with a tripod. I panicked and only made things worse."

## Doing work similar to that of foreign correspondents, but at greater risk.

Days later, a group of men approached Rahimi's father at the village mosque. "They told my dad, 'Your son is working with infidels,'" Rahimi said. Animosity for Afghans who work with Americans can run deep. "Powerful people in my village tribe see my work with foreigners as a major crime and that I'm more guilty for the deterioration of Afghanistan than any foreigner," he said. "I'll be targeted if I go back."

Zahori said that when he walks the streets and bazaars of Kabul with a Western journalist, he hears Afghans whisper insults his way. "I've been called a spy and a shoe-licker of foreigners by my people," he said. It's a stigma that will not likely disappear. "I expect the work that these Afghans are doing now will be considered even more ugly if the Taliban come back to power," said Abdul Mujeeb Khalvatgar, director of the Afghan media advocacy group Nai.

The dangers to the press in Afghanistan are unique worldwide in that international media have borne the brunt of deadly attacks. Two-thirds of those killed in Afghanistan since the war began were foreign journalists; of the seven Afghan journalists killed during that period, five worked for international news organizations. Elsewhere in the world, even in countries embroiled in conflict, local journalists working for local news outlets have had the highest fatality rates.

International news media rely on local assistance all over the world, but most heavily in hot spots such as Iraq, Somalia, and Afghanistan. These local colleagues—some established journalists, some not—serve as interpreters, guides, and conduits to sources. The work is extremely dangerous: CPJ has documented the deaths of more than 70 local support workers worldwide since 2003, with the heaviest fatalities coming in Iraq.

For Afghans based full-time in the provinces, danger is always near. Away from Kabul's relative safety bubble, they live in areas where insurgent groups can hold sway. Any hint of their work with foreigners could prompt retaliation. Many give their Western colleagues Muslim-sounding names when adding their numbers to their cell phones. To keep their occupations hidden, particularly in volatile areas such as Kandahar, Afghanistan's main city in the south, they lie to their relatives about their work.

"The vast majority of the country's default position is to be suspicious or hostile toward Americans or anyone working with them," said Quil Lawrence, Kabul bureau chief for the U.S. media outlet NPR.

Everyone takes precautions. "You must figure out the possible risks through long conversations," said Alissa Rubin, Kabul bureau chief for *The New York Times*. She asks her Afghan colleagues many questions: Is it too dangerous for them to report from their home province? Would it be safer to report the story remotely, phoning a source instead of going in person? If they do head out to meet a source, is there a chance that, this time, he might sell them out to kidnappers? "And it's not only the Taliban that I'm worried about," said Rubin. "I get far more worried when we write about

official corruption, the government, and links to organized crime. That's extremely dangerous. We're talking more about criminal networks, less ideological and more ruthless and daring."

Indeed, Zahori said that after he helped *The New Yorker*'s Dexter Filkins report on corruption within Kabul Bank, one of Afghanistan's largest financial institutions, he expected reprisals, perhaps from the discredited, but still powerful, bank executives themselves. When the story came out in February, Zahori went underground. He changed his routines, altered his commute along Kabul's dusty city streets, and turned off his cell phone for

............................................

## What will happen after 2014, when NATO forces are scheduled to leave?

............................................

several days. When he restarted his phone, he didn't answer unrecognizable calls. "I'm not worried about myself, but about my family," Zahori said. Like many Afghans, he lives with his immediate and extended family in a compound in an unsecured area of Kabul. "If something happens, I might send the family to Pakistan. I don't know what I would do, really."

For many, the overriding concern is what will happen after 2014, when NATO forces are scheduled to leave and, with them, numerous foreign correspondents and bureaus. Add to this the possibility of the Taliban's regaining power. "We've been working with foreigners and will be the first ones punished," said Hashim Shukoor, a 27-year-old pediatrician who has worked since 2003 with foreign media, including McClatchy. "We're extremely concerned about our future. We see it as dark with no light inside."

Worried, some Afghans are searching for a way out. Local journalists said that conversations often revolve around visas, international scholarships, and other opportunities abroad. But no legal exit is guaranteed. "What's clear is that it's time to leave," said Rahimi, "especially for those of us maligned or defamed by working with foreigners." Rubin, his boss, is also worried. "What's going to happen to the Afghans we've worked with?" she said. "This needs thinking through now."

A small number of Afghan journalists have found safe havens, albeit temporarily, in Europe. One organization, Sweden's Fojo Media Institute, has offered shelter to Afghan journalists, as it has to reporters from countries such as Pakistan and Colombia. Fojo also facilitates medical care and psychological counseling. "But we should be considered a last resort, a short-term solution," said Johan Romare, Fojo's international director.

Scholarships can be another way out. In 2009, Samim won a scholarship offered to Afghans to earn a master's degree in communications at the University of Ottawa in Canada. More than 300 people applied for the five slots, which were offered in partnership with the Open Society Foundation. Samim's wife and three children have since received visas and have joined him in Canada. But their visas came only after myriad letters of support from the foreigners Samim met during his work as a journalist, and with the direct backing of a Canadian member of parliament. "I got lucky," said Samim, who is now applying for asylum with his family. "My kids don't want to go back. They feel the danger that still exists back home."

The path is less certain for Afghan journalists seeking U.S. visas. "There's always this dubious question about whether they're really a journalist," Rubin said. Indeed, the Obama administration's new, more rigorous background checks for visa applicants have lengthened backlogs. The process could take years. (In 2008, the U.S. Congress approved the Refugee Crisis in Iraq Act, which allowed Iraqis affiliated with U.S. government agencies and media outlets to apply for direct resettlement to the United States. A special visa program has been established for Afghanistan as well, but it is not open to Afghan journalists.)

Some journalists said that U.S. news organizations should band together and apply pressure on Washington to expedite visas for their Afghan colleagues. "There's an obligation on the part of Western news organizations to help their Afghan employees if things start turning for the worse," Landay said. "It's these very Afghans who have helped us do our jobs. They've been crucial in helping us inform Americans about the war."

Zahori isn't hopeful. "Look, my country has been labeled as a factory for terrorism," he said. "It'll take a lot to convince a consulate official that I'm not a terrorist. You have to be rich or politically connected to get a U.S. or European visa."

Both Zahori and Rahimi are applying to U.S. journalism schools. Inculcated with the drive to report, Rahimi said: "I believe that working with the media, exposing the corruption, will help my people even more so than medicine. I know the dangers, but journalism is my passion."

*Monica Campbell is a San Francisco-based freelance journalist and former CPJ consultant. She reported from Afghanistan in early 2011.*

# As Security Field Matures, The Risks Multiply

*By Frank Smyth*

Less than 20 years ago, the field of journalist security did not exist. "There was no security, no body armor, no training," said Heather Allan, head of newsgathering for Al-Jazeera English and a former NBC News bureau chief.

In the 1990s, journalists' deaths in the Balkans and Africa underscored "the need for a systematic approach to journalists' physical security," said Bruce Shapiro, executive director of the Columbia University-based Dart Center for Journalism & Trauma. The shock of the September 11 attacks and the wars in Afghanistan and Iraq made the journalist security field, at least for a time, a growth industry.

Today, the need for safety preparation has never seemed greater. Traditional threats to journalists persist at the same time that new dangers are either emerging or becoming apparent. Sexual assault, civil unrest, organized crime, digital security, and trauma are all recognized challenges to press freedom and safety, and leading news organizations are either modifying the military-oriented training courses, or developing their own security practices and curriculum. Still, money for security training is limited, and employers struggle to adapt their preparation to the myriad dangers. "We've quickly had to change our view of security," said David Verdi, vice president of worldwide newsgathering for NBC News.

"We need a more nuanced approach," said Judith Matloff, a veteran foreign correspondent and independent journalist security trainer who recently became director of the North American branch of the London-based nonprofit International News Safety Institute. "What is the best training for a situation? We need to do assessments of needs, as opposed to taking the approach that there is one solution for all."

For more than a decade, many journalists took HEFAT, or Hostile Environments and Emergency First Aid Training, courses taught largely by British Royal Marines and other elite U.K. forces. Yet the most dangerous situation for journalists historically has not been combat coverage, but local reporting on sensitive topics such as crime, politics, and corruption. Since 1992, nearly three out of four journalists killed worldwide were murdered, mostly within their own nations, according to CPJ research. Another one in five was killed in combat or related situations, with the balance killed while covering street demonstrations or other violent, nonmilitary assignments.

Those proportions have changed significantly over the past two years, during which growing numbers of journalists have been killed covering violent street protests. By 2011, about 40 percent of media fatalities came during coverage of street demonstrations, many during the series of popular uprisings that swept the Arab world. And that shift in the dangers facing journalists has raised a new set of challenges for the profession.

........................................

*More fatalities are occurring during coverage of street demonstrations.*

........................................

The international community spends about $250 million a year on media development around the world, said Rodney Pinder, executive director of the International News Safety Institute and a former Reuters Television News executive. "They are training them to be professional journalists, and risk their lives," Pinder said. "But they don't train them how to protect themselves."

Al-Jazeera correspondents and crews have been on the front lines of breaking news in nations such as Tunisia, while citizen journalists have been feeding footage and other news to the Doha-based network from nations such as Syria. "We're worried about injury, how to get people out," said Al-Jazeera news chief Allan. Kidnapping is another major concern. Every one of her foreign correspondents must compile regular risk assessments. The preparation requirements are even more stringent for Al-Jazeera journalists covering Mexico, a nation plagued by pervasive violence. "We have to see [the assessment] before they go out the door. Where are you going? Who are you meeting? How are you traveling there? Where are you sleeping at night?" she said. "People disappear there. Journalists are soft targets."

Few attacks more strongly underscore the need for a new approach than the sexual assault of CBS News correspondent Lara Logan in Egypt's Tahrir Square in February 2011. That case "drove the point home—that we must prepare our journalists not only for the battlefield but for all of the various new threats they face when covering the news," said Larry Rubenstein, a veteran photojournalist who recently became Thomson Reuters' general editorial manager for safety and logistics.

Indeed, *Time* magazine's veteran foreign correspondent Vivienne Walt recently told the Canadian Broadcasting Corporation about her experience taking a HEFAT training course. "We were taught all sorts of things, from dressing wounds to recognizing different kinds of artillery, to what to do in a kidnap situation," she said. "What was really striking was there was never any discussion about the particular problems pertaining to women."

Organized crime groups, corrupt government officials, and terrorist organizations pose another kind of threat. "There is a difference between preparing war correspondents and training local journalists covering urban violence or organized crime," said Rosental Alves, former managing editor of *Jornal do Brasil* and director of the Knight Center for the Americas at the University of Texas at Austin.

## Tailoring training to specific needs such as coverage of crime, corruption.

Journalists are regularly targeted for murder in nations such as Iraq, Mexico, the Philippines, Russia, Pakistan, and Somalia. Worldwide, the murderers get away with it in nearly nine out of 10 cases. The victims are overwhelmingly local journalists, cut down within their own communities. "Local journalists in emerging democracies living amidst civil conflict go home to their families who are also at risk," said the Dart Center's Shapiro. "Press freedom advocates need to be looking at ways to do more for local journalists."

In Peru, the nonprofit news outlet IDL-Reporteros is developing its own security curriculum. Journalists take classes twice a week for eight weeks to learn Krav Maga, the self-defense system designed for close-quarter fighting adopted by the Israeli military. "This is obligatory," said Gustavo Gorriti, editor of IDL-Reporteros and one of Latin America's most respected investigative journalists. (Gorriti himself was abducted for two days in 1992 by Peruvian intelligence agents.) Gorriti said journalists are also trained how to spot a tail.

Another nonprofit, investigative journalism group, the Balkans-based Organized Crime and Corruption Reporting Project, has its own security training practices. "We believe the most dangerous indicator is that someone is following your reporter," said Advising Editor Drew

Sullivan. The group's security protocols include surveillance detection and ways to approach and interview potentially violent groups and figures. "You have to do some counter-surveillance measures. Ours are not very sophisticated, but you have to start somewhere."

A related threat is electronic interception. Government agencies have spied on journalists in nations from China to Colombia and Iran to Eritrea. In these countries and others, foreign correspondents, local journalists, and bloggers alike face the prospect of having their email, Facebook, and Twitter accounts monitored, their communications with sources, editors, and others intercepted, the data on their hard or flash drives stolen or copied, and their movements tracked, perhaps through cell phones or other devices. Criminal syndicates often possess the same capabilities. The lifting of such information rarely leaves a trace.

There is still great need for training in combat awareness and emergency first aid. Veteran photojournalists Chris Hondros and Tim Hetherington were killed in an attack in April in Misurata, Libya. Hetherington's colleagues say he bled to death from an open wound to the femoral artery, consistent with a video of his body on a hospital gurney showing a blood-soaked wound to the right inner thigh.

Several colleagues told CPJ that they wonder whether Hetherington could have been saved. A trained responder could conceivably reach into an open femoral wound to apply pressure above the artery break to stop

the bleeding. But this would be difficult under the best of circumstances, let alone in the back of a speeding pickup truck carrying three wounded journalists. A tourniquet would be another option, at the likely cost of losing the leg. But few journalists carry tourniquets and even fewer are trained how to use them.

The 2011 meltdown and radiation leak from a nuclear power plant in Fukushima, Japan, raised another set of contingencies that experts have barely addressed. Leading firms such as the U.K.-based Centurion Risk Assessment Services have provided training on biological and chemical warfare protection, but not on radiological disasters. The leading nonprofit International News Safety Institute lists providers of chemical, biological, radiological, and nuclear protection equipment.

## Security is a core function of any news organization, one executive says.

One area in which many international news organizations have provided better support for journalists in recent years is coping with stress and trauma. Years ago, said Al-Jazeera's Allan, "I think every journalist was supposed to suck it up." Allan, a journalist of 30 years, said attitudes toward trauma are different today. "There are signs, and you can help people," she said.

"We seek out leaders in the field of trauma," said Santiago Lyon, a veteran photojournalist and photography director at The Associated Press. NBC news executive Verdi said he now brings in female and male experts from both the counseling and law enforcement fields who are experienced in addressing trauma as well as rape as part of NBC's security training.

"Security in all its forms is simply a part of the core function of companies that are putting journalists in the field," Verdi said. "It's no longer discretionary. It's not an adjunct or ancillary function. It's a core function of being a journalist. It has to be considered up front on how to cover different regions of the world."

*Frank Smyth is CPJ's senior adviser for journalist security. He has reported on armed conflicts, organized crime, and human rights in El Salvador, Guatemala, Colombia, Rwanda, Eritrea, Ethiopia, Sudan, and Iraq. Smyth is also founder and executive director of Global Journalist Security, a firm that provides consulting and training services.*

Africa

# Africa

PHOTO CREDITS

*Section break: In Johannesburg, photographers come under attack by supporters of an African National Congress youth leader. (Daniel Born/The Times)*

*Page 53: Ethiopia's Meles Zenawi and China's Wen Jiabao toast their collaboration. (AFP/ Adrian Bradshaw)*

*Page 57: A protest against South Africa's "secrecy bill." (AP/Schalk van Zuydam)*

*Page 61: Kenyan police are accused of widespread extrajudicial killings, including the murder of reporter Francis Nyaruri. (AFP/Tony Karumba)*

RESEARCH CREDITS

*Country reports in this chapter were researched and written by Mohamed Keita, CPJ's Africa advocacy coordinator, and Tom Rhodes, CPJ's Nairobi-based East Africa consultant.*

# In Africa, Development Still Comes At Freedom's Expense

## By Mohamed Keita

Tommo Monthe, a seasoned Cameroonian diplomat, appeared at a human rights forum alongside the U.N. high commissioner for human rights and extolled the primacy of ... development. "Poverty is a challenge to the enjoyment of rights," Monthe declared at the October 2011 event at U.N. headquarters. "Roads, pumps, railroads, all kinds of development equipment in Africa are keys to the enjoyment of such rights." Back home, Cameroonian authorities have detained and harassed dozens of journalists in recent years for scrutinizing the use of public funds intended for just that kind of infrastructure. One, editor Cyrille Germain Ngota Ngota, died in state custody in 2010, having been imprisoned for investigating alleged public corruption in the oil sector.

More and more, African leaders are arguing that freedom of the press and human rights are unattainable so long as poverty persists. They cite their plans, real and otherwise, to eradicate poverty as reason to suppress media scrutiny and dissident voices. Taking a cue from China, which has an expanding role on the continent as an investor and model, they stress social stability and development over openness and reform. As a result, national priorities, public spending, and corruption go unquestioned. Political dissent is stamped out, and the tales of people left out of economic development, particularly in rural areas, go untold.

In January, for example, the outgoing African Union chairman, President Bingu wa Mutharika of Malawi, signed into law an amendment to the country's penal code giving the information minister unchecked authority to block the reporting of any news the government deems not to be in the public's interest. The move came as members of the ruling party were seeking a number of court injunctions to stop investigative reporting about the management of public funds, including the payment of large salaries to public servants. Media and civil society groups have challenged the constitutionality of the amendment, and its application was suspended pending a determination by the High Court.

"Poverty has made people cynical about human rights and democracy," said Faith Pansy Tlaluka, the African Union special rapporteur on freedom of expression. But she noted the inherent connection between press freedom and achievement of the Millennium Development Goals, the eight anti-poverty benchmarks that world leaders committed in 2000 to reach by 2015. "It is hardly possible to address the [goals] without citizen participation, freedom of expression, and information."

Yet many African leaders continue to offer a false choice between stability and press freedom, justifying press restrictions by invoking the primacy of economic development. In March, Gambian President Yahya Jammeh bluntly warned journalists in such terms. "If you're interested in development, you want peace and stability, then you don't have anything to fear from me," Jammeh said. Calling himself "a dictator of development," Jammeh said he would not sacrifice Gambian stability for freedom of expression or freedom of the press. "You have a *positive* role to play in national development, peace, and stability," he told journalists. The warning sought to deter the local press from reporting on human rights abuses as the government pursued an aggressive international marketing campaign to revive its tourism sector.

...............................................

## In Uganda, Museveni tries to criminalize negative economic news coverage.

...............................................

In May, Ugandan President Yoweri Museveni accused local and international media of endangering national economic interests by covering the brutal repression of opposition-led protests over high fuel prices. Calling independent media "irresponsible" and "enemies of Uganda's recovery," Museveni asserted that coverage "scared away some of the tourists who were planning to come here," as well as foreign investors. Museveni's government has introduced a proposal to parliament to criminalize reporting that the government considers "economic sabotage."

Echoing Museveni's rhetoric, Equatorial Guinea President Teodoro Obiang asserted in July that critical press coverage was to blame for hindering Africa's progress. "Africa is moving towards development in order to move beyond the bad image that some media use," said Obiang, whose government seized unflattering footage of slums from a ZDF German television crew in June. Speaking about the country he has ruled for more than 32 years, all the while stifling press freedom and dissent, Obiang claimed citizens held "widespread satisfaction" with its progress. To spread this message further, the government hired international public relations firms to issue glowing press releases about strides in development, according to news reports. But in fact, the country remained in the bottom third of many development indicators, including the Mo Ibrahim Index, which assesses governance quality, Transparency International's Corruption Perceptions Index, and the U.N. Development Programme's Human Development Index. The nation ranked poorly even as an oil boom and Chinese infrastructure investment fueled Equatorial Guinea's economy.

China overtook the West as Africa's biggest trading partner in 2009, according to news reports, and the most imposing symbol of China's influence could be China State Construction Engineering Corp.'s massive US$150 million expansion of the headquarters of the African Union. A 2006 Beijing summit between Chinese and African leaders laid the groundwork for cooperation, an alternative to dependence on the West with its requirements for human rights and reform.

Of the 11 African economies identified by the World Bank as among the world's fastest growing in 2011, only five—Ghana, Botswana, Mozambique, Tanzania, and Nigeria—have achieved a decent record of press freedom in CPJ's assessment. The others—Ethiopia, the Democratic Republic of Congo, Angola, Zimbabwe, Rwanda, and Republic of Congo—took an authoritarian approach to the press that was much like that of Beijing. Combined, those countries received more than one-fifth of China's total foreign direct investment in 2010, according to Chinese government data.

Following the path of Chinese leaders, the former Marxist rebels who have ruled Ethiopia since 1991 have blocked websites featuring dissenting political views with what is "the most extensive" Internet censorship infrastructure in sub-Saharan Africa, according to Rebekah Heacock, a project coordinator with OpenNet Initiative, which monitors filtering and surveillance globally. Prime Minister Meles Zenawi has imprisoned dissidents and enacted laws severely restricting the press, political opposition, and civil society; like China, Ethiopia is one of the foremost jailers of journalists in the world.

## Nations benefiting from China's investments are following its repressive lead.

"We do not follow the liberal democratic principles which the Western countries are pushing us to follow," asserted Deputy Prime Minister Hailemariam Desalegn in an October 2010 interview with the U.S. government-funded broadcaster Voice of America. "Our strategy is totally different from the Western way or approach, because we have to get out of this rampant poverty as soon as possible." In July, before a panel of the U.N. Human Rights Committee in Geneva, Genenew Assefa, a senior political adviser to Ethiopia's government, indicated that for the administration, development trumps human rights. Speaking about the government's five-year development plan, Assefa said, "It is premised on the notion that without the well-being, without food security, all the other democratic rights would be hollow. A starving people, huh? Priority should be given to overcoming abject poverty and providing every citizen security to life, and that is the direction that my country is going."

In April, Zenawi announced plans to build Africa's largest hydroelectric dam on the Blue Nile. According to news reports, the dam is part of a five-year growth plan that focuses on, among other things, energy and telecommunications infrastructure. (The Chinese company ZTE Corp. has installed and financed a US$1.5 billion telecom network in Ethiopia, news reports said.) Former Ethiopian President Negasso Gidada said in an October interview with *The Christian Science Monitor* that the ruling party is so convinced that only its leadership can lead the country to prosperity that it believes "all other organizations should be brought on board or eliminated."

Critical media outlets are apparently among those organizations. Beginning in June, authorities invoked a vague and unsubstantiated plot to destroy electrical and telecommunications infrastructure as reason to arrest four critical local journalists under the country's far-reaching anti-terrorism law. Columnist Reeyot Alemu of the weekly *Feteh*, for instance, had criticized the country's development plan for paying scant attention to democratization and human rights, and dissident blogger Eskinder Nega criticized Zenawi's diplomacy with Egypt over the dam project, according to CPJ research. A former journalist with Ethiopia's government-controlled state media, speaking on condition of anonymity for fear of reprisals against relatives still in Ethiopia, told CPJ that ruling party officers appointed to senior editorial positions discouraged journalists from carrying out investigative reports critically examining the government's plan. "They told me the media promotes development," the former journalist said.

A 2010 University of Oxford study on China's influence on African media cited "the partially overlapping ideas of 'positive reporting' in China and 'developmental journalism' in Africa, both of which stress the importance of focusing on collective achievements and offering citizens tools to contribute to national development rather than reporting on divisive issues or sensational negative news." The report noted that the Chinese intensified training of African journalists beginning in 2005, in an engagement that "privileges state media over private media in contrast with the Western focus on supporting civil society or private press."

......................................................

*Ethiopia jails journalists to suppress coverage critical of its development plans.*

......................................................

Africa's "developmental journalism" emerged in the post-independence, Cold War era of the 1960s and 1970s. "Development journalism supposedly was an effort to report on development, but it usually turned out to be propaganda-based, often designed solely to favor a particular government," said veteran reporter and journalism professor Arnold Zeitlin. In the view of veteran Zimbabwean journalist Bill Saidi, post-independence governments in southern Africa still expect the media to provide developmental journalism. "Criticism of the government is considered 'unpatriotic' and 'disloyal,'" he said.

In South Africa, which is China's largest trading partner in sub-Saharan Africa, the ruling African National Congress has castigated the independent press as unethical, biased, and Western-influenced in response to media scrutiny of its record on poverty, crime, and corruption. In June, government spokesman Jimmy Manyi announced a new policy to use state advertising expenditures to reward media outlets that "told the truth" about the party's anti-poverty achievements, according to news reports.

The next month, Sports Minister Fikile Mbalula accused the local media of practicing "British-style" journalism by scrutinizing the private business dealings of ruling party youth leaders, who he said "have raised contentious issues for the benefit of the majority of our people, who are black and landless."

Andrew Kanyegirire, a former journalist who is now head of communications for an Africa Union agency that promotes both democracy and development, said the journalistic concept of "being detached, being truthful, being neutral, reporting what you see, doing things in interest of being a watchdog" has become "un-African" in the eyes of some leaders and opinion-makers.

*Neutral, watchdog reporting has become 'un-African' in the eyes of leaders.*

"At a continental level, the '80s were a lost decade in terms of development, with the famine for instance. The '90s were about establishing good governance, democracy as a basis for development, with elections, free press, human rights, civil liberties," said Kanyegirire. The 2000 commitment to the Millennium Development Goals, he said, marked a shift. "As far as I am concerned, we were going back to the '60s, '70s, where the end goal was development," Kanyegirire said. "Here, the expectation is that all key sectors, agencies, spheres of society focus on development—that applies to media and journalists. There is a veiled, implicit call to pay credence to the father of the nation, or mother of the nation."

This notion has stretched as far as sports coverage. During a March press conference after Cameroon's loss to Senegal in a soccer match, Cameroonian striker Samuel Eto'o snapped at Senegalese reporter Moussa Tandian after the journalist raised a critical question about the team's disappointing performance. "You journalists, certain journalists like you, you who do not want Africa to advance, you who do not want Cameroon to advance, you are always negative. Try to change a little," Eto'o said, pointing at Tandian.

Even some in the Western donor community have seemed to weigh the importance of development against that of human rights. When a journalist from the Swedish newspaper *Dagens Nyheter* questioned Swedish International Development Cooperation Minister Gunilla Carlsson about Stockholm's US$37 million aid to Ethiopia in light of Addis Ababa's imprisonment of two Swedish reporters, Carlsson said: "We have been clear about what we say are major deficits in democracy and human rights.

At the same time, Prime Minister Meles Zenawi is successful in fighting poverty and has assumed major responsibility in climate negotiations."

But injustices have sprung from the pursuit of development detached from human rights and free expression. In an August 2011 report, the U.N. secretary-general examined African nations' progress in line with the

*Injustice springs from the pursuit of development detached from human rights.*

democracy and development goals outlined in the New Partnership for Africa's Development, a plan charted by AU heads of state in 2001. The U.N. report found "strong economic growth and improvement in social development indicators, especially in health and education" but also cited ongoing violations of human rights and "the systematic exclusion of significant portions of society from institutions of political governance."

In a May editorial in the Ethiopian newspaper *Addis Fortune*, Kenichi Ohashi, former Ethiopia country director for the World Bank, warned of the consequences of development without democracy. "The long-run stability and resilience of any system come from continual adaptation to changing circumstances. That in turn requires the free flow of information,

even when the message is not what the top leaders hoped to hear, and the space for vigorous contestation of ideas."

South African journalist Joe Thloloe, who was repeatedly imprisoned during apartheid in a career that has spanned more than 50 years, observed, "It's not an either/or." One can be democratic and "at the same time ensure that you don't go hungry," he said. "If the press doesn't highlight the wrongs in society, in addition to good things happening, there's nobody who will be paying attention to the wrongs and devoting time to resolve them."

## In South Africa, an ANC bill would cloak government operations in secrecy.

That concept is in danger now. In South Africa, the ANC has pushed legislative measures to criminalize investigative journalism and allow officials to classify as secret virtually any piece of government information in the name of "national interest." The National Assembly approved the controversial bill in November, sending it to the National Council of Provinces for consideration in late year. Under the proposed measures, investigative reports on government shortcomings, such as a May 2 *Daily Dispatch* story on the poor living conditions of citizens in Eastern Cape, could be suppressed. "Seventeen years after the dawn of democracy, the people of Malepelepe have yet to taste most of the fruits of democracy in the form of development," reads the story, which quotes a resident named Nofundile Dawuse as saying, "Nothing has changed. I still live in poverty. We don't have water. I do not have electricity. I use candles and paraffin."

*Mohamed Keita is advocacy coordinator for CPJ's Africa program. He regularly gives interviews in French and English to international news media on press freedom issues in Africa and has participated in numerous international panels. He conducted a fact-finding mission to Senegal and Mali in 2011.*

# Murder in Remote Kenya Reverberates Across Nation, World

*By Tom Rhodes with reporting
from Clifford Derrick*

By the edge of Kodero Forest in remote western Kenya, local hunters discovered the body of 31-year-old newspaper reporter Francis Nyaruri, decapitated and grotesquely disfigured, his hands tied behind his back to render him helpless. It was January 29, 2009, two weeks after the reporter had gone missing while on a trip to Kisii, about 30 kilometers from his home in Nyamira.

The gruesome killing haunts his wife. "The eyes were not even there—they had been gouged out," Josephine Kwamboka Nyaruri recounted in an interview with CPJ. "Even his lower jaw was missing." At the time of the murder, Nyaruri had just finished a story accusing a police official of corruption in the construction of facilities in Nyamira and elsewhere. It wasn't his first piece questioning the performance and integrity of national police officials stationed in western Kenya.

A CPJ investigation, which included a review of law enforcement documents and interviews with people involved in the case, found evidence that senior officials engaged in a large-scale effort to obstruct the investigation into Nyaruri's murder. "There is strong suspicion that police officers could have executed the deceased," Attorney General Amos Wako wrote in a June 2009 letter, one of several official documents that also raise the likelihood of direct police culpability.

But nearly three years later, no police official has been charged or even questioned in the killing. Two men are being tried on murder charges, but Nyaruri's colleagues and relatives believe that if the suspects were involved at all, they were bit players in a larger conspiracy. The murder comes against a backdrop of widespread extrajudicial killings in Kenya, which led U.N. Special Rapporteur Philip Alston to conclude in February 2009 that "Kenyan police are a law unto themselves, and they kill often and with impunity." The Kenya National Human Rights Commission continues to wage a campaign to highlight police impunity in extrajudicial killings.

(Kenyan police are also implicated in a 1991 attack on photojournalist Wallace Gichere, who was severely injured when he was thrown from a third-story window. Gichere died in 1998.)

Despite the remoteness of its setting, the murder also reflects global issues for the press. Nine of 10 journalist murders worldwide involve local reporters such as Nyaruri, CPJ research shows. About 30 percent of victims worldwide had investigated corruption in the months before their deaths. Government officials are suspected in one in four journalist murders across the globe. And, as in the Nyaruri case thus far, journalist murders are carried out with impunity 88 percent of the time.

"The murder of Nyaruri could be conducted with impunity because none of the perpetrators feared arrest from authorities," Nyaruri family lawyer Andrew Mandi told CPJ. "That's because they represented the local authorities."

## Public officials are suspects in one in four journalist murders worldwide.

The original investigating officer, Inspector Robert Natwoli, appeared to make fairly quick progress in the case. By March he had questioned a suspect, taxi driver Evans Mose Bosire, and by May he had detained another man, Japeth Mangera, a reputed member of a local gang known as the *sungusungu*. Originally a sort of community security force with ties to police, the *sungusungu* had increasingly turned criminal and murderous over the years.

In a statement to national police in Kisii on March 12, 2009, Bosire said he drove Nyaruri to the home of a Kisii town councilor named Samuel Omwando on the day of the killing. Omwando had promised Nyaruri a "big story," according to Bosire, who said two police officers and two *sungusungu* members had gone along for the ride. Nyaruri grew nervous during the trip and attempted to leave, Bosire said in his statement, prompting one officer to strike the reporter with the butt of his gun. Bosire said the group dragged Nyaruri to the local councilor's house in the neighboring town of Suneka and severely beat him. Around 7:30 p.m., the group took Nyaruri to Kodero Forest and killed him, Bosire said, although the statement did not provide details about the evident brutality used in the killing. The assailants dumped the body just meters from the road, and Bosire drove the group back to Kisii, the taxi driver said.

Held for several weeks, Bosire was never formally charged. He was granted leave for a family visit in late May 2009 and disappeared. (Later, a

CPJ reporter who called Nyaruri's former cell phone spoke to an individual who identified himself as Bosire. The individual hung up as the reporter began asking questions, apparently turning off the phone afterward.) Mangera, the second suspect, was found wearing a cap belonging to Nyaruri when officers picked him up, police records show. Mangera told police he had no involvement in the killing, although he pointed to two other potential suspects, according to his May 26, 2009, statement to police. Charged with murder, he remained in custody in late 2011, along with another *sungusungu* member who was detained later.

Omwando moved to an undisclosed location as the investigation got under way, local journalists told CPJ. Calls to a phone number identified as belonging to Omwando went to a disconnected service. There is no record that investigators ever questioned Omwando.

Journalists in western Kenya told CPJ that Nyaruri's murder has cast a pall over their reporting, prompting many to resort to self-censorship. With a few exceptions, most local journalists have been too fearful to speak out on Nyaruri's behalf.

Although Nyaruri used a penname, Mong'are Mokua, while reporting for the private *Weekly Citizen* newspaper, he was not a cautious reporter. "He reported on issues of corruption involving the police and local municipal officials in Nyamira. This made him an enemy to many," recalled Samuel

Owida, a friend and former reporter for Kenya's main daily, *The Nation*.

"He just wouldn't be intimidated by anyone," KTN reporter Fred Moturi said, "but he also didn't take any precautions. Often, he would rush to a story without letting others know what he was rushing to. He would just hang up the phone and he was off before we knew where he was going."

Derided by establishment journalists as part of the "gutter press" for its sensational and sometimes thinly reported coverage, the *Weekly Citizen* also produced hard-hitting stories on subjects ignored by Kenya's major newspapers, said Esther Kamweru, former director of the Nairobi-based Media Council, an industry ombudsman's office.

....................................................

## *Nyaruri had produced hard-hitting stories about alleged police corruption.*

....................................................

One of those stories focused on the construction of housing for police recruits in Nyamira and two other locations, a project valued at 20 million shillings (US$203,252). Nyaruri caught wind of allegations that substandard iron sheets were being used for roofing on the project. His story in the *Weekly Citizen* accused Lawrence Njoroge Mwaura, the national police officer in charge in Nyamira, of defrauding the government in the construction.

The story was published on January 19, 2009, four days after Nyaruri went missing, but its findings were widely known beforehand. Before the piece was published in the *Weekly Citizen*, Nyaruri had discussed his conclusions on two local radio stations, Egesa FM and Citizen Radio, family lawyer Mandi said. Nyaruri had taken on the police before, notably in a 2008 piece accusing Mwaura of using police vehicles to transport prostitutes, the lawyer said. The reporter's father, Peter, said police officials had threatened Nyaruri after the 2008 story appeared, forcing him into hiding for several weeks.

Mwaura was not happy with such critical coverage, according to Mandi, who said he witnessed the officer threaten Nyaruri in early January 2009. "One day when I was in the company of Francis we met the police chief as he was going to his house for lunch. He confronted Francis in my presence and warned him of dire consequences if he did not stop writing about him," Mandi told CPJ. Inspector Natwoli also recalled his supervisor expressing dissatisfaction with Nyaruri in a December 2008 conversation. "He simply told me that the government was not happy with the way Nyaruri was writing stories about the police that embarrassed the government. ... He then informed me that Nyaruri was to be dealt with once and for all."

In an interview with CPJ, Mwaura denied that either conversation took place as recounted. He said that he bore no ill will toward Nyaruri and that he had no knowledge of why the reporter was murdered or by whom. "In fact, Nyaruri was my best friend. I had no single problem with this young man," Mwaura said. "He did not die in my district. I don't really know for sure why he was killed."

Life became increasingly difficult for Inspector Natwoli after he arrested the two suspects in spring 2009. "Soon after, Mwaura and his deputy came to my station and ordered that I be charged with disciplinary offenses of idling, negligence, disobeying lawful orders, and acts prejudicial to good order and discipline in the force," Natwoli stated in an affidavit he filed in connection with the murder investigation. Natwoli was transferred out of the jurisdiction in June, the first in a series of transfers involving officers assigned to the case.

Natwoli told CPJ he continued to face threats from police and *sungusungu*—including an episode in which shots were fired at his home—prompting him to go into hiding briefly and eventually to leave the police force entirely. "For simply carrying out my professional duties, my life was turned upside down," Natwoli told CPJ.

......................................................

## *The officer who probed Nyaruri's murder found himself under attack.*

......................................................

Throughout the summer of 2009, the head of the national police force, Commissioner Hussein Ali, authorized the transfers of several other police officers assigned to the case. No explanations were given at the time, and deputy police spokesman Charles Owino later told CPJ he could not comment on the transfers. But the transfers clearly undermined the investigation, according to local journalists and lawyers. "The investigation is at a complete standstill," prosecutor Mary Oundo told CPJ in October 2010. "All those investigating it in the beginning were transferred."

In his 2009 findings, U.N. Special Rapporteur Alston singled out Commissioner Ali for obstructing investigations into extrajudicial police killings. Describing a climate of "zero internal accountability," Alston went on to say, "the police who kill are the very same police who investigate police killings." Alston urged that Ali be dismissed, although President Mwai

Kibaki decided instead to name him chief executive of the Kenyan postal service. By late 2011, the International Criminal Court at The Hague was questioning Ali about his alleged role in the rampant violence that followed the disputed presidential election of December 2007.

Ali did not return messages left at his postal service office seeking comment for this story. Kenya police spokesman Eric Kiraithe denied official obstruction in the Nyaruri murder. "There is no senior officer who is under any obligation whatsoever to protect an officer who has broken the law," Kiraithe said.

As early as June 2009, however, Attorney General Wako directed the investigating officer to examine the potential role of Mwaura in Nyaruri's murder. "From his conduct, it is clear that he must have participated in the crime in one way or another," Wako said in a letter. "He should therefore be investigated."

## A U.N. official finds a Kenyan police culture of zero accountability.

The directive does not appear to have been followed. The senior criminal investigative officer now assigned to the case, Sebastien Ndaro, said he could not arrest Mwaura, but he declined all other comment. Wako, who stepped down in September 2011, was himself heavily criticized by Alston for his ineffectual handling of extrajudicial police killings. Mwaura was transferred to a similar supervisory position in Turkana.

In February 2010, police did arrest a second suspected *sungusungu* gang member in relation to Nyaruri's murder. The suspect, Wilfred Nyambati, denied any involvement and said he was traveling at the time, according to a police statement.

The case dragged on because of procedural delays—one judge abruptly postponed a 2010 hearing, saying he wasn't taking new cases—before the two suspects were finally brought to court in November 2011. At the hearing, Peter Nyaruri testified that his son had confided that Mwaura had threatened his life. Proceedings were adjourned until March 2012.

"God help Kenya" was the last voicemail greeting that Francis Nyaruri recorded on his cell phone in January 2009, recounted Jack Nduri, an old friend. Nduri said he tried to call Nyaruri on the day of the murder. "At that point he must have known he was going to be killed. His phone was switched off soon after I made that call."

For Nyaruri's family and colleagues, divine intervention seems more likely now than any human action to bring the perpetrators to account. "I have lost hope we will see any justice in this case," said the reporter's wife, Josephine. "They are just playing games." *Nation* reporter Owida, whose reporting helped expose Nyaruri's murder, said he has endured threatening phone calls warning him that he will "share Nyaruri's fate."

........................................

## *Kenya's strong civil society can reshape law enforcement gone awry.*

........................................

But it does not have to be that way. "While the existing situation is bad, it is far from intractable," Alston wrote back in 2009. "If it so chooses, Kenya can significantly reduce the prevalence of unlawful killings. Much of the institutional and legal structures needed to carry the reform process forward are in place. ... Kenyan citizens are politically engaged, and civil society is professional and serious and contributes substantially to the protection of human rights by monitoring abuses and proposing reforms."

CPJ has written to President Kibaki and Prime Minister Raila Odinga to appeal for a full and thorough prosecution. Due to Inspector Natwoli's early detective work, much of the investigation is well documented. It is not too late for justice for Francis Nyaruri, and it's not too late for Kenyan citizens to wrest back a law enforcement system that has been turned on its head.

*Tom Rhodes is CPJ's Nairobi-based East Africa consultant. Clifford Derrick is a freelance writer and former CPJ consultant.*

# Angola

Youth-led and social media-fueled protests demanding reform challenged President José Eduardo Dos Santos, who marked 32 years in power. Parliament, controlled by Dos Santos' MPLA party, considered legislation to "combat crime" in information and communication technology. The bill, pending in late year, would stiffen penalties for defamation and would criminalize electronic dissemination of "recordings, pictures, and video" of any individual without the subject's consent. In nationally televised remarks targeting citizen journalists, Dos Santos lashed out at the use of the Internet to organize "unauthorized demonstrations to insult, denigrate, provoke uproar and confusion." (One YouTube user called Kimangakialo posted more than 150 clips of protests.) In the same April address, Dos Santos claimed journalists enjoyed unfettered freedom to criticize his leadership. But CPJ research shows that security forces assaulted, detained, and obstructed independent journalists covering protests and official functions. Powerful public figures and officials used security forces and the courts to settle scores with reporters investigating allegations of abuse of power, corruption, or misconduct. Two journalists, Armando José Chicoca and William Tonet, were sentenced to prison over their critical coverage; they were free on appeal in late year. José Manuel Gimbi faced intimidation from security forces while reporting from the militarized, oil-rich enclave of Cabinda. Denial-of-service attacks targeted the exile-run websites *Club-K* and *Angola24horas*, taking them off-line in October.

KEY DEVELOPMENTS

» Internet "crime" bill would restrict newsgathering, social media.

» Arrests, assaults, obstruction climb, limiting coverage of corruption.

KEY DATA

## 25 Attacks, 2011

CPJ research charted a significant rise in attacks on the press in 2011. Cases of assault, censorship, detention, and threats jumped more than three-fold over 2010. Many involved journalists covering anti-government protests.

### Attacks over time, according to CPJ research:

| | |
|---|---|
| 2007 | 4 |
| 2008 | 4 |
| 2009 | 7 |
| 2010 | 7 |
| 2011 | 25 |

# 2 Independent newspapers

Officials of the ruling MPLA, their family members, and businesses aligned with the party have controlling interest in all but two of Angola's private newspapers, according to CPJ research.

**2 independent papers:**

*Agora*

*Folha 8*

**7 papers supportive of MPLA:**

*O Pais*

*Expansão*

*Exame*

*Angolense*

*A Capital*

*Semanário Angolense*

*Novo Jornal*

# 2 Independent broadcasters

In addition to controlling the national public broadcasters, officials of the ruling MPLA control all but two private radio stations, according to local journalists.

**2 independent stations:**

Radio Ecclésia

Radio Despertar

**8 stations supportive of MPLA:**

Rádio Nacional de Angola

Televisão Publica de Angola

FM Rádio LAC

FM Radio Comercial de Cabinda

FM Radio 2000

FM Radio Morena

Rádio Mais

TV Zimbo

# 8 Years prison penalty

The pending Internet bill proposed a stiff penalty for those "who without consent provide, transmit, make available, or distribute recordings, films, and photographs of another person through a system of information." At least four existing laws criminalize journalistic activities.

**Restrictive laws:**

1886   Colonial-era penal code sets a six-month prison penalty for defaming officials.

2002   State Secrecy Law imposes a two-year prison penalty for possession of official documents deemed sensitive.

2006   Press Law allows courts to suspend media outlets for a year.

2010   State Security Crime Law sets a two-year prison penalty for "words, images, writings, or sound insulting" to the president or official institutions.

# 10 Killed since 1992

Ten journalists have been killed for their work in Angola over the last two decades, according to CPJ research. Many of the deaths occurred during the country's 27-year civil war.

**A breakdown of fatalities since 1992:**

7   Journalists murdered

2   Journalists killed in crossfire

1   Journalist killed on a dangerous assignment

0   Arrests in the killings

# Cameroon

The government sought to curtail popular protests and related news coverage as President Paul Biya extended 29 years of rule in an October election. Having consolidated power through constitutional amendments that removed term limits and stacked the membership of the election oversight agency with loyalists, Biya swept 78 percent of the vote in a poll marked by low turnout and allegations by the United States and France that irregularities occurred. Twenty-two opponents, none competitive, split the rest of the balloting. With Biya's overwhelming dominance of the political and journalistic space, social media became the primary means to criticize his record on political repression, poverty, and corruption. In February, government spokesman Issa Tchiroma Bakary summoned journalists to his office and accused Cameroonian social media users, many of whom were based abroad, of "manipulating" young people to destabilize the country. A month later, the government temporarily shut down a Twitter-via-SMS service to foil possible protests. Security forces obstructed journalists covering the violent dispersal of small-scale protests, although citizen journalists posted several videos to YouTube that showed heavy-handed police tactics. Throughout the year, public figures used their influence to prosecute journalists investigating corruption. At least three critical journalists were detained for varying periods.

KEY DEVELOPMENTS

» Journalists detained for investigating official misconduct, harassed for covering protests.

» Government demonizes social media users, criminalizes certain online speech.

KEY DATA

O **Arrests in Ngota death**
Editor Germain Cyrille Ngota Ngota, 38, of the private newspaper *Cameroon Express*, died in Kondengui Prison on April 22, 2010, while being held on fabricated charges of falsifying a government document.

Ngota was arrested with three other journalists after they sent questions to a senior presidential adviser about a confidential government memo. Despite an international outcry, no one was held accountable for Ngota's death.

## 0 Permitted political programs

In a September decree, the Communications Ministry told independent news broadcasters not to air any political or debate programs ahead of an October election. Under a 2000 decree, the government can impose penalties for violations of such directives.

### Restricting broadcast media by decree:

**6** Month suspension of a broadcast license for violating a ministerial directive.

**100** Maximum broadcast radius in kilometers for broadcasters providing local news coverage.

**13** Members appointed by the communications minister to a board tasked with reviewing broadcast licenses. The board has 13 members.

## 3 Licensed TV stations

Due to hefty licensing fees imposed by a 2000 decree, the overwhelming majority of domestic private broadcasters operate without official licenses, according to CPJ research. Under a de facto policy of "administrative tolerance," the government allows most private stations to operate without a license. But it then selectively enforces the regulations to silence critical news coverage at politically sensitive periods.

## 9 Broadcasters silenced, 2003-11

Intervening at politically sensitive times, the Communications Ministry has ordered critical independent broadcasters off the air for failure to pay licensing fees. In doing so, the ministry abandoned its usual policy of "administrative tolerance." Most of the stations returned to the air after months-long suspensions.

### Silencing critical news coverage:

**February 19, 2003**: RTA and Canal 2

**March 14, 2003**: Magic FM

**May 23, 2003**: Freedom FM

**November 14, 2003**: Radio Veritas

**February 21, 2008**: Equinoxe Télévision

**February 28, 2008**: Magic FM

**August 17, 2009**: Sky One Radio

**October 6, 2009**: Démenti FM

## 4 Years in prison

Responding to a growing, critical blogosphere, Biya and the National Assembly enacted legislation in December 2010 that set a prison penalty of up to four years for electronic dissemination of unverified news and recordings of political speech without the subject's consent, according to CPJ research.

# Democratic Republic of Congo

Incumbent Joseph Kabila claimed victory in a November presidential election marred by widespread voting irregularities and a spike in attacks on news outlets. While international observers questioned the results, Kabila forces launched a crackdown on dissent. Attacks on the press were concentrated in the capital, Kinshasa, and surrounding Bas Congo province. Supporters of incumbent President Joseph Kabila's PPRD party and his administration intimidated journalists favorable to chief rival Etienne Tshisekedi; pro-opposition media were targeted in a series of arson attacks. In August, Kabila consolidated his grip on the media by appointing members of a new regulatory board charged with enforcing press laws and meting out penalties. Journalists criticized Kabila for stacking the 15-member agency with government allies, according to news reports. Across the vast nation, powerful local officials and their security forces carried out attacks on the press with impunity in reprisal for critical coverage. And in the country's strife-torn, mineral-rich east, a journalist was murdered amid murky circumstances.

KEY DEVELOPMENTS

» Attacks on press hit a five-year high ahead of November presidential elections.

» For fifth consecutive year, a journalist is murdered in eastern DRC.

KEY DATA

14 **Assaults in Bas Congo**

Many of the anti-press attacks in Bas Congo were physical assaults, CPJ research shows. The police and ruling party supporters carried out most of the violence.

0 **Officials arrested, 2006-11**

A number of government officials have been accused of attacking or threatening journalists, but the Kabila administration has not held any of them accountable, CPJ research shows.

**Four attacks, no accountability**

2006 Republican Guard soldiers assaulted a journalist.

2007 The education minister was accused of ordering police to beat journalists who were in his office for an interview.

2008 Ruling party militants assaulted five cameramen.

2011 A ruling party member of parliament was taped threatening a journalist.

# 2 Missing, 1998-2011

At least two news media workers have gone missing, according to CPJ research. In neither case have police uncovered information about the individuals' whereabouts.

## Media workers who vanished

**1998** Belmonde Magloire Missinhoun, a Benin national and owner of the independent financial newspaper *La Pointe Congo*, was last seen being arrested after a traffic accident with a military vehicle in Kinshasa.

**2003** Acquitté Kisembo, a 28-year-old medical student serving as a fixer for Agence France-Presse, was reported missing in the northeastern Ituri region, a dangerous and unstable area.

# 34 Press violations in Bas Congo

CPJ documented numerous instances of official censorship, assault, intimidation, detention, imprisonment, and legal harassment targeting journalists in Bas Congo province, home of the capital.

## The five provinces with the most anti-press attacks in 2011:

| | |
|---|---|
| Bas Congo | 34 |
| Katanga | 18 |
| East Kasai | 12 |
| West Kasai | 6 |
| North Kivu | 5 |

# 8 Killings by uniformed forces, 2005-11

CPJ has documented eight journalist deaths between 2005 and 2011. One murder was in direct retaliation for the journalist's work; CPJ is investigating the other cases to determine whether they were work-related. There was one common thread: In all of the cases, the killers wore uniforms of the security forces. CPJ research found that official investigations fell short in the collection and handling of forensic evidence, in transparency and scope, and in their failure to determine motives.

## Killings by uniformed assailants:

**November 3, 2005**: Franck Kangundu in Kinshasa. Motive unconfirmed.

**July 8, 2006**: Bapuwa Mwamba in Kinshasa. Motive unconfirmed.

**June 13, 2007**: Serge Maheshe in Bukavu. Motive confirmed as work-related.

**August 9, 2007**: Patrick Kikuku Wilungula in Goma. Motive unconfirmed.

**November 21, 2008**: Didace Namujimbo in Bukavu. Motive unconfirmed.

**August 23, 2009**: Bruno Koko Chirambiza in Bukavu. Motive unconfirmed.

**April 5, 2010**: Patient Chebeya in Beni. Motive unconfirmed.

**June 22, 2011**: Witness-Patchelly Kambale Musonia in Kirumba. Motive unconfirmed.

# Equatorial Guinea

News and information is tightly controlled in Equatorial Guinea, which CPJ has identified as one of the world's most censored nations. Nearly all news media are owned and run by the government or its allies. One independently owned newspaper circulates in the country, but it must practice self-censorship; no independent broadcasters operate domestically. Even in this rigid environment, authorities fearful of the implications of Arab unrest censored news coverage of the protests. President Teodoro Obiang continued efforts to alter his international image, assuming presidency of the African Union and reviving his effort to establish an "Obiang Prize" in life sciences under the auspices of UNESCO. For the second time, UNESCO suspended consideration of the prize after a global campaign by human rights and freedom of expression groups. As he marked his 32 years in power, Obiang declared there are "no" human rights violations in his country. But his administration suspended a state radio presenter for a mere reference to a "leader of the Libyan revolution." Authorities also urged the owners of television sets in public places not to show international satellite channels covering the Arab unrest, according to local journalists. Security agents detained a German TV crew and deleted footage of an interview with an opposition leader and pictures of children playing in slums.

KEY DEVELOPMENTS

» Authorities impose a news blackout on coverage of Arab uprisings.

» Obiang rebuffed in an effort to alter his image with a UNESCO prize.

KEY DATA

## 0 Broadcast reports of uprisings

The government banned news of Arab unrest on tightly monitored national airwaves and on television sets in public places, according to local journalists. CPJ has ranked Equatorial Guinea as the fourth-most-censored nation in the world.

## 10 Press freedom violations, 2011

CPJ documented at least 10 cases in which authorities arrested, censored, or obstructed journalists. Officials were particularly sensitive to coverage of poverty, obstructing at least three journalists who tried to document the issue.

# $1.2 Million

**Public relations fees**

The government paid three Washington-based public relations firms a total of US$1,192,329.50 between April and October 2010 to produce positive news about Equatorial Guinea, according to a report by the U.S. Department of Justice.

0 **Independent domestic broadcasters**

All television and radio are directly run by the government or controlled through its allies, CPJ research shows.

**A dearth of independent news sources:**

1 Independent newspaper

0 Independent television

0 Independent radio

1 Correspondent for international media

**Breakdown of attacks in 2011:**

4 Arrests

4 Cases of censorship

1 Case of obstruction

1 Case of retaliatory harassment

# $3 Million Prize

Drawing on his considerable wealth, Obiang tried to establish a self-named prize in life sciences under the auspices of UNESCO. The international agency postponed consideration of the proposal after human rights groups said Obiang's poor record contradicted UNESCO's values.

**A prize not to be:**

**2008:** Obiang offered UNESCO US$3 million for a self-named International Prize for Research in the Life Sciences.

**May 2010:** Thirty freedom of expression organizations expressed opposition. A month later, laureates of the UNESCO/Guillermo Cano World Press Freedom Prize joined in opposition.

**October 2010:** UNESCO indefinitely suspended the prize pending "consultations among all parties."

**July 2011:** At a summit in Equatorial Guinea, African Union heads of state passed a resolution urging UNESCO to reverse its decision.

**September 2011:** Republic of Congo and Ivory Coast requested that UNESCO's executive board adopt the prize immediately.

**October 2011:** UNESCO deferred action on the prize, and set up a working group to continue consultations.

# Eritrea

No independent press has operated in this Red Sea nation since a September 2001 government crackdown on dissent that led to the imprisonment of 11 leading journalists without charge or trial and the enforced closure of their publications. President Isaias Afewerki's administration has consistently refused to account for the whereabouts, legal status, or health of the jailed journalists, or even confirm reports that some have died in custody. All of the journalists are held without access to their families or lawyers. The only media allowed to operate in the country are under the control of Information Minister Ali Abdu, who enforces rigid control of information and ideas through intimidation and imprisonment. Even state media journalists have braved border guards' shoot-to-kill orders to escape the country. Government agents abroad harass and intimidate media outlets established by exiled journalists. The government's egregious actions drew condemnation from the European Parliament in September 2011, the latest in a series of international censures.

KEY DEVELOPMENTS

» For 10 consecutive years, nation is the leading jailer of journalists in Africa.

» Using ruthless tactics, state maintains absolute control over news coverage.

KEY DATA

## 28 Imprisoned as of December 1, 2011

Eritrea is Africa's leading jailer of the press and the second worst worldwide, trailing only Iran, according to CPJ research.

### World's worst jailers in 2011:

| 42 | Iran | 12 | Burma |
|----|------|----|-------|
| 28 | Eritrea | 9 | Vietnam |
| 27 | China | | |

## 47 In exile, 2001-11

Vast repression has driven dozens of journalists out of the country over the past decade, according to a CPJ study.

The study takes into account journalists who flee due to work-related persecution, who remain in exile for at least three months, and whose whereabouts and activities are known to CPJ.

# 3,751 **Days Dawit Isaac imprisoned**

As of December 31, 2011, Swedish-Eritrean journalist Dawit Isaac had been held more than 3,700 days in a secret prison without charge or trial. He was among a group of 11 journalists who were taken into custody in 2001 as part of a widespread crackdown that shut the independent press. Isaac was briefly freed in 2005 only to be placed back in prison within two days.

## Timeline in the Isaac case:

**September 23, 2001**: Arrested in crackdown on dissent.

**November 19, 2005**: Released, called family in Sweden.

**November 21, 2005**: Imprisoned again without explanation.

**January 11, 2009**: News reports said he was hospitalized.

**May 2009**: Afewerki said Isaac would not be given a trial and that he made a "very big mistake."

**April 2010**: Former prison guard said Isaac was in poor health.

**August 1, 2010**: Senior official accused Isaac of "very serious crimes" but provided no details.

**September 2011**: European Parliament resolution called for immediate release of Isaac.

# 0 **Independent news media**

All print, television, and radio news outlets are directly controlled by the government, CPJ research shows. The government's control over the flow of information is near total.

## An absence of independent news media:

0 Correspondents for international media

0 Locally hosted independent news websites

0 Independent newspapers, television stations, radio stations

# 6th **Most censored nation**

CPJ ranked Eritrea as one of the most censored nations in the world in a 2006 survey. The government's ruthless repression has shielded its leaders from scrutiny.

## CPJ's Most Censored Nations:

1. North Korea

2. Burma

3. Turkmenistan

4. Equatorial Guinea

5. Libya

6. **Eritrea**

7. Cuba

8. Uzbekistan

9. Syria

10. Belarus

# Ethiopia

Trumpeting economic growth on par with India and asserting adherence to the authoritarian model of China, Prime Minister Meles Zenawi pushed an ambitious development plan based in part on ever-hardening repression of critical journalists. The government aggressively extended application of a 2009 anti-terrorism law, designating rebel and opposition groups as terrorists and criminalizing news coverage of them. Authorities were holding seven journalists in late year on vague accusations of terrorism, including two Swedes who reported on separatist rebels in the oil-rich Ogaden region, and three Ethiopians with critical views of the ruling party. The government provided no credible evidence against the journalists, and both Zenawi and state media proclaimed the journalists' guilt before trial proceedings started. The Human Rights Committee of the U.N. High Commissioner for Human Rights raised numerous questions about the use of the terror law in its periodic review of Ethiopia's record. In November, government intimidation led to the closing of the independent *Awramba Times* and forced two of its journalists, including 2010 CPJ International Press Freedom Awardee Dawit Kebede, to flee the country. Another journalist fled into exile in September after his name appeared in unredacted U.S. diplomatic cables released by WikiLeaks. Police threatened to arrest the journalist after the cable showed he had spoken to U.S. diplomats about a potential press crackdown.

KEY DEVELOPMENTS

» Government broadens use of terror law, criminalizes coverage of opponents.

» Wary of Arab uprising, authorities censor, jail independent journalists.

KEY DATA

## 79 In exile, 2001-11

Ethiopia has driven more journalists into exile over the past decade than any other nation in the world, according to CPJ research. Official harassment and the near-constant threat of imprisonment have compelled dozens of journalists to flee.

**Top nations from which journalists have fled:**

| | |
|---|---|
| **Ethiopia** | **79** |
| Somalia | 68 |
| Iran | 66 |
| Iraq | 55 |
| Zimbabwe | 49 |

4 **International journalists jailed**

Two Swedish journalists reporting on separatist rebels were convicted on terrorism charges and sentenced to 11 years in prison apiece. Two Eritrean journalists remained in government custody on vague terrorism accusations after being jailed in 2007. With seven jailed in all, Ethiopia's crackdown propelled it into the ranks of the world's leading jailers of the press.

**World's worst jailers in 2011:**

| | |
|---|---|
| Iran: | 42 |
| Eritrea: | 28 |
| China: | 27 |
| Burma: | 12 |
| Vietnam: | 9 |
| Turkey: | 8 |
| Syria: | 8 |
| **Ethiopia:** | 7 |

99% **Ruling party control of parliament**

The ruling Ethiopian Peoples' Revolutionary Democratic Front (EPRDF) controls all but one of 547 seats in the House of Peoples' Representatives. Since 2008, the chamber has enacted three laws restricting independent media, political opposition, and civil society organizations. The party's grip on the chamber mirrors its dominance of the media and political scenes.

7 **Imprisoned on December 1, 2011**

Imprisonments in Ethiopia rose in 2011 in concert with its aggressive extension of terror laws. Dissent, and even coverage of dissent, was conflated with treason.

**Imprisoned in Ethiopia over time:**

| | |
|---|---|
| 2007 | 2 |
| 2008 | 2 |
| 2009 | 4 |
| 2010 | 4 |
| 2011 | 7 |

1 **Internet service provider**

With investments from China's ZTE Corp. and France Telecom, the government retained monopoly control over state-owned Ethio Telecom, allowing it to conduct the most substantial filtering of Internet sites in sub-Saharan Africa, according to CPJ research and the OpenNet Initiative. Censorship of online media secured authorities a spot in CPJ's May report on the world's worst online oppressors.

**CPJ's 2011 Online Oppressors:**

| | |
|---|---|
| Iran | China |
| Belarus | Tunisia |
| Cuba | Egypt |
| **Ethiopia** | Syria |
| Burma | Russia |

# Gambia

Years of brutal repression by President Yahya Jammeh's administration have gutted Gambia's once-vibrant independent press and driven numerous journalists into exile. In August, the government forced Taranga FM, the last independent radio station airing news in local languages, to halt its coverage. The move came ahead of an October presidential election in which Jammeh faced no viable opponent and brooked no dissent. Official repression has taken many forms over the years, including arbitrary arrests, censorship, forced closures of media outlets, verbal and physical intimidation, arson attacks, and prosecutions under restrictive legislation. These actions, coupled with impunity in attacks on media houses and journalists, have reduced the domestic news media to a handful of newspapers that operate under intense fear and self-censorship. While marketing the country internationally as an idyllic tourism destination, the government ignored two rulings by a West African human rights court: one ordering the release of reporter "Chief" Ebrima Manneh, who disappeared in state custody after his 2006 arrest, and another compelling the government to pay compensation to a journalist for illegal detention and torture.

KEY DEVELOPMENTS

» Radio station forced to drop news; no independent broadcaster remains.

» Whereabouts of reporter detained by government remain a mystery.

KEY DATA

## 17 In exile, 2001-11

Violence and intimidation have driven many of the Gambia's best journalists out of the country. Despite its small size, Gambia is 13th worst among all nations worldwide in the number of journalists who have fled into exile, according to CPJ research.

**Nations from which journalists have fled:**

| | |
|---|---|
| Ethiopia | 79 |
| Somalia | 68 |
| Iran | 66 |
| Iraq | 55 |
| Zimbabwe | 49 |
| Eritrea | 47 |
| Sri Lanka | 25 |
| Cuba | 25 |
| Colombia | 20 |
| Haiti | 18 |
| Rwanda | 18 |
| Uzbekistan | 18 |
| **Gambia** | **17** |

## 4 Presidential threats, 2006-11

With words of contempt and intimidation, Jammeh periodically threatened the media, chilling journalists into fear and self-censorship, according to CPJ research and news reports.

**Jammeh's hostile words:**

**September 2006**: "The whole world can go to hell. If I want to ban any newspaper, I will."

**July 2009**: "Any journalist who thinks that he or she can write whatever he or she wants and go free is making a big mistake. If anybody is caught, he will be severely dealt with."

**September 2009**: "I will kill you, and nothing will come out of it. We are not going to condone people posing as human rights defenders to the detriment of the country."

**March 2011**: "If I have to close any newspaper because you have violated the laws, I will close it. ... I will not *billahi wallahi*, sacrifice the interests, the peace and stability and well-being of the Gambian people at the altar of freedom of expression, or freedom of press, or freedom of movement, or freedom of whatever."

## 0 Arrests in media attacks

Impunity in anti-press attacks has been complete over the past decade. No arrests or convictions have been made for arson attacks on media houses, the murder of a prominent journalist, and the shooting death of another.

## 5 Years disappeared

Manneh disappeared in government custody after he was arrested in his newsroom by agents of the National Intelligence Agency. Despite eyewitness accounts of Manneh's arrest and subsequent sightings of the journalist in custody, Gambian officials have consistently denied having any knowledge of his whereabouts. That changed in October 2011, however, when Justice Minister Edward Gomez said Manneh was alive. He offered no details.

## 6 Outlets banned, 1998-2011

The administration has silenced numerous independent news sources over the years, imposing temporary or permanent bans. Outlets that were allowed to resume operation often eliminated news coverage or began exerting intense self-censorship.

**Outlets temporarily or permanently closed:**

**1998**: Citizen FM (Resumed operation without news coverage)

**2005**: Sud FM (Closed)

**2006**: *The Independent* (Closed)

**2008**: Radio France Internationale (Allowed to resume operations)

**2010**: *The Standard* (Resumed operation with self-censorship)

**2011**: Taranga FM (Resumed operation without news coverage)

# Ivory Coast

After the disputed November 2010 presidential elections, incumbent Laurent Gbagbo and rival Alassane Ouattara, whom the United Nations recognized as the winner, waged a months-long struggle for power led by partisan media outlets. The fight was centered in the economic capital, Abidjan, where Gbagbo controlled the national media and security forces. Ouattara enjoyed the support of a handful of newspapers and set up an improvised television station in the hotel where he was protected by U.N. peacekeepers. Both sides targeted rival outlets with reprisals, forcing numerous journalists into hiding. A journalist and a media worker were murdered in the violence. Fighters loyal to Ouattara clashed with Gbagbo troops for control of the national public broadcaster Radiodiffusion Télévision Ivoirienne in March and April, damaging studios and transmitters and knocking the station off the air, according to news reports and local journalists. While media movements were limited during the final battle for Abidjan, some citizen journalists provided exclusive footage of explosions and military operations by posting unedited videos on social media. With Gbagbo's April 11 capture, Ouattara assumed power and promised reconciliation, but his administration jailed a pro-Gbagbo TV host on antistate charges and his forces ransacked and occupied media outlets loyal to the former president. Journalists seen as sympathetic to Gbagbo faced continued harassment.

KEY DEVELOPMENTS

» Partisan media outlets, journalists are attacked in presidential power struggle.

» Ouattara pledges reconciliation, but his government retaliates against pro-Gbagbo media.

KEY DATA

### 87 Attacks in power struggle

CPJ documented dozens of assaults, detentions, threats, instances of censorship, kidnappings, and murders of journalists stemming from the presidential standoff that ended in April.

**Attacks by month:**

13 January

22 February

37 March

15 April

## 11 Evacuated from Abidjan

With the assistance of CPJ and the local Ivorian Committee to Protect Journalists, the U.N. peace-keeping force airlifted journalists trapped by heavy fighting in Abidjan to the northern city of Bouaké on March 30. All of the journalists resumed work after the fighting ended, but some faced continuing reprisals from the new government.

**New government, old repression:**

5   Former media personalities charged with antistate crimes for supporting Gbagbo.

8   Journalists whose assets the Ouattara government froze on accusations of supporting Gbagbo.

10   Pro-Gbagbo media outlets suspended since Ouattara took power.

## 2 Killed in 2011

A journalist and a media worker, both working for pro-Gbagbo outlets, were murdered by Ouattara supporters.

**Two politically inspired killings:**

**February 28, 2011**: A mob of Ouattara supporters dragged Marcel Legré, a printing press employee for La Refondation, publisher of the pro-Gbagbo newspaper *Notre Voie*, out of his home and hacked him to death in the Abidjan suburb of Koumassi.

**May 8, 2011**: Forces loyal to Ouattara killed Sylvain Gagnetau Lago, an assistant editor with community station Radio Yopougon, during a sweep in the Yopougon district of Abidjan, a former stronghold of Gbagbo.

## 4 Imprisoned on December 1, 2011

The most prominent detainee was former state journalist Hermann Aboa, host of a political talk show that had favored Gbagbo. In July, he was imprisoned on antistate crimes. Authorities had not disclosed evidence to back the charges as of late year.

**Timeline in the Aboa case:**

**April 11, 2011**: Aboa fled to Ghana on the day Gbagbo was captured.

**April-May**: Ouattara government officials assured CPJ that pro-Gbagbo media outlets and journalists had nothing to fear.

**June 13**: A state prosecutor froze the assets of 97 people accused of supporting Gbagbo, including Aboa, according to news reports.

**June 14**: Aboa returned to Ivory Coast, heeding Ouattara's call for exiles to return.

**July 21**: Aboa was arrested on antistate charges after filing a petition to unfreeze assets.

**July 27**: In a press conference at U.N. headquarters, Ouattara accused Aboa of hosting a program that "called on hate, hatred." CPJ found the accusations baseless after reviewing footage of Aboa's program.

# Malawi

President Bingu wa Mutharika signed a penal code amendment that allows the government to ban any publication it deems "not in the public interest." Authorities did not immediately use the new tactic, but local journalists said the law's existence had created a chilling effect. Government officials also made use of court injunctions to silence critical coverage of public officials' financial dealings. Authorities and ruling party supporters pushed back aggressively against coverage of nationwide protests over rising fuel costs and diminishing bank reserves: Police and security officers beat and detained journalists; the government blocked the transmissions of four private radio stations; and suspected ruling party supporters damaged two vehicles belonging to the private Zodiac Broadcasting Corp. The managers of a critical online news outlet, *Nyasa Times*, said they experienced a denial-of-service attack that took down their website during the protests.

## KEY DEVELOPMENTS

» Authorities censor, violently suppress coverage of nationwide protests.

» Officials use the courts to block critical stories, while a new law allows publication bans.

## KEY DATA

### 22 Assaulted in 2011

CPJ research found a surge of anti-press violence in 2011, occurring largely during nationwide protests in July.

**Journalists assaulted over time in Malawi:**

2007: 1

2008: 2

2009: 0

2010: 0

2011: 22

### 84% Attacks by police

Police were overwhelmingly behind attacks against the press in Malawi. Officers were involved in 84 percent of cases monitored by CPJ over the past five years.

**Behind the attacks, 2007-11:**

21: Police

2: Government officials

1: Ruling party supporter

1: Other

## 2 Injunctions against publisher

Nation Publications Ltd., publishers of the independent *The Nation*, *Weekend Nation*, and *Nation on Sunday*, was targeted with two court injunctions in March that blocked publication of articles that would have detailed allegations of tax evasion and disclosed a senior official's salary.

**March 11**: A regional governor, Noel Masangwi, obtained a High Court injunction to block a *Nation* story that alleged he avoided paying taxes of more than 36 million kwacha (US$237,000), according to local reports. Masangwi did not publicly respond to the accusation.

**March 30**: The treasury secretary got a High Court injunction blocking *Weekend Nation* from revealing his salary package, according to local reports. Secretary Joseph Mwanamvheka was earning four million kwacha per month (US$26,000), according to local reports.

## 716,400

**Internet users, 2009**

Despite being one of the poorest countries in Africa, Malawi has seen Internet use grow considerably, according to World Bank Development Indicators. The figure represents about 5 percent of the country's overall population. A flurry of news websites have emerged in recent years.

**Internet users over time, according to the World Bank:**

| 2005 | 52,500 |
| 2006 | 59,700 |
| 2007 | 139,466 |
| 2008 | 316,100 |
| 2009 | 716,400 |

## 11 Detained without charge, 2007-11

Malawian police have held a number of journalists in short-term detentions without formal charge in an effort to silence critical coverage, CPJ research shows. No journalist was formally charged in these cases.

**Short-term detentions without charge over time:**

| 2007 | 1 |
| 2008 | 3 |
| 2009 | 3 |
| 2010 | 1 |
| 2011 | 3 |

# Rwanda

Authorities pursued an aggressive legal assault against critical journalists, using laws that ban insults against public officials and abusing anti-genocide laws to silence independent voices. President Paul Kagame's close relations with Western governments continued to shield him from criticism over his administration's poor press freedom record. In February, a panel of High Court judges sentenced two editors of the now-closed independent weekly *Umurabyo* to lengthy prison terms on charges of "genocidal ideology" related to articles detailing ethnic divisions in the security forces. In June, the Supreme Court sentenced in absentia Jean-Bosco Gasasira, editor of the independent *Umuvugizi*, to a prison term of two and a half years on insult charges stemming from an opinion piece that unfavorably compared Kagame to Zimbabwean leader Robert Mugabe. Gasasira had fled the country in 2010, joining one of the region's largest press diasporas. Another independent weekly editor, Nelson Gatsimbazi, fled the country in September, also fearing imprisonment. The government's aggressive actions left a subdued and largely state-dominated press landscape. A small number of critical websites remained, but they were subjected to regular government blocking.

KEY DEVELOPMENTS

» Two independent journalists receive heavy prison sentences.

» Director of independent weekly flees the country as a press exodus continues.

KEY DATA

## 7 Major defamation cases, 2008–11

Public officials and prominent business figures have used criminal and civil defamation complaints and a politicized judiciary to silence independent journalists, CPJ research shows. In the seven major defamation cases heard in the past four years, the press has lost every time.

## Defamation cases over time in Rwanda:

2008 2

2009 1

2010 2

2011 2

# 18 In exile, 2001-11

Facing prison sentences and harassment, Rwandan independent journalists have steadily fled the country.

## Nations from which journalists have fled:

| | |
|---|---|
| Ethiopia | 79 |
| Somalia | 68 |
| Iran | 66 |
| Iraq | 55 |
| Zimbabwe | 49 |
| Eritrea | 47 |
| Sri Lanka | 25 |
| Cuba | 25 |
| Colombia | 20 |
| Haiti | 18 |
| **Rwanda** | **18** |
| Uzbekistan | 18 |

# 2 Imprisoned on December 1, 2011

High Court judges sentenced Agnès Uwimana, editor of *Umurabyo*, to 17 years in prison and Saidati Mukakibibi, the weekly's deputy editor, to seven years.

## Imprisoned over time in Rwanda:

| | |
|---|---|
| 2007 | 1 |
| 2008 | 0 |
| 2009 | 0 |
| 2010 | 0 |
| 2011 | 2 |

# 7 Suspensions of outlets, 2007-11

Whether ordered by the state or self-imposed, local and international media houses have faced suspensions. Some have been as short as one month, but others have been indefinite.

**June 2007**: Information Minister Laurent Nkusi suspended the license of the independent *Weekly Post* on vague allegations that it used false documents in its license application. The paper, in circulation for one issue, never published again.

**October 2007**: The Rwanda Independent Media Group, publisher of three weeklies, suspended publication for two weeks to protest remarks by two ministers claiming the company worked for "opposition forces."

**March 2008**: The Media High Council issued a one-year suspension to the independent Kinyarwandan weekly, *Umuco*, for insulting Kagame.

**April 2009**: The government suspended the BBC's Kinyarwandan programming for a month on trumped-up anti-genocide charges.

**April 2010**: The state-run Media High Council suspended the independent weeklies *Umuseso* and *Umuvugizi* for six months for insulting Kagame.

**August 2011**: The Kinyarwandan-language independent bimonthly *Ishema* suspended publication for a month after getting threats concerning an opinion piece that called Kagame a "sociopath."

# Somalia

L ocal and international journalists faced persistent, deadly violence, with both targeted murders and crossfire killings reported. Four soldiers with the African Union peacekeeping mission fired on a Malaysian humanitarian aid convoy in September, killing one journalist and injuring another. The AU mission in Somalia suspended the soldiers and returned them to their home country of Burundi for potential trial. Despite improved security in the capital, Mogadishu, journalists across the country continued to flee into exile to avoid threats and violence. Al-Shabaab militants and other insurgents continued to shutter independent radio stations in southern and central Somalia. Growing insecurity in the semi-autonomous region of Puntland led to increased attacks and arrests of journalists. In Somaliland, President Ahmed Mahmoud Silyano reneged on his 2010 campaign pledge to uphold press freedom and initiated a series of state-sponsored criminal defamation cases against the region's private press.

KEY DEVELOPMENTS

» AU forces kill Malaysian journalist; Somalia is region's deadliest nation.

» Press freedom violations rise in Puntland and Somaliland.

KEY DATA

## 9 Radio stations shut since 2007

Insurgents, notably militants with Al-Shabaab, have routinely shuttered stations deemed critical of their operations, seizing the properties for use in spreading their own propaganda. A government-allied militia, Ahlu Sunna Wal Jama'a, also seized a radio station.

**Radio stations shut over time:**

| | |
|---|---|
| 2007: 1 | 2010: 2 |
| 2008: 2 | 2011: 1 |
| 2009: 3 | |

## 22 Killed since 2007

Local and international journalists and media support staff face myriad dangers in a country gripped by violence and instability. Journalists have been murdered or killed in crossfire on a regular basis.

**Deaths in Somalia over time:**

2007: 7

2008: 2

2009: 9

2010: 2

2011: 2

# 2nd Impunity Index ranking

With at least 10 unsolved murders of journalists in the last decade, Somalia has the worst rating in Africa and the second worst worldwide in combating deadly attacks on the press, CPJ's Impunity Index shows.

**World ranking on CPJ's 2011 Impunity Index:**

1:  Iraq

**2:  Somalia**

3:  Philippines

4:  Sri Lanka

5:  Colombia

6:  Afghanistan

7:  Nepal

8:  Mexico

9:  Russia

10:  Pakistan

11:  Bangladesh

12:  Brazil

13:  India

# 68 In exile, 2001-11

Facing threats, attacks, and harassment, Somali journalists have fled the country by the dozens over the past decade, according to CPJ's annual report on exiled journalists. The exodus has decimated the local press corps and left a significant void in coverage seen internationally. Worldwide, only Ethiopian journalists have fled in higher numbers over the past decade, according to CPJ research.

**Top nations from which journalists have fled:**

| | |
|---|---|
| Ethiopia | 79 |
| **Somalia** | **68** |
| Iran | 66 |
| Iraq | 55 |
| Zimbabwe | 49 |
| Eritrea | 47 |
| Sri Lanka | 25 |
| Cuba | 25 |
| Colombia | 20 |
| Haiti | 18 |
| Rwanda | 18 |
| Uzbekistan | 18 |

# 7 Defamation cases in Somaliland

Despite 2010 campaign pledges to uphold press freedom, Somaliland authorities routinely filed politically motivated criminal defamation complaints to silence critical reporting. Seven cases were filed in 2011 alone, CPJ research shows.

**Newspapers targeted in 2011:**

*Hargeisa Star* (three times)

*Saxafi*

*Waheen*

*Ogaal*

*Yool*

# South Africa

The ruling African National Congress bridled at news media scrutiny of its record on poverty, crime, and corruption, which raised concerns about the durability of post-apartheid democratic reforms. In June, the government announced a new policy to use state advertising expenditures to reward supportive media outlets. Members of the ANC's youth wing tried to intimidate media outlets that examined the affluent lifestyle and private business dealings of its fiery former leader, Julius Malema. Youth members assaulted journalists covering Malema's appearance at a party hearing convened to discuss his hard-line statements. President Jacob Zuma, who traveled to Libya twice in support of Muammar Qaddafi, was criticized for failing to hold Libyan officials accountable in the case of Anton Hammerl. Loyalist forces killed the South African photojournalist in April, but Libyan officials withheld information about Hammerl's death for many weeks. In October, South African officials acknowledged that police had tapped the phone conversations of journalists Mwazili Wa Afrika and Stephan Hofstatter. The two faced persistent threats and intimidation related to a 2010 story on police corruption. The ANC pushed several restrictive legislative measures, including a bill that would allow officials to classify virtually any piece of government information in the name of "national interest." The National Assembly approved the bill in November, sending it to the National Council of Provinces for consideration in late year.

KEY DEVELOPMENTS

» Amid the ANC's anti-press rhetoric, assaults on journalists climb.

» Ruling party pushes secrecy bill, other restrictive legislation.

KEY DATA

## 11 Zuma defamation suits, 2006-11

President Zuma has made a practice of intimidating the press through defamation suits. Although no lawsuits were reported in 2011, local news outlets documented a series of defamation complaints filed by Zuma over the past several years.

## 10 Anti-press salvos

Throughout 2011, the ANC Youth League issued statements demonizing the independent press. In October, for example, the league said Talk 702 Radio and the daily Sowetan had spread "desperate and disgusting lies." They had reported that Malema used a vehicle instead of walking with protesters during a protest march.

# 4 Bills restricting news media

The National Assembly considered at least four bills in 2011 that would restrict press freedom, according to local journalists and the Media Institute of Southern Africa. Despite heavy local and international criticism, ANC leaders insisted that broad, new media legislation was needed.

**Four restrictive bills:**

**Protection of Information Bill**: Often dubbed the "secrecy bill," it would allow authorities wide discretion to classify information deemed "in the national interest." Journalists who report on classified information would face up to 25 years in prison.

**Protection from Harassment Bill**: The measure would bar individuals, including journalists, from pursuing someone in a way vaguely described as unreasonable. The South African National Editors Forum said the legislation could be used to block journalists' inquiries. A five-year prison penalty was proposed.

**Public Services Broadcasting Bill**: The measure would provide the government wide powers to regulate broadcast content, local journalists told CPJ. The legislation also obligates community radio stations to partner with local governments, locate their studios at municipal offices, and have government officials serve on their boards.

**Independent Communications Authority Act Amendment Bill**: Local journalists were concerned the legislation would undermine the independence of the authority, which oversees electronic and broadcast licenses. The proposal would allow the Information Ministry to appoint and evaluate members of the authority.

# 16 Assaults in 2011

Assaults against journalists increased sharply in 2011, CPJ research shows. Members of the ANC's Youth League were believed to be responsible for about two-thirds of the assaults.

**Attacks over time in South Africa:**

2007:   2
2008:   2
2009:   2
2010:   3
2011:   16

# 4.4 million
**Internet users, 2009**

Internet use has crept upward since 2005, according to the World Bank Development Indicators. With a population of nearly 50 million, though, South Africa offers considerable untapped Internet potential.

**Internet use over time, according to the World Bank:**

2005: 3.5 million      2008: 4.2
2006: 3.7              2009: 4.4
2007: 4.0

# Uganda

Police and security agents engaged in widespread physical attacks on local and foreign journalists during the general election campaign and its aftermath. Incumbent President Yoweri Museveni was elected to a fourth term in the February vote, which was marred by reports of intimidation and vote-buying. Reporters covering opposition candidates were at particular risk: Security agents shot two journalists covering opposition or protest rallies, leaving one reporter hospitalized. In April and May, authorities assaulted at least 25 journalists covering nationwide, opposition-organized protests over rising prices. Museveni publicly criticized foreign and local media for their coverage of the protests, saying the reports damaged the country's economic interests. Police raided the independent weekly *Gwanga* in May and briefly detained four journalists on the tenuous claim that its possession of a civil society newsletter could somehow incite public violence. *Gwanga* did not resume regular publication.

KEY DEVELOPMENTS

» Presidential election marred by anti-press violence; two journalists shot, dozens assaulted.

» Nationwide protests over rising prices lead to anti-press attacks and censorship.

KEY DATA

## 10 Held without charge, 2007-11

CPJ research shows the majority of detentions by state security operatives are conducted without formal charge, in apparent disregard of the Ugandan Constitution's 48-hour pre-trial detention limit.

**Held without charge over time:**

2007: 0          2010: 5

2008: 1          2011: 1

2009: 3

## 17 Short-term detentions, 2007-11

CPJ research shows police and state security operatives routinely detained journalists for periods ranging from several days to several weeks in an effort to cow the press from reporting on sensitive issues.

**Detentions over time:**

2007: 0          2010: 7

2008: 3          2011: 3

2009: 4

# 41 Attacked in 2011

Presidential and parliamentary elections in February and a swearing-in ceremony in May were marred by physical attacks on local and international journalists. Further attacks against the press came after opposition party leaders organized nationwide protests, called the Walk to Work campaign. CPJ documented at least 41 attacks.

**Breakdown of violence:**

23 Attacked while covering election campaign

7 Attacked while covering civil society protests

3 Attacked while covering student protests

8 Attacked at other events

# 25 Attacks by state agents

State agents and ruling party officials were responsible for at least 25 physical attacks against journalists in 2011, CPJ research shows. But people suspected to be working for authorities also contributed to anti-press violence, accounting for another 11 assaults, CPJ found.

**Breakdown of responsibility:**

21 Police and security agents

4 Public officials aligned with the ruling party

11 Suspected ruling party supporters

5 Other individuals

# 89% Museveni's share, state media election coverage

State-run broadcasters devoted the large majority of their election coverage to Museveni, according to a media monitoring survey conducted by the European Commission. Private broadcasters tilted toward the main opposition candidate, Kizza Besigye, but were more even-handed than state media.

**How they covered the race, according to the European Commission:**

**UBC Television** (state)
Museveni: 409 minutes / Besigye: 27 minutes

**UBC Radio** (state)
Museveni: 158 minutes / Besigye: 43 minutes

**NTV** (private)
Museveni: 118 minutes / Besigye: 164 minutes

**WBS** (private)
Museveni: 128 minutes / Besigye: 184 minutes

**Simba FM** (private)
Museveni: 75 minutes / Besigye: 55 minutes

**CBS** (private)
Museveni: 19 minutes / Besigye: 16 minutes

# Zimbabwe

Although official anti-press harassment continued a gradual decline from its peak after the disputed 2008 elections, a highly restrictive legal framework has kept domestic, independent news sources to a mere handful. The fractious coalition between Robert Mugabe's ZANU-PF and Morgan Tsvangirai's MDC failed to implement the media reforms they had pledged to undertake in their 2008 power-sharing deal, leaving in place repressive laws such as the Access to Information and Privacy Protection Act. At least six journalists faced criminal defamation charges, including two staffers from the weekly *Standard* who were detained after covering a politician's arrest. Assailants broke into the offices of *NewsDay* and *Masvingo Mirror*, stealing computer hard drives and storage discs. Both break-ins followed critical coverage; no suspects were arrested in either case. Fearing the influence of revolutions in North Africa, authorities detained dozens of civil society members for watching footage of the Egyptian revolution at a public gathering. The European Union named six state media journalists among 200 Zimbabweans subject to sanctions for allegedly promoting violence during the 2008 polling.

KEY DEVELOPMENTS

» Official harassment is down slightly, but restrictive laws and regulatory system remain.

» Government raises accreditation fees and lags on issuing private broadcast licenses.

KEY DATA

## 2 Private broadcast licenses

Although the power-sharing agreement of September 2008 allows private broadcasting, it was only in 2011 that the Broadcasting Authority of Zimbabwe began calling for applications. Of the applications received, the authority granted licenses to only two radio station applicants, Zimpapers Talk Radio and AB Communications, both closely linked to the ruling ZANU-PF party.

## 1 Arrest under AIPPA, 2011

Arrests under the repressive accreditation law declined since the post-election crackdown of 2008, when police detained more than a dozen journalists, CPJ research shows. Still, one AIPPA-related arrest was reported in 2011. Police arrested photographer Blessed Mhlanga in July for taking images without accreditation. Mhlanga was soon released after producing accreditation documents.

# 49
### In exile, 2001-11

Official repression drove at least 49 journalists into exile over the past decade, the fifth-highest number in the world, according to a CPJ study. Most of the exodus occurred in the first half of the decade.

**Top nations from which journalists have fled:**

| | |
|---|---|
| Ethiopia | 79 |
| Somalia | 68 |
| Iran | 66 |
| Iraq | 55 |
| **Zimbabwe** | **49** |
| Eritrea | 47 |
| Sri Lanka | 25 |
| Cuba | 25 |
| Colombia | 20 |
| Haiti | 18 |
| Rwanda | 18 |
| Uzbekistan | 18 |

# $6,000
### Fee for international outlets

In January 2011, authorities significantly raised the accreditation fees for international news media outlets and their local correspondents.

**Steep jumps:**

**300%** Increase in fee to open an international news media bureau. International news outlets must pay US$6,000, up from US$2,000. Renewals went from being free to costing US$5,000.

**400%** Increase in accreditation fee for Zimbabwean journalists working for foreign media. The fee quadrupled from US$100 to US$400. The renewal of accreditation went from being free to costing US$300.

**100%** Increase in fee for southern African media outlets operating in Zimbabwe. The fee increased from US$1,000 to US$2,000.

# 7
### Obstruction cases, 2011

Several cases of obstruction were reported during the year, according to CPJ research. Officials blocked reporters from covering news events in some instances. In others, authorities and ruling party supporters prevented newspaper vendors from selling critical publications.

**Cases of obstruction over time:**

| | |
|---|---|
| 2007 | 0 |
| 2008 | 8 |
| 2009 | 2 |
| 2010 | 1 |
| 2011 | 7 |

# Africa Regional Data

**4**

Journalists
Killed in 2011

**301**

Journalists
In Exile 2001-11

**112**

Journalists Killed
Since 1992

**43**

Imprisoned on
December 1, 2011

**68**

Unsolved Journalist
Murders Since 1992

**4**

Missing as of
December 31, 2011

Americas

# Americas

PHOTO CREDITS

*Section break: In Santiago, tear gas envelopes photographers covering a protest by Chilean students. (Reuters/Ivan Alvarado)*

*Page 99: Ecuador's president, Rafael Correa, uses state media to attack press outlets such as the national daily* La Hora, *which he rips in half at a public conference. (El Universo)*

*Page 107: Mexican President Felipe Calderón Hinojosa pledged action to deter anti-press attacks, but his government has accomplished little. (AP/Marco Ugarte)*

*Page 110: A Mexican soldier at a busy Veracruz highway intersection, where more than 30 bodies were brazenly dumped. (AP/Felix Marquez)*

RESEARCH CREDITS

*Country reports in this chapter were researched and written by CPJ Research Associate Sara Rafsky, with reporting by Senior Program Coordinator Carlos Lauría.*

# Shunning Public Interest, State Media Advance Political Goals

*By Carlos Lauría*

Riots at an infamous Venezuelan prison in June escalated into gun battles between hundreds of troops and inmates, killing at least 22 people. The crisis lasted four weeks, drew widespread media coverage, and sparked a war of words between the government and the opposition. Supporters of President Hugo Chávez, including the influential talk show host Mario Silva, accused the press of "manipulating" the situation and called for an investigation. Silva, host of the late-night show "La Hojilla" (The Razor) on state-owned Venezolana de Televisión (VTV), accused critical broadcaster Globovisión of calling for an uprising in the prisons and fomenting public anxiety. He suggested the network was trying to destabilize Venezuela.

Silva's accusations prompted the National Telecommunications Commission (Conatel) to open an investigation into Globovisión's coverage. On October 18, the regulator fined Globovisión more than US$2 million, citing the country's highly restrictive Law on Social Responsibility in Radio and Television. Using Silva's broadcasts as a springboard, Conatel found the station falsely claimed that members of the National Guard had "massacred" prisoners and that its reporting could have provoked riots in other prisons. Globovisión called the charges baseless and stood by its reporting.

Silva, who often refers to Globovisión as "Globoterror," is a close Chávez adviser who dedicates his show to character assassination of opposition figures, critical reporters, media executives, and free press activists. After the Caracas-based daily *El Nacional* published an article on the murder of Silva's bodyguard, he called the paper's editor, Miguel Henrique Otero, a "coward and a swine," repeatedly insulted members of his family, and accused him of supporting the failed 2002 coup against Chávez. Otero filed a defamation suit against Silva, which is pending.

Silva's publicly funded program has become the most notorious example of a regional trend in which state-owned media are used not only for political propaganda, but also as platforms for smear campaigns against critics, including journalists. In politically polarized Latin American countries such as Venezuela, Ecuador, and Nicaragua, elected leaders have invested in large multimedia holdings, building bulky official press conglomerates that further their personal political agendas, CPJ research shows.

The pattern defies regional and international standards. Free press advocates believe state media should be politically independent in order to provide citizens with information free of commercial, state, or political influence. Indeed, public media should be "independent of the executive branch; truly pluralistic; universally accessible; with funding adequate to the mandate provided for by law; and they must provide community participation and accountability mechanisms at the different levels of content production, distribution, and receipt," the Inter-American Commission on Human Rights' special rapporteur for freedom of expression said in a 2009 report.

.................................................

*International standards say state media should serve all sectors of society.*

.................................................

That document echoes the 2007 Joint Declaration on Diversity by the United Nations, the Organization of American States, the Organization for Security and Co-operation in Europe, and the African Commission. "The mandate of public service broadcasters should be clearly set out in law and include, among other things, contributing to diversity, and serving the information needs and interests of all sectors of society," the declaration states.

Venezuela, Ecuador, and Nicaragua all lack laws mandating that state media serve the public interest. "Public media have not been conceived in our countries as a quality alternative for the dissemination of information or response to cultural diversity," wrote Guillermo Mastrini, a media specialist at the University of Buenos Aires in Argentina, in an analysis of public media and communication rights.

Leaders of the three nations often describe private media executives as the "oligarchy" or the "business elite," people tied to transnational conglomerates and determined to skew coverage in favor of the political opposition, business, or other special interest groups. Governments in these countries justify their actions against journalists—who are often denied access to officials and events—by accusing private media of being enemies of the people.

Analysts say Venezuela in particular has tried to replicate aspects of the Cuban communications model, where the government owns and controls all media, uses them for propaganda and to oppose foreign criticism, and vilifies independent journalists and bloggers. This is worrisome because Cuba was, until recently, one of the world's leading jailers of journalists. Those who try to work independently in Cuba are harassed, detained, threatened with prosecution or jail, or barred from traveling. Government websites accuse independent bloggers of receiving money from foreign-based opposition groups. Cuba's constitution recognizes only "freedom of speech and the press in accordance with the goals of the socialist society."

At the same time, Cuban government policy has severely restricted domestic Internet infrastructure, with only a small portion of the population allowed Internet at home. The vast majority are required to use state-controlled access points and undergo identity checks and heavy surveillance. Access to non-Cuban sites is restricted. Venezuela, too, will eventually control all communications, including the Internet, suggests Antonio Pasquali, a scholar with Venezuelan Central University. "The telephone and Internet will be our last instruments of freedom," he said.

Venezuela still has private outlets that exercise their right to present different points of view. Three national dailies—*El Universal*, *El Nacional*, and *Tal Cual*—provide critical coverage, as do a handful of Caracas papers and magazines, several regional publications, and a number of online news sites. But of the three private television stations, only Globovisión still carries news shows and airs criticism of the government. RCTV, once the

largest TV network and a tough critic of the administration, was forced off the air in 2007 in a politicized regulatory action. Two years later, Conatel used a legal technicality as a pretext to strip the licenses of more than 30 radio and television stations, silencing a chorus of critical voices.

"Venezuela's communications model clearly emulates Cuba," said Otero of *El Nacional*.

......................................................

## *Venezuela emulates the Cuban model, the most repressive in the hemisphere.*

......................................................

Through more than a decade in power, Chávez has proclaimed himself a socialist "revolutionary" leading poor Venezuelans in a struggle against the elites, including the media. But it took the Venezuelan president a few years to realize that his ability to cling to power rests on dominating the media. Until the failed 2002 coup, the state communications apparatus was composed of the Radio Nacional de Venezuela network, VTV, and the official news agency Venpres (now AVN). Since then, the government has invested hundreds of millions of bolívares in state-owned and community media projects, including TV and radio stations, newspapers, and websites. Since 2003, it has financed the startup of ViVe TV, a nationwide cultural and educational television network; ANTV, which broadcasts National Assembly sessions on the airwaves and on cable; AN radio; Ávila TV, a regional channel run by the city of Caracas; Alba TV and Alba Ciudad FM; YVKE Mundial Radio; La Radio del Sur; the newspaper *Correo del Orinoco*; and the news website *Aporrea*. Venezuelan Social Television Station, known as Tves, began broadcasting on May 28, 2007, a day after RCTV was pulled off the air. In July 2005, the government launched its most ambitious media project, Telesur, a 24-hour news channel that officials see as an alternative to CNN. Venezuela owns 51 percent of the channel; the governments of Argentina, Cuba, Uruguay, Ecuador, Nicaragua, and Bolivia own minority stakes.

The administration continues to subsidize state media heavily. In July, deputies of the socialist party authorized a loan of 700 million bolívares (US$166 million) aimed at supporting the state media apparatus, news reports said. Communications and Information Minister Andrés Izarra has long acknowledged that the government's strategy is aimed at "achieving the state's communication and information hegemony." By expanding state and community media, officials contend, the government is fulfilling citizens' constitutional guarantee of plural information. But Marcelino Bisbal, a professor at Universidad Católica Andrés Bello, said the administration perceives communication as a way to educate the people in socialism, its ultimate goal. "For this government, information is about creating one sole truth, one sole communication, one sole information, one sole culture," Bisbal wrote in a media analysis.

Ecuadoran President Rafael Correa has followed closely in Chávez's footsteps. When Correa took office in early 2007, state media consisted only of Radio Nacional de Ecuador. The administration erected an ambitious press machinery in just a few years. The 2008 government takeover of two private television stations, TC Televisión and Gama TV, and several other media outlets served as the starting point for this remarkable growth. The outlets were owned by Grupo Isaías, whose principals, Roberto and William Isaías, allegedly owed $661 million to Ecuador after the 1998 collapse of Filanbanco, their financial institution. The stations draw nearly 40 percent of the country's news audience.

At the time of the takeover, Correa pledged to sell the media assets to recover money owed to Ecuadorans, but he has never done so. Neither did he keep his promise to preserve the outlets' editorial independence. "All those media are used for government propaganda," said Tania Tinoco, an anchor with the privately owned television station Ecuavisa.

........................................

## Correa has plowed public funds into a massive state media operation.

........................................

Ecuador's media landscape remains diverse and vibrant, CPJ research shows. Hundreds of radio stations operate around the country, among them community and indigenous broadcasters in provincial regions. Five private television networks—Ecuavisa, Teleamazonas, RTS, Telerama, and Canal Uno—and more than 35 daily newspapers offer a wide range of opinions, analyses, and political perspectives, CPJ's analysis found.

But year by year, the Correa administration has plowed public funds— the amount has never been disclosed—into assembling a massive state media operation that now consists of numerous TV stations (TC Televisión, Gama TV, and Ecuador TV, plus cable stations CN3 and CD7), radio stations (Radio Pública de Ecuador, Radio Carrousel, Radio Super K 800, and Radio Universal), newspapers (*El Telégrafo, PP El Verdadero,* and *El Ciudadano*), magazines (*La Onda, El Agro, Valles,* and *Samborondón*), and a news agency (Agencia Pública de Noticias del Ecuador y Suramérica, known as Andes). "The state has transformed itself as a communications player, from being irrelevant when Correa took office to now having a leading role," said César Ricaurte, executive director of the local press group Fundamedios.

The administration's official stance is that state media should have editorial independence. "The public media are relatively new in Ecuador, and the government is trying to improve their administration and seek their editorial independence," Doris Soliz, minister of political coordination, told CPJ. "But the media belong to the state, not to the government."

........................................

*A policy that calls for independence, but a practice of political confrontation.*

........................................

In practice, however, Correa has used state media as a platform to discredit journalists who oppose his policies. The president often devotes his regular Saturday radio broadcasts to verbal assaults against media companies and individual journalists. The outlets most frequently targeted are the national dailies *El Universo*, *La Hora*, *El Comercio*, and *Expreso*, along with the television network Teleamazonas. The president has described critics as "ignorant," "trash-talking," "liars," "unethical," "mediocre," "ink-stained hit men," and "political actors who are trying to oppose the revolutionary government." With this stream of abuse, Correa has managed to influence public opinion while avoiding debate on issues related to corruption and government transparency.

In Nicaragua, President Daniel Ortega mimics the steps taken by Chávez and Correa, gradually exerting more control over people and institutions, including the press, and casting the private media as enemies. The Sandinista-led government uses the official media apparatus—Channel 4, Channel 8, Channel 13, the radio station Nueva Radio Ya, and the news website *El 19*—to conduct character attacks against critics. These efforts are supported by an email news service called *Nicaragua Triunfa*—and the FSLN-owned Radio Sandino. Well-known critical journalists like former *El Nuevo Diario* editor Danilo Aguirre have been labeled "fascists." Carlos Fernando Chamorro, host of the show "Esta Semana" (This Week) on private television station Channel 12, has been investigated and accused of money laundering in what CPJ described as a politicized inquiry intended to restrict news coverage on government corruption.

The investigations and name-calling are part of an aggressive campaign to obstruct and marginalize independent media. Nicaragua is home to more than 100 private radio stations and several television stations, including channels 2, 10, 11, and 12. Cable television is available in the main urban centers. There are two national dailies, *La Prensa* and *El Nuevo Diario*, both of which are harshly critical of Ortega, along with the weekly *Confidencial*, and several online publications.

But government officials maintain contact with only the handful of pro-government outlets controlled by the president's family or party. Criminal defamation lawsuits against independent journalists are routine, and the administration has manipulated government advertising in ways intended to punish critical media and reward allies, a 2009 CPJ report found.

The June launch of Channel 13 Viva Nicaragua, a 24-hour television news network owned by the Ortega family and run by Ortega's children Luciana, Camila, and Maurice Ortega Murillo, is one instance of the president's aim to control the flow of information. Promoted as an outlet focused on "social themes," the station offers the official perspective to the exclusion of opposition voices. For example, an October piece on an epidemic of dengue fever focused entirely on the national campaign to prevent the disease and provided no information on the death toll or number of people who contracted the disease in 2011.

.......................................

*Epidemic coverage that highlights government action and forgets human toll.*

.......................................

Nicaraguan journalists said the Ortega family has created a prosperous media empire in the last five years. Son Rafael Ortega Murillo, who heads a company called Nueva Imagen, negotiated the family's access into Nicaraguan TV by partnering with Mexican businessman Ángel González in 2007. Carlos Enrique and Daniel Edmundo Ortega Murillo direct Channel 4; Juan Carlos Ortega Murillo directs Channel 8; and Maurice Ortega Murillo directs the TV production company RGB Media, according to press reports. President Ortega's wife, Rosario Murillo, is his communications strategist and top press adviser.

Leaders of other nations have exploited state media for political purposes. In Bolivia, President Evo Morales has been frank in saying his government takes advantage of state broadcasting to thwart perceived private media distortions. And in Argentina, critics say the television show "6, 7, 8" on state-run Channel 7 has launched witch hunts against unsympathetic journalists. On this roundtable show, five journalists and two guests regularly disparage coverage by the mainstream press, portraying reporters and news outlets as political actors and opposition. They have used social media to call on government supporters to take to the streets to protest mainstream coverage.

The concept of state media as public service—taken from the European model of entrusting organizations to act in the general interest and giving them enough autonomy to prevent political interference—has yet to be applied in Latin America. But some analysts point out encouraging regional developments, particularly in television. Televisión Nacional de Chile (TVN), Channel 22 in Mexico, and TV Cultura in Brazil have been put forward as examples of outlets that belong to the state but have accomplished their primary public service goal.

............................................

*The concept of state media as public service is only beginning to take root.*

............................................

An announcement in July by Salvadoran President Mauricio Funes that state media would be reformed to grant official outlets unprecedented legal autonomy was seen by media analysts and press advocates as a positive step toward ending the role of government media as mouthpieces for ruling administrations. The reforms, developed in collaboration with the World Bank, are aimed at promoting the "public good," as expressed by Andrew Leyton, representative of the multilateral lending institution. The World Bank will give financial support to the rebuilding of old equipment from state radio and television. Funes said the first step will involve creation of Radio El Salvador Internacional and a news agency. David Rivas, secretary of communications for the Salvadoran presidency, said that for years, state radio and television have been "subject to political whims." The Funes administration, Rivas said, is seeking to give state media independence so they can fulfill their goal of public service.

*Carlos Lauría is CPJ's senior program coordinator for the Americas. A native of Buenos Aires, he is a widely published journalist who has written extensively for* Noticias, *one of the world's largest Spanish-language newsmagazines. In 2011, Lauría conducted a fact-finding mission to Ecuador.*

# Calderón Fails,
# And the Mexican Press Is Dying

*By Mike O'Connor*

On his living room couch, his two sons nearby, Jorge Medellín could barely endure the torturous thoughts coursing through his mind. He grasped his wrists, he rocked roughly on the couch, he bounded across the room and then returned to sit. He was nearly certain that he was going to be assassinated for what he had written about a Mexican Army general in the newspaper *Milenio*. There was nothing much to the story, really, but the general came off looking bad. Medellín, who had covered national security issues for 15 years, interpreted anonymous comments posted to his story on the paper's website as death threats. He did not believe his government would protect him. In fact, he believed that if he were killed, it would be on orders of military officers who could count on Mexico's near-complete record of failing to solve the murders of journalists.

Mexican journalists take the smallest hint of a threat seriously because they know that killing a reporter is so easy to get away with. The word for this is impunity—killing with no consequences. None for the killer, at least. But the consequences for the Mexican people are that journalists are afraid to report the news.

It was this reality that made Medellín suffer so. He thought he might well leave his wife a widow and his sons fatherless for writing a story that was only mildly in-depth, but even so crossed the line of what is permitted. "What was wrong with me?" Medellín said. "Why didn't I realize what would happen? I know these people." He had already gone to his friends in the military and civilian intelligence to ask for protection. But not even his friends could be sure that federal bodyguards would not be bought off. "They tell me they can't trust their own people, because if I am killed nothing would be investigated," Medellín told CPJ that afternoon, November 1, 2010.

It was an important moment in the struggle against impunity in Mexico. Just five weeks earlier, President Felipe Calderón Hinojosa had promised

CPJ, the Inter American Press Association, and the entire country that he would move assertively to protect a besieged press corps. A federal journalist protection program would be established, a new special prosecutor would bring killers to trial, and new legislation would make anti-press violence a federal crime.

But over the course of 2011, a CPJ investigation has found, Calderón and his administration have failed at nearly every turn.

......................................................

## Has the president lost the political will to tackle the impunity crisis?

......................................................

The case of Jorge Medellín, who so profoundly mistrusts his government that he would rather go it alone than have federal bodyguards, illustrates the depth of the crisis. The federal government's befuddled, yearlong launch of its "Protection Mechanism" for journalists under threat, combined with the inability of an understaffed special prosecutor to gain a single conviction in a press murder, has bred deep cynicism among journalists. Many also see the president's commitment to federalization of anti-press crimes as evaporating, leaving investigations to state police forces universally seen as more corrupt than their federal counterparts. Has the president, they ask, lost the political will to tackle the problem?

Back on September 22, 2010, Calderón was unequivocal. "We categorically reject any attack against journalists because it is an assault against democratic society," Calderón told a delegation from CPJ and the Inter American Press Association. At that point, 32 journalists and media support workers had been murdered or had disappeared in Mexico since Calderón had taken office in December 2006.

In the meeting with the press groups, the president unveiled what his administration called the Protection Mechanism, a program giving immediate help to journalists under threat, from supplying something as simple as a cell phone to call a police hotline, to providing more intensive help such as bodyguards or relocation. Officials initially spoke of hundreds of people seeking protection, considering that journalists in so many parts of the country are under threat.

But by October 2011, the Mechanism had only eight cases. Five of the people on the case list told CPJ that the protection was inept, sporadic, or nonexistent. The identities of the other three were not disclosed to CPJ.

And by October 2011, Medellín had given up on the program. Because he was afraid of federal bodyguards, the program had asked the Mexico

City government to help with protection. But the city's attorney general refused, saying it wasn't his job. That left the task to city police patrols— not much of a barrier to an assassination team. But even those patrols didn't come around for many days, Medellín told the Protection Mechanism committee overseeing his case. When patrols finally did start coming, they always arrived between noon and about 1 p.m., hardly a deterrent, he told the committee.

CPJ attended several of the closed-door committee meetings with a promise to keep the proceedings confidential unless Medellín gave permission to disclose them. For months, he said he was afraid to make his case public; then, in October, Medellín said he was too disgusted with the Mechanism to stay silent and granted permission, he said, so that the public would know it was a failure. The program had ensnared Medellín in hours of procedural meetings involving about a dozen bureaucrats each time, seven such sessions in which he heard many promises but was never given any real protection. It's a very good thing there was never an assassination attempt, he said.

Medellín said he doesn't know what became of the investigation into the threats against him. That wound up with the federal attorney general's organized crime unit, which he said refused to tell him what it might have found out. "If they had anything, they'd tell me," Medellín said. "So the silence is a confession of failure." Unit officials did not return CPJ's phone calls seeking comment.

The months of meetings to discuss plans that never seemed to work

symbolize not only the Protection Mechanism's problems, but also the Calderón administration's overall failures. Calderón gave the job of organizing the Protection Mechanism to the Secretariat of Government, the most powerful office in his cabinet. But three other cabinet secretariats that are to contribute resources to the Mechanism have fought for power or sought to delay implementation of the program, according to three officials who have been involved in yearlong negotiations that they described as bitter and unproductive.

·················································

## Mexican officials concede the Protection Mechanism is a shell of a program.

·················································

These officials say it is only a shell of a program, with no agreed-upon rules and only ad hoc responses to journalists' problems. It is not at all clear how the program's budget was spent—or even what was budgeted. Felipe Zamora, the undersecretary of government who was in charge of the program, insisted the first-year budget was $11 million pesos (a little less than US$1 million), although other senior officials working on the program said more than double that amount had been set aside.

Zamora referred CPJ's detailed questions about expenditures to his private secretary, who did not respond to a written request for budget information. (Zamora later died in a November helicopter crash that took the lives of several government officials.) However the money was spent, there was little to show for it. Said one ranking official working on the program: "The Mechanism has no power. Half of the members want it to fail because being responsible is too much trouble. The whole thing means nothing."

Even if the program was working perfectly on the federal level, it still bases much of its budget and hope on getting states to supply resources such as bodyguards for cases within their jurisdiction. Such reliance reflects an optimism bordering on irrationality; very few reporters will trust their state police for protection. But matters are not even to that point yet—most states have not signed agreements to cooperate.

In an interview prior to his death, Undersecretary Zamora told CPJ that while implementation was taking longer than expected, the government could not afford the luxury of slacking off. "All beginnings are difficult," he said, "but we can't use that as a pretext for avoiding responsibility."

But where, critics ask, is Calderón when this program is in such trouble? Why can't he direct his own cabinet to make the program work?

A spokesman for Calderón did not respond to CPJ's email and phone requests for comment.

In a bulky sweatshirt and jeans, a young journalist clinked a spoon around her cup at a restaurant on the edge of Mexico City. She stared into her coffee as if it held the answer to the difficult decision confronting her. It was February 12, 2011.

The 28-year-old and some colleagues had come upon firsthand information identifying the killers in the recent murder of a provincial journalist. But the woman told CPJ that she and the others were deathly afraid. What if the killers learned what information the journalists had? The journalists didn't trust the state police to investigate the case or keep them safe. Going to local authorities, they thought, would actually put them in far more danger. "It's all one mafia there," she said. So, they made a pact to stay silent.

For some time she thought there was no reason to tell police what she knew because, after all, there was no reason to think the killers would ever be punished. But for all the logic against it, the woman gambled. Finishing her coffee that February day, she decided to go to the special federal prosecutor for crimes against freedom of expression and tell him what she knew. (Her identity and other identifying aspects of the crime are being withheld here because the case was under investigation in late year.)

*Most journalist killings remain in the hands of corrupt or fearful state police.*

Murder is a state crime, so most journalist killings remain in the hands of corrupt or fearful state police, who have compiled a record of near-complete failure. But the federal special prosecutor can claim jurisdiction if a violation of federal law, such as use of an assault rifle, occurs during the course of the crime. The special prosecutor's office was able to take up this case because witnesses had been threatened.

The special prosecutor, Gustavo Salas Chávez, has 103 cases, almost all involving relatively minor issues such as unjustified detentions. But Salas, who was assigned only seven investigators, will be judged not on the small cases but on whether he solves any of the 11 murders and disappearances of journalists he says are in his jurisdiction. So far, he has not brought anyone to justice in those cases. Salas took over in early 2010 after ineffectual terms by two previous special prosecutors. In contrast, Salas has been a demanding boss, working his employees late into the night, bringing his investigators in on the weekends, and churning though them with firings and resignations, according to interviews with staff members. Salas declined to comment for this report, saying that his boss, Attorney General Marisela Morales, refused to let him speak to CPJ.

As it turned out, federal authorities had briefly looked into the case before the female journalist arrived at the special prosecutor's door. State police had handed them a tidy case file that depicted the victim as being caught in a love triangle and targeted by a jealous husband. The file did not include other, seemingly pertinent information. Friends of the victim, for example, said he had been engaged in a dispute with a local official whom he had continually criticized in his news coverage.

When the journalist arrived at federal offices with her own information, investigators questioned her for hours with a CPJ representative present, as she had requested. Convinced that her story was credible, investigators went to the scene of the killing. CPJ led investigators to another journalist who had information about the murder, along with witnesses to other aspects of the case. By late year, federal authorities said they were close to wrapping up their investigation, although no arrests had been made.

In the meantime, legislation making anti-press violence a federal crime, which Calderón had vowed to push forward, moved very slowly in Congress. The Chamber of Deputies passed a bill in November but many steps

remained. That the proposal came in the form of a constitutional amendment complicated chances for passage; amendments require not only a two-thirds vote by both chambers of Congress but approval by a majority of the state legislatures.

Although the measure did not progress far in Congress, state officials had already geared up opposition to a plan they saw as giving too much power to the federal government, according to Manuel Clouthier, a member of the Chamber of Deputies from the National Action Party, or PAN. Many journalists working in the deadliest areas say state politicians had another, powerful motive: Keeping journalists afraid keeps the press from investigating them. Calderón could not even secure passage of a bill to increase penalties in the few instances in which anti-press attacks are already federal crimes. That effort passed in the lower house but failed in the Senate.

..................................................

*For state officials, there is a powerful motive to keep journalists afraid.*

..................................................

By law, Calderón has a single term. It ends on December 1, 2012, with the coming year's political agenda to be dominated by the campaign leading up to July's presidential election, and a steady loss of power for the lame-duck leader.

In the city of Veracruz, reporters and photographers huddled in a large coffee shop overlooking the Gulf of Mexico. It's a morning ritual: trading tips, insults, and jokes. But this morning, October 7, 2011, was different. The day before, 36 bodies were found in several places in the city and its suburbs. Phantom-like murderers were haunting Veracruz and, it seemed, members of the press corps were among the targets.

The string of killings had begun on June 20, leaving the press and public fearful of what would happen next and angry at state officials who they believed were incompetent or complicit. It wasn't that they had evidence to support those beliefs: they had no evidence of anything, actually, except for all the bodies turning up. The deputy editor of the main newspaper, *Notiver*, his wife, and son were all found shot to death in their home. A few weeks later, on July 26, the body of a *Notiver* police reporter was found, tortured and decapitated. Then, on September 21, more than 30 bodies were brazenly dumped at one of the area's busiest highway intersections during afternoon rush hour.

None of the reporters in the coffee shop knew anything more because state officials, they said, either refused to discuss the murders or issued inaccurate information. More than that, there were no police beat reporters left in town. They were the ones with the sources to get at the truth, but after the murders of *Notiver* deputy editor Miguel Angel López Velasco and reporter Yolanda Ordaz de la Cruz, the city's entire police beat, about 15 reporters, fled town. So the "news" was coming from government handouts and releases from the Mexican Navy, which is headquartered in the city and was taking part in the investigations. Although none of the remaining reporters believed the handouts, none was doing much digging because of the risk. The public, too, was uninformed, except for the rumors traded on Twitter and Facebook.

## The events terrorizing citizens, the city's most important story, went uncovered.

Understanding how things could come to this requires a bit of background. The most consistent account of how organized crime took over Veracruz starts in 2007, when the Zetas criminal gang came to town and petrified or corrupted police and local officials into letting it operate. The press was controlled in the same way, reporters agreed, although they would speak only anonymously. "When we were threatened, we knew there were no honest authorities left to protect us," one said. "We began to cover the news the way we were told by the Zetas."

The first thing that meant, reporters said, was no stories about the Zetas. So no stories about how the city was being taken over. When the journalists were murdered in 2011, it was assumed that some other criminal group moving into town had seen them as too close to the Zetas. But one photographer acknowledged, "We actually have no idea." It was the logical next step when journalists are killed with impunity: The events terrorizing the city, the most important story for its citizens, could not be covered.

Across Mexico, by the end of 2011, the toll of journalists and media workers killed or disappeared stood at 48 since Calderón took office. At least 13 of the victims were killed in direct relation to their work, CPJ research shows, nearly all after trying to cover Mexico's vast web of crime, drugs, and official corruption. No convictions had been reported in any case. Only five countries worldwide had more unsolved journalist murders on their ledgers at year's end. Just eight Mexican journalists under threat had been granted government protection in 2011, with five calling it ineffectual. The numbers, and the bodies, are adding up.

The Calderón administration took action in 2011 but made no progress, leaving journalists with no reason to believe the climate of impunity would change any time soon. The Protection Mechanism was more promise than reality, while the special prosecutor's office was badly understaffed and limping. Both efforts could have brought change, but they ended up as forgotten commitments. The idea of taking anti-press crimes away from corrupt state authorities still made sense, but the president couldn't get it through Congress. As a practical matter, Calderón's ability to effect change lessens as each day brings the election of a new president closer. It is that person in whom journalists will likely have to place their hopes.

*Mike O'Connor, a Mexico City-based journalist, is CPJ's representative in Mexico. He is the co-author of the 2010 CPJ special report,* Silence or Death in Mexico's Press.

# Argentina

The Supreme Court of Justice ruled in March that the government should apply reasonable balance in the distribution of state advertising. Ruling in a case brought in 2006 by Editorial Perfil, the country's largest magazine publisher, the court sought to rein in the government's long-standing practice of rewarding supportive news media with state advertising while punishing critical media by withholdings ads. Nonetheless, Perfil and other critics alleged that President Cristina Fernández de Kirchner, who won re-election in October, continued the system of unequal distribution. Relations between Grupo Clarín, the nation's largest media conglomerate, and the Kirchner government worsened in March after demonstrators, including members of the Teamsters, blocked trucking exits at *Clarín*'s printing facilities, preventing the paper from distributing its Sunday edition. Circulation of the national daily *La Nación* was also disrupted for several hours. In December, Kirchner signed a measure bringing the country's sole newsprint manufacturer, Papel Prensa, under government regulation. Publishers groups said it was another attack on *Clarín* and *La Nación*, which own a majority stake in the company. The local press group Foro de Periodismo Argentino documented a series of abuses in the country's interior, including an attack on a radio journalist, a case of arson, and an episode in which a camera crew was fired upon. A federal court sentenced 16 former military members in October to jail terms ranging from 18 years to life in prison for the murder of journalist Rodolfo Walsh and 85 others during the 1976-83 Argentine dictatorship.

### KEY DEVELOPMENTS

» Supreme Court tells government to end inequitable distribution of official advertising.

» Blockade at printing facilities disrupts circulation of two national dailies.

### KEY DATA

## 7 Justices backing Editorial Perfil

In a landmark ruling for press freedom, the seven Supreme Court justices decided unanimously that all media should receive official advertising. The decision upheld a 2009 ruling by a federal appeals court that said withholding government advertising from Editorial Perfil publications violated freedom of the press as guaranteed in the Argentine constitution. Editorial Perfil said the government was discriminating against its publications due to their critical reporting.

## 1 Complaint of noncompliance

In October, Editorial Perfil filed a court complaint that alleged the government had not complied with the March Supreme Court decision calling for equitable official advertising. The publishing company asked that then-Chief of Staff Aníbal Fernández and Media Secretary Juan Manuel Abal Medina be fined.

### Official advertising since the Supreme Court decision, according to *Perfil*:

**8** Official advertisements placed in the daily *Perfil* from March until October.

**1** Of the eight advertisements, one attacked the newspaper itself.

## 16 Years of litigation

In December, the Inter-American Court of Human Rights ruled in favor of two journalists with the newsweekly *Noticias* in the court's first case weighing privacy rights against reporting on matters of public concern. The case began in 1995 when former President Carlos Saúl Menem, filed a lawsuit alleging the journalists had violated his privacy by reporting on his child from an extramarital affair. Argentina's Supreme Court had ruled in Menem's favor in 2001.

## 18 Provinces with abuses

While many press freedom issues are centered in the capital, Buenos Aires, the press group Foro de Periodismo Argentino (Fopea) documented abuses in 18 Argentine provinces in the first half of 2011. Abuses included threats, assaults, attacks against media facilities, confiscation of equipment, and obstruction of coverage.

### Provinces with the highest number of abuses:

**12** Buenos Aires province

**7** Santa Fe

**6** Salta

**5** Chaco

**4** Each: Misiones, San Juan, Mendoza, and Río Negro

## 1 Newspaper edition blocked

The leading national daily *Clarín* was prevented from distributing its Sunday, March 27, edition by union demonstrators who blocked exits at its printing plant. Circulation of the nation's other major daily, *La Nación*, whose adjacent facilities were targeted, was delayed by four hours. Union members claimed they were protesting workplace discrimination, but *Clarín* denied any such labor dispute and pointed to a pattern of government harassment and union interference at the plant.

# Brazil

In provincial areas where law enforcement is weak, reporters were vulnerable to attack for their coverage of corruption. In urban centers,
journalists faced risks while covering organized crime and drug trafficking. Two journalists were killed in direct relation to their work in 2011,
and CPJ was investigating the circumstances in four other killings. The
uptick in deadly violence pushed Brazil back onto CPJ's 2011 Impunity
Index, which highlights countries with unsolved journalist murders. Politicized judicial rulings continued to hinder coverage of sensitive issues.
A censorship order against the daily *O Estado de S. Paulo* remained in
place more than two years after it was first imposed, barring the paper
from reporting on a corruption inquiry involving the family of Senate
President José Sarney. In November, President Dilma Rousseff signed
into law an access-to-information measure that regulates the classifica-
tion of documents and imposes a maximum withholding period of 50
years for top secret files. The bill was lauded as an important step for
government transparency and a helpful tool for journalists covering
corruption.

KEY DEVELOPMENTS

» Lethal violence against provincial journalists covering corruption is
   unrelenting.

» Judicial censorship continues to restrict coverage on issues of public
   interest.

KEY DATA

## 224 Online removal demands

In the first half of 2011, Brazilian
authorities issued 224 takedown orders to Google, more than any other
country in the world.In August, a
judge in the state of Ceará froze
US$130,000 in Google's domestic
bank accounts for noncompliance
with a takedown order of anonymous blog posts that accused a
local mayor of corruption.

**Countries with the most
takedown demands,
January–June 2011:**

| | |
|---|---|
| **224** | **Brazil** |
| 125 | Germany |
| 92 | United States |
| 88 | South Korea |
| 69 | Taiwan |

## 2.5 Years of censorship order

The court order against the São Paulo daily *O Estado de S. Paulo*, imposed in July 2009, forbids the paper from reporting on a corruption probe involving the Sarney family.

Judicial censorship has been a widespread problem in Brazil, CPJ research shows.

## More on Brazilian censorship:

**6** Cases of judicial censorship in six-month period in 2011, according to the Inter American Press Association, or IAPA.

**US$1,700** Fine placed against Radio Cultura for every report it aired on a construction company accused of corruption, according to IAPA.

## 2 Killed in 2011, motive confirmed

Newspaper publisher Edinaldo Filgueira was gunned down on June 15 after running a poll on his blog that reflected dissatisfaction with the local government, CPJ research found.

Television cameraman Gelson Domingos da Silva was shot and killed November 6 while covering a confrontation between state police and suspected drug traffickers in Rio de Janeiro.

## Nonfatal attacks against journalists in 2011:

**1** Journalist attacked by gunman.

**2** Drive-by shootings of journalists' cars and and homes during one week in October, according to the Inter American Press Association.

## 12th CPJ Impunity Index ranking

## 19 Killed since 1992

The Brazilian press has faced persistent violence over two decades, CPJ research shows. The 19 work-related fatalities in that period make Brazil the third deadliest country in the Americas, behind only Colombia and Mexico.

Coverage of government corruption has been particularly dangerous in Brazil.

## A closer look at killings in Brazil:

**56%** Suspected to have been committed by government officials

**68%** Victims who covered government corruption

**44%** Victims who were threatened beforehand

# Colombia

While lethal anti-press violence has slowed considerably in recent years, the press freedom landscape remains troubled. Journalists continue to be attacked and threatened with such frequency that some are compelled to flee to safer locations within Colombia or into exile. A journalist in Arboletes was murdered in June, although the motive was unclear. In this violent context, press groups feared the potential consequences of statements made by former President Álvaro Uribe, who described veteran reporters Juan Forero and Claudia Julieta Duque as "terrorist sympathizers" after they wrote critical stories about the Uribe administration in *The Washington Post*. The national intelligence agency's illegal espionage against journalists and other critics, a legacy of the Uribe administration, continued to be the subject of investigation. But progress was slow, with cases pending against more than 20 defendants in late year. In a blow to press freedom, the Supreme Court in May upheld defamation provisions in the penal code.

KEY DEVELOPMENTS

» Threats against journalists on the rise, prompting some to relocate.

» Former President Uribe's anti-press rhetoric sparks concern.

KEY DATA

## 1 Murdered in 2011, motive unconfirmed

Freelance journalist Luis Eduardo Gómez was murdered June 30 in Arboletes. CPJ is investigating to determine whether the motive was work-related. At least 43 journalists have been killed in Colombia in direct relation to their work since 1992; another 32 have been killed in unclear circumstances. Despite recent improvements, Colombia remains one of the world's most dangerous places for the press.

## Deadliest countries for journalists since 1992:

1. Iraq
2. Philippines
3. Algeria
4. Russia
5. **Colombia**
6. Pakistan
7. Somalia
8. India
9. Mexico
10. Afghanistan

# 5 th Impunity Index ranking

CPJ's Impunity Index found that Colombia is the world's fifth worst nation in combating deadly anti-press violence, with 11 unsolved murders over the past decade.

# 20 In exile, 2001-11

Mary Luz Avendaño fled Colombia in 2011 after receiving threats related to her reporting on drug trafficking.

CPJ's annual survey of exiled journalists found that 20 Colombian editors and reporters were forced to leave the country in the past decade.

**Top nations from which journalists have fled, 2001-11:**

| 79 | Ethiopia |
|---|---|
| 68 | Somalia |
| 66 | Iran |
| 55 | Iraq |
| 49 | Zimbabwe |
| 47 | Eritrea |
| 25 | Sri Lanka |
| 25 | Cuba |
| 20 | **Colombia** |
| 18 | Haiti |
| 18 | Rwanda |
| 18 | Uzbekistan |

# 94 Threats in 2011

The regional press group Foundation for Freedom of the Press (FLIP) found that the number of threats against journalists rose in 2011 after a decline the previous year. FLIP defines threats as direct intimidation of a journalist or the individual's family.

**Threats in Colombia over time as documented by FLIP:**

| 2007 | 85 |
|---|---|
| 2008 | 71 |
| 2009 | 74 |
| 2010 | 49 |
| 2011 | 94 |

# 5 Convictions in spying scandal

Five former officials of the national intelligence agency DAS were convicted in connection with an illegal espionage program that targeted critical journalists, opposition politicians, and others from 2003 to 2009.

**An ongoing inquiry:**

22 DAS officials awaiting trial or being investigated, including former deputy director José Miguel Narváez, who is also accused of masterminding the 1999 murder of journalist Jaime Garzón.

5 Prominent journalists whose emails and phone calls the authorities have acknowledged were intercepted.

# Cuba

Official repression in Cuba remains the most intense in the hemisphere. Although the last of the 29 independent journalists imprisoned in the 2003 Black Spring crackdown was released in April, the government's restrictive practices persist. Official censorship is codified in law and closely enforced. The government persecutes critical journalists with arbitrary arrests, short-term detentions, beatings, smear campaigns, surveillance, and social sanctions. Despite the island nation's low Internet penetration, the battle for free expression is being waged almost entirely online. The government has enlisted a legion of official bloggers to counteract a vibrant independent blogosphere. A fiber-optic cable project will enable the introduction of high-speed Internet. The launch of broadband service, which faced delays in 2011, will improve the island's government-approved Internet connections, but will not extend connectivity to the general public.

KEY DEVELOPMENTS

» Last Black Spring detainee freed from prison, but official repression is significant and ongoing.

» Fiber-optic cable project sets stage for broadband Internet, although general public will not benefit.

KEY DATA

## 18 Forced into exile, 2010-11

CPJ research found that Cuba and Iran led the list of countries from which journalists were forced to leave in 2010-11. Most of the Black Spring detainees were sent to Spain as a condition of their release from prison.

Life in exile has been marked by economic and professional challenges for the exiled Cuban journalists.

**Top countries from which journalists fled, 2010–11:**

| | |
|---|---|
| 18 | **Cuba** |
| 18 | Iran |
| 5 | Eritrea |
| 5 | Ethiopia |
| 3 | Somalia |
| 3 | Democratic Republic of Congo |
| 3 | Pakistan |

# 50 Cases of repression

CPJ research found that independent journalists were regularly harassed, obstructed, and detained in March and April 2011, a period with two sensitive political milestones.

The actions prevented these reporters from covering the Communist Party Congress in April and the eighth anniversary in March of the Black Spring crackdown.

## Highlights from the cases:

**11** Arrests carried out with violence

**12** Journalists subjected to house arrest

# 15.1% Internet penetration

Penetration remained relatively low, with the International Telecommunication Union estimating about 1.5 million users. Internet connections are mostly in government offices, universities, and other officially approved locations.

## Domestic Internet penetration over time:

| | |
|---|---|
| 2007 | 11.1 percent |
| 2008 | 11.7 |
| 2009 | 12.9 |
| 2010 | 14.3 |
| 2011 | 15.1 |

# 0 Imprisoned on December 1, 2011

Intense international advocacy efforts and long-term negotiations led by the Catholic Church and the Spanish government resulted in the release of the last journalist jailed in the Black Spring crackdown, CPJ research shows.

# 1,000 Official bloggers

The government estimates that it has enlisted 1,000 bloggers to promote official views and denounce critical journalists. Many official bloggers are government employees, and all enjoy easy, low-cost access to official Internet connections, CPJ research shows.

## A field tilted toward the government:

**40** Estimated number of critical journalistic blogs, CPJ research shows, all of which are hosted on overseas servers.

**US$8** Approximate hourly cost of uncensored Internet connections at hotels.

## US$70 million

Cost of fiber-optic cable project, financed by the Venezuelan government and laid by the French company Alcatel-Lucent. It will improve existing connections in government offices, universities, and other official sites but will not increase overall connectivity.

# Ecuador

The press freedom climate continued its sharp decline under President Rafael Correa. In September, a CPJ special report concluded that Correa's policies had transformed the country into one of the hemisphere's most restrictive nations for the press. In March, Correa brought a criminal libel complaint against senior managers of *El Universo*, the country's leading critical daily. The case, which centered on a biting opinion column that condemned Correa's actions in a 2010 standoff with police, resulted in convictions, prison sentences, and multimillion-dollar fines against the managers. The managers were free on appeal in late year. Other government officials also used the nation's archaic criminal defamation laws to try to silence journalists. The president made frequent use of *cadenas*, presidential addresses that pre-empt all private broadcast programming nationwide, to smear individual journalists and news outlets. Although *cadenas* have traditionally been used to deliver information in times of crisis, they have become a forum for political confrontation under Correa. The administration used other tactics to supplant independent voices with its own perspective, repeatedly ordering individual broadcasters to give over portions of their news programming to government "rebuttals." In a May referendum, voters approved ballot measures that would allow the administration to regulate news content in vaguely defined areas and force media owners to divest other holdings.

KEY DEVELOPMENTS

» *El Universo* managers sentenced to jail in libel case brought by Correa.

» Administration pre-empts programming to promote political agenda, attack critical journalists.

KEY DATA

2 **Restrictive ballot measures**
At a May referendum, voters narrowly approved a series of administration-backed ballot questions, including two that harm press freedom. Voters approved in concept a communications law that would, in turn, create a media regulatory council. The precise text of the law was being debated by the National Assembly in late year. The other ballot measure bars private national media companies, executives, and main shareholders from holding assets in other companies.

# 1,025 *Cadenas, 2007–2011*

Ecuadoran television was pre-empted more than a thousand times for *cadenas* since Correa came to power, according to Fundación Ethos, a nonpartisan Mexico-based research organization.

## *Cadenas* breakdown:

**150** Number of hours devoted to *cadenas* under Correa as of May 2011, according to Fundación Ethos.

**3** *Cadenas* devoted to discrediting the authors of the book *El Gran Hermano* (Big Brother), which detailed allegations of official corruption, CPJ research shows. Correa has also sued the authors for US$10 million.

# 17 **State news outlets**

When Correa took office in 2007, state media consisted of a single radio network. Since then, the administration has built one of the region's most extensive state media operations, which serves largely as a presidential megaphone.

## State media operations:

5 Television stations
4 Radio stations
3 Newspapers
4 Magazines
1 News agency

# 148 **Press freedom violations, 2011**

The press group Andean Foundation for Media Observation & Study, known as Fundamedios, documented nearly 150 press freedom violations as of November 2011. They include physical and verbal attacks, threats, harassment, arbitrary lawsuits and judicial decisions, coerced pre-emption, and obstruction.

## Press freedom violations, according to Fundamedios:

| Year | Violations |
|------|------------|
| 2008 | 22 |
| 2009 | 103 |
| 2010 | 151 |
| 2011 | 148 |

# 3 **Years sentenced to jail**

*El Universo* executives Carlos Pérez Barriga, César Pérez Barriga, and Nicolás Pérez Barriga, along with opinion editor Emilio Palacio, were sentenced to prison and multimillion-dollar fines in July. Palacio, who resigned, later fled to the United States.

## Damages in *El Universo* case:

### $40 million

Total Pérez Barriga brothers, Palacio, and newspaper must pay.

### $80 million

Total sought by Correa, when he appealed the sentence.

# Guatemala

Journalists increasingly practiced self-censorship as Mexican drug cartels expanded their presence in Guatemala. In May, criminals in four provinces hung banners in public places, threatening journalists with harm if gang activities were covered. A television journalist in southern Escuintla province was killed under unclear circumstances after receiving several threats. While the rise of criminal groups posed a growing risk, journalists also faced danger for coverage of official corruption and domestic security issues. In the southwestern city of Quetzaltenango, a television journalist and his family escaped injury when their van came under gunfire. The reporter had received death threats related to his coverage of police corruption. A columnist in the western city of Panajachel was forced to relocate after receiving a series of intimidating text messages concerning her coverage of a citizen security committee. The local press group CERIGUA documented an increase in press freedom violations in the months leading up to the November presidential elections, as well as a number of assaults and threats against journalists on Election Day. Otto Pérez Molina, a retired general running on the conservative Patriotic Party ticket, defeated businessman Manuel Baldizón in a runoff. Facing a murder rate among the highest in the world, Pérez pledged a tough approach on crime.

KEY DEVELOPMENTS

» As drug cartel influence expands, journalists face a growing threat.

» Press freedom violations climb: Columnist forced to relocate, reporter fired upon.

KEY DATA

15 **Press freedom violations**

The local press group CERIGUA documented 15 abuses against the press in the first six months of 2011.

Nineteen violations were documented in all of 2010.

**Breakdown of 2011 violations:**

9 Threats

2 Cases of obstruction

2 Attacks

1 Murder

1 Harassment

## 3 Arrests for threats

In May, three reputed members of the Zetas crime syndicate were arrested in the city of Quetzaltenango on charges of hanging banners with anti-press messages such as: "Tone it down, before the war is with you." Similar banners were found in Petén, Baja Verapaz, and Huehuetenango provinces. A week earlier, the press had covered the massacre of farm workers in Petén province. The Zetas organization, which originated in Mexico, has made considerable inroads in Guatemala in recent years.

### A massacre and a warning:

27   People killed in widely covered massacre in May.

4   Provinces where public messages threatening the press were found.

## 53% Violations by officials, politicians

CERIGUA found that more than half of the 2011 violations were committed by government authorities or politicians. Criminal groups accounted for only one case because Guatemalan journalists were practicing self-censorship, CERIGUA said.

### Attack by source:

5   Officials

2   Political party members

1   Organized crime

1   Security agent

3   Unknown

3   Others

## 1 Killed, motive unconfirmed

Yensi Roberto Ordoñez Galdámez, a television reporter and teacher, was stabbed to death in May 2011. CPJ continues to investigate to determine if the motive was work-related.

### Breakdown of fatalities in Guatemala over time:

5   Journalists killed, motive confirmed, since 1992.

13   Journalists killed, motive unconfirmed, since 1992. CPJ continues to investigate.

## 1 Forced to relocate

Newspaper columnist Lucía Escobar fled Panajachel after intimidation and harassment in connection with a piece that suggested a citizen security committee might have been behind the disappearance of a local resident. Escobar alleged the committee, an independent group formed to help protect the community, had begun using extralegal measures to enforce its own code of conduct.

### Other threats against journalists:

3   Shots fired at television journalist Oscar de León's minivan while he drove with his family. No one was injured. De León also received multiple death threats.

6   Intimidating text messages sent to Lucía Escobar over five days.

# Honduras

The Honduran press continued to suffer the violent fallout of the 2009 coup that ousted Manuel Zelaya. Four broadcast journalists were murdered in 2011 under unclear circumstances. CPJ is investigating to determine whether the killings were work-related. A climate of violence and widespread impunity has made the country one of the most dangerous in the region. The government's stance on media killings has worsened the situation. Authorities have minimized crimes against journalists and been slow and negligent in pursuing the culprits. No progress was reported in solving the murders of three journalists killed in direct relation to their work in 2010, CPJ research shows. A Truth and Reconciliation Commission composed of Honduran and international representatives delivered its much-anticipated report on the military-led overthrow of Zelaya. The commission labeled the takeover a coup—a decision met with controversy in Honduras—but it also accused Zelaya of improperly ignoring a Supreme Court decision concerning presidential term limits. The report found major press freedom violations during the coup, including the torture of journalists and the takeover of media premises.

KEY DEVELOPMENTS

» Post-coup violence and impunity cause ongoing damage to press freedom.

» Truth and Reconciliation Commission finds major anti-press attacks in 2009 coup.

KEY DATA

## 5 Murders, motive confirmed, since 1992

CPJ research shows at least five journalists have been murdered in direct relation to their work since 1992.

Thirteen others have been killed in unclear circumstances, and CPJ continues to investigate.

## A closer look at Honduran murder cases:

80% Committed with full impunity

60% Of victims threatened beforehand

60% Of victims worked in television

## 7 Police attacks, 2011

Journalists covering a tumultuous nationwide teacher strike faced harassment, detention, and violent attacks from police during a two-week period in March and April, CPJ research shows.

**Breakdown of harassment:**

1 Journalist detained

1 Journalist grazed by a bullet

3 Journalists injured by tear gas or rubber bullets

2 Journalists who had a tear gas canister thrown at their vehicle

## 3 Radio stations harassed

At least three community radio outlets that featured critical news coverage faced harassment in January 2011, according to CPJ research. Community stations have been vulnerable to threats and harassment in recent years.

**Breakdown of harassment:**

**La Voz Lenca and Guarajambala**: The OAS special rapporteur for freedom of expression said a government contractor cut electricity to these two radio stations, likely in reprisal for their critical content.

**Faluma Bimetu**: This station took itself off the air for 12 days after facing harassment from local officials concerning its leadership. The station had criticized local land development projects.

## 12 Major attacks, 2009 coup

A July 2011 report by the government-sponsored Truth and Reconciliation Commission found that the military committed major violations of freedom of expression.

**From the report:**

5 Military occupations of media facilities

2 Journalists tortured

5 Media organizations subjected to persecution, threats, and attacks

## 7 Attacks, 2011

CPJ research shows that *La Tribuna* General Manager Manuel Acosta Medina, Voz de Zacate Grande Director Franklin Meléndez, and Radio Uno Director Arnulfo Aguilar were the targets of armed violence. In addition, four journalists were murdered under unclear circumstances.

The murder victims were: television journalist Héctor Francisco Medina Polanco, media owner Luis Ernesto Mendoza Cerrato, and radio journalists Nery Geremías Orellana and Luz Marina Paz Villalobos.

**Breakdown of attacks:**

1 Attempted break-in of journalist's home by gunmen

2 Shootings of journalists

4 Murders, motives unconfirmed

# Mexico

Criminal groups exerted extraordinary pressure on the press as they extended their control over virtually every sector of society. Journalists were killed or disappeared, media outlets were bombed and threatened. Pervasive self-censorship was a devastating consequence of this environment. In an information vacuum, journalists and citizens increasingly used social media to inform their communities. The murder of a Nuevo Laredo reporter was the first case documented by CPJ worldwide in which a person was killed in direct relation to reporting done on social media. At least three journalists were granted political asylum in the United States and Canada, and several others sought refuge in other countries. Several major news organizations agreed on a professional code in which they set protocols for journalists at risk and pledged not to be propaganda tools for criminals. But President Felipe Calderón Hinojosa's administration failed to implement effective reforms. Despite efforts to rejuvenate the office of the special prosecutor for crimes against free expression, anti-press violence went virtually unpunished. The government's new journalist-protection program was widely seen as ineffective. And while the Chamber of Deputies passed a bill to federalize anti-press crimes, the legislation remained pending in late year.

KEY DEVELOPMENTS

» Violence continues unchecked as administration fails in reform efforts.

» Murder is first worldwide in retaliation for reporting done on social media.

KEY DATA

3 **Murders in 2011, motive confirmed**

Maria Elizabeth Macías Castro, Luis Emanuel Ruiz Carrillo, and Noel López Olguín were killed in direct retaliation for their reporting, CPJ research found. Four other journalists were murdered in unclear circumstances. CPJ is investigating to determine if the motives were work-related.

**Killed in direct relation to journalism in Mexico:**

| | |
|---|---|
| 2 | 2007 |
| 2 | 2008 |
| 3 | 2009 |
| 3 | 2010 |
| 3 | 2011 |

# 8 Protected in government program

The administration's new protection program for journalists under threat was widely seen as ineffectual and beset by bureaucratic rivalries. Only eight journalists were provided help by October 2011, and most said the protection was of little value.

## Breakdown of the program:

**Hundreds** Projected enrollment in the program.

**8** Journalists enrolled.

**5** Enrolled journalists who said the protection was ineffectual.

## 11 million pesos (US$840,000)

First-year budget for the protection program, according to official figures.

# 2 Missing in 2011

Editor Marco Antonio López Ortiz was abducted in Acapulco in June, while police reporter Manuel Gabriel Fonseca Hernández went missing in Acayucán in September. Mexico has the highest number of missing journalists in the world over time.

## Missing journalists in Mexico over time:

| | |
|---|---|
| 2006 | 2 |
| 2007 | 2 |
| 2009 | 1 |
| 2010 | 3 |
| 2011 | 2 |

# 0 Murder convictions by special prosecutor

The office of the special prosecutor for crimes against freedom of expression was restructured in 2010 and placed in the hands of a new administrator, Gustavo Salas Chávez, in an effort to improve its record of ineffectiveness. Nonetheless, the new office had no immediate success in prosecuting journalist murders.

## The special prosecutor's caseload and staff:

**103** Total number of cases, most involving minor issues

**11** Cases of murders or disappearances

**7** Investigators assigned to the office

# 8th Impunity Index rating

CPJ's Impunity Index found that Mexico is among the world's worst nations in combating deadly anti-press violence, with at least 13 unsolved murders over the past decade.

## World ranking on CPJ's Impunity Index:

1. Iraq
2. Somalia
3. Philippines
4. Sri Lanka
5. Colombia
6. Afghanistan
7. Nepal
8. **Mexico**

# Peru

Press freedom suffered notable setbacks in 2011. In the run-up to the presidential election in June, journalists reported an alarming rise in attacks and threats in response to campaign coverage. In northern Peru, one journalist was murdered in reprisal for his work, while two others were killed under unclear circumstances. Trial courts convicted four journalists under archaic criminal defamation laws, with one reporter imprisoned for more than six months until his conviction was overturned on appeal. President Ollanta Humala pledged upon assuming office in July to be a "defender of human rights, freedom of the press, and freedom of expression." In July, Congress passed a bill that would eliminate jail terms for defamation, but by late year the president had not signed the measure into law.

KEY DEVELOPMENTS

» Authorities use criminal defamation laws to jail, harass journalists.

» Anti-press violence grows. Numerous pre-election attacks reported.

KEY DATA

## 1 Murdered in 2011, motive confirmed

Television reporter Pedro Alfonso Flores Silva, who had covered local government corruption in the northwestern province of Casma, was shot on September 6 and died two days later. Two other journalists were killed in 2011 in unclear circumstances. Radio host Julio Castillo Narváez was gunned down on May 3, and José Oquendo Reyes was killed on September 14. CPJ was investigating the murders to determine whether they were work-related.

### Historical information:

7 Peruvian journalists murdered in direct relation to their work since 1992

3 Fatalities in 1992

1 Fatality in 1993

1 Fatality in 2004

1 Fatality in 2007

1 Fatality in 2011

# 193 Days in prison

Broadcast journalist Paul Segundo Garay Ramírez was jailed on April 19 on charges of defaming a prosecutor in Coronel Portillo. He was initially sentenced to a three-year prison term. On October 28, the Supreme Court tossed out the conviction, citing flawed evidence. A key audiotape, the court found, had not been properly authenticated.

# 4 Criminal defamation convictions

In addition to Garay, three other journalists were convicted in 2011 on criminal charges of defaming public officials in critical news coverage. Peru's defamation laws are increasingly out of step with regional trends.

**A year of defamation cases:**

**July**: Reporter Hans Francisco Andrade Chávez was convicted on charges of defaming an official in Chepén; an appeals court overturned his conviction in October on procedural grounds.

**September**: TV and radio station owner Gaston Medina was given a suspended prison sentence and fined on charges of defaming a local congressman.

**November**: Broadcast journalist Teobaldo Meléndez Fachín received a suspended prison sentence and fine on charges of defaming a local mayor.

# 2 Congressional access violations

In two cases, Peruvian courts ruled that Congress had violated the country's access-to-information law by withholding records related to alleged malfeasance by members. Courts ruled that Congress must turn over information requested by the regional press group Instituto Prensa y Sociedad (IPYS). Congress had not complied with either ruling by late year.

**Information delayed:**

**7-12** Days allotted by Peruvian law to process information requests.

**4** Years it took IPYS to win a court ruling confirming that the public should have access to a Congressional debate that led to sanctions against a member.

**2** Years it took to win a court ruling confirming the public should have access to records concerning an allegedly unauthorized Congressional payment.

# 8 Pre-election attacks or threats

CPJ documented eight cases in May in which journalists were assaulted, threatened, or harassed in response to their coverage of the June 5 presidential race.

# United States

A federal judge ruled in favor of reporter James Risen, who invoked his First Amendment rights to protect a confidential source. The Reporters Committee for Freedom of the Press and other groups called the ruling an important victory for the press. The Department of Justice, which appealed the decision, continued to take an aggressive approach in filing criminal charges against people who leak classified information. U.S. journalist groups were also troubled that increasing numbers of case documents were being sealed by the Supreme Court. CPJ reported that the State Department fell short in its first year of implementing the Daniel Pearl Freedom of the Press Act, which requires that press freedom issues be incorporated into the agency's annual country reports on human rights. WikiLeaks was in the headlines again when it disclosed thousands of classified, unredacted U.S. diplomatic cables. An Ethiopian journalist was forced to flee his country after he was cited in a cable. Police in five cities arrested reporters and photographers covering Occupy Wall Street demonstrations, often claiming the journalists did not have sufficient accreditation. At least three other journalists covering Occupy events were attacked by protesters or police officers.

KEY DEVELOPMENTS

» Two convicted for orchestrating 2007 murder of editor Chauncey Bailey.

» Government secrecy troubles U.S. journalism groups.

KEY DATA

0 **Detained by U.S. abroad**
This was the first full calendar year since 2003 in which no journalist was held in U.S. custody abroad, CPJ research shows. Beginning in 2004, U.S. military forces held numerous journalists in Iraq, Afghanistan, and Guantánamo Bay on vague assertions that they posed security threats. They were all held without charge or due process.

**Imprisoned by U.S. forces abroad, as documented on CPJ's annual December 1 surveys:**

|  | |
|------|---|
| 2005 | 5 |
| 2006 | 2 |
| 2007 | 2 |
| 2008 | 1 |
| 2009 | 1 |
| 2010 | 0 (A detainee was released |
| 2011 | 0 in February 2010) |

## 2 Convictions, Bailey murder

Two men were convicted in June on charges of orchestrating the 2007 murder of editor Chauncey Bailey in Oakland. Yusuf Bey IV, found guilty of ordering the murder, and accomplice Antoine Mackey were later sentenced to life in prison. The gunman, who pleaded guilty in 2009, is serving a 25-year sentence.

**Journalists killed over time in the United States:**

| 1992 | 1 |
|------|---|
| 1993 | 1 |
| 2001 | 2 |
| 2007 | 1 |

## 1 Targeted after U.S. cable leak

Ethiopian journalist Argaw Ashine was forced to flee his country after WikiLeaks disclosed a U.S. diplomatic cable in which his name appeared. Ethiopian police interrogated Ashine when the cable disclosed that he had told U.S. diplomats about a potential press crackdown.

**WikiLeaks breakdown:**

**2** Requests made by CPJ to WikiLeaks in 2010 to redact names of journalists cited in cables. WikiLeaks promptly complied.

**251,287** Number of unredacted U.S. diplomatic cables that became available in September 2011.

## 20 Attacks, arrests at Occupy protests

As police nationwide rounded up protesters demonstrating in allegedly unauthorized places, they also detained journalists covering the events. Press accreditation was at the center of several cases as police refused to acknowledge journalists who did not carry what they considered to be official accreditation. Assaults were also reported, including an attack in Oakland that left a cameraman with a concussion.

**17 Arrests**. Police arrested journalists in New York, Oakland, Nashville, Richmond, and Milwaukee.

**1 Attack by police**. In New York, a Fox 5 crew was hit by pepper spray and police batons as protesters broke past barriers and police sought to contain them.

**2 Attacks by protesters**. In Oakland, several men assaulted KGO cameraman Randy Davis as he was trying to film the aftermath of a fatal shooting at a protest site. In New York, a demonstrator seized a reporter's microphone.

## 24 Supreme Court records sealed, 2010–11

The Supreme Court has sealed an increasing number of records and documents in recent years, according to the Reporters Committee for Freedom of the Press.

# Venezuela

President Hugo Chávez Frías' administration continued its systematic campaign to stifle critical reporting through regulatory, judicial, and legislative avenues. The telecommunications regulator fined Globovisión, the country's sole critical television station, more than US$2 million for its coverage of deadly prison riots in June and July. The regulator invoked the Law on Social Responsibility in Radio and Television, one of the region's most restrictive measures. Prosecutors brought criminal charges against two executives of a critical weekly concerning a satirical article and photo montage that depicted high-ranking female officials as playing roles in a "cabaret" directed by Chávez. The weekly was briefly shut, and one executive was imprisoned for nearly three months. The Chávez administration used its extensive state media operation to spread political propaganda and wage smear campaigns against its critics. Chávez's announcement that Cuban doctors had found and removed a cancerous tumor fueled speculation about the country's political future as the October 2012 presidential election approached. Official information about the president's health was scarce and treated as if it were a state secret.

## KEY DEVELOPMENTS

» Wielding regulatory and judicial tools, government targets critical broadcaster, weekly.

» President's health problems treated as state secret, fuel speculation ahead of 2012 vote.

## KEY DATA

### 82 Days in prison

Leocenis García, owner of the weekly *6to Poder*, was detained in August after his paper ran a satirical article that compared senior female officials in the Chávez administration to cabaret dancers. He was charged with incitement to hatred, insulting officials, and denigrating women. García was freed in November, but charges were pending.

### Breakdown of *6to Poder* case

1 Week ban placed on *6to Poder* by a judge after the article's publication.

2 Days that *6to Poder* executive Dinorah Girón was jailed on the same charges. She was released but was ordered to appear in court every 15 days.

# $2.16 million

**Fine against Globovisión**

Conatel, Venezuela's telecommunications regulator, fined Globovisión for its coverage of a tense 27-day standoff between government troops and prisoners at the country's El Rodeo II Prison in the city of Guatire. Regulators alleged the station violated the Law on Social Responsibility in Radio and Television.

**Breakdown of Globovisión case:**

**7.5%** Proportion of fine in relation to Globovisión's annual income

**269** Times that Globovisión broadcast interviews with relatives of prison inmates

**8** Members of Conatel's 11-member social responsibility directorate who are executive branch appointees

# 13 Rejected U.N. recommendations

The administration rejected all 13 recommendations concerning freedom of expression that were made during the country's Universal Periodic Review before the U.N. Human Rights Council in October.

The recommendations, part of a larger human rights package, had called for the adoption of access-to-information legislation and the repeal of laws that criminalize insulting a public official.

# 6 Email, Twitter accounts hacked

Six critical journalists and columnists, including 2010 CPJ International Press Freedom Awardee Laureano Márquez, saw their Twitter accounts hacked in September. The hackers, going under the name N33, effectively took over the accounts. The group said it was independent of the government but was defending Chávez's honor, according to the International Press Institute. Eight opposition politicians and activists were also targeted.

# 1 Killed in 2011, motive unconfirmed

The body of Wilfred Iván Ojeda, a political columnist and opposition activist, was found in a vacant lot, gagged, hooded, and bound, with a gunshot to the head, according to local investigators. CPJ was investigating to determine whether the killing was related to his journalism.

**Breakdown of Universal Periodic Review recommendations:**

**148** Total number of recommendations

**95** Recommendations accepted (others were being considered)

**0** Recommendations accepted concerning freedom of expression

**38** Recommendations rejected, including all 13 freedom of expression items

# Americas Regional Data

**8**

Journalists
Killed in 2011

**84**

Journalists
In Exile 2001-11

**140**

Journalists Killed
Since 1992

**0**

Imprisoned on
December 1, 2011

**94**

Unsolved Journalist
Murders Since 1992

**11**

Missing as of
December 31, 2011

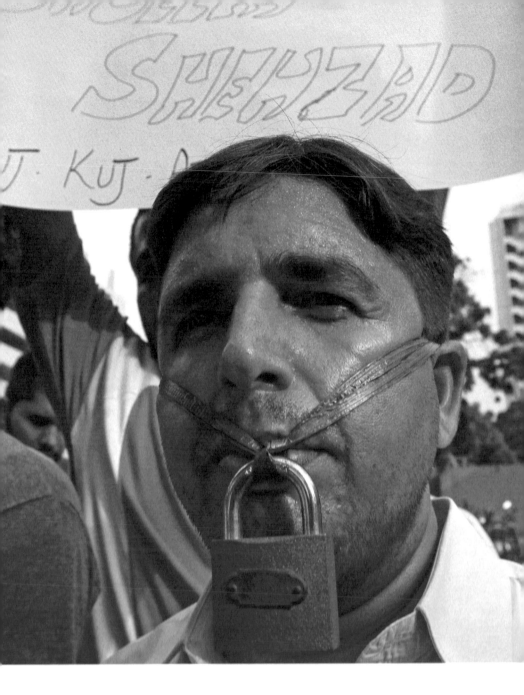

Asia

# Asia

PHOTO CREDITS

*Section break: A rally in Karachi demands justice in the murder of Saleem Shahzad. (AP/ Shakil Adil)*

*Page 141: A demonstrator holds a poster with the photo of slain Pakistani journalist Wali Khan Babar and the question, "Why?" (AP/Mohammad Sajjad)*

*Page 151: Ai Weiwei speaks to journalists at his home in Beijing after the government held him incommunicado for nearly three months. (AP/Ng Han Guan)*

*Page 159: An advocate for the Maguindanao massacre victims appears at a court hearing near several police officers charged in the killings. (Reuters/Romeo Ranoco)*

RESEARCH CREDITS

*Country reports in this chapter were written and researched by CPJ Asia Program Coordinator Bob Dietz, Senior Research Associate Madeline Earp, and Bangkok-based Senior Southeast Asia Representative Shawn W. Crispin.*

# Under Siege, Pakistani Media Look Inward for Solutions

*By Bob Dietz*

Speak to journalists in newsrooms or in the field in Pakistan and you will hear stories and opinions about killed and missing colleagues. Within their circle, reporters and editors readily share theories on the identities of perpetrators and their motives. Some whisper of threats they have received. By email, a few send "If I am killed" messages to friends, telling of threats and fears, their suspicions of possible killers and accusations of intent, founded and unfounded. Some ask for assistance in hiding from pursuers or moving between cities. Others want help to flee the country. Some have already gone.

Their concern is quite real because colleagues are being abducted, beaten, and killed in Pakistan at a rate higher than anywhere else in the world. While a few journalists simply disappeared, the bodies of most victims turned up soon after their death, their corpses apparently meant to serve as a warning to others.

The record is brutal. Pakistani journalists are vulnerable prey for many of the violent actors in their country—militant and extremist groups, criminals and thugs, street-level political groups in densely populated cities like Karachi, and, despite official denials, the military and security establishment. In 2010, Pakistan ranked as the world's deadliest country for journalists, and with 41 dead since CPJ started keeping detailed records in 1992, it ranks historically as the sixth worst in the world. The pace was similar in 2011, coupled with an apparent increase in death threats to journalists. Though some cases have drawn international attention and been subjected to high-profile investigations, all but one remain unsolved. Except when some of the men complicit in the murder of *Wall Street Journal* reporter Daniel Pearl were brought to justice after his 2002 beheading, there has been perfect impunity for those who kill journalists in Pakistan.

Decades of ineffectual governments demonstrate that journalists cannot expect justice should they become targets of any of the country's many violent actors. But within Pakistan's vibrant and financially successful media culture, some professional groups are taking proactive steps that, coupled with the manpower and financial support of media houses, could help address these problems without the government. In the meantime, some journalists will continue to censor themselves, give up the profession, or flee the country.

## Shahzad's reporting had angered military and intelligence officials.

The most prominent murder in 2011 was that of Saleem Shahzad, 40, who disappeared on May 29, soon after a two-part article about Al-Qaeda infiltration in Pakistan's navy appeared in *Asia Times Online*. His body was found on May 31 floating in an irrigation canal near the town of Mandi Bahauddin, about 75 miles (120 kilometers) south of the capital, Islamabad. His white Toyota Corolla was parked nearby.

Shahzad's book, *Inside the Taliban and Al-Qaeda*, had been released about 10 days before he was beaten to death. In it, he used insider information to link a small cadre of military officers to fundamentalist groups. Shahzad's reporting angered some factions within the military and intelligence community, but he had been diligently promoting his book on Pakistan's contentious political television programs despite the rising threat level. He was reported missing when he failed to show up at one of those televised panels, where he had intended to discuss the *Asia Times Online* piece, which claimed that Al-Qaeda was behind the 17-hour siege at a naval air base in Karachi on May 22. According to Shahzad, the attack came after the military refused to release a group of detained naval officials suspected of being linked to militant groups.

Earlier in April, three navy buses carrying recruits were blown up via remote-control devices in Karachi, the large port city where the navy is headquartered. In retrospect, those attacks were most likely the precursor to the all-out assault on the base, and Shahzad had said so. Further, his disclosures came just a few weeks after the U.S. killing of Osama bin Laden deep within Pakistani territory.

For months, Shahzad had been telling friends that he was trading text messages with intelligence agents and had been summoned to meetings with them. He had been directed to stop reporting on security matters that caused trouble for the military. Shahzad told a friend, Ali Dayan Hasan, a researcher for Human Rights Watch in Pakistan, that he had been threatened by a top official during an October 2010 meeting at the headquarters of the government's powerful Inter Services Intelligence Directorate, or ISI.

Hasan said Shahzad had sent him a note describing the meeting "in case something happens to me or my family in the future." Hameed Haroon, president of the All Pakistan Newspaper Society and one of Shahzad's former employers, told Human Rights Watch that he received a similar message about the same time.

Given those threats, it is understandable that friends who raced to see Shahzad's body before he was buried told CPJ that his face and neck showed signs of torture. But, according to the post-mortem report, it seems likely that Shahzad was not tortured until he died, at least not in a manner that would be used if his assailants were seeking to extract information from him. Instead, he was most likely beaten to death quickly and brutally in a manner that would intimidate other journalists.

His killing had the apparently desired chilling effect: Many journalists in Pakistan openly admit they were intimidated. Reporters covering security matters said they had received the sorts of threats and abuse that Shahzad had been receiving. Others started talking of threats from other sources, including ground-level political groups in restive areas such as Karachi, Baluchistan, and the Federally Administered Tribal Areas. For some, intimidation is part of the cost of doing business, and they have learned when to dial back a story to avoid more serious consequences. Their editors understand. The result is an institutionalized self-censorship that undercuts the power of Pakistan's historically assertive news media.

"You don't know what it is like to spend all your time worrying about an attack and where it might come from," said one journalist who spoke on condition of anonymity for fear of reprisal. "The fear affects more than just your reporting. It makes you worry about the safety of your family. It is a powerful thing that takes over your life."

..................................................

*Fear affects more than reporting, a journalist says. It takes over your life.*

..................................................

After Shahzad disappeared and in the weeks after his death, the journalism and human rights communities accused the ISI of complicity. The agency denied involvement, but public anger forced President Asif Ali Zardari to form a five-member commission headed by Supreme Court Justice Mian Saqib Nisar to hear testimony. (Similar panels have been convened in other killings and attacks on journalists. None have been conclusive.)

Before Shahzad's death, Pakistan's patriotic and nominally pro-military media had stepped up criticism of the military and intelligence establishments with portrayals of official ineptitude in the Karachi naval attack and the U.S. raid on bin Laden. The criticism escalated after Shahzad's murder, but eventually the story moved on. The United States stirred up nationalist resentments with increased rhetoric about ISI support for certain factions of the Taliban, and the Pakistani media began to speculate about a U.S. invasion of Pakistan. By fall, the press had returned to its earlier, pro-military stance. The special inquiry into Shahzad's death had issued no findings by late year.

There was precedent for Shahzad's murder. In December 2005, freelancer Hayatullah Khan, who for years had been under threat from government officials and militant groups in North Waziristan, took photographs of the remnants of an American-made Hellfire missile that had hit a house inside Pakistan, apparently targeting senior Al-Qaeda figure Hamza Rabia. Khan's pictures for the European Pressphoto Agency directly contradicted the Pakistani government's claim that Rabia had died in a blast caused by explosives in the house. At the time, the military-backed government of President Pervez Musharraf was denying that the United States was violating Pakistani territory with military operations inside its borders. Khan supplied some of the first proof of what later came to be common knowledge.

Like Shahzad six years later, Khan was abducted and died a violent death after discrediting the military. He was grabbed by gunmen on December 5, 2005, the day after his pictures were published worldwide. On June 16, 2006, he was found in his hometown of Miran Shah. His body had multiple gunshot wounds and had been ritually shaved in the Islamic manner used to prepare a corpse for burial, family members told CPJ. On his left hand dangled the distinctive sort of handcuff used by the military.

Musharraf ordered an investigation, in this case by High Court Justice Mohammed Reza Khan. The judge delivered his report in September 2006, but the results have never been made public. In July 2007, then-Interior Minister Aftab Ahmed Khan Sherpao and then-Secretary of the Interior Syed Kamal Shah pledged in a meeting with CPJ in Islamabad to release the report. The call for publication continued to be made over the years. On May 3, 2011, World Press Freedom Day, in a meeting with President Zardari and Interior Minister Rehman Malik, CPJ made the request again. The report has yet to be released.

..................................................

## In 2006, a high-profile murder led to a high-level probe with no result.

..................................................

Khan's death still resonates with journalists in Pakistan. As CPJ reported in the 2009 series, "The Frontier War," reporters have faced pressure from all sides to censor their work amid the deepening conflict along the border with Afghanistan. While those journalists remaining in the Federally Administered Tribal Areas have become a major source for news on fatalities from U.S. drone strikes, reporting on the struggles between militant factions, villages, and religious groups is highly restricted. Many local journalists have left the profession or report on only the most benign topics.

The intimidating effect of threats and attacks, not to mention deaths, drives some journalists to leave the country altogether. Since December 2010, CPJ's Journalist Assistance program has processed requests for help from 16 Pakistani journalists who have received threats from police, military, paramilitary, and political organizations. Fearing for their safety, most have asked that their individual cases go unpublicized. After Shahzad's death, requests for assistance started to climb, a trend that continued through late year.

Waqar Kiani, 32, who in the past had been a local correspondent for the British newspaper *The Guardian*, survived two assaults before resolving to leave Pakistan. In 2008, he was abducted in Islamabad by suspected intelligence agents, blindfolded, beaten, and burned with cigarettes. His ordeal ended 15 hours later when he was dumped 120 miles (180 kilometers) outside the city. Kiani told CPJ his abductors had threatened to rape his wife and post the video on YouTube if he told anyone what had happened. Traumatized, Kiani continued to freelance, telling only his closest friends and colleagues of the ordeal. He did not go public with the story until, caught up in the public anger surrounding Shahzad's death, he gave an interview to *The Guardian* about his own abduction and torture, then discussed it on political talk shows.

On the night of June 18, 2011, a few weeks after Shahzad's killing, a police van pulled Kiani over and ordered him out of his car. They wanted to search it, the officers said. As he stepped out, he told CPJ, four officers started to beat him with sticks and a rubber whip. They taunted him: "You want to be a hero? We'll make you a hero. We're going to make an example of you," the journalist said. Kiani was beaten on his face and back so badly that Declan Walsh, *The Guardian*'s Pakistan correspondent at the time, raced to the scene to transport him to a nearby hospital.

## The intimidating effect of attacks is driving journalists out of the country.

Soon after Kiani's second beating, Interior Minister Malik ordered separate judicial and police inquiries. But after Islamabad Senior Superintendent of Police Tahir Alam said preliminary investigations showed that police were not involved in the attack, the investigations stopped. Kiani lowered his profile as a journalist and with the help of *The Guardian*, he left the country for a few months, waiting for the threat to fade.

After Kiani returned to Pakistan, he told CPJ, he was convinced that he and his family remained under threat. He left Pakistan a few weeks after returning home. Temporarily separated from his family, he was seeking asylum in a European country in late year.

Another Pakistani journalist, Malik Siraj Akbar, is now based in Washington. He fled Pakistan because of military action in his native Baluchistan province, where secessionist groups battle each other and the Pakistani military, and where his exposure of military abuses would, he believed, make him a target. Soon after he was given political asylum in the United States, he told CPJ, "While I know the life of an asylum-seeker is often marked with extraordinary hardships, demise of one's professional career, and complete disconnection with friends and families, I believe no story is worth dying for."

The Pakistani security services are far from the only suspects in cases of attacks on journalists. Sometimes it is impossible to narrow down who may be responsible because of the sheer number of potential culprits. On May 10, about 700 miles (1,100 kilometers) due north of Karachi, in the Federally Administered Tribal Areas along the border with Afghanistan, Nasrullah Khan Afridi was killed when his car exploded in a crowded market in Peshawar. According to his colleagues at the Tribal Union of Journalists (Afridi was the union's president), he had been receiving threats for years from just about every combatant group along the border with Afghanistan—the government, Taliban groups, gun runners, and the military. No one knows whom to blame for the targeted killing of this prominent regional reporter who worked for Pakistan Television and the Urdu-language *Mashreq*.

...........................................

*Exile is filled with hardship, says one journalist, but no story is worth dying for.*

...........................................

Luckier than Afridi was television reporter Naveed Kamal. Two assailants shot at him in April on his way home from the small, low-budget cable TV station Metro One where he was a reporter. The motorcycle-riding gunmen fired repeatedly, hitting him with one round to the right cheek that shattered his jaw and exited his left cheek. Lying on a bed recovering at his parents' house in Karachi, Kamal told CPJ that police had conducted only a desultory investigative interview with him. He said he fully expected there would be no arrest made in his case. The last story Kamal had covered described the flags and banners that political groups were flying over specific neighborhoods—an indicator of the turf wars in Karachi among partisan and criminal organizations. Kamal said he did not know which group went after him or why. Although he later returned to work, he faced ongoing threats that forced him to switch beats.

The most fully, but still unsuccessfully, investigated journalist murder case of 2011 was the January 13 killing of Wali Khan Babar, a popular general news reporter in Geo TV's Karachi bureau. He was gunned down after filing a report on gang violence in the city, the country's most violent. In April, a few widely publicized arrests of low-level suspects were made; all were members of the Mutahida Qaumi Movement, or MQM, the country's third largest political party. But after four witnesses to the killing were shot and killed, as well as the brother of the police officer leading the investigation, the case went fallow. A spokesman for the prime minister's office told reporters that it considered Babar's murder a provincial matter, with the federal government having no role in continuing or ending the investigations. Because the suspected mastermind reportedly lives abroad, local authorities say the case is the federal government's responsibility. A perfect jurisdictional Catch-22 has stalled the investigation.

Sitting at his desk in Geo's newsroom, News Director Azhar Abbas picked his words carefully. "No less a person than the home minister [Malik] has named the MQM in the killing of Wali Khan Babar," he said. "The arrests in the case so far are linked to the MQM, and the MQM has not distanced itself from the killing. The onus is now on the MQM to say if it was involved or not." The MQM has denied any involvement in Babar's death.

## A perfect jurisdictional Catch-22 stalls the investigation into one murder.

When Zardari met with a CPJ delegation on World Press Freedom Day, he pledged that he would address Pakistan's appalling record for unprosecuted murders of journalists. So far his government has taken no action, in some cases because it apparently chooses not to, in others because it has no control over the actors. But the milieu in which Zardari rules and journalists operate is reeling out of control. A May report from the Center for Strategic International Studies identified 2,113 terrorist attacks, 369 clashes between the security services and militants, 260 operational attacks by the security forces, 135 U.S. drone attacks, 69 border clashes, 233 bouts of ethno-political violence, and 214 inter-tribal clashes in 2010. In all, more than 10,000 people died and about the same number were injured. The data being compiled by other organizations for 2011 looked to be similar.

With violence at a high level, special investigations proving fruitless, and an ineffective, impotent government unable or unwilling to protect them, Pakistani journalists have come to realize they must act on their own. Already, there are noteworthy instances of unity: When Umar Cheema, a prominent political reporter for the English-language daily *The News* (and a recipient of CPJ's International Press Freedom Award), was abducted on September 4, 2010, held overnight, stripped, beaten, humiliated, and abused before being bound and dumped on a roadside, the English-language daily *Dawn*, a direct competitor of *The News*, voiced its solidarity and anger. In an editorial, *Dawn*'s staff wrote: "No half-hearted police measures or words of consolation from the highest offices in the land will suffice in the aftermath of the brutal treatment meted out to journalist Umar Cheema of *The News*. This paper's stand is clear: The government and its intelligence agencies will be considered guilty until they can prove their innocence."

Founded more than 50 years ago, the Pakistan Federal Union of Journalists and its local chapters have long been a source of protest and pressure on the government when it comes to journalists' safety. The groups regularly turn out to protest attacks on colleagues in other cities, and there is a strong identity of journalism as a profession and a culture. The country's abysmal record of impunity has strengthened the groups' resolve, if not its ability to reconfigure Pakistan's culture of violence.

Journalists and media companies have put some basic steps in place. To remind reporters and photographers to take precautions while covering everyday violence, *Dawn* displayed posters and distributed handbooks for field crews with safety tips drawn from detailed guides by CPJ, the International Federation of Journalists (IFJ), and other international journalist organizations. IFJ has prepared posters in Urdu. *Dawn*'s sister organization, Geo TV, has done something similar and is backing up the guidelines by sending select staff members abroad to get practical, if expensive, training that they pass on to their colleagues. The Khyber Union of Journalists issued its own coverage guidelines after the double bombing of a market in Peshawar on June 11 that killed two reporters.

*The milieu in which journalists operate is reeling out of control.*

Concerned by the violence, after meeting with President Zardari and Interior Minister Malik on May 3 and 4, CPJ hosted a discussion on May 5 in Karachi. Haroon, who is chief executive of Dawn Media Group along with heading the All Pakistan Newspapers Society, led a conversation about the creation of a press organization to monitor and compile data on anti-press attacks. Haroon wants to create a hub of experts and gather knowledge about the assaults, kidnappings, and murders of journalists over the years.

Others in Karachi have a similar idea. The Citizen Police Liaison Committee is a private organization, run by the local business community. It supports a 24-hour hotline to police and the Interior Ministry. The idea arose in the 1990s when the abductions of wealthy businessmen in Karachi were a serious problem. The committee met with some success in solving the problem, though it was far from a total success. Zaffar Abbas, the editor of *Dawn*, suggested that a similar model would work for members of the journalist community when threatened or in immediate danger. Amin Yousuf, the Pakistan Federal Union of Journalists secretary-general at the Karachi Press Club, said the union would be interested in working with such a group. The task is to bring the two ideas together.

Pakistan's media are vibrant, with the larger groups commercially successful and the smaller ones proving viable over the long term. Large and small, they are owned by strong-willed, successful businesspeople with

...............................................

*For now, solutions will have to be found by people in the profession.*

...............................................

deep political connections, part of the country's ruling class. For now, whatever solutions exist will have to be found by people in the profession. Among their many challenges will be confronting a government unable and unwilling to stand up for a free press.

*Bob Dietz, coordinator of CPJ's Asia program, has reported across the continent for news outlets including CNN and* Asiaweek. *He led a CPJ mission to Pakistan in April and May 2011.*

# Amid Change, China Holds Fast To Information Control

*By Madeline Earp*

As popular uprisings unfolded across the Middle East and North Africa, Chinese Communist Party leaders prepared for a 2012 leadership handoff by fiercely suppressing homegrown protests. Online opposition was their greatest concern. China's individual Internet users passed 500 million in 2011, according to the state-affiliated China Internet Network Information Center. Activists had long used digital tools to criticize the government; in 2011, citizens embraced them to protest a series of public safety scandals, particularly the government's response to a high-speed rail crash in July. Criticism that began on social media sites facilitated some unusually aggressive press coverage.

"You can draw a parallel with the Occupy Wall Street movement," Zhang Ping, a columnist forced from his job in January for outspoken analysis of political and media issues, told CPJ. "Often online protesters have no clear goal, no organization, ideology, or financial support. They resort to methods that are frowned upon in regular society in order to seek justice they can't find through regular channels. This generation of young Chinese people didn't occupy Tiananmen, but they are occupying the Internet."

Despite the growth of Internet tools such as Twitter-like microblogs that gained attention inside and outside China, there are few tangible results of this activism. Indeed, the expansion of public debate may create an illusion of increased political participation. Though analysts expect some loosening of information control in the long term, it seems likely that censorship will only tighten in the coming year, given an anticipated clampdown on microblog providers and legal revisions under way to facilitate the secret detention of activists.

"While things at the moment are very repressive, I think we are going to see an era of big sociopolitical change in China, sooner after the leadership change than we might expect, because this follows the logic of China's overall development," Kerry Brown, who heads the Asia program at the British think tank Chatham House, told CPJ.

In 2011, censorship was strengthened around sensitive domestic or global events. Images of Egypt's pro-democracy demonstrators beamed around the world from Tahrir Square were blocked in China. The association with student-led Tiananmen Square protests in 1989, which leaders violently suppressed and subsequently banned from public discourse, was only part of the danger foreseen by propaganda officials. Soon, there were unsigned calls for political demonstrations, dubbed "the Jasmine revolution," on Chinese-language websites.

................................................

## Images of Tahrir Square seen around the world are blocked in China.

................................................

The goals of this revolution were modest: Protesters indistinguishable from pedestrians would stroll through city centers around China on a series of Sundays, demanding reform rather than regime change. Yet Communist leaders were reminded of Liu Xiaobo's Charter 08, an online political petition with widespread support among intellectuals. In China, the Charter prompted Liu's 11-year imprisonment on antistate charges; abroad, it garnered him the Nobel Peace Prize in 2010.

Foreign journalists looking to cover protests in Beijing and elsewhere found a few dozen dissenters outnumbered by security agents. Demonstrations remained discreet—one man laid a jasmine flower outside a Beijing McDonald's on February 20, according to *The New York Times*—but security officials manhandled and detained several international reporters for a few hours each, threatening to revoke their accreditation. A Bloomberg journalist who was punched and kicked by men in plainclothes required hospital treatment.

Some abusive Twitter messages accused foreign reporters of "stirring things up." (Twitter is blocked in China, but is heavily used by activists through proxy networks overseas.) Other online commentators mocked the authorities' exaggerated response, which confirmed the threat of unrest even as officials publicly denied it. Regulations forbidding foreign journalists to report without permission near protests appeared on a city website. One tall Western journalist was told to leave a protest for "obstructing traffic," *The Atlantic* reported.

Meanwhile, the government began a pre-emptive crackdown on known government critics. Dozens of online writers, lawyers, and activists were detained, harassed, or disappeared. Security agents detained at least two individuals, Liang Haiyi in northern Heilongjiang province and Hua Chunhui in eastern Jiangsu, for reposting details about the rallies on social networks. Other reprisals were handed down for comments on unrelated, though sensitive, issues, including political reform and media control. At least four professional journalists in the comparatively freewheeling media environment of southern Guangdong province were "side-shuffled" or given "leave," euphemisms for dismissal, which colleagues used to avoid further injunctions.

The detentions of prominent activists Ran Yunfei and Ai Weiwei resulted in extrajudicial punishment rather than criminal charges, a development that came to characterize the crackdown. Security officials placed Ran, a prominent Sichuan-based online commentator, in custody on February 20, and indicted him in March on charges of inciting subversion of state power. CPJ has documented several cases in which writers, including Liu Xiaobo, were convicted on that charge in relation to critical articles. The criticisms on Ran's blog left him vulnerable. "It's not that I want to ... criticize government and society day after day," he said. "If this were a regular democracy, I would not have that kind of zeal. But I was born in calamity-stricken China." In August, he was released under residential surveillance. Authorities either lacked evidence to prosecute, or considered the threat of re-arrest an adequate deterrent. Other detentions concluding in residential surveillance, also translated as house arrest or soft detention, included those of writer Yang Hengjun and lawyer and blogger Xu Zhiyong.

The punishment of Ai followed a similar arc. Ai documented social injustice in his work and online writing, noting the names of children killed as shoddy school buildings collapsed amid solid government offices during the 2008 Sichuan earthquake. Many believed his renown at home and overseas would protect him. But on April 3 he disappeared at the Beijing airport while preparing to board a flight to Hong Kong, and police raided his home, confiscating computers. A handful of supporters also vanished, including freelance journalist Wen Tao, who was quietly released later in the year. Ai was held incommunicado for nearly three months.

## In the case of Ai Weiwei, police reinterpret the meaning of 'house arrest.'

Unlike Ran, Ai was never formally detained or charged, although state media said he had confessed to tax evasion. A May 20 report from the official Xinhua News Agency said Ai was under residential surveillance, but he was not at his home. Neither was he in a jail or a detention center, his wife told foreign journalists. Police seemed to have reinterpreted house arrest, which can be imposed for six months without charge, to mean arrest at a location of their choosing. Ai later told reporters he had been watched around the clock, including during bathroom breaks. He remained under observation after release.

CPJ decried this treatment, which contravened domestic as well as international law, and encouraged the United States and the European Parliament to do the same. China's indirect response came in August. A National People's Congress committee announced draft revisions to China's criminal code that would legalize the practice of "residential" surveillance outside the suspect's home, without access to family members and lawyers, in antistate crimes. The changes are expected to be adopted in 2012, according to a research note prepared by Flora Sapio of the Centre of Advance Studies on Contemporary China in Italy, and Annabel Egan of the Irish Center for Human Rights' EU-China Human Rights Network. The approval process for covert detentions would be "significantly less stringent than those which currently apply to detention," the note said.

China human rights analyst Joshua Rosenzweig told CPJ that there is not yet enough data to establish a definite trend of surveillance over criminal prosecutions—and pointed out that abuse of residential surveillance has occurred in China for decades. But he agreed that "police appear to have been using 'non-residential' residential surveillance more often recently." It represented, he argued, a more flexible measure:

"Enforced disappearance is more a means of intimidation, a punishment in itself. If the intimidation doesn't succeed (and there's actually a case, however flimsy, that can be pursued) then the police have the option, after six months, of forwarding the case for prosecution."

The development is also an answer to Internet activists adept at documenting surveillance. Shanghai-based dissident and writer Feng Zhenghu updated Twitter followers about his security detail. Supporters helped formerly jailed lawyer and activist Chen Guangcheng and his wife broadcast video of their enforced home isolation in February, despite severed Internet and phone access. "Since the rise of the Web, blogs, and Twitter … we have got our voice," Chen told viewers. "It is almost impossible to block all the information."

The propaganda department's battle to block information met its biggest challenge of the year in July, when one of China's long-awaited new bullet trains rear-ended another near Wenzhou in southeastern Zhejiang province, killing at least 40 people. Leaders had touted the train as a "miracle" of development. The word was to haunt the subsequent coverage, as the usual propaganda regulations on covering disasters were sent to news outlets: Don't cast blame, laud the government's response, and emphasize miracles.

........................................................

## *Propaganda officials try to promote 'miracles' in train crash coverage.*

........................................................

Meanwhile, a flood of firsthand accounts of the crash hit the Internet. Official explanations—a lightning strike, signal failure—were retracted or contradicted. Online photographs showed authorities burying the wreckage instead of investigating it for flaws, fueling rumors of a Ministry of Railways cover-up. In a week reminiscent of the days after the 2008 Sichuan earthquake, many editors broke rules to get reporters on the scene. Readers called compliant news outlets to account: Internet commentators were furious that state mouthpiece *People's Daily* and three other newspapers ran coverage of a military ceremony on front pages the day after the accident, according to the Hong Kong-based *EastSouthWestNorth* blog.

Journalists chased Ministry of Railways spokesman Wang Yongping and demanded a press conference. A propaganda "miracle," in the form of a 2-year-old rescued after survival was declared impossible, became a focal point of the encounter. Accounts online said a rescue worker defied orders in order to save her, casting the official search in a less flattering light.

Asked for comment, Wang could only repeat that her discovery was miraculous. "It was not a miracle," one reporter yelled back. Defending the burial of the train, Wang inadvertently undermined the official explanation, that it facilitated the rescue effort, by saying: "Whether you believe it or not, I believe it." The words became an instant meme that Internet users shared in jokes, cartoons, and even a music video. They sealed his fate: Wang was reassigned to a position in Poland, although he retained his rank.

As they had after the Sichuan earthquake, propaganda authorities intensified regulations and censorship, but not before some strongly worded criticisms were made public. *A Southern Metropolis Daily* analysis carried the headline, "Some Freaking Miracle!!!" The Beijing-based *Economic Observer* ran an eight-page special report after the second round of regulations. Even the *People's Daily* cautioned against development at the expense of safety, employing the phrase "blood-smeared GDP." Government broadcaster CCTV suspended "24 Hours" news producer Wang Qinglei after his July 26 show not only covered Wenzhou, but referenced other scandals subject to censorship, like the Sanlu company's sale of milk made protein-rich with a chemical contaminant in 2008. "Can we drink a glass of milk that's safe?" the program asked, according to a *Shanghaiist* blog translation. "Can we stay in an apartment that will not fall?" Wang was equally outspoken on his microblog.

................................................

## A news program asks: Can we drink a glass of milk that's safe?

................................................

Public safety prompted other online clashes. In August, microblog sites deleted images and suspended some accounts for revealing the scale of demonstrations in Dalian, Liaoning province, over a storm-damaged chemical plant. China media analyst Jeremy Goldkorn listed 11 major local media stories involving food adulterated with dangerous substances in 2011, including watermelons exploding from growth hormones, pork chemically treated to pass as beef, and waste oil resold to restaurants for cooking. A Ministry of Health threat to blacklist reporters spreading "wrong information" about food in June caused an outcry. "Food won't be safe unless journalists are," the *Economic Observer* wrote. In September, while investigating the use of recycled oil for consumption, Luoyang TV journalist Li Xiang asked his microblog followers why safety inspectors had failed to find the gangs reportedly running the scam in Henan province. The following week he was stabbed to death walking home from karaoke. CPJ is still investigating the motive; police treated the death as a robbery, but other microblog users said he had been targeted for his reporting.

In response to online dissent, local governments promised systemic change but rarely delivered. After Wenzhou, three Shanghai railway officials were dismissed, but victims accused the government of delaying its promised investigation. Public trust was further undermined in September, when city subway operators said a signal failure had caused a crash that injured nearly 300 passengers. Foreign journalists reported that the Dalian chemical plant was still operating in October, two months after local authorities responded to protests with a pledge to shut it down.

........................................................

## The edgiest debates are usually found on the Sina microblog, Weibo.

........................................................

The edgiest debates over these scandals could usually be found on the Sina microblog, Weibo. Twitter, initially popular for the same reason, was blocked in 2009. Other local copycats have been shut down or controlled with licenses contingent on monitoring and censorship. With 200 million users, Sina is a huge commercial player, resilient to pressure. But as Weibo was increasingly credited with propelling stories from the fringe into the mainstream, information officials began to reassert control. In August, Beijing's Communist Party Secretary Liu Qi visited company headquarters, and Sina suspended two accounts for alleged rumor-mongering the following week. In October, the Communist Party Central Committee issued a directive stating, "We should strengthen the guidance and management of tools such as social networking and instant messaging applications," according to international news reports. Earlier that month, state media, citing the State Internet Information Office, said one person had been held for 15 days and another detained for "spreading rumors" online. It was not clear which sites the individuals had used. "There's still plenty of edgy stuff on Weibo," media analyst Goldkorn told CPJ by email in October. "But rumors of a real name registration system and clampdowns are continuing." Sina declined media interviews, and a Sina spokesman did not respond to CPJ's emailed request for comment.

During the year, outgoing Premier Wen Jiabao, a proponent of political reform, was among the few establishment figures who said that allowing public criticism would strengthen, not weaken, the party. "We must establish the conditions under which [people] can criticize and supervise the government," he told reporters at the National People's Congress in March, according to a translation by the China Media Project.

Future leaders may yet choose to follow in Wen's footsteps. As Internet penetration grows, Chinese leaders increasingly find themselves accountable to an online citizenry accustomed to access, engagement, and disputation. "Wen Jiabao's sentiments are right," Chatham House's Brown said. "I think history will see him having the last laugh, because the next leadership will be much more authentically reformist."

## Will leaders be accountable to an online citizenry accustomed to engagement?

Yet with sensitive political appointments likely in 2012, there is little hope for short-term improvement. The Chinese Communist Party holds its National Congress to announce major directives and party appointments every five years. In 2012, President Hu Jintao is expected to hand off to Xi Jinping, the Politburo Standing Committee's current No. 6. His appointment as head of state by delegates of the annual March legislative session, the National People's Congress, would follow in 2013. Analysts have identified the present No. 7, Li Keqiang, as Premier Wen Jiabao's likely replacement.

The standing committee's remaining seven incumbents all reach the traditional retirement age of 68 this year, opening the door to a generational overhaul. Yet the nine youngest of the existing 24-member Politburo, who are best placed to enter the top tier, are, like Xi and Li, likely to secure promotion by emphasizing traditional party values, including information control.

*Madeline Earp, senior research associate for CPJ's Asia program, is the author of the 2010 CPJ special report, "In China, a debate on press rights." She has studied Mandarin in China and Taiwan, and graduated with a master's degree in East Asian studies from Harvard.*

# Undue Process
# In Maguindanao Massacre Trial
*By Shawn W. Crispin*

Monette Salaysay and Rowena Paraan spoke out when they saw potential injustice in the ongoing Maguindanao massacre trial. A news report had alleged that a main suspect, Zaldy Ampatuan, the suspended governor of the Autonomous Muslim Region of Mindanao, might have bribed appellate court judges to approve his motion to be dropped as a defendant. In a case awash in allegations that witnesses had been bribed, threatened, and attacked, Salaysay, the widow of slain journalist Napolean Salaysay, and Paraan, a respected press freedom advocate, had some questions for the judicial system. Why, they asked at a public protest in March, did two appellate judges not recuse themselves from deliberations as they had with an earlier motion involving another Ampatuan clan leader?

The reaction the women generated when they questioned the court illustrates why many here see a justice system turned on its head. Citing rules that shield Philippine court proceedings from conduct seen as degrading the legal system, Appellate Court Justice Danton Bueser said the two women had abused their right to free expression and were potentially in contempt of court, which could bring fines and prison sentences. In his contempt resolution, Bueser wrote that the remarks by Salaysay and Paraan were "unfounded and malicious, intended to put the members of the court and the court itself in a bad light." The appeals court eventually rejected the dismissal motion filed on behalf of Zaldy Ampatuan, but the contempt resolution against the two women was still pending in late year. Ampatuan's attorney, Redemberto Villanueva, denied the bribery allegations in published remarks and chimed in that Philippine case law shows that "freedom of expression and speech is not unlimited."

For Paraan, secretary-general of the National Union of Journalists of the Philippines, the message was clear. "The charges are intended to intimidate those who are most vocal in criticizing how the trial is going and most active in pushing for justice for the massacre victims," Paraan told CPJ.

"The contempt charge may have a chilling effect on the victims' families since they are not used to this kind of fight."

Nearly two years since the Maguindanao massacre—an orgy of violence in which 32 journalists and media workers were among 57 people ambushed and killed—the fight for justice has simultaneously intensified in rhetoric and bogged down in technicalities. Legal stalling tactics, a fractured prosecution, and slow-moving courts have conspired against a speedy trial. Resolutions like the one lodged against Salaysay and Paraan have threatened to curb public scrutiny of the landmark prosecution.

......................................................

## A battle intensifies in rhetoric while bogging down in technicalities.

......................................................

Despite the case's high international profile and pronouncements by President Benigno Aquino that justice would be swiftly served, the Maguindanao prosecution has conformed to a disturbingly familiar pattern for media killings in the Philippines: A journalist is killed; local law enforcement officials are lax or complicit; witnesses and complainants are intimidated, bribed, or attacked; the defense employs stalling tactics to break the will and resources of victims' families; the case goes unsolved and the culture of impunity is reinforced. The Philippines ranked third worst on CPJ's 2011 Impunity Index, which calculates unsolved media killings as a percentage of each country's population.

Journalists and advocates believe that a successful prosecution of the Maguindanao massacre would break the cycle of impunity and make the Philippines a safer place to report the news. There have been certain signs of a breakthrough. Eleven members of the powerful Ampatuan clan, who stand accused of planning and carrying out the mass killing, have been arrested and detained, marking a break from past media murders in the Philippines in which influential suspects leverage political clout to elude arrest and trial. The detained include Andal Ampatuan Jr., mayor of the town that bears his family's name and the case's main suspect.

In June, the government's Anti-Money Laundering Council issued a freeze order on the assets and bank accounts of 28 Ampatuan clan members and close associates, a move prosecution attorneys believe will undermine their ability to finance their legal defense or influence witnesses. That same month, the Supreme Court granted a petition filed by two local press groups—the National Press Club of the Philippines and the Alliance of Filipino Journalists—asking that the Quezon City Regional Trial Court hearing the case be designated a "special court" with no duties beyond Maguindanao massacre hearings.

There have been other, less hopeful signs. Although proceedings began in January 2010, the trial court was still hearing arguments on bail rather than on the merits of the case. Only 70 of the case's 195 suspects had been arraigned by late 2011. (Evidence presented in the bail proceedings, including eyewitness testimony, will be recycled when the case is heard, prosecutors told CPJ.) Weak law enforcement has also weighed against the prosecution's case: 100 suspects remained on the loose in late 2011, with many believed to be evading arrest in the remote, mountainous areas of Maguindanao province where the Ampatuan clan still wields considerable political influence.

By late year, several jailed suspects, including a group of police officials and members of the Ampatuans' private armed militia, had filed motions for their release on bail due to what they argued was a lack of evidence. And an organization of victims' family members raised concern over reports that Zaldy Ampatuan was negotiating with the Aquino administration to become a state witness in an unrelated electoral fraud case against former President Gloria Macapagal-Arroyo, potentially in exchange for dropping the Maguindanao charges against him.

Defense lawyers representing Ampatuan clan members have filed a series of motions challenging the legal basis of the charges, including conspiracy to commit mass murder. A group of alleged gunmen under the

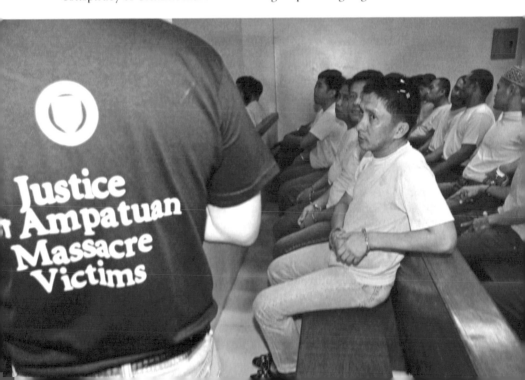

Ampatuans' command filed a habeas corpus motion that contends they were illegally arrested and misidentified as suspects in the case.

Romel Bagares, a private legal associate working with the prosecution, told CPJ that defense lawyers have employed "box techniques," in which they lure prosecutors into courtroom commitments that are difficult to fulfill and then file motions when the commitments aren't met. When prosecution witnesses have taken the stand, Bagares said, the defense has postponed cross-examination on technical grounds, including not receiving witnesses' background information in a timely manner. He noted that if a witness were killed or went missing before being cross-examined, his or her testimony would be nullified under Philippine court rules. At least one prosecution witness was murdered in unclear circumstances after bail proceedings began.

## Defense lawyers file motions challenging the very foundation of the case.

Philip Sigfrid Fortun, the defense attorney representing suspects Andal Ampatuan Sr. and Andal Ampatuan Jr., rejected suggestions that the defense has purposefully stalled the trial. In response to written questions from CPJ, Fortun said defense attorneys have tried to expedite the proceedings, proposing twice-weekly court hearings and the submission of judicial affidavits in place of time-consuming direct examination of witnesses. "If there is anyone interested in having the cases move at a faster clip, it is the defense lawyers whose clients are in jail for close to two years," Fortun said.

According to press freedom advocates monitoring the trial, the flurry of motions and petitions has fragmented and overstretched a prosecution team in which private lawyers have been called in to assist their under-resourced public counterparts. Some private prosecution lawyers have worked on the case on a pro bono basis and have been able to do so only part-time. On the other side, a team of 15 private defense attorneys filed on average three new motions per week, each of which required the prosecution to submit written responses and replies in court. In cases in which prosecution witnesses have given damaging testimony, defense lawyers have filed perjury and mandamus petitions, according to private prosecutor Prichy Quinsayas.

Prosecutors and advocates say the sudden death by heart attack of Leo Dacera, the public prosecutor and witness protection chief, in 2010 has left a leadership vacuum that has undermined the prosecution team's unity and morale. Tensions came to a head in March 2011 when private prosecutors working alongside their state-assigned counterparts clashed openly over courtroom tactics.

Nena Santos, a private prosecutor representing 27 complainants in the case, openly accused state prosecutors of soft-pedaling questions to defense witnesses at bail proceedings. Justice Secretary Leila de Lima soon ordered a revamp of the prosecution panel, removing lead prosecutor Richard Anthony Fadullon and others from the public prosecution team. De Lima told the *Philippine Daily Inquirer* that the Fadullon-led team had been lacking in "zeal, aggressiveness, and dynamism" and that her revamp aimed to bridge "irreconcilable differences" between public and private lawyers handling the case. She named assistant regional prosecutor Peter Medalle to head the new team.

The slow progress and splits between public and private prosecutors have raised doubts about the Aquino administration's ability to achieve justice. In a statement released on the first anniversary of the massacre, Aquino said the resolution of the cases would be a "litmus test" of the country's justice system. Two years since the massacre, observers and advocates estimate that without a strong executive push, including a sweeping revision of courtroom rules, the complex case could stretch out a decade or longer.

*State and private prosecutors clash openly over courtroom tactics.*

To expedite the proceedings, advocates and lawyers say, the government should also allocate more resources. Quinsayas, a private prosecution attorney involved in the case on behalf of the Freedom Fund for Filipino Journalists, told CPJ that public prosecutors have to carry their usual workload on top of the massacre trial and that they are not given extra allowances to cover its expenses. She noted that the prosecution was assigned just one support staff member to handle the case's voluminous clerical work. And it was only in October 2011, nearly two years into the case, that Justice Secretary de Lima provided a working area for the exclusive use of the prosecution panel.

The Center for Media Freedom and Responsibility, a local press freedom group, has argued that the defense team has strategically stalled the proceedings by filing a deluge of motions, including at least six demanding that the presiding judge recuse herself. The Center, the Freedom Fund, and the National Union of Journalists have long advocated a review of court rules that have been exploited by defendants to weaken their trials, pursue legal loopholes, or create procedural missteps that would allow them to escape prosecution. The three groups have held meetings with both the previous Arroyo government and the incumbent Aquino administration at which they have sought ways to reform court rules.

Of particular concern is Rule 65, which allows defendants to file limitless motions of *certiorari*, a writ seeking higher court review of a lower court's ruling, jurisdiction, or discretion. The motions have historically been lodged to stall or subvert court proceedings in media murder cases. Top defendants in the 2005 murder of investigative journalist Marlene Esperat used *certiorari* motions to challenge their arrest warrants and, as a result, were able to stall the beginning of their trial by nearly two years.

Former Palawan Gov. Joel Reyes filed a petition for *certiorari* in October 2011 to try to stop a new investigation into allegations that he planned the killing of journalist Gerry Ortega. His petition argued that de Lima, three state prosecutors, and the journalist's widow, Patria Ortega, "gravely abused" their discretion in requesting and ordering a reinvestigation. The Center for Media Freedom and Responsibility notes that Philippine law defines grave abuse of discretion as "the capricious and arbitrary exercise of judgment"—a highly subjective characterization that defense lawyers are free to assert repeatedly during proceedings.

......................................................

## *Under one rule, limitless motions seeking higher court review.*

......................................................

Filing an endless stream of such motions seems to be at the heart of the Ampatuans' legal defense. A group of arraigned Ampatuan family members filed a petition of *certiorari* in September claiming that the court that heard their bail proceedings had abused its discretion by issuing warrants for their arrests. The defendants requested that proceedings be halted until their petition is resolved, although the Court of Appeals has allowed bail hearings to continue while the matter is pending.

The defense lawyers "are trying to prolong the case so that the media and public lose interest," said Melanie Pinlac, who monitors the case for the Center for Media Freedom. "They are trying to make the victims' families feel tired and lose hope."

Defense attorney Fortun argues that the use of *certiorari* petitions is restricted by current rules. If the Court of Appeals is willing to entertain the petitions, he said, then they legally represent issues critical to the case. He contends that such petitions are often necessary because critical media reports have unfairly prejudiced public opinion against his clients. "They have convicted them beyond a reasonable doubt," Fortun said. "Anything less than conviction could generate a lynch mob effect against the court system and lawyers."

................................................

*A risk that the public will lose interest and prosecutors their resolve.*

................................................

Aquino administration officials have maintained that they cannot intervene directly to expedite the judicial process, citing a constitutional separation of powers among the executive, legislative, and judicial branches. Press freedom advocates have countered that Aquino could initiate a review of particular court rules that have been exploited to delay the Maguindanao proceedings. Private prosecution associate Bagares and others argue that Aquino could also exercise his executive authority to expedite the arrests of the more than 100 suspects still at large.

Press advocates see a growing risk that the defense team's dizzying array of petitions and resolutions will eventually break the resolve of overstretched prosecutors and cause the media to lose interest in the case. Aquino has repeatedly said he views the case as a test of the Philippine judiciary's ability to dispense justice. But without a greater commitment of government resources and attention from his own office, it's a test the Philippines could easily fail.

*Shawn W. Crispin, CPJ's senior Southeast Asia representative, is the author of the 2010 special report, "Impunity on trial in the Philippines," and has conducted several missions to the Philippines as part of CPJ's Global Campaign Against Impunity. The Global Campaign Against Impunity is underwritten by the John S. and James L. Knight Foundation.*

# Afghanistan

A s NATO and Afghan military forces faced off with militant groups,
the news media worked in a hostile and uncertain environment. Two
journalists were killed for their work, both during major insurgent attacks.
Accusations of widespread fraud marred the second post-Taliban parliamentary elections, which were resolved only by a presidential decree that
ousted several apparent winners. International aid organizations continued
to pump resources into developing local media, although many Afghan
outlets faced severe challenges in sustaining their work. In May, diplomatic
missions circulated a memo to international journalists warning of possible
kidnappings, though the threat never materialized. Three France 3 television crew members were released in June after 18 months in Taliban captivity. Abductions, which had spiked in 2009 and continued into 2010,
appeared to decline during the year. Afghanistan's mass media law, introduced in Parliament in 2003, has yet to be enacted because of political
stalemate. Under discussion were several draft versions, most of which
threatened to be more restrictive.

KEY DEVELOPMENTS

» As violence persists, two journalists are killed in crossfire.

» Abductions show decline; French-Afghan TV crew freed by Taliban.

KEY DATA

## 5 Freed from captivity

Two French journalists and
three Afghan colleagues were freed
by their Taliban captors in mid-
2011. Stéphane Taponier and Hervé
Ghesquière, journalists with the
French public service channel France
3, and Afghan interpreter Reza Din
were released on June 29 after a
lengthy captivity. Their local driver
and fixer had been quietly released a
few weeks earlier. The crew members
had been working on a story about
road reconstruction east of Kabul
when they were seized in late 2009.

## Recent, long captivities:

**547** Days that Taponier, Ghesquière, and Din were held by
the Taliban in 2009-11.

**223** Days that U.S. journalist
David Rohde and Afghan
reporter Tahir Ludin spent in
Taliban captivity in 2008-09.

**167** Days that British journalist
Asad Qureshi spent in captivity in Pakistan in 2010.

**157** Days that Japanese journalist
Kosuke Tsuneoka spent in captivity in Afghanistan in 2010.

## 2 Killed, 2011

In July, a U.S. soldier shot Ahmad Omaid Khpalwak, a reporter for the BBC and Pajhwok Afghan News, in the aftermath of a Taliban attack on government buildings in Tarin Kot. The soldier mistook Khpalwak for an insurgent. Farhad Taqaddosi, a cameraman for Iran's Press TV, died in September of injuries sustained in a Taliban attack on prominent international buildings in Kabul. Afghanistan is the 10th deadliest nation for the press since 1992.

## 6th Impunity Index ranking

At least seven journalist murders have gone unsolved over the past decade, making Afghanistan one of the world's worst nations in combating deadly anti-press violence, according to CPJ's 2011 Impunity Index. The index calculates unsolved murders as a percentage of each country's population.

## 80% Violence, anti-government forces

Measuring all types of violence, the Brookings Institution found that anti-government forces were behind an increasing proportion of attacks in recent years. In the first six months of 2011, anti-government actors accounted for the vast majority of all types of violence.

## 24 Killed since 1992

Fatalities in Afghanistan have run counter to many worldwide trends, CPJ research shows. International journalists constitute about two-thirds of victims, a proportion far higher than global trends. Murders made up only about half of the fatalities—far lower than the worldwide proportion—with deaths in combat and other dangerous assignments constituting the rest.

### A closer look at fatalities in Afghanistan since 1992:

VICTIMS

**67** percent were international journalists, well above the worldwide proportion of 13 percent.

TYPE OF DEATH

**54** percent were murders, 38 percent occurred in combat, and 8 percent stemmed from dangerous assignments. Worldwide, 71 percent of media fatalities were murders.

FREELANCERS

**21** percent of victims were freelancers, above the worldwide proportion of 14 percent.

TAKEN CAPTIVE

**54** percent of murder victims were taken captive first, well above the worldwide rate of 23 percent.

# Burma

Burma's news media remained among the most restricted in the world, despite the transition from military to civilian rule and President Thein Sein's vow to adopt a more liberal approach. The Press Scrutiny and Registration Department reviewed all local news journals prior to publication, censoring a vast array of topics. Criticism of the government and military was forbidden, although censors allowed more coverage of opposition leader Aung San Suu Kyi and some political and economic topics. Authorities exercised control with a vengeance: The nation was still among the world's worst jailers of the press. Exile-run media continued to fill the news gap, but at a high cost: At least five undercover reporters for exile media were imprisoned. Regulations adopted in May banned the use of flash drives and VoIP communication services in Internet cafés.

KEY DEVELOPMENTS

» Civilian government takes no significant steps on press freedom.

» New restrictions imposed at Internet cafés; censorship still pervasive.

KEY DATA

## 12 Imprisoned on December 1, 2011

With the number of imprisoned journalists virtually unchanged, the new civilian government's record reflected no improvement from the oppressive approach taken by the military junta.

**Imprisoned in Burma over time:**

| | |
|------|----|
| 2007 | 7 |
| 2008 | 14 |
| 2009 | 9 |
| 2010 | 13 |
| 2011 | 12 |

## 0.2% Internet penetration, 2009

With limited infrastructure, costly connections, and severe online restrictions, Burma has the world's fourth lowest Internet penetration rate, according to the most recent data from the International Telecommunication Union, or ITU.

**Lowest Internet rates worldwide, according to ITU data:**

1. North Korea: 0 percent

2. East Timor: 0.21

3. Liberia: 0.07

4. **Burma: 0.22**

5. Sierra Leone: 0.26

# 174 Publications censored

Strict censorship continued to force the nation's 174 newspapers and journals to publish weekly rather than daily. Censors reviewed all content prior to publication, typically ordering the removal of numerous articles. Censors also compelled editors to publish state-prepared news and commentaries that presented the government in a glowing light. CPJ has ranked Burma as the second-most-censored nation in the world.

## CPJ's Most Censored Nations list:

1. North Korea

**2. Burma**

3. Turkmenistan

4. Equatorial Guinea

5. Libya

6. Eritrea

7. Cuba

8. Uzbekistan

9. Syria

10. Belarus

# 2 DVB journalists sentenced

Two undercover reporters for the Democratic Voice of Burma were handed long prison sentences in 2011, CPJ research shows. Authorities have targeted exile media reporters in response to their censorship-evading reports, according to CPJ research. Burma remained among the world's five worst jailers of the press.

## World's worst jailers on CPJ's 2011 survey:

| | |
|---|---|
| 1. Iran | **42** |
| 2. Eritrea | **28** |
| 3. China | **27** |
| **4. Burma** | **12** |
| 5. Vietnam | **9** |

# 0 Arrests in Nagai case

Authorities have failed to hold anyone accountable for the killing of Japanese photojournalist Kenji Nagai, who was shot by troops while filming an armed government crackdown on street demonstrators on September 27, 2007, according to CPJ research. Burma has seen other instances of deadly official violence against the press.

## Deaths attributable to the government:

**1997** U Hla Han, a staff member of the state-owned newspaper *Kyemon*, died in government custody. DVB reported that he had been tortured.

**1997** U Tha Win, another *Kyemon* staff member, also died in custody amid allegations of torture.

**2007** Nagai was shot by government troops.

# China

Authorities blocked reporting of unrest occurring around the world, from Inner Mongolia to the Occupy movement. More than half of the 27 journalists imprisoned on December 1 were from Tibet and Xinjiang, reflecting crackdowns after earlier unrest in minority regions. After online calls for Arab Spring-style demonstrations, dubbed the Jasmine revolution, CPJ documented the worst harassment of foreign journalists since the 2008 Olympics, including beatings and threats. Police detained dissidents—including outspoken artist Ai Weiwei—and writers they feared could galvanize protests, often without due process, and kept them under surveillance after release. Draft revisions to the criminal code would allow alleged antistate activists to be held in secret locations from 2012. Officials obstructed reporting on public health and food safety issues, among other investigations. President Hu Jintao's U.S. visit and two bilateral dialogues, one on human rights, made little headway on press freedom, but domestic activists successfully challenged censorship using digital tools, especially microblogs.

KEY DEVELOPMENTS

» Fearing unrest, authorities crack down on critics. Minority journalists are also targeted.

» Growth of social media, particularly microblogs, tests Internet censorship.

KEY DATA

## 200 million
### Weibo accounts

The Twitter-like provider supported 56.5 percent of China's microbloggers in 2010, according to state media.

Authorities began intensifying control of Sina corporation's Weibo after users shared news faster than authorities could censor it.

## 6 Guangzhou sanctions

Traditionally lenient Guangzhou authorities suspended Southern Media Group colleagues Zhang Ping, Chen Ming, and Song Zhibiao; *Time Weekly*'s Peng Xiaoyun; and *Nanfang Chuang*'s Chen Zhong and Zhao Lingmin. Each was disciplined for critical commentary.

# 17 Jailed minority journalists

More than half of China's imprisoned journalists were ethnic minorities. Detentions of Tibetan and Uighur freelancers leapt after regional violence in 2008 and 2009. Information about trials is heavily censored.

## A growing clampdown on ethnic press:

**2007**    1 of 29 journalists behind bars was ethnic Uighur.

**2008**    3 of 28 jailed reporters were ethnic minorities, after the arrest of two Tibetans.

**2009**    6 of 24 journalists behind bars came from ethnic groups in the wake of riots in Tibet.

**2010**    15 of 34 imprisonments involved ethnic minorities, as six Uighur arrests followed unrest.

# 27 Imprisoned on December 1, 2011

China ceded its position as the world's leading jailer of journalists, a distinction it shared with Iran in 2010. Yet cases of journalists and activists under "soft detention" in their homes increased. Hong Kong's Chinese Human Rights Defenders reported more than 200 such detentions in March; almost all were subsequently lifted, the group said.

# 81 Days Ai detained

Documentarian Ai and associates disappeared in April, to international condemnation. State media accepted his irregular arrest. Though penalized for allegedly delinquent taxes, he was never charged. Newspapers debated draft legalization of secret detentions for 2012.

## Systematic harassment of government critics:

**52**    Individuals detained from mid-February to December, Chinese Human Rights Defenders said.

**171**    Days blogger Ran Yunfei was imprisoned before being released to residential surveillance.

**3**    One-day disappearances of lawyer and blogger Xu Zhiyong, reported on May 7, May 20, and June 22.

**2**    Delays to writer Chen Wei's antistate prosecution for insufficient evidence, Radio Free Asia reported.

**100**    Unidentified individuals guarding activist Chen Guangcheng under residential surveillance in October, according to Human Rights in China.

# India

Although the motives remained unconfirmed in late year, the murders of Chhattisgarh's Umesh Rajput and Mumbai crime reporter Jyotirmoy Dey reminded colleagues of the risk of violence. India remained on CPJ's Impunity Index, a ranking of countries in which journalists are murdered regularly and authorities fail to solve the crimes. Violent clashes between insurgents and government forces in states such as Kashmir challenged reporters' ability to work. In a mid-year report, *The Hoot*, a media issues website, recorded nine journalist assaults between January and May, including four in Orissa, where industrialization and Maoists had each displaced local residents. Authorities retaliated against critical reporting with antistate charges: Two journalists were jailed for allegedly supporting rebels after they criticized the impact of anti-Maoist campaigns on civilians. Journalists who exposed police ineptitude and corruption faced jail time. Politicians and businessmen muzzled reporters with legal action, including defamation, which authorities failed to decriminalize. Internet penetration was relatively low but growing, prompting the government to pass regulations that could suppress online dissent.

## KEY DEVELOPMENTS

» Impunity in journalist murders fosters further anti-press violence.

» Authorities nationwide allege antistate activity to justify media harassment.

## KEY DATA

### 11 Blocked websites

Two U.S.-based news sites, *Indymedia* and *IndyBay*, were among those that Bangalore's Center for Internet and Society found had been blocked domestically in April. Critics said new regulations banning ill-defined "harmful" online content could increase censorship.

### 2 Imprisoned on December 1, 2011

Freelancer Lingaram Kodopi documented anti-Maoist violence by police in Chhattisgarh. Mumbai magazine editor Sudhir Dhawale criticized Chhattisgarh's anti-insurgent militia. Both journalists awaited trial in late year on retaliatory charges.

# 10 Killed in Kashmir since 1992

The state's historically poor press freedom record declined again after violence contesting Indian rule during the summer of 2010 brought tighter government restrictions.

## A chokehold on coverage:

**5,000** Subscribers to an SMS news service that were affected when a June 2010 government blockage was extended into 2011. Officials later reinstated non-journalistic SMS services.

**5** Kashmir newspapers denied government advertising for "anti-national" riot coverage, *India Today* reported.

**0** Journalists interviewed in February by the weekly *Tehelka* who said police had honored curfew passes allowing them to report during times of restricted movements.

**5** Journalists covering protests who were assaulted or detained by authorities in August and November.

**2** Journalists refused entry. U.S.-based Alternative Radio's David Barsamian, known for his analyses of Kashmir, was turned back at New Delhi airport; and Gautam Navlakha, editorial consultant of *Economic and Political Weekly*, was sent home to New Delhi from the summer capital, Srinagar.

# 2 Pledges to decriminalize defamation

In January, M. Veerappa Moily, minister of law, and in February, Ambika Soni, minister of information and broadcasting, promised journalists that decriminalization was forthcoming. It did not materialize in 2011.

## A range of legal attacks:

**1** Night in jail spent by *Prabhatkiran* cartoonist Harish Yadev after Muslims took offense to his drawing of a politician. *Prabhatkiran* said the politician instigated the complaints, *Hindustan Times* reported.

**6** Gujarat police who summoned journalist Rahul Singh to court in January for tampering with evidence. Singh had exposed a mass grave of 2002 Gujarat riot victims, *Open* magazine reported.

**5** Days in detention spent by Tarakant Dwivedi under the Official Secrets Act after he detailed faulty weapons storage in a *Mumbai Mirror* article.

# 13th Impunity Index ranking, 2011

Seven murders from the past decade remain unsolved, making India one of the worst countries in the world at combating deadly anti-press violence, CPJ's Impunity Index showed.

# Indonesia

With no work-related deaths reported in 2011, Southeast Asia's largest economy and most populous country pulled back from its record high of three fatalities in 2010. The country's vibrant media remained under threat, however, particularly in remote areas. Banjir Ambarita, a contributor to the *Jakarta Globe*, suffered serious injuries in a March stabbing in apparent reprisal for coverage that linked police to a prisoner sex abuse scandal. No prosecutions were brought in the case by late year. CPJ research shows that corruption was an extremely dangerous beat for reporters; corruption itself was widespread, according to international monitors. Three men were acquitted in the 2010 murder of TV journalist Ridwan Salamun in remote Maluku, with no new arrests made. In June, the Supreme Court acquitted *Playboy Indonesia* publisher Erwin Arnada, who had been unjustly jailed for eight months on politicized charges of public indecency. While Internet penetration was a relatively low 9.1 percent, Indonesia had the world's second largest number of Facebook subscribers. Legislation passed by the Senate in October would give the intelligence agency expansive new powers to tap telephones and track other communications. The measure awaited President Susilo Bambang Yudhoyono's signature in late year.

KEY DEVELOPMENTS

» Journalists in remote areas vulnerable; one seriously hurt in stabbing.

» Corruption is widespread—and a very dangerous beat for reporters.

KEY DATA

## 2nd Facebook use

Although the country lags in Internet penetration, social media platforms were widely used. In 2011, Indonesia ranked second worldwide in total Facebook users, according to the social media statistics aggregator Socialbakers.

**Top five in Facebook use as of November 2011:**

| | |
|---|---|
| United States | 156 million |
| **Indonesia** | **40.8 million** |
| India | 38 million |
| United Kingdom | 30.5 million |
| Turkey | 30.4 million |

# 100th Global corruption ranking

Transparency International ranked Indonesia in the bottom half of its 2011 Corruption Perceptions Index. Indonesia's ranking of 100 out of 178 compared poorly to other Southeast Asian nations.

**Transparency International's 2011 Global Corruption ranking:**

| | |
|---|---|
| Singapore | 5 |
| Malaysia | 60 |
| Thailand | 80 |
| **Indonesia** | **100** |
| Philippines | 112 |
| Vietnam | 129 |

(The higher the number, the greater the level of corruption)

# 9.1% Internet penetration

Penetration remained low due to geographic dispersion and weak infrastructure. Data from the International Telecommunication Union put Indonesia's penetration below several other Asian nations:

**Regional Internet penetration, according to ITU data:**

| | |
|---|---|
| South Korea | 83.7 percent |
| Japan | 80 |
| China | 34.3 |
| Vietnam | 27.6 |
| Philippines | 25 |
| **Indonesia** | **9.1** |
| India | 7.5 |

# 0 Killed in 2011

No journalists were killed in 2011, although a reporter was stabbed after reporting on possible police sexual abuse of prisoners. No charges were brought in the assault. Journalists in provincial areas remained targets of violence.

**Media fatalities in Indonesia over time:**

| | |
|---|---|
| 2007 | 0 |
| 2008 | 0 |
| 2009 | 1 |
| 2010 | 3 |
| 2011 | 0 |

# 75% Victims who covered corruption

CPJ data show that Indonesian journalists covering corruption have been at great risk. Two-thirds of those killed for their work since 1992 had reported on official corruption.

**Beats covered by victims in Indonesia:**

| | |
|---|---|
| 75% | Corruption |
| 38% | Politics |
| 13% | Business |
| 13% | Crime |
| 13% | Culture |

(The data add up to more than 100 percent because more than one beat applied in some cases.)

# Nepal

Anti-media attacks and harassment flourished in a power vacuum left by the ruling coalition's political struggles. Baburam Bhattarai of the Unified Communist Party of Nepal (Maoist) became prime minister in August, securing support with his proposal to offer amnesty for war crimes, including journalist murders. Four assailants were convicted in two separate journalist slayings, but masterminds remained unpunished as authorities struggled to address the nation's entrenched culture of impunity. Of several assaults on journalists, at least one caused life-threatening injuries. Journalists received threats nationwide for their reporting, many from politicians or political youth groups. Assailants targeted at least six newspaper offices and burned hundreds of newspapers to limit distribution.

KEY DEVELOPMENTS

» Political in-fighting fosters anti-press violence.

» Maoists seek amnesty for civil war crimes, codifying impunity.

KEY DATA

## 4 Convictions

Local courts sentenced four individuals to life imprisonments for the unrelated murders of Birendra Shah and Uma Singh. In both cases, though, masterminds evaded detention and trial.

### A persistent record of impunity:

6 Journalists murdered since 2002.

4 Cases in which no convictions have been won.

2 Cases in which assailants have been convicted.

0 Cases in which masterminds have been convicted.

## 7th Impunity Index ranking

With journalist murders going un-solved, Nepal is among the worst nations worldwide in combating impunity, CPJ's Impunity Index shows.

### World ranking on CPJ's 2011 Impunity Index:

1. Iraq
2. Somalia
3. Philippines
4. Sri Lanka
5. Colombia
6. Afghanistan
7. **Nepal**

## 3 Bones broken

Youth members of the Communist Party of Nepal (Unified Marxist Leninist) assaulted *Nagarik* journalist Khilanath Dhakal in June in reprisal for his coverage of political violence, news reports said. The assailants broke Dhakal's nose in multiple places. The newspaper itself faced retaliation for its reporting.

## 4 Years missing

Armed men abducted Prakash Singh Thakuri, a Kanchanpur district freelancer, in 2007 in retaliation for perceived pro-monarchy reporting. Many press advocates presume him to have been killed. Maoists in government blocked investigations of three youth cadres, according to the local press freedom group Freedom Forum.

### A case on and off track:

2006   The Comprehensive Peace Agreement ended the civil war.

2007   Thakuri was abducted. His wife, Janaki, filed a report with Kanchanpur police.

2009   The Maoist-led government directed authorities to drop the case, saying the peace agreement precluded prosecution, according to Freedom Forum.

2011   Nepal's Supreme Court overturned the decision, and a Kanchanpur court reinstated the case.

## A newspaper under attack:

175   Copies of *Nagarik* and sister paper *Republica* burned by a CPN-UML youth group on June 11.

1   Public threat issued by a CPN-UML youth chairman. On August 13, the youth chairman demanded that *Nagarik* be closed and its editor jailed.

## 4 Prime ministers in 4 years

The Constituent Assembly was tasked in 2008 with drafting a constitution and an electoral system for the new democratic republic. But the assembly has foundered, and successive leaders have failed to secure cross-coalition support.

### A revolving government door:

3   Information and communications ministers in 2011.

4   Extensions granted to the Constituent Assembly after it was supposed to finish its work in 2010.

17   Rounds of parliamentary votes needed to elect Jhalanath Khanal of the Communist Party of Nepal (Unified Marxist Leninist) as prime minister in February. The subsequent election of Bhattarai came more easily, taking just one vote.

# Pakistan

Meeting with a CPJ delegation in May, President Asif Ali Zardari committed his government to the pursuit of justice in journalist murders. But with seven journalists killed, five in targeted killings, Pakistan was the world's deadliest country for the press for the second consecutive year. High-profile investigations into the drive-by shooting of Wali Khan Babar in January and the abduction and fatal beating of Saleem Shahzad in May yielded no prosecutions, replicating the country's long-standing record of impunity in journalist murders. Intelligence officials were suspected of complicity in the Shahzad case and other anti-press attacks. With Zardari's government unwilling or unable to protect journalists, media organizations stepped up efforts to protect reporters working in the field. But widespread violence in Baluchistan, the Federally Administered Tribal Areas, Karachi, and the Swat Valley—combined with the war in Afghanistan—made the challenge exceptionally difficult. At least three Pakistani journalists fled into exile during the year.

KEY DEVELOPMENTS

» Zardari pledges to reverse record of impunity; unpunished killings continue.

» Pakistan remains the world's deadliest nation for press; threats and assaults become more common.

KEY DATA

## 10th Impunity Index ranking

Pakistan is one of the world's worst nations in combating deadly, anti-press violence, CPJ's Impunity Index shows.

Journalist murders have gone unpunished over the last decade with just one exception, the killing of *Wall Street Journal* reporter Daniel Pearl in 2002. At least 14 journalist murders have gone unpunished during that timeframe.

### World ranking on CPJ's 2011 Impunity Index:

1. Iraq
2. Somalia
3. Philippines
4. Sri Lanka
5. Colombia
6. Afghanistan
7. Nepal
8. Mexico
9. Russia
10. **Pakistan**

# 41 Killed since 1992

With 41 work-related fatalities, Pakistan is the world's sixth deadliest nation for the press since 1992, CPJ research shows.

## Deadliest nations, 1992–2011:

1. Iraq          151

2. Philippines   72

3. Algeria       60

4. Russia        53

5. Colombia      43

**6. Pakistan    41**

7. Somalia       36

8. India         27

9. Mexico        27

10. Afghanistan  24

# 12,643 Civilian fatalities, 2007-11

Journalists were covering an exceptionally violent story, as shown by data from the Pakistan Institute for Peace, which monitors terrorist attacks and other acts of violence across the country.

## A closer look at violence, according to institute data:

24,171   Civilians injured, 2007-11

3,393    Violent incidents, 2010

2,113    Militant attacks, 2010

# 1 Prosecutions after special inquiries

Over the past decade, the government has commissioned at least six high-level, special investigations into attacks on journalists, CPJ research shows. In only one case, however, has a special inquiry led to a prosecution.

## Many investigations, little result:

2002   Daniel Pearl, killed, prosecution brought

2006   Hayatullah Khan, killed, no prosecution

2010   Umar Cheema, attacked, no prosecution

2011   Saleem Shahzad, killed, no prosecution

2011   Wali Khan Babar, killed, no prosecution

2011   Waqar Kiani, attacked, no prosecution

# 7 Killed in 2011

As violence escalated throughout Pakistan, the risks to journalists increased dramatically, CPJ research shows. At least 29 journalists have been killed in Pakistan in direct relation to their work since 2007.

## Journalists killed over time in Pakistan:

2007: 5      2009: 4      2011: 7

2008: 5      2010: 8

# Philippines

Despite high levels of press and Internet freedom, provincial journalists worked under constant threat of reprisal. Two broadcast journalists, Gerardo Ortega and Romeo Olea, were shot and killed for their reporting. Both cases were unsolved by year's end, underscoring the country's third worst ranking on CPJ's 2011 Impunity Index, which calculates unsolved journalist murders as a percentage of a country's population. The vow of President Benigno S. Aquino III to reverse the trend went unfulfilled as legal proceedings in the 2009 Maguindanao massacre, in which 32 media workers were ambushed and slain, stalled amid numerous defense motions to disqualify witnesses and suppress outside scrutiny. In another high-profile case, an appeals court denied a dismissal motion filed by two government officials accused of plotting the 2005 murder of reporter Marlene Garcia-Esperat. Although the decision cleared the way for arrests, the long-running prosecution has been beset by delays. Press advocates were critical of a new freedom of information bill, which they said would curtail access to official documents.

KEY DEVELOPMENTS

» Prosecution stalls in landmark Maguindanao massacre case.

» Provincial journalists face persistent violence; two murders reported.

KEY DATA

## 2 Killed in 2011

Two radio journalists were killed in direct relation to their reporting in 2011, according to CPJ research. Half of the 72 Philippine journalists killed since 1992 worked in radio, CPJ's data show. The 2011 killings add to the country's long record of deadly anti-press violence.

## 2nd Deadliest country

At least 72 journalists have been killed for their work since 1992, making the Philippines the second deadliest country in the world for journalists, CPJ research shows. Fatalities include murders, along with deaths on dangerous assignments.

### Media fatalities in the Philippines over time:

| 2006 | 2007 | 2008 | 2009 | 2010 | 2011 |
|------|------|------|------|------|------|
| 4 | 0 | 2 | 33 | 2 | 2 |

# 3rd Impunity Index rating

At least 56 journalist murders have gone unsolved over the past decade, making the Philippines the world's third worst nation in bringing the perpetrators of media killings to justice, CPJ's Impunity Index shows.

**World ranking on CPJ's 2011 Impunity Index:**

1. Iraq
2. Somalia
3. **Philippines**
4. Sri Lanka
5. Colombia
6. Afghanistan
7. Nepal
8. Mexico
9. Russia
10. Pakistan

# 25% Internet penetration, 2010

With its far-flung island geography and underdeveloped landline systems, Internet penetration has lagged behind several of the country's Asian neighbors, according to data compiled by the International Telecommunication Union, or ITU.

**Internet penetration over time, according to the ITU:**

| | |
|---|---|
| 2006 | 5.7 percent |
| 2007 | 6 |
| 2008 | 6.2 |
| 2009 | 9 |
| 2010 | 25 |

# 8th Highest Facebook use

Although the country has lagged in Internet penetration, its residents have quickly adopted social media platforms. The Philippines ranks among the world's top 10 in total Facebook users, according to social media statistics aggregator Socialbakers.

**Top 10 in Facebook use as of November 1, 2011:**

United States
## 156 million

Indonesia
## 40.8 million

India
## 38 million

United Kingdom
## 30.5 million

Turkey
## 30.4 million

Brazil
## 30.4 million

Mexico
## 30.1 million

**Philippines**
## 26.7 million

France
## 23.2 million

Germany
## 21.6 million

# Sri Lanka

The government's effort to silence critical media has been brutally effective as politically motivated deaths, attacks, and disappearances go uninvestigated and unprosecuted. The sister websites *Groundviews* and *Vikalpa* became the last independent news sites based in Sri Lanka, after a series of attacks on *Lanka eNews*. Arsonists attacked the offices of *Lanka eNews* in January, and authorities arrested the site's Colombo-based editor Bennet Rupasinghe in March. The site continued to publish from London but was blocked domestically. Authorities have turned the notion of law enforcement on its head, obstructing justice in numerous anti-press attacks. Prime examples are the unsolved 2010 disappearance of cartoonist Prageeth Eknelygoda, and the unsolved 2009 murder of prominent editor Lasantha Wickramatunga. Anti-press violence continued in 2011. In July, Gnanasundaram Kuhanathan, news editor of the Tamil-language daily *Uthayan*, was assaulted in northern Sri Lanka by assailants wielding iron bars. News media access to northern, predominantly Tamil areas remained severely restricted. The government and Tamil secessionists rejected allegations that they committed human rights violations during the long civil war, but independent coverage of the abuses was limited.

## KEY DEVELOPMENTS

» Critical website banned, leaving just two independent, domestic news sites.

» Impunity in anti-press attacks widespread; another assault goes unpunished.

## KEY DATA

### 1 Missing

The 2010 disappearance of *Lanka eNews* cartoonist Prageeth Eknelygoda has gone virtually unexamined, according to CPJ research. Eknelygoda was also a political reporter for the opposition website.

### 9 Murdered in Rajapaksa era

CPJ data show that since Mahinda Rajapaksa became prime minister in April 2004, and then later president, nine journalists have been murdered in politically charged circumstances.

# 4th Impunity Index ranking

Sri Lanka is one of the worst nations in the world in combating anti-press violence, according to CPJ's Impunity Index. The index calculates unsolved journalist murders as a percentage of each country's population. Authorities have obtained no convictions in any of nine murders in the past decade.

# 25 In exile, 2001-11

Violence and intimidation have forced Sri Lankan journalists to flee in high numbers. Despite its small size, Sri Lanka ranks among the leading nations from which journalists have fled, CPJ research shows.

**Top nations from which journalists have fled, 2001-11:**

| Ethiopia | 79 |
|---|---|
| Somalia | 68 |
| Iran | 66 |
| Iraq | 55 |
| Zimbabwe | 49 |
| Eritrea | 47 |
| Cuba | 25 |
| **Sri Lanka** | **25** |
| Colombia | 20 |
| Haiti | 18 |
| Rwanda | 18 |
| Uzbekistan | 18 |

# 12% Internet penetration, 2010

Sri Lanka's Internet usage rate tripled from 2007 to 2010, according to the International Telecommunication Union, or ITU. With the shutdown of *Lanka eNews*, the nation has only two domestic websites, *Groundviews* and its sister *Vikalpa* with Sinhala and Tamil content, that are critical of the government.

**Internet penetration rates in South Asia, according to the ITU:**

Maldives

## 28.3 percent

Pakistan

## 16.8

**Sri Lanka**

## 12

India

## 7.5

Nepal

## 6.8

Afghanistan

## 4

Bangladesh

## 3.7

# Thailand

Journalists faced significant restrictions, particularly online, despite democratic elections and a change in government. Outgoing Prime Minister Abhisit Vejjajiva cracked down on partisan media, shutting radio stations and detaining Somyot Preuksakasemsuk, editor of a newsmagazine aligned with the anti-government United Front for Democracy Against Dictatorship. New premier Yingluck Shinawatra wielded the country's strict *lèse majesté* laws by censoring websites and Facebook pages, and harassing Internet users who posted online material critical of the monarchy. Chiranuch Premchaiporn, editor of the news website *Prachatai*, faced a possible 50 years in prison under the draconian 2007 Computer Crimes Act for anonymous anti-royal remarks that were posted to one of her site's comment sections. The case was pending in late year. A reporter was killed in September while covering bombings in the country's insurgency-plagued southern region, a fatality that continued the country's recent spate of media deaths. The government opened a new inquiry into the fatal shooting of Reuters cameraman Hiro Muramoto during 2010 protests in Bangkok, but authorities left unresolved the case of a second international journalist killed in the 2010 unrest, Italian photographer Fabio Polenghi.

KEY DEVELOPMENTS

» Online repression intensifies; thousands of pages censored, editor on trial.

» Violent trend continues with one fatality; two 2010 killings unresolved.

KEY DATA

## 74,686 Blocked Web pages

The Ministry of Information and Communications Technology censored nearly 75,000 Web pages between the enactment of the 2007 Computer Crimes Act and the end of 2010, according to Thailand's independent iLaw project. More than 75 percent of the blocked pages were said to contain anti-royal content.

### Growing online censorship, as recorded by iLaw:

| YEAR | COURT ORDERS | CENSORED WEB PAGES |
|---|---|---|
| 2007 | 1 | 2 |
| 2008 | 13 | 2,071 |
| 2009 | 64 | 28,705 |
| 2010 | 39 | 43,908 |

# 9 Journalists killed since 1992

At least nine journalists have been killed in direct relation to their work in Thailand since 1992. Fatalities have increased in recent years along with rising political tensions, CPJ research shows. In 2011, newspaper reporter Phamon Phonphanit died from severe burns suffered while covering bomb blasts in Sungai Kolok.

**Work-related fatalities in recent years:**

| | |
|---|---|
| 2007 | 0 |
| 2008 | 3 |
| 2009 | 0 |
| 2010 | 2 |
| 2011 | 1 |

# 1 Imprisoned on December 1, 2011

A clampdown on partisan media and anti-royal commentary saw the jailing of Somyot. With his imprisonment, Thailand appeared on CPJ's annual prison census for the first time.

**Imprisoned in Thailand on CPJ's annual census:**

| | |
|---|---|
| 2007 | 0 |
| 2008 | 0 |
| 2009 | 0 |
| 2010 | 0 |
| 2011 | 1 |

# 875 Lèse majesté cases

The number of *lèse majesté* complaints filed to lower courts has spiked since a 2006 military coup, according to Thai court records. Thailand's *lèse majesté* laws prohibit criticism of the royal family and set prison penalties up to 15 years, making them among the most severe in the world.

**Lèse majesté cases filed 2006-10:**

| | |
|---|---|
| 2006 | 30 cases |
| 2007 | 126 cases |
| 2008 | 77 cases |
| 2009 | 164 cases |
| 2010 | 478 cases |

# 16th World ranking, Facebook use

As authorities ramped up website censorship, bloggers and alternative news providers migrated to platforms such as Facebook. With more than 12 million users, Thailand ranked 16th globally in total Facebook usage, according to Socialbakers data.

**Facebook use in the region:**

| | |
|---|---|
| Indonesia | 40.8 million users |
| India | 38 |
| Philippines | 26.7 |
| **Thailand** | **12.4** |
| Malaysia | 11.7 |
| Taiwan | 10.7 |
| Australia | 10.6 |

# Vietnam

Vietnam intensified a media crackdown targeting online journalists and bloggers, reasserting the government's near-total control of domestic news media. Authorities arrested and detained five bloggers and contributors to online news publications, bringing to nine the number of journalists behind bars. Political bloggers Pham Minh Hoang and Vi Duc Hoi were both given harsh prison sentences on antistate charges related to their writings. Authorities continued to hold and deny visitation privileges for blogger Nguyen Van Hai even though his prison sentence expired in October 2010. A new executive decree that came into force in February gave the government greater powers to penalize journalists, editors, and bloggers who reported on issues deemed sensitive to national security. An "accusation" bill passed in November was designed to force journalists to reveal the identities of confidential sources critical of government agencies.

KEY DEVELOPMENTS

» Several bloggers imprisoned in clampdown on political dissent.

» New regulations give authorities greater power to curb sensitive reporting.

KEY DATA

## 27.6% Internet penetration

Internet penetration rates have been relatively flat over the past several years, according to data from the International Telecommunication Union, or ITU.

**Internet penetration over time, according to the ITU:**

| | |
|---|---|
| 2006 | 17.2 percent |
| 2007 | 20.8 |
| 2008 | 23.9 |
| 2009 | 26.5 |
| 2010 | 27.6 |

## 5 Bloggers jailed in 2011

Authorities imprisoned five online journalists during 2011, intensifying their crackdown on political dissent, according to CPJ research. Four other online journalists had been detained prior to 2011.

**Imprisoned in Vietnam on CPJ's annual census:**

| | |
|---|---|
| 2007 | 2 |
| 2008 | 2 |
| 2009 | 1 |
| 2010 | 5 |
| 2011 | 9 |

# 5th
### Worst jailer of journalists

At least nine journalists were behind bars when CPJ conducted its worldwide census on December 1, 2011.

All nine of the reporters imprisoned in Vietnam published blogs or contributed to online news publications.

## World's worst jailers on CPJ's 2011 survey:

1. Iran — 42

2. Eritrea — 28

3. China — 27

4. Burma — 12

5. **Vietnam** — **9**

# 6th
### Worst nation for bloggers

CPJ ranked Vietnam among the worst countries in the world to be a blogger. Detentions, harassment, and severely restrictive laws have earned the country the designation.

## CPJ's Worst Countries for Bloggers:

1: Burma

2: Iran

3: Syria

4: Cuba

5: Saudi Arabia

6: **Vietnam**

7: Tunisia

8: China

9: Turkmenistan

10: Egypt

# 1
### Unsolved murder

Authorities failed to solve the death by burning of journalist Le Hoang Hung, a reporter with the *Nguoi Lao Dong* (Laborer) newspaper who reported on local corruption issues.

Dong's murder was the first work-related fatality in Vietnam since CPJ began compiling detailed statistics in 1992.

## Murdered journalists over time:

2007 — 0

2008 — 0

2009 — 0

2010 — 0

2011 — 1

# Asia Regional Data

**13**

Journalists
Killed in 2011

**81**

Journalists
In Exile 2001-11

**238**

Journalists Killed
Since 1992

**51**

Imprisoned on
December 1, 2011

**156**

Unsolved Journalist
Murders Since 1992

**3**

Missing as of
December 31, 2011

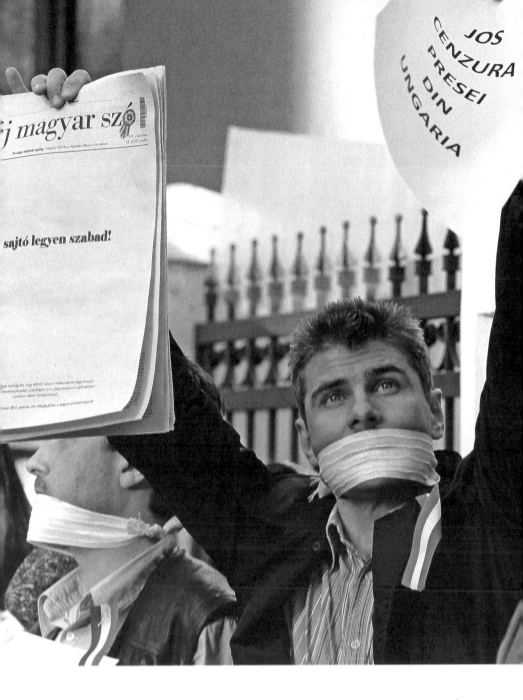

Europe and
Central Asia

# Europe and Central Asia

PHOTO CREDITS

*Section break: In Romania, a protest against Hungary's highly repressive media law. (Reuters/Radu Sigheti)*

*Page 191: Until his last days in office, Italy's Silvio Berlusconi pursued restrictive legislation known as the "gag law." (Reuters/Alessandro Garofalo)*

*Page 201:* Novaya Gazeta *editor Dmitry Muratov is guarded about progress in the murder investigation into his paper's renowned reporter Anna Politkovskaya. (Reuters/Sergei Karpukhin)*

RESEARCH CREDITS

*Country reports in this chapter were researched and written by Nina Ognianova, CPJ's Europe and Central Asia program coordinator, along with CPJ Research Associate Muzaffar Suleymanov, CPJ's Brussels-based senior adviser, Jean-Paul Marthoz, and CPJ's U.K.-based consultant, Elisabeth Witchel.*

# Cracks in the Pillar
# Of European Press Freedom

*By Jean-Paul Marthoz*

European officials tend to be proud of the state of press freedom in the European Union. Most EU member states sit at the top of international freedom-of-expression rankings, and the adoption in December 2009 of the Lisbon Treaty, the constitutional basis of the EU, has enshrined freedom of the press as legally binding. Physical attacks against journalists are rare, and in intergovernmental forums, EU member states usually stand up for freedom of expression.

But while the reality in Europe is light-years away from that of the most repressive countries, the gap is widening between "model countries" such as Finland or Sweden and others such as Hungary, Romania, Greece, or Bulgaria that are on the wrong side of the press freedom rankings. France, which has a vibrant and inquisitive media, has also registered a worrying slide in its press freedom record.

"We are quite concerned by the deteriorating conditions of press freedom in a number of EU countries, in particular in some of the new member states like Hungary or Bulgaria," said Tanja Fajon, a Slovenian member of the European Parliament. "In recent years we have recorded growing political pressures, harassment, and even attacks against journalists. The lack of transparency in the ownership of the media, the economic crisis, and the rise of right-wing populist movements have created a worrying environment for the exercise of independent journalism," said Fajon, who is a member of the Progressive Alliance of Socialists and Democrats, the second largest group in the European Parliament, and vice chairwoman of its Media Intergroup.

"Despite the European Union's commitment to the values of press freedom and human rights as set out in numerous treaties and declarations, its institutions—Council, Parliament, and Commission—are often restrained by member states who jealously guard their jurisdiction over media policy," said Aidan White, a media analyst and former general secretary of the

Brussels-based International Federation of Journalists. "There has been little effort to create a single, harmonized culture of press freedom across the region. The Council and the Commission often remain silent in the face of press freedom violations and concerns."

In recent years, some European governments have shown a propensity to tighten control on the media. Post-9/11 anti-terror laws have created a more chilling environment for press freedom and access to information. There is widespread concern, writes Sheffield University Professor William Horsley, "that some anti-terrorism legislation restricting freedom of expression is too broad, fails to define clear limits to authorities' interference, or lacks sufficient procedural guarantees to prevent abuses."

The EU Data Retention directive, in particular, has been denounced by free-speech advocates as a threat to independent watchdog journalism. It obliges telecommunications companies to store citizens' telecommunications data for six to 24 months and allows police and security agencies armed with a court order to request access to IP addresses and time of use of emails, phone calls, and text messages.

The protection of sources is the major battleground of press freedom in Europe. Although they celebrate the role of a free press as the pillar of a vibrant democracy, some governments are particularly eager to defang investigative journalism and do not refrain from using the resources of the state and dirty tricks to silence whistleblowers or intimidate muckrakers.

In France, for example, the secret services, under direct orders from President Nicolas Sarkozy's office, required telecommunications companies to provide the phone records of a *Le Monde* journalist, Gérard Davet, as the interior minister eventually admitted. Davet had published incriminating documents on the Bettencourt saga, a highly publicized case involving, in part, allegations of illegal contributions to Sarkozy's 2007 presidential campaign by the richest woman in France, Liliane Bettencourt. In October 2011, this affair led to the indictment of the director of the Central Directorate of Internal Intelligence, Bernard Squarcini, on charges of "illegally collecting data and violating the confidentiality of sources of a journalist."

In Portugal, senior members of the Strategic Defense and Intelligence Services (SIED) illegally secured access to journalist Nuno Simas' mobile phone calls and messages. Acting on their own initiative and without any judicial warrant, according to the weekly *Expresso*, the agents were trying to identify Simas' sources for an article published in the newspaper *Publico* about alleged tensions between SIED, Portugal's foreign intelligence agency, and SIS, its domestic agency.

In September 2011, U.K. police questioned *Guardian* reporter Amelia Hill over her investigation into the hacking of the voicemail of celebrities and private citizens by Rupert Murdoch's now-defunct *News of the World*. Scotland Yard also invoked the Official Secrets Act to try to force the reporter to reveal her confidential sources. The police eventually withdrew their bid.

........................................................

*Some member states jealously guard their jurisdiction over media policy.*

........................................................

Governments confronted with economic downturn and social malaise have shown signs of nervousness and intolerance. Embattled political leaders continually on the lookout for electoral support tend to see independent and critical journalism as a potential threat to their ability to retain office. In France, Sarkozy granted himself the prerogative of directly appointing the directors of the influential public television channels, a measure seen by journalist associations as an attempt to influence political coverage in the run-up to the 2012 presidential elections.

Before being forced from office in November, Italian Prime Minister Silvio Berlusconi had tried to domesticate the RAI public service system, leaving most of the independent watchdog function to a few newspapers

SILVIO BERLUSCONI

and the blogosphere. Eager to stop leaks on corruption investigations and his sex scandals, Berlusconi had also proposed a gag law that would impose heavy fines and prison terms on journalists publishing police wire-tapped material before the opening of a trial.

Governments have also sometimes lost nerve when confronted with demonstrators and rioters. In August 2011, at least six photojournalists were verbally abused, assaulted, or beaten by the Spanish police while covering social protests and demonstrations against Pope Benedict's visit to the country. Reporters have been subject to police violence in Greece as well.

## Governments lose nerve when confronted with demonstrators and rioters.

After the disturbances that rocked British cities in August 2011, Conservative Prime Minister David Cameron threatened to shut down social media if there were further street protests, under the pretext that the riots had been coordinated on Twitter and Facebook. He backed down under pressure from press freedom groups and civil libertarians. But the BBC, Sky News, and ITN were forced to hand over to the police hundreds of hours of un-broadcast footage of the riots after being served with court orders by Scotland Yard. "We are there to report news for the public, not to be used as a source of evidence for the police to prosecute people," protested Barry Fitzpatrick of the National Union of Journalists.

In such contexts, journalists are also targeted by rioters who see them as political adversaries or police auxiliaries. Attacks or threats against journalists were reported during the English disturbances in August and the Greek protests in October.

Tensions over religious issues also affect freedom of expression, with some media apparently exercising self-censorship to avoid being accused of inciting hatred or being the target of violent reprisals. On November 2, 2011, the Paris offices of *Charlie Hebdo*, a satirical weekly, were fire-bombed and its website was hacked after it published a "Charia Hebdo" issue "guest-edited by Prophet Muhammad" that took potshots at radical Islam. The attack triggered a rowdy debate on the limits of freedom of expression and responsibility of the press regarding sensitive issues such as religion and ethnicity.

A blasphemy law was enacted in Ireland in 2010, and similarly vague legislation on "religious insults" or "religious vilification" is still on the books in a number of European countries, including Austria, Greece, Malta, the Netherlands, and Poland.

Press freedom can also be threatened by violent groups. In Spain, although the ETA separatist armed group declared a "permanent truce" in January 2011, at least 19 media professionals working in the Basque country were still under police protection in late 2011, according to the Spanish Federation of Journalists Associations. In countries such as Italy, powerful criminal groups are major threats to journalists, forcing reporters to self-censor or go underground. The Neapolitan journalist and writer Roberto Saviano, the best-selling author of *Gomorrah*, a book that exposed the Camorra's (local mafia) business and connections, has been given permanent police protection.

The state of press freedom is also shaped by the economics of the media. "Concentration of ownership and the buying up of media groups by pro-government players are worrisome trends across Europe, and particularly in countries like Italy or Bulgaria," said Edward Pittman, program coordinator at the Open Society Media Program. "These trends limit the plurality of views, threaten truly independent journalism, and foster self-censorship in the coverage of important public interest issues."

...........................................

## *Concentration of media ownership is a worrisome trend across Europe.*

...........................................

Still, the crudest attempts at controlling or intimidating the media have usually been met with sharp resistance. In France, journalists are vying to unveil political corruption or influence-peddling whatever political party is on the firing line. In Portugal's Simas case, the daily *Publico* counter-attacked by filing a complaint for violation of privacy. In the United Kingdom, the police action against Hill, a reporter for the center-left *Guardian*, was roundly rebuked even by pro-Conservative media outlets such as *The Daily Mail* and *The Times*.

In matters of press freedom, the European Union is largely a two-tier or two-speed community. In many of the Eastern European countries that joined the EU, as well as in accession countries such as Croatia or Turkey, press freedom is far from being firmly established.

"The EU enlargement process over the past 15 years has seen countries with a weak tradition of press freedom welcomed into the Brussels family," the analyst White said. "In all of these countries problems remain, particularly over a lack of transparency in media ownership, a tendency among politicians of all colors to interfere in journalism, and flawed systems of media regulation, particularly covering public broadcasting."

In the Western Balkans, in particular, politicization of the media corrodes public debate and an atmosphere of intimidation is fostered by strong populist and nationalistic movements either in government or in the opposition. Criminal organizations also constitute a major threat. Journalists have been threatened, violently assaulted, and murdered in Bulgaria, Croatia, Greece, Hungary, Kosovo, Serbia, and Turkey.

The most direct political attack against the letter and the spirit of a free press within the EU has come from Hungary. Viktor Orban's conservative government rammed through Parliament a new press law in late 2010 and a new constitution in April 2011 that were denounced as starkly illiberal by civil rights and press freedom groups. "As a candidate country, Hungary would have been obliged to reform its media law before it would have been allowed in," said former Belgian minister Guy Verhofstadt, the leader of the Alliance of Liberals and Democrats in Europe, the third largest group at the European Parliament.

## Complacency on press freedom issues has come back to haunt the EU.

The Hungarian case indicates that the EU remains wary of putting in place the mechanisms that would force recalcitrant member states to respect the values and standards laid out in the Lisbon Treaty. "The European Commission has requested only cosmetic changes in the Hungarian legislation," said Fajon, the European Parliament member. "The digital agenda commissioner, Neelie Kroes, has addressed only technical aspects of the law although the Hungarian government was directly challenging the fundamental values of the EU."

The Hungarian media law, parts of which were struck down by the country's Constitutional Court in late year, has also highlighted the need to be more forceful in negotiations with candidate countries. A key test of the EU's commitment to these principles is how seriously it considers press freedom as a yardstick to judge candidate countries' compliance with the so-called Copenhagen criteria, the list of requirements—a functioning democracy, market economics, and implementation of EU law—with which nations have to comply before joining the Union.

Recently, however, the European Union has looked past press freedom violations when this suited its "other and more substantive interests," in the words of one EU official. In 2006, EU officials eager to complete the accession of Romania and Bulgaria played down the failings of these aspiring countries in the fields of press freedom and good governance. This complacency has come back to haunt the EU. As the European Federation of Journalists put it in May 2011: "In Romania, journalists have to challenge a national security strategy that considers journalists a threat to the state, and in Bulgaria, investigative journalists are threatened and sometimes physically assaulted." The victims have included Bulgarian crime writer Georgi Stoev, who was shot dead in 2008, and television journalist Sasho Dikov, whose car was blown up outside his Sofia apartment on October 13, 2011.

The European Commission promises to be tougher in its negotiations with the remaining candidate countries. Although it has given the green light to Croatia, a country plagued with violence against investigative journalists, "the enlargement commissioner, Stefan Fule, is thinking of singling out press freedom as a more explicit benchmark for accession," said Katinka Barysch, deputy director of the Centre for European Reform.

"Press freedom is becoming a priority for the EU and in particular for the European Parliament," Fajon said. "Two committees of the European Parliament are preparing reports on press freedom and freedom of expression in EU member states and in the rest of the world."

Concern for press freedom is guiding the assessment of Turkey's conformity with EU standards. The latest progress reports published by the European Commission, backed by stern appraisals of Turkey's press freedom record by Thomas Hammarberg, the commissioner for human rights at the Council of Europe, have been more critical than in years past. (Turkey, which has reinforced its economic power and is playing an increasingly active role on the international scene, still does not appear ready to take its cue from Brussels.) The more severe approach might also be applied to Macedonia, where the ruling nationalist government has bullied opposition and dissident media and, according to press freedom groups, used taxation laws to silence political rivals in the press.

On the positive side, emblematic cases like anti-terror legislation, the Hungarian press law, or the French secret services' spying on journalists have energized press freedom groups around pan-European campaigns, boosting their clout with European institutions and national governments. The increased cross-border cooperation has helped raise local issues of press freedom to the level of the European Union. The European Parliament held a succession of hearings on the state of media in the region at the behest of press freedom groups. And in late November, delegations of international and national press freedom groups visited Hungary and Macedonia to support embattled local journalists.

"Press freedom groups across Europe are keenly aware that everything is interconnected: If Hungary gets away with cherry-picking the worst pieces of EU legislation to draft its press law, it will inevitably lead other countries to follow this bad example," said the Open Society's Pittman.

Indeed, something positive has emerged from these controversies, suggests Renate Schroeder, co-director of the European Federation of Journalists. "While [in] years past no one seemed to care about press freedom within the EU, Neelie Kroes, the EU digital agenda commissioner, at least reacted a little bit on the Hungarian case and the European Parliament acted," Schroeder said. The announcement by the European Commission in early October that it was opening a high-level inquiry into press freedom might "just be for show," as the *EUObserver* reported, but it demonstrates that the commission has been forced to listen to the warnings of journalists' groups and concerned members of the European Parliament.

......................................................

*If Hungary gets its way, other countries will follow its bad example.*

......................................................

EU journalists can also refer cases to the European Court of Human Rights, an institution linked to the Strasbourg-based Council of Europe, whose rulings apply to all EU member states. The court has often ruled in favor of press freedom and freedom of expression and has developed EU-wide norms and jurisprudence.

Still, the lack of common standards and initiatives between the various European institutions that deal with press freedom is a challenge. "The Council of Europe's human rights commissioner as well as the representative on freedom of the media" at the Organization for Security and Co-operation in Europe "are doing great work," Schroeder said, "but there is not enough coordination with the European Union, which has the tools—the Lisbon Treaty, the Charter of Fundamental Rights—to effectively defend freedom of the press in its member states."

Further, fighting legal battles as they arise will not be enough to contain or roll back negative trends. "A proactive strategy is needed in order to protect media pluralism and independence," Pittman said. "In Eastern Europe, in particular, ways have to be found to assure the sustainability of truly independent media that are able to resist massive pressures from the state, large corporations, and criminal organizations."

The state of press freedom inside the European Union is crucial to the EU's credibility in public diplomacy. In its external relations, the EU tries to present itself as a beacon of democracy and as a world leader in respect to freedom of speech. This commitment is generally respected by the EU in the context of intergovernmental institutions such as the U.N. Human Rights Council or UNESCO; European countries usually battle attempts to impose resolutions on the "defamation of religion" and fight maneuvers to establish prizes in the name of dictators, such as the proposed UNESCO/ Teodoro Obiang Prize, named for and funded by the president of Equatorial Guinea.

Still, many European countries have also shown a readiness to put aside press freedom in their external relations. Few European governments openly protested when authoritarian Arab rulers appeared solidly installed in their presidential palaces. France, the United Kingdom, and Italy waited until the last moment before jettisoning Ben Ali, Mubarak, and Qaddafi. Cozy relationships with African strongmen are still the rule between Paris and its former colonies, despite promises to support good governance and civil liberties. Until recently, the United Kingdom has also refrained from openly criticizing allied countries such as Rwanda or Ethiopia for their very poor records on press freedom. And Spain's socialist government has remained soft in its assessment of Cuba's dire press freedom conditions, though it did work to win the release of imprisoned Cuban journalists in 2010 and 2011.

................................................

## *Press freedom inside the EU is crucial to the Union's global credibility.*

................................................

Press freedom is often excised from the human rights dialogues that the EU holds with powerful and prickly countries like Russia or China. During bilateral summits, some committed officials are sometimes able to raise objections behind closed doors and inquire about the fate of imprisoned journalists, but such touchy subjects are not allowed to emerge in public events or to hamper trade deals.

The EU and its member states, like other democracies, appear torn between principles and realpolitik. Even as EU-funded human rights experts train journalists to secure their Internet communications against state-sponsored hacking or denial-of-service attacks, European trade officials allow the export to authoritarian countries of technology to monitor, track, and repress these very dissidents and independent writers. While the European Commission proclaims its commitment to press freedom, many European countries have been toughening their asylum procedures, at the risk of compromising the safety and the rights of foreign journalists under threat.

Two December 2011 initiatives should bring more consistency to EU foreign and trade policy by incorporating Internet freedom as a key objective. The European Parliament approved an Internet Freedom Fund aimed at empowering online journalists to circumvent censorship, while Kroes launched a "No-Disconnect" strategy designed to help human rights defenders communicate safely and anonymously. The challenge for advocates is to constantly monitor EU initiatives, linking the Union's internal performance to its foreign policy.

Press freedom advocates rely on the commitment of the European Parliament, an institution that has been endowed with new prerogatives by the Lisbon Treaty, to bridge the gap between rhetoric and policy. The parliament has consistently awarded its prestigious Sakharov Prize for Freedom of Thought to independent journalists and writers in authoritarian states. The parliament and its major political groups have also held frequent hearings on attacks against press freedom and adopted many resolutions condemning abuses, like the Eritrean government's jailing of journalists, the harassment of dissidents in China, or impunity in Russia.

"How can the EU be credible if it allows Hungary to undermine freedom of expression and tolerates encroachments on the press in countries like France or Italy?" said Schroeder of the European Federation of Journalists. "The best way for the EU to help independent journalists abroad is also to fully respect inside its own borders the principles of freedom of expression, which it is so keen to preach abroad."

Norway, which is not an EU member state, is seen by many press freedom groups as an inspiration. After the Utoya Island massacre carried out in July by far-right militant Anders Behring Breivik, the country's authorities solemnly reaffirmed their belief in freedom of expression as a pillar of democratic society.

Norwegian Prime Minister Jens Stoltenberg sent a strong message to governments tempted to exploit dramatic events in order to muzzle independent journalism and restrict freedom of expression, stating, "Our country will stake its course with the strongest weapons in the world: freedom of speech and democracy."

*CPJ Senior Adviser Jean-Paul Marthoz is a Belgian journalist and writer. He is a foreign affairs columnist for* Le Soir *and journalism professor at the Université de Louvain-la-Neuve.*

# Despite Progress,
# Impunity Still the Norm in Russia

*By Nina Ognianova*

On September 28, 2010, Aleksandr Bastrykin, Russia's top investigating official, told a visiting CPJ delegation that it was "a matter of honor" for his agency to solve a string of journalist murders committed under the country's current administration. "It is a matter of proving our professionalism," he said. Bastrykin admitted his team of investigators had made a mistake "rushing" the case of murdered *Novaya Gazeta* journalist Anna Politkovskaya to court two years earlier. This time, he said, detectives were doing a thorough job, gathering solid evidence that would hold up to the scrutiny of a jury trial.

The meeting demonstrated a notable shift in tone; Bastrykin was more open in his interaction with CPJ than any Russian official had ever been. His agency, the Investigative Committee of the Russian Federation, which is tasked with solving serious crimes, announced two days later that it was reopening five closed or suspended inquiries into journalist murders. The decision, a spokesman said, was prompted by the meeting with CPJ. Cautious hopes were kindled that Russian authorities were starting a new chapter—not only in tackling the murder cases but also in communicating with the public.

More than a year later, however, the rhetoric is largely unmatched by results.

Investigators won convictions in one case—the double murder in Moscow of *Novaya Gazeta* reporter Anastasiya Baburova and human rights lawyer Stanislav Markelov—and they made progress in solving the slaying of Politkovskaya, the highest profile of the 20 journalist murders committed since 2000. In the double murder, a jury declared two defendants guilty in April 2011 and sentenced them to lengthy prison terms. In Politkovskaya's case, authorities announced the arrest and indictment of the suspected gunman in mid-2011, then detained a retired police lieutenant colonel and charged him with helping carry out the killing.

By late year, the circle of suspects in the 2006 Politkovskaya murder was growing, but the mastermind who had sent the assassin to her doorstep remained unidentified. In the Baburova-Markelov case, investigators said the two people convicted in the 2009 murders had a number of accomplices, yet those suspects remained at large. And the death toll grew yet again in December, when an assassin gunned down Gadzhimurad Kamalov, founder of the Dagestani weekly *Chernovik*, which had investigated government corruption, human rights abuses, and Islamic radicalism.

Failure to prosecute the masterminds perpetuates impunity, even in cases where significant initial progress is made. The heart of the problem is a lack of political will and an apparent link between political power and criminality. "The impunity the masterminds enjoy—this is the main part of the mechanism, which breeds new murders," said Sergey Sokolov, deputy editor of *Novaya Gazeta*. And when impunity is the norm, journalists stay away from topics that could get them in trouble. "The most effective protection for a journalist nowadays is self-censorship," said Grigory Shvedov, editor of the online news outlet *Kavkazsky Uzel* (Caucasian Knot), which maintains a network of correspondents in the volatile North Caucasus region. "This is why we are seeing fewer and fewer examples of independent, investigative journalism." His agency is not relenting, but his correspondents face severe risks.

At an October 4 Council of Europe discussion on journalist protection, Sokolov was asked how those who order attacks on the press are able to evade justice. "Why aren't they held accountable?" he said. "Because, one way or another, these are people connected to power, which in turn means that they are connected to big money and criminality. Unfortunately, no one has been able to untangle this skein."

The latest Politkovskaya murder inquiry has exposed just how tangled that skein is. Two suspects in the case are former high-ranking police officers indicted on charges that they used official resources to organize the murder. One is retired Lt. Col. Dmitry Pavlyuchenkov, who was head of surveillance at Moscow's Main Internal Affairs Directorate, the city's police force, at the time of the slaying. Using their ties to criminal figures, the former police officials formed a gang to kill Politkovskaya, the investigation found. Dmitry Muratov, *Novaya Gazeta*'s editor, said his newspaper's own investigation reached similar conclusions. "The department for which Pavlyuchenkov worked is one of the most secretive, closed police subdivisions," Muratov told the news agency RIA Novosti in September. "It is a department that carried out surveillance, determined people's whereabouts, and tapped their conversations."

Pavlyuchenkov and his subordinates "de facto privatized the capacities of their posts and leased out, if you will, the services of their office," Muratov said. "For instance, for US$100 an hour, anyone could buy the services of this department if they had access to Pavlyuchenkov and his team." After Pavlyuchenkov was indicted, Muratov said: "We can now reveal that Pavlyuchenkov used the official cars of his police department to carry out surveillance of Anna Politkovskaya to determine her address and usual routes."

How the official Politkovskaya investigation proceeds will show whether Russian investigative authorities have truly moved toward independence or whether they are still bound by the powerful influences that stop them from exposing the truth. Muratov, if welcoming of the recent headway, remains cautious. He and his *Novaya Gazeta* staff have more experience than any other newsroom in Russia in seeking justice for colleagues; five journalists and a lawyer for the paper have been murdered in retaliation for their work since 2000. In each case, the paper did its own journalistic investigation. The day that authorities detained Pavlyuchenkov, officials also announced they had "information about the suspected mastermind of the crime." In response, Muratov urged vigilance. "I am uncomfortable with the quickness and lightness with which investigators started talking about the mastermind," Muratov told the local press on August 24. "I just know what such loud statements turn out to be. ... I think we can expect some politically motivated actions."

As if to confirm Muratov's apprehension, the business daily *Kommersant* reported in September that Pavlyuchenkov had named Boris Berezovsky, an exiled Russian oligarch and a staunch Kremlin critic, as the mastermind of Politkovskaya's murder. Bastrykin's office neither confirmed nor denied that his agency was pursuing that angle. In response, Anna Kachkayeva,

the Politkovskaya family lawyer, said her clients "did not need an assigned mastermind in the case."

Berezovsky's name first appeared in connection with Politkovskaya's killing when, speaking in Germany days after the murder, then-President Vladimir Putin attributed the crime to "certain persons who are hiding abroad from Russian justice [and] have long nurtured plans to sacrifice someone in order to create a wave of anti-Russian feelings and do Russia harm." (Berezovsky was convicted of embezzlement in Russia, charges he has disputed as politically motivated. Moscow has long sought his extradition from the United Kingdom, to no avail.) Colleagues and supporters of Politkovskaya have brushed off the Berezovsky theory as nonsensical. Lyudmila Alekseyeva, a veteran human rights defender and chairwoman of the Moscow Helsinki Group, told the German public broadcaster Deutsche Welle in October: "I think this is a trick of the investigators in order to distract us from the real people behind the murder. Berezovsky is no angel and I have little sympathy for him, but what we have here is speculation and conjecture and I wonder who is taking advantage of that."

Colleagues have reason to be skeptical. More than two years after another *Novaya Gazeta* reporter, Natalya Estemirova, was abducted in Chechnya and found murdered in Ingushetia, her killers walk free. The investigation into the July 15, 2009, killing of Estemirova, a Grozny-based journalist and human rights defender, started off on the right track only to get derailed, her colleagues at *Novaya Gazeta* and the human rights organization Memorial told CPJ. At a July press conference in Moscow, they presented the results of their independent investigation, which revealed numerous apparent flaws in the official inquiry.

At the time of the murder, Estemirova was investigating the possible involvement of Chechen police officers in the July 7, 2009, public execution of Rizvan Albekov in the village of Akhkinchu-Borzoi. She was the first journalist reporting on the case. The Investigative Committee initially focused on the story as the likeliest reason Estemirova was murdered, colleagues said. In their report, "Two Years After the Killing of Natalya Estemirova: Investigation on the Wrong Track," *Novaya Gazeta*, Memorial, and the International Federation for Human Rights found that lead investigator Igor Sobol had sought information from the local prosecutor's office about Albekov's killing and local police abuses.

But investigators inexplicably stopped pursuing the lead in early 2010. The current inquiry, the report's authors said, has focused on Alkhazur Bashayev, a rebel leader whom Chechen authorities say was killed in a 2009 special operation. Bashayev was allegedly angered by Estemirova's investigation into accusations that he and other separatists were recruiting young men in a Chechen village. But the report by Estemirova's colleagues raised dozens of questions about the official theory. How could the car allegedly used to kidnap Estemirova contain no sign of a struggle? How was the unsophisticated suspect able to falsify the police identity card that Chechen police claim to have found in the Bashayev home, along with the murder weapon?

What happened to the genetic material collected from under Estemirova's fingernails that likely contained the DNA of her killers? The material, the report said, showed that Estemirova struggled with at least three attackers, one of whom was a woman. But investigators ordered only one type of DNA testing, which could neither categorically confirm nor disprove the involvement of Bashayev. In the process of testing, the report's authors said, the DNA samples were depleted, making further testing nearly impossible. It is possible, however, to compare the completed test results against other potential suspects—such as the police officers implicated in the Albekov execution. Why hasn't this been done?

The Investigative Committee did not respond in detail to the report, instead issuing a statement that said the findings "are not based on facts but are simply the subjective opinion of persons who do not possess the necessary competence, do not have information, and do not have access to all of the materials of the criminal case." The Investigative Committee did not explain what it found concerning the possible link to Estemirova's reporting on the extrajudicial killing of Chechen resident Albekov. The committee did not respond to CPJ's written request for comment on the Estemirova investigation.

CPJ spent three months in Russia in 2011, reporting on the investigations into journalist murders and other attacks on the press. Colleagues of Estemirova and individuals close to the official inquiry told CPJ that Moscow investigators are obstructed from working in Chechnya. "They know who the killers are, and they say that in private conversations. But they are simply unable to proceed," said a person tracking the investigation who spoke on the condition of anonymity because he was not authorized to discuss the case publicly. The person did not elaborate on the obstruction.

The North Caucasus is the most dangerous assignment for reporters in Russia. Politkovskaya, Estemirova, Kamalov, and another murdered journalist, *Forbes Russia* Editor Paul Klebnikov, all were investigating corruption and human rights abuses in the region. In two of the cases, suspicions have fallen on Chechnya's administration, specifically the republic's president, Ramzan Kadyrov. The reporting by Politkovskaya and Estemirova implicated local security and law enforcement officials in human rights abuses, as it did with the military men known as Kadyrovtsy for their devotion to the Kadyrov clan. Kadyrov had made no secret of his hostility toward both journalists and the organizations they represented—Memorial and *Novaya Gazeta*. In March 2008, for instance, Kadyrov summoned Estemirova for a meeting and asked her a series of questions about her family, including her teenage daughter. According to Human Rights Watch, Kadyrov told the journalist: "Yes, my arms are in blood up to my elbows. And I am not ashamed of it. I killed and will kill bad people. We are fighting the enemies of the people." Estemirova's daughter was relocated after that meeting, and the journalist herself briefly traveled away from home.

At the September 2010 meeting with the Investigative Committee, CPJ asked Bastrykin and his team whether they had questioned the Chechen president as part of the Estemirova and Politkovskaya murder inquiries. Yes, investigators said, but they had not found evidence of his involvement.

The lack of resolution in the slayings of Politkovskaya, Estemirova, and Klebnikov does not bode well for lesser-known provincial cases, such as the murders of two consecutive editors of the muckraking newspaper *Tolyattinskoye Obozreniye* in the industrial city of Togliatti. The handling of those cases—lower in profile and subject to local political influence—further test Russia's commitment to the rule of law.

Valery Ivanov and Aleksei Sidorov, killed 18 months apart in the early 2000s, had edited a publication unique for Togliatti, boldly exposing corruption, organized crime, and government wrongdoing in Russia's carmaking capital. At the time of their killing, colleagues said, both had been investigating alleged police misappropriation of assets that had belonged to the late crime boss Dmitry Ruzlyayev. Despite witnesses to both killings, testimony from family and colleagues, a common compelling lead, and *Tolyattinskoye Obozreniye* articles brimming with characters who could have been angered by the paper's critical coverage, investigators did not arrest a single suspect in Ivanov's murder and tried an innocent man in 2003 in Sidorov's murder. The trial, which ended in an acquittal, revealed multiple flaws in the police investigation, including a coerced confession and disregarded evidence. Neither murder, authorities said at the time, was related to the editors' work. Ivanov, they said, was killed because of a business dispute; Sidorov in a street brawl.

Both cases were dormant until, seven years later, the federal Investigative Committee reopened and moved them out of Togliatti to the jurisdiction of the regional Investigative Committee in Samara, a move that was supposed to shield the inquiries from powerful local interests. The news was welcomed by relatives and colleagues of Ivanov and Sidorov.

Two months after reopening the cases, the Samara Investigative Committee announced progress. Officials said evidence suggested the editors' killings were linked to two other murders in Togliatti; shortly after, the agency said it had identified a circle of five suspects. This seemed to be a long-overdue step in the right direction. But the initial publicity that stirred attention at home and abroad was followed by months of silence. In mid-year, CPJ traveled to Samara and Togliatti on a fact-finding mission, meeting investigators as well as the victims' colleagues and families. Despite the rhetoric, CPJ found, the new investigations had yielded no tangible results.

"They make a first step, some symbolic gesture, but then there is no follow-up," Yelena Ivanova, Valery Ivanov's widow, told CPJ. She said a detective with the Samara Investigative Committee met with her in October 2010 to offer assurances that her husband's killers would be brought to justice. She said she had not heard from the committee since. Vladimir Sidorov, father of slain Aleksei Sidorov, is equally skeptical of the new investigation. "The system is a corporate organism," he said, one in which an investigator's good work is often negated. "An individual cannot do anything on their own."

Meeting with CPJ in June, top officials with both the Samara and the Togliatti investigative committees said they had pursued every lead, questioned every witness, and considered all evidence in the murders of Ivanov and Sidorov. Yet no arrests had been made. As in Estemirova's killing, investigators issued an arrest warrant in the Ivamov case for a man widely believed to be dead. Russian news reports say the suspect, a reputed contract killer named Sergey Afrikyan, was killed after an assassination attempt went awry. No suspects have been named in the Sidorov case. And no mastermind has been identified in either murder.

"Authorities must do more than live by a calendar of anniversaries," Nadezhda Prusenkova, *Novaya Gazeta*'s press secretary, told CPJ. Whenever the next journalist murder anniversary nears, she said, a spokesman issues a statement that the investigation continues and "that measures are being taken." The public is temporarily appeased until the next date that calls attention to the cases.

Statements are not enough; the families and colleagues of the victims are tired of them. A better tone has been helpful, but thus far the official promises have fallen far short of achieving justice. Without tangible results—the prosecution and conviction of all those behind violent attacks on journalists—enterprising, independent journalism in Russia has a bleak future.

*Nina Ognianova, CPJ's Europe and Central Asia program coordinator, conducted a three-month fact-finding mission to Russia in 2011 as part of CPJ's Global Campaign Against Impunity and at the invitation of the Russian Union of Journalists. CPJ's Global Campaign Against Impunity is underwritten by the John S. and James L. Knight Foundation.*

# Azerbaijan

Four years after Eynulla Fatullayev was imprisoned on a series of fabricated charges, and more than a year after the European Court of Human Rights ordered his immediate release, the editor finally walked free. In an interview with CPJ, Fatullayev praised the international community for its sustained support. Attacks against domestic journalists covering sensitive subjects continued with impunity. Freelance reporter Rafiq Tagi, who wrote critically about Islamist politics and government policies, died after being stabbed on a Baku street. Two reporters for the pro-opposition newspaper *Azadlyg* were beaten in reprisal for their work, while the editor of the independent newspaper *Khural* was jailed in late year on retaliatory charges. Hostility toward international reporters was on the rise: Members of a Swedish television crew working on a human rights documentary were deported; a U.S. freelancer and a British researcher were assaulted; and a photojournalist was denied entry based on her Armenian ethnicity.

KEY DEVELOPMENTS

» International pressure prompts release of unjustly jailed editor.

» Domestic journalists face violence; foreign press obstructed.

KEY DATA

## 4 International journalists obstructed

In April, a three-member team with the Swedish public broadcaster Sveriges Television was detained while reporting on a protest rally. The crew, which had traveled to Baku to film a documentary on human rights and freedom of speech, was expelled despite having valid Azerbaijani visas. Separately, Diana Markosian, a freelance photographer for *Bloomberg Markets* magazine, was denied entry to Azerbaijan in July. Authorities cited her Armenian ethnicity as reason.

## Recent hostility toward international reporters:

**January 2009:** The government barred local radio transmissions of three international broadcasters: the BBC, along with the U.S. government-funded Radio Free Europe/Radio Liberty and Voice of America. All three had aired programming in Azerbaijan for at least 15 years.

**May 2010:** Unidentified men at Baku International Airport seized footage from a Norwegian television reporter and a cameraman who were working on a film about freedom of expression in Azerbaijan.

# 1,497 Days Fatullayev was jailed

Authorities arrested Fatullayev after he wrote an article that accused the government of complicity in the murder of his colleague, Elmar Huseynov. Several other journalists have served extended prison terms on retaliatory charges during President Ilham Aliyev's tenure.

# 36% Internet penetration

With government censorship rampant in the broadcasting sector, an increasing number of consumers have been going online for independent information. Internet penetration is three times what it was in 2006. Most users, however, are concentrated in the capital, Baku, and other large urban centers, according to the International Telecommunication Union, or ITU.

**Internet penetration over time, as documented by the ITU:**

| 2006 | 12 percent |
|------|-----------|
| 2007 | 14.5 |
| 2008 | 17 |
| 2009 | 27 |
| 2010 | 36 |

# 6 Reporters attacked, 2011

The fatal stabbing of Tagi in November underscored a year of heightened violence against local and international journalists. Amanda Erickson, a U.S. freelance contributor to *The Washington Post* and *The New York Times*, and Celia Davies, a British staffer at the Institute for Reporters' Freedom and Safety, were attacked outside their Baku apartment building in June. Ramin Deko and Seimur Khaziyev, reporters for the pro-opposition *Azadlyg*, were beaten 10 days apart in early spring. And assailants targeted the home of Idrak Abbasov, a journalist with the Institute for Reporters' Freedom and Safety, in September. The attacks are unsolved.

**Assaults against journalists over time:**

| 2007 | 1 |
|------|---|
| 2008 | 2 |
| 2009 | 0 |
| 2010 | 0 |
| 2011 | 6 |

# 1 Independent TV station

Of the nine television stations broadcasting nationwide, only ANS TV was independent. The others were owned directly by the state or controlled by administration allies. Because of its editorial policy, ANS has been subjected to repeated censorship through the years.

# Belarus

After a rigged December 2010 presidential vote, authoritarian leader Aleksandr Lukashenko unleashed two waves of repression against critics and political opponents, one in early year and one in summer. The KGB and police raided independent newsrooms and journalists' homes, confiscated reporting equipment, and jailed independent reporters. Politicized courts handed suspended prison terms to prominent journalists Irina Khalip and Andrzej Poczobut. Police used brutal force against reporters who covered nationwide anti-government protests. Critical news websites experienced multiple denial-of-service attacks and official blocking. The suspicious 2010 death of Aleh Byabenin, founder of the pro-opposition news website *Charter 97*, remained unexamined. With a domestic economy suffering, Lukashenko promised to free jailed critics if the European Union lifted travel and trade sanctions. During a year of relentless attacks on journalists, the Lukashenko administration reinforced its reputation as Europe's most repressive regime for the press.

KEY DEVELOPMENTS

» Widespread crackdown on news media prompts U.S., EU sanctions.

» *Charter 97* Editor Natalya Radina forced into exile, receives CPJ Press Freedom Award.

KEY DATA

## 2 News sites blacklisted

In April, the general prosecutor's office ordered Internet service providers to block the pro-opposition news websites *Charter 97* and *Belarussky Partizan*, according to local press reports. The government's censorship of online media secured Belarus a spot in CPJ's May report on the world's worst online oppressors.

## 114 Pieces of equipment seized

Authorities raided newsrooms and seized equipment in an effort to silence critical coverage.

Andrei Bastunets, a lawyer for the Belarusian Association of Journalists, told CPJ the crackdown was the harshest attack on press freedom he had witnessed in his 14-year tenure.

# 95 Detained in summer crackdown

Police targeted reporters and activists as they clamped down on anti-Lukashenko protests held weekly from late May to late July, according to the Belarusian Association of Journalists, or BAJ.

**Two infamous days:**

July 3   Nationwide protest rallies sparked an especially strong government crackdown against both demonstrators and the journalists covering the events.

July 6   Protesters regrouped for another set of demonstrations. So did police. In all, 48 journalists were detained while covering the two days of protests, BAJ reported.

# 108 Days KGB occupied Khalip's home

After her release from detention, authorities placed Khalip under strict house arrest, with two KGB agents stationed at her apartment around the clock. Khalip, a correspondent for the Moscow newspaper *Novaya Gazeta* and wife of opposition candidate Sannikov, was eventually convicted of "organizing and preparing activities severely disruptive of public order," for her coverage of the post-election unrest.

# 39 Days Natalya Radina was jailed

Authorities arrested the editor hours after the election and indicted her on fabricated charges of organizing mass disorder. Thousands of Belarusians had protested the presidential vote, prompting Lukashenko to order the arrest of critical journalists, activists, and opposition candidates. Facing international outcry, the KGB released Radina in January. She later left the country.

**A lopsided presidential vote:**

79.65   Percentage of vote cast for Lukashenko, according to the official totals.

2.43   Percentage cast for Andrei Sannikov, the main opposition candidate. He was arrested after the vote and sentenced to five years in prison in May, the BBC reported.

1.78   Percentage cast for opposition candidate Vladimir Neklyayev. Police beat and arrested Neklyayev after the vote. In May, he was sentenced to a suspended two-year prison term, Al-Jazeera reported.

**Balance:** Split among other candidates, or cast for no candidate at all.

# France

France's press freedom record continued a downward slide, in large part because authorities attempted to violate the confidentiality of journalists' sources and interfere with editorial decisions. Most of the recent cases stemmed from the "Bettencourt affair," the alleged illegal financing of the presidential party by the billionaire Liliane Bettencourt. In 2010, President Nicolas Sarkozy's office ordered the secret services to identify sources leaking information about the matter to the press. Journalists from major media outlets were targeted, and the secret services obtained the phone records of a *Le Monde* journalist. In October, the director of domestic intelligence was charged with violating the secrecy of correspondence and confidentiality of sources. Press-government relations were further strained during the 18-month abduction of two France 3 journalists in Afghanistan, which ended in June. Élysée Palace and the army had criticized the "recklessness" of the reporters. In November, the Paris offices of *Charlie Hebdo* were firebombed and its website was hacked after the satirical weekly published a spoof edition "guest-edited" by Prophet Muhammad.

KEY DEVELOPMENTS

» Security services spy on journalists investigating the financing of Sarkozy's party.

» Intelligence chief charged with violating confidentiality of journalistic sources.

KEY DATA

## 1 Finding for *Le Monde*

In September 2010, *Le Monde* announced it was filing lawsuits alleging that the Sarkozy government unlawfully used the country's intelligence services to identify a source for journalist Gérard Davet, who had been covering the Bettencourt affair. An appellate court ruled in favor of *Le Monde* in December 2011.

## 3 Investigated in spy scandal

In late 2011, Investigating Magistrate Sylvie Zimmerman was questioning Bernard Squarcini, head of domestic intelligence; Philippe Courroye, a state prosecutor; and Fréderic Péchenard, France's chief of police, as part of an inquiry into the illegal surveillance of *Le Monde*'s Davet. Squarcini was charged on October 17.

## 2 Lawsuits withdrawn

In November 2010, the satirical weekly *Le Canard enchaîné* and the news website *Mediapart* accused Sarkozy's office of directly supervising espionage against journalists covering the Bettencourt affair. Sarkozy's chief of staff and the head of domestic intelligence sued the two news outlets for defamation in late 2010. By June 2011, as the government's own actions came under fire, the complaints were withdrawn.

### Other legal attacks on French media:

**November 2008:** Paris police detained and abused Vittorio de Filippis, a former editor of the newspaper *Liberation*. Police interrogated him for five hours without a lawyer in a 2006 libel case, and forced him to undergo strip searches.

**June 2010:** A Paris prosecutor indicted Augustin Scalbert, a journalist with *Rue89*, on charges of "stealing and keeping" a video that showed Sarkozy reprimanding public television journalists for not giving him enough airtime. *Rue89* had published the video two years earlier. Scalbert faced up to five years in jail. The case was pending in late 2011.

**July 2011:** *Rue89* prevailed in a defamation lawsuit filed by Lola Karimova, daughter of Uzbek President Islam Karimov. The outlet had called the Uzbek leader "a dictator" in a 2010 article. Karimova had demanded 30,000 euros (US$41,500) in damages.

## 547 Days in Afghan captivity

Stéphane Taponier and Hervé Ghesquière, two journalists with the French public service channel France 3, were freed on June 29, 2011, after being held by the Taliban in the Kapisa region of Afghanistan since late 2009. Three Afghan colleagues were also released.

### Others who endured recent, long captivities:

**223** Days U.S. journalist David Rohde and Afghan colleague Tahir Ludin spent in Taliban captivity in 2008-9.

**167** Days British journalist Asad Qureshi spent in captivity in Pakistan in 2010.

**157** Days Japanese journalist Kosuke Tsuneoka spent in captivity in Afghanistan in 2010.

## 80.1% Internet penetration, 2010

Data from the International Telecommunication Union, or ITU, show that penetration has climbed significantly since 2006. France has adopted tough legislation on Internet file-sharing, and it applies to the Web its strict laws on defamation and hate speech.

# Hungary

On January 1, 2011, the day Hungary assumed the rotating presidency of the European Union, a restrictive new media law came into force. The law created a National Media and Infocommunications Authority—staffed with appointees of the ruling Fidesz party—that was given vast powers to regulate news media. The law established heavy fines for violations such as carrying "imbalanced news coverage" or running content that violates "public morality." The law applied to all news media, reaching beyond national borders to foreign outlets "aimed at the territory of Hungary." The measure triggered protests in Hungary and throughout Europe, where it was seen as violating the Charter of Fundamental Rights enshrined in the Lisbon Treaty. Hungarian lawmakers agreed to minor changes in response to pressure from the European Commission. In December, the country's Constitutional Court struck down a provision that would have obliged journalists to reveal confidential sources. The court also exempted print media from the law as of May 2012, although it left intact most other anti-press provisions. The domestic media scene reflected deep polarization between supporters and adversaries of the center-right Fidesz. Political pressures were rife in public broadcasting: In July, 570 employees of the four state-run media companies were dismissed, representing about 16 percent of the workforce. Authorities reassigned the broadcast frequency of the largest opposition radio station, Klubradio, to an entertainment broadcaster in December, citing a higher bid.

KEY DEVELOPMENTS

» Highly restrictive media law assailed by public, court, and EU.

» Leading opposition radio outlet loses its broadcast frequency.

KEY DATA

## 200 Million forint fine

The media law set very high fines. Outlets with "significant power of influence," such as national television channels, can face penalties of up to 200 million forints (US$886,000).

**Maximum fines for other types of media:**

**National dailies:**
25 million forints (US$110,000)

**Internet news portals:**
25 million forints

**Weekly and monthly publications:**
10 million forints (US$44,000)

## 1 EU resolution

In March 2011, the European Parliament adopted a resolution condemning Hungary's new media law. This indictment of a member state was followed by another resolution, in July, that criticized Hungary's new constitution.

**Two votes of opposition:**

**March 10:** Parliament called on Hungary to repeal the media law, which it found incompatible with EU laws and other European conventions.

**July 5:** After heated debate, members adopted a resolution criticizing the revised Hungarian constitution for failing to respect EU non-discrimination standards and for weakening governmental checks and balances. The resolution also chided Hungary for revising the constitution in haste and without sufficient transparency.

## 65.3% Internet penetration

Online use has increased at only a modest rate, according to data from the International Telecommunication Union, or ITU.

**Internet penetration over time as gauged by the ITU:**

|  |  |
|------|-------------|
| 2006 | 47 percent |
| 2007 | 53.3 |
| 2008 | 56 |
| 2009 | 61.8 |
| 2010 | 65.3 |

## 1 Media law revision

Parliament amended the law to placate the European Commission, but its changes were nominal, exempting bloggers from a balanced reporting requirement and softening registration rules. More substantively, the Hungarian Constitutional Court struck down a provision that would have eliminated legal protection for confidential sources.

**Media law timeline:**

**December 21, 2010:** The Hungarian Parliament adopted the media law. Opposition and civil society groups were excluded from the debate.

**January 1, 2011:** The law took effect.

**January 7:** The European Commission met with Hungarian officials to seek clarifications and ensure the law respects EU legislation.

**March 7:** Hungary made cosmetic changes to appease critics.

**March 10:** The European Parliament adopted a resolution demanding substantive changes to the law.

**October 23:** In Budapest, thousands demonstrated in defense of press freedom.

**December 20:** The Constitutional Court declared portions of the law unconstitutional, but left content restrictions and hefty fines intact.

213

# Italy

Silvio Berlusconi's government crumbled in November amid the country's economic crisis, ending a tenure marked by manipulation and restriction of the press. As prime minister and media owner, Berlusconi owned or controlled all of Italy's major national television channels, ensuring news coverage favorable to his administration. He worked methodically for three years to enact controversial legislation to prevent print and online media from publishing embarrassing information about alleged corruption in his government and his dalliances with young women. Even in the final days of his tenure, Berlusconi sought to revive a bill that would have limited the use of police wiretaps, penalized journalists for publishing the contents of wiretaps, and forced websites to publish "corrections" to information considered damaging to a person's image within 48 hours of receiving a complaint. Parliament had already postponed action on the measure, termed Berlusconi's "gag law," in 2010. In Perugia, prosecutor Giuliano Mignini used Italy's harsh defamation laws to intimidate journalists, authors, and media outlets—in Italy and the United States—that reported critically about his performance in two high-profile cases.

KEY DEVELOPMENTS

» As Berlusconi is forced out, he still pushes bill banning wiretap coverage.

» Journalists covering Meredith Kercher murder trial face official retaliation.

KEY DATA

## 3 TV controlled by Berlusconi

Through his media company, Mediaset, Berlusconi owned the commercial national television stations Canale 5, Italia 1, and Retequattro. Before resigning as prime minister, Berlusconi also controlled the public national television channels Rai 1, Rai 2, and Rai 3, part of the RAI broadcasting network. Mediaset and RAI together have dominated Italy's viewership and advertising market since the 1990s, which gave Berlusconi a virtual monopoly on the broadcast media landscape.

## Most popular Italian media, according to the European Journalism Centre:

**Print:** National dailies *Corriere della sera* and *La Repubblica* were the leaders in circulation.

**Television:** Mediaset and RAI channels together attracted 90 percent of Italy's audience.

**Radio:** The divisions of RAI, Radio Uno, and Radio Due shared the top spots in terms of listenership.

**Online**: News websites with the highest number of visitors were the Italian version of MSN, *Virgilio, Libero*.

# 53.7% Internet penetration

Compared with other members of the European Union, Italians have been slower to embrace new media and the Internet, according to research by the International Telecommunication Union, or ITU.

**Internet penetration in the EU's six founding nations, according to the ITU:**

| | |
|---|---|
| Netherlands | 90.7% |
| Luxembourg | 90.6% |
| Germany | 81.8% |
| France | 80.1% |
| Belgium | 79.3% |
| Italy | 53.7% |

## 6 Defamation threats

Perugia prosecutor Mignini has sued or threatened to sue several individuals and media outlets critical of his record. The threats, which have had a chilling effect on the press in Italy and the United States, stemmed from coverage of Mignini's performance in two high-profile murder investigations—the Monster of Florence case and the November 2007 slaying of British exchange student Meredith Kercher.

## 1 Blogger attacked

Squadra Mobile—the local police unit in charge of the Kercher murder investigation—harassed, assaulted, and detained Frank Sfarzo in retaliation for critical reporting and commentary on his blog, *Perugia Shock*. The blog was later ordered removed.

## 1 Closed in protest

In October 2011, Wikipedia disabled its Italian website to protest the revival in parliament of a controversial bill that would, in part, order online media to publish corrections—within 48 hours of a lodged complaint and without the right to appeal—if the online material is deemed damaging to the plaintiff's image.

**Recent press freedom protests in the EU:**

**March 2008:** Slovakia's six leading dailies published identical, front-page calls against a restrictive press bill.

**October 2009:** Tens of thousands of Italians rallied in Rome against Berlusconi's attempts to censor critical journalists and his excessive control over the media.

**January 2011:** Thousands of Hungarians protested in Budapest against the country's restrictive media law.

# Kazakhstan

The convictions of three men in the 2009 murder in Almaty of prominent Kyrgyz journalist Gennady Pavlyuk was a bright spot in Kazakhstan's otherwise grim press freedom record. The government has yet to reform its media laws in line with international standards, despite its promises to the Organization for Security and Co-operation in Europe, or OSCE. To the contrary, the upper chamber of parliament approved a bill in December requiring international broadcasters to register with the government and imposing limits on foreign content aired by local cable carriers. Editor Ramazan Yesergepov continued to serve a three-year prison term on fabricated charges of collecting state secrets after a local court denied him early release. In November, an Almaty court convicted reporter Valery Surganov on defamation charges stemming from an article alleging police improprieties; the court imposed severe restrictions on his movements as penalty. The cases were a sobering reminder of the cost of critical journalism. In April, President Nursultan Nazarbayev won a fourth term in an election so uncompetitive that he took 95 percent of the vote, according to official results. OSCE monitors criticized the restrictive media climate in the run-up to the vote.

KEY DEVELOPMENTS

» Assaults, politicized lawsuits, newspaper confiscations limit press freedom.

» Convictions in 2009 murder mark a high point in anti-impunity efforts.

KEY DATA

## 3 Convictions in 2009 murder

In October, an Almaty court found a former Kyrgyz security agent and two accomplices guilty in Pavlyuk's abduction and murder, sentencing them to prison terms ranging from 10 to 17 years, international press reports said. The court said the killing was motivated by Pavlyuk's journalism, but it did not specify a reason or name a mastermind, the regional news website *Fergana News* reported.

## 1 Imprisoned on December 1, 2011

Ramazan Yesergepov, editor of the independent weekly *Alma-Ata Info*, remained in prison on antistate charges, according to CPJ research. Yesergepov's newspaper published two memos from the KNB, the Kazakh security service, that showed high-ranking agents conspiring to influence a prosecutor and a judge in a tax-evasion case.

## 4 Assailants in brutal attack

The unidentified men used baseball bats and a non-lethal traumatic pistol against Orken Bisen and Asan Amilov of the Internet-based, opposition broadcaster Stan TV. The two were covering a strike by oil and gas company workers in the western city of Aktau. The assailants stole the journalists' equipment and video footage in the October attack, Stan TV said.

### Attacks over time, according to CPJ and Adil Soz, the Almaty-based media foundation:

**2007:** 1 independent journalist assaulted in the southern city of Shymkent.

**2008:** 1 opposition journalist stabbed in Almaty.

**2009:** 2 journalists attacked, 1 murdered in Almaty.

**2010:** 1 journalist beaten in western Kazakhstan.

**2011:** 2 Stan TV journalists attacked.

## 3 Newspaper confiscations

On three occasions—in January, March, and October—authorities confiscated or bought off the print runs of the independent weekly *Respublika-Delovoye Obozreniye*, according to the press freedom group Adil Soz. Authorities did not provide an explanation, Adil Soz reported. The critical outlet has long been at odds with authorities, CPJ research shows.

## 5 Million tenge damages awarded

An Almaty court ruled in favor of Saltanat Akhanova, wife of Kazakhstan's financial police head, in a defamation lawsuit against editor Gulzhan Yergaliyeva and her news website *Guljan*. The damages, equivalent to US$33,800, stemmed from *Guljan* articles that described foreign assets allegedly held by Akhanova. The plaintiff had sought 2.6 billion tenge.

### Notable damage awards, according to Adil Soz:

**2008:** 30 million tenge (US$200,000) against journalist Almas Kusherbayev and the independent newspaper *Taszhargan*. Member of Parliament Romin Madinov filed suit over an article that said his business interests had benefited from his legislative work.

**2009:** 60 million tenge (US$400,000) against the independent daily *Respublika*. Plaintiff BTA Bank filed suit over an article saying the institution was facing financial pressure from foreign investors.

**2010:** 20 million tenge (US$135,000) against journalist Lukpan Akhmediyarov and the independent newspaper *Uralskaya Nedelya*. The plaintiff, a company named Tengiz NefteStroy, later decided to withdraw its claim.

# Kyrgyzstan

A s President Roza Otunbayeva declared her commitment to press freedom, parliament decriminalized libel, eliminating a tool used by authorities in the past to suppress critical journalism. But rising violence, censorship, and politically motivated prosecutions marred the year in Kyrgyzstan. Parliament ordered state agencies to block domestic access to the critical website *Fergana News*, although the order was not immediately implemented. Ahead of the October 30 presidential vote won by Almazbek Atambayev, legislators ordered domestic broadcasters to screen foreign-produced programming and remove content that could insult the candidates. An investigative commission under the auspices of the Organization for Security and Co-operation in Europe found Kyrgyz authorities complicit in the ethnic conflict that gripped the south in June 2010. The conflict continued to cast a dark shadow over press freedom. Authorities brought trumped-up extremism charges against two ethnic Uzbek media owners, who went into exile after being compelled to give up their news assets. Another ethnic Uzbek journalist, Azimjon Askarov, was serving a life prison term on fabricated charges despite international calls for his release. Legislators banned local media from publishing images of the conflict on its anniversary.

KEY DEVELOPMENTS

» Parliament decriminalizes libel, but moves to censor foreign news coverage.

» Ethnic Uzbek journalists targeted with legal reprisals; 2010 conflict casts long shadow.

KEY DATA

8 **Assaulted in 2011**
In a June public letter, 40 journalists and press freedom advocates demanded that authorities investigate and solve continuing attacks against journalists, according to local press reports. Anti-press violence was on the rise in 2011, according to CPJ research.

**Attacks over time in Kyrgyzstan:**

|  | |
|------|---|
| 2007 | 5 |
| 2008 | 0 |
| 2009 | 5 |
| 2010 | 6 |
| 2011 | 8 |

## 0 Uzbek broadcasters

After the June 2010 conflict, ethnic Uzbek media owners Khalil Khudaiberdiyev and Dzhavlon Mirzakhodzhayev faced attacks, harassment, and retaliatory prosecution. Authorities forced Khudaiberdiyev to sell his company, Osh TV. Mirzakhodzhayev suspended operation of Mezon TV and the newspapers *Portfel* and *Itogi Nedeli*. The outlets had produced news in Uzbek, as well as in Russian and Kyrgyz. As both owners fled the country, the country's largest ethnic minority was left without access to news in its native language.

### A loss of Uzbek-language news:

**10** At least 10 electronic and print media outlets in southern Kyrgyzstan produced reports and programming in Uzbek language before the 2010 conflict, local sources told CPJ.

**1** In September, the Kyrgyz Foreign Ministry denied accreditation to a journalist with the Uzbek service of the U.S. government-funded Radio Free Europe/Radio Liberty, the reporter told CPJ.

## 11 Denied election accreditation

In July, Kyrgyzstan's Central Elections Commission excluded Web-based news agencies from the list of media accredited to cover the presidential campaign and the October 30 vote, the Bishkek-based Media Policy Institute reported. Tuigunaly Abdraimov, the commission chairman, said the agency would not issue the accreditations because it did not have regulatory power over online outlets.

## 1 Imprisoned on December 1, 2011

Press freedom and human rights groups, including CPJ, believe the charges against Askarov were fabricated in retaliation for his reporting on ethnic conflict and the abuse of detainees in southern Kyrgyzstan. Kyrgyzstan's Supreme Court rebuffed his appeal in December, according to regional press reports.

### Askarov case timeline:

**June 15, 2010:** Jalal-Abad police arrested Askarov on charges of incitement to ethnic conflict.

**August 12, 2010:** Regional prosecutors indicted Askarov on charges that included incitement to ethnic hatred, calls to mass disorder, and complicity in a police officer's murder.

**September 15, 2010:** Despite procedural violations and allegations that Askarov was tortured in custody, a regional court sentenced him to life in prison.

**November 10, 2010:** A regional court denied Askarov's appeal. Due to poor health, the journalist was transferred to a prison hospital.

**December 20, 2011:** In a ruling seen as a major blow to press freedom, the Supreme Court rejected Askarov's appeal.

# Russia

A uthorities detained at least six journalists covering December protests over flawed parliamentary elections, but in a rare phenomenon Kremlin-controlled television reported on demonstrations that brought tens of thousands of Muscovites onto the streets. In December, a gunman killed the founder of the weekly *Chernovik*, the 20th work-related murder in Russia since 2000. CPJ advocated extensively against impunity in anti-press attacks, calling on the European Commission to press the issue in meetings with Prime Minister Vladimir Putin. Authorities made progress in two murder cases. In April, two suspects were found guilty in the 2009 murders of journalist Anastasiya Baburova and human rights lawyer Stanislav Markelov; in May, the defendants were sentenced to lengthy prison terms. The suspected gunman and several suspected organizers in the 2006 killing of Anna Politkovskaya were indicted. But impunity prevailed in the savage beatings of journalists Mikhail Beketov and Oleg Kashin. Authorities retaliated against one international reporter. Luke Harding, Moscow correspondent for *The Guardian* of London, was barred from re-entering the country in February after writing about U.S. diplomatic cables disclosed by WikiLeaks that described Kremlin officials in unflattering terms.

KEY DEVELOPMENTS

» Convictions help impunity rate, but another murder is reported.

» As tens of thousands protest election, journalists are detained.

KEY DATA

## 2 Convictions in Baburova killing

In April, a Moscow jury found ultranationalists Nikita Tikhonov and Yevgeniya Khasis guilty of murdering Baburova and Markelov. In May, a judge sentenced Tikhonov, the convicted gunman, to life in prison and his accomplice, Khasis, to an 18-year term. In only two of 19 journalist slayings since 2000 have authorities obtained murder convictions.

## 1 Killed in 2011

An assassin ambushed Gadzhimurad Kamalov, founder of the independent Dagestani weekly *Chernovik*, which had probed sensitive topics such as government corruption, human rights abuses, and Islamic radicalism. Although deadly, anti-press violence had slowed in the two years prior to the slaying, Russia remained one of the deadliest nations for the press. Dagestan, with four journalist murders since 2000, is especially dangerous.

# 3 Years' recovery for editor

Neighbors found Beketov, editor of an independent newspaper, lying unconscious in a pool of blood in the front yard of his home in Khimki on November 13, 2008. Attackers struck to kill: They broke his skull, smashed the fingers of both hands, broke his legs, and left him for dead in the freezing cold. Beketov spent three weeks in a coma and underwent multiple operations including leg and finger amputation. He also lost his ability to speak. No one has been arrested in the attack.

# 9th Impunity Index ranking

CPJ's Impunity Index calculates unsolved journalist murders as a percentage of each country's population. In 2011, Russia showed a slight improvement in its Impunity Index ranking due to the convictions in Baburova's killing.

## World ranking on CPJ's 2011 Impunity Index:

1: Iraq
2: Somalia
3: Philippines
4: Sri Lanka
5: Colombia
6: Afghanistan
7: Nepal
8: Mexico
**9: Russia**
10: Pakistan
11: Bangladesh
12: Brazil
13: India

# 2 Arrests in Politkovskaya case

In June, authorities indicted Rustam Makhmudov, the suspected gunman in Politkovskaya's killing. Two months later, investigators arrested a retired police lieutenant colonel on charges he helped carry out the crime. Two other suspects—already in custody in other cases—were named conspirators. Arrests in journalist murders are rare.

## Other cases in which officials have identified suspects:

**In July,** two years after the killing of journalist and human rights defender Natalya Estemirova in the North Caucasus, investigators announced that the sole suspect in her murder was a Chechen separatist whom regional authorities had previously declared killed in a special operation. That theory has been disputed by Estemirova's colleagues and relatives.

**In June**, Samara Investigative Committee head Vitaly Gorstkin told CPJ that investigators had identified a suspected gunman in the April 2002 murder in Togliatti of newspaper editor Valery Ivanov. Gorstkin said the suspect is believed to have fled Russia. Relatives and colleagues are skeptical; the suspect is widely believed to have been killed.

# Tajikistan

Investigative journalists were targeted with retaliatory arrests and debilitating lawsuits, marking a decline in press freedom conditions. Makhmadyusuf Ismoilov, a reporter for the independent weekly *Nuri Zindagi*, was imprisoned for nearly a year on defamation charges related to stories on government corruption in the northern Sogd region. BBC correspondent Urinboy Usmonov spent a month in jail after security agents arrested him on extremism charges stemming from his reports on the banned Islamist group Hizb-ut-Tahrir. The independent newspaper *Asia Plus* and reporter Ramziya Mirzobekova faced a civil lawsuit from a senior Interior Ministry official who accused them of spreading false information in a story about a man who died in government custody, press reports said. And a Dushanbe-based independent newspaper, *Paykon*, was forced to close after a state agency won a sizable judgment in a defamation case related to a letter alleging corruption. In September, President Emomali Rahmon ended the requirement that senior officials convene quarterly press conferences, diminishing already-limited access to leaders.

KEY DEVELOPMENTS

» Authorities use extremism, defamation charges to retaliate against critical reporters.

» Spate of lawsuits seeking disproportionate damages; one newspaper forced to shut.

KEY DATA

## 1 Newspaper forced to close

Marshals in Dushanbe raided *Paykon* and seized newsroom equipment in April, the U.S. government-funded Radio Free Europe/Radio Liberty reported. The seizure represented fulfillment of a 2009 court verdict that ordered *Paykon* to pay 300,000 somoni to the Agency on Standardization, Metrology, and Certification, also known as Tajik-standart. A month after the raid, the newspaper was forced to close.

**July 2009:** *Paykon* published a letter from a local businessman who accused the agency of corruption.

**October 2009:** A district court in Dushanbe ordered *Paykon* to pay 300,000 somoni in damages to Tajikstandart.

**January 2010:** An appeals court upheld the verdict against *Paykon*.

**April 2011:** Marshals raided *Paykon* offices, confiscated equipment.

# 31 Days Usmonov jailed

Tajikistan's security service, known as the KNB, arrested Usmonov on charges of belonging to the banned Hizb-ut-Tahrir. Unable to prove their charges, authorities amended them twice before releasing him on bail in July. On October 14, a Sogd regional court convicted Usmonov and sentenced him to three years in jail. The court, facing international outcry, immediately granted Usmonov amnesty and set him free the same day.

## Timeline in the Usmonov case:

**June 13:** KNB agents arrested Usmonov and alleged that he belonged to Hizb-ut-Tahrir.

**June 20:** Usmonov was charged with making "public calls to overthrow Tajikistan's constitutional regime," his lawyer told regional reporters.

**June 29:** Authorities dropped the initial charges against Usmonov, according to press reports.

**July 13:** Prosecutors finished their inquiry against Usmonov, amending the charges again.

**July 14:** Usmonov was released on bail.

# 2 Years of imprisonment

Defamation through mass media is a criminal offense carrying a potential prison penalty of two years. Insult, another criminal offense, also carries significant penalties.

# 1 million
## Damages in somoni sought from *Asia Plus*

An interior ministry general sought damages equivalent to US$210,000 against reporter Mirzobekova concerning a December 2010 article alleging that a 30-year-old detainee had died from abuse in police custody. Facing an outcry, the plaintiff dropped the case in October 2011. But research by the National Association of Independent Media of Tajikistan shows government officials regularly target critical journalists with complaints seeking disproportionate damages.

# 11 Months Ismoilov jailed

Authorities imprisoned Ismoilov in November 2010 on politicized charges that included defamation and insult. The charges stemmed from an August 2010 article alleging government corruption, abuse of power, and mismanagement of funds. Nearly a year later, a Sogd regional court convicted Ismoilov and fined him 35,000 somoni (US$7,300). In December, an appeals court upheld the conviction but lifted the fine.

# Ukraine

The government failed to deliver on President Viktor Yanukovych's promises to investigate official harassment of news media and ensure justice in the 2000 murder of online journalist Georgy Gongadze. Prosecutors indicted former President Leonid Kuchma on abuse-of-office charges in connection with the Gongadze slaying, alleging that he had ordered subordinates to silence the journalist. But after the Constitutional Court found that a key audiotape was inadmissible, a trial court in Kyiv dismissed the case in December. The ongoing trial of Aleksei Pukach, the former Interior Ministry general charged with strangling Gongadze, was marked by irregularities, delays, and secrecy. The developments were seen as significant setbacks in the fight against impunity. As in past years, the domestic press faced persistent danger as reporters endured threats, physical attacks, and censorship. Investigators reported no progress in the case of Vasyl Klymentyev, an editor who went missing in 2010 after reporting on alleged local corruption. Kharkiv-based cable television carriers stopped carrying programming from the independent news outlet ATN in August, according to press reports. ATN said regional authorities pressured the carriers to drop its critical news coverage.

KEY DEVELOPMENTS

» Gongadze prosecution falters as charges against Kuchma are dismissed.

» Domestic press face persistent threats; critical editor remains missing.

KEY DATA

1 **Missing since 2010**

Authorities reported no progress in the disappearance of Klymentyev, editor of the Kharkiv-based newspaper *Novyi Stil*, who was last seen on August 11, 2010. At least three other journalists for Ukrainian news outlets have gone missing since 1996, according to CPJ research.

**Journalists missing over time:**

**1996:** Vitaly Shevchenko, Andrei Bazvluk, and Yelena Petrova, three journalists for the Kharkiv-based television outlet Lita-M, disappeared while reporting in Chechnya.

**2010:** Klymentyev was reported missing in Kharkiv.

## 2 Convictions in brutal attack

In April, a court convicted two defendants in the March 2010 assault on Vasyl Demyaniv, editor of the independent newspaper *Kolomyiskiy Vestnik*, press reports said. The court declared robbery the motive. Demyaniv decried the verdict, telling reporters the defendants were innocent and that he was attacked in retaliation for his critical reporting on local government in the western city of Kolomyya. Journalists have pointed to broad impunity in anti-press attacks, an assertion supported by CPJ research on journalist murders.

### Justice in Ukrainian journalist murders:

5 Journalist murders since 1992

3 Cases with no convictions, complete impunity

2 Cases in which assailants were convicted, but no masterminds

0 Cases in which both assailants and masterminds were convicted

## 11 Years Gongadze case pending

Kuchma was long accused of having ordered Gongadze's murder, but it took prosecutors more than a decade to indict the former leader. In September 2010, investigators announced that the late Interior Minister Yuri Kravchenko had ordered the killing. Kravchenko was found dead in 2005 with two gunshot wounds to the head. Authorities said Kravchenko had committed suicide, a claim greeted at the time with wide skepticism.

## 2 Appeals of frequency denials

The independent broadcasters TVi and Channel 5 said they would appeal Ukraine's politicized denial of broadcast frequencies by bringing a case to the European Court of Human Rights. The broadcasters alleged that Valery Khoroshkovsky, head of Ukraine's National Security Service, had improperly influenced the decision in order to benefit a rival company, the Inter Media Group. News accounts said Inter Media was owned by Khoroshkovsky and run by his wife.

## 12 Assaults in 2011

The Institute of Mass Information, a Kyiv-based press freedom group, documented at least a dozen assaults directly related to journalism. Ukrainian officials, however, appeared to play down the incidence of anti-press violence. Addressing parliament in March, Interior Minister Anatoly Mogilev told lawmakers that the vast majority of attacks against journalists were not work-related, according to local press reports.

### Assaults on journalists over time, according to IMI research:

| | |
|---|---|
| 2007 | 8 |
| 2008 | 17 |
| 2009 | 9 |
| 2010 | 13 |
| 2011 | 12 |

# United Kingdom

The *News of the World* phone-hacking scandal and subsequent public inquiry raised concerns that public interest journalism could suffer from efforts to curtail unethical practices through regulation. While investigating related police leaks, Scotland Yard invoked the Official Secrets Act to pressure a journalist to reveal sources for her coverage of the scandal. Authorities ultimately backed down from the unprecedented effort. Several journalists came under attack while covering mass riots in urban areas in August. Prime Minister David Cameron said news outlets must hand over raw footage of rioters and suggested the government restrict social media tools to curb street violence. The government drafted a defamation bill aimed at reforming the U.K.'s much-criticized libel laws. The measure had yet to go through parliament.

KEY DEVELOPMENTS

» Reporters, photographers attacked while covering urban riots.

» Revelations of phone-hacking prompt public inquiry into media practices.

KEY DATA

## 11 Attacks during riots

Attacks were reported against journalists covering mass riots that erupted in August. Sky News reporter Mark Stone was chased by rioters and forced to flee during disturbances near Clapham Junction in London; BBC and Sky News reporters had to retreat when their vehicles had windows smashed in Croydon; and rioters knocked down and kicked Michael Russell, a reporter for the *Ealing Gazette*, before taking his camera on Ealing Broadway. In June, photographer Niall Carson was shot and injured while covering clashes in Belfast.

## 1 Unsolved killing since 1992

No one has been brought to justice in the murder of Martin O'Hagan, an investigative journalist with the Dublin newspaper *Sunday World*, who was shot outside his home in the Northern Ireland town of Lurgan on September 28, 2001.

**Journalists killed with impunity in the European Union since 1992:**

| | |
|---|---|
| Greece | 1 |
| Spain | 1 |
| **United Kingdom** | **1** |

# 38
### Resettled in the U.K.

The United Kingdom is one of the world's top five safe havens for journalists fleeing threats of violence, imprisonment, or harassment for their work in their home countries, CPJ research shows.

## Top host countries for exiled journalists, 2001-11:

| | |
|---|---|
| United States | 180 |
| Kenya | 66 |
| **United Kingdom** | **38** |
| Sweden | 32 |
| Canada | 29 |

# 140:1
### Libel costs, England vs. Europe

A University of Oxford study found that the average libel lawsuit costs defendants exponentially more in England than in the rest of Europe. U.K. libel laws strongly favor the plaintiff and enable a damaging practice known as "libel tourism," the practice of shopping for a jurisdiction with laws that are advantageous for plaintiffs.

In March 2011, the Ministry of Justice published a draft libel bill that aims to reform libel laws to better defend the public interest.

## Noteworthy libel cases, as documented by the Libel Reform Campaign:

**500,000 pounds:** Fees *The Guardian* paid fighting a libel lawsuit by a South African businessman whose practices were criticized in the paper in 2007. The amount was equivalent to US$801,778. *The Guardian* prevailed, but recouped only a portion of its costs.

**165,000 pounds:** Damages awarded to an exiled Tunisian politician in a 2007 suit against the Dubai-based broadcaster Al-Arabiya. The station had accused the plaintiff of having links to Al-Qaeda. The amount was equivalent to US$264,500.

**50,000 pounds:** Damages a Ukraine-based news website was ordered to pay a Ukrainian businessman in 2008. The site, which had no more than a few dozen U.K. readers, had written about the businessman's upbringing. The amount was equivalent to US$80,000.

**10,000 pounds:** Damages awarded to a Saudi financier in a suit against Israeli-American author Rachel Ehrenfeld. Her 2003 book had accused the plaintiff of funding terrorist groups. The amount was equivalent to US$16,000.

# Uzbekistan

Authoritarian leader Islam Karimov marked Media Workers Day by calling for an independent domestic press, the state news agency UzA reported, but his long-standing policies of repression belied such statements. The regime is a persistent jailer of journalists, often ranking among the worst in the region. Embattled reporter Abdumalik Boboyev faced official obstruction when he tried to travel to Germany; officials cited his prosecution in 2010 on charges of "insulting the Uzbek nation" as reason. Two other reporters faced retaliation after they participated in media seminars outside Uzbekistan. In the face of official intimidation, domestic media complied with censorship regulations and refrained from covering the popular uprisings that swept the Middle East and North Africa. Mindful of the role the Internet played in the Arab revolutions, Uzbek authorities expanded their list of internally blocked news websites and created a state commission to censor content in the Uzbekistan domain.

KEY DEVELOPMENTS

» With five journalists in prison, Uzbekistan is the region's worst jailer of the press.

» Authorities impose wide Internet censorship, block numerous news sites.

KEY DATA

## 5 Imprisoned on December 1, 2011

CPJ's analysis has found that all of the imprisoned journalists have been convicted on fabricated charges and sentenced in retaliation for their critical reporting on regional authorities and government policies. Among those in custody is Salidzhon Abdurakhmanov, a reporter jailed on falsified drug charges after exposing police corruption.

## Imprisonment timeline:

**1999:** Muhammad Bekjanov, Yusuf Ruzimuradov, *Erk*; sentenced to 14 and 15 years in jail respectively. They have been jailed longer than any other journalist worldwide.

**2002:** Gayrat Mehliboyev, freelance; sentenced in 2003 to seven years, and then in 2006 to six years in prison.

**2008:** Abdurakhmanov, *Uznews*; sentenced to 10 years.

**2009:** Dilmurod Saiid, freelance; sentenced to 12.5 years.

## 3 Months Boboyev denied visa

Boboyev was found guilty in 2010 on charges of "insulting the Uzbek people" in a series of articles for the U.S. government-funded Voice of America. To honor his work and recognize his persecution, a German foundation awarded Boboyev a fellowship that started in April, regional press reports said. Authorities obstructed his trip by denying him the exit visa needed to leave Uzbekistan. International advocacy prodded authorities to grant the visa in June.

### Others charged with "insulting the Uzbek people":

**January 2009:** Maksim Popov, civic activist, psychologist.

**January 2010:** Umida Akhmedova, independent documentary filmmaker, photographer.

**July 2010:** Vladimir Berezovsky, Russian editor of the news website *Vesti*.

## 18 In exile, 2001-11

At least 18 journalists facing threats, harassment, and imprisonment have fled Uzbekistan over the past decade, according to CPJ research. Among those who have fled are the author Dina Yafasova and Galima Bukharbaeva, a 2005 recipient of CPJ's International Press Freedom Award. Uzbekistan is among the world's worst nations in forcing journalists to flee, CPJ research shows.

## 29 News sites blacklisted, 2011

In August, Uzbek authorities blocked domestic access to at least 29 Russian and international news websites and online broadcasters, the independent website *Uznews* reported. Authorities had long blocked access to regional news websites such as *Uznews* and *Fergana News*, along with international sites such as those of the BBC and Deutsche Welle.

### Among the 2011 blacklisted websites:

- Russian dailies *Kommersant*, *Nezavisimaya Gazeta*, and *Izvestiya*

- Russia-based radio stations Ekho Moskvy and Mayak

- Other international outlets, including *The Financial Times*, *The New York Times*, and Reuters

## 1 Rights group expelled

At a June hearing, Uzbekistan's Supreme Court ordered the closing of the Tashkent office of the New York-based Human Rights Watch. By documenting ongoing human rights abuses, HRW's Uzbekistan researchers had provided vital news about the tightly controlled nation. After the regime cracked down on critics in the wake of the 2005 Andijan massacre, HRW was the only international human rights group to maintain an office in Uzbekistan.

# Europe and Central Asia
# Regional Data

| | |
|---|---|
| **2** | **39** |
| Journalists Killed in 2011 | Journalists In Exile 2001-11 |
| **132** | **8** |
| Journalists Killed Since 1992 | Imprisoned on December 1, 2011 |
| **66** | **11** |
| Unsolved Journalist Murders Since 1992 | Missing as of December 31, 2011 |

Middle East
and North Africa

# Middle East and North Africa

PHOTO CREDITS

*Section break: Plainclothes police harass a cameraman during a Cairo protest. (AP/Ben Curtis)*

*Page 235: Photographers take cover during November protests in Tahrir Square. (AFP/ Mahmud Hams)*

*Page 245: Turkish Prime Minister Recep Tayyip Erdoğan, buoyed by a landslide election victory, has led an attack on press freedom. (AP/Boris Grdanoski)*

*Page 251: Iranian photographer Javad Moghimi Parsa experienced repression before going into exile. (Photo courtesy Parsa)*

RESEARCH CREDITS

*Country reports in this chapter were researched and written by Dahlia El-Zein, research associate for CPJ's Middle East and North Africa program, with reporting from CPJ Program Coordinator Mohamed Abdel Dayem.*

# From Arab Uprisings, Five Trends to Watch

*By Mohamed Abdel Dayem*

At the trial of deposed President Hosni Mubarak, Egypt's print media were banned from reporting on testimony by the de facto head of state, Field Marshal Hussein Tantawi. But the testimony—in which Tantawi contradicted an earlier public statement by the military that it had defied orders to shoot protesters—was reported by bloggers and others on Twitter. With the news broken, traditional media seized on the opportunity to run their own stories that otherwise would have been off-limits.

"New media in this instance furthered the free flow of information because they are not bound by the restrictive laws constricting professional newsgatherers," said Yasser al-Zayyat, an Egyptian journalist, lecturer, and analyst. "Print media can then provide depth on an issue they were initially prevented from covering."

Media in the Middle East and North Africa, which had been inching toward pluralism in recent years, contributed to the destabilization and demise of deep-rooted autocracies in 2011. In turn, the dramatic political shifts in the region changed conditions for journalists in ways unimaginable a year earlier. The convergence of traditional and new media is among the major trends emerging after the fall of Zine El Abidine Ben Ali's Tunisian regime in the opening days of 2011.

While these trends favor free expression, they are filled with ambiguity. Much will depend on the political configurations to emerge after the revolutionary dust has settled. In the meantime—because control of national narratives will determine the success or failure of the region's popular uprisings—journalists will find themselves the targets of new and evolving threats. Here are five trends to watch:

**New and traditional media converge:** The rise in citizen-generated video footage was central to the ability of mainstream media to cover the revolutions. In turn, had the citizen content not been amplified by traditional media, particularly television, Tunisia's revolution might have been snuffed out. "Broadcasters simply would not have been able to adequately cover the Arab uprisings without the daily contributions of citizen journalists," said Mourad Hashim, New York correspondent and former Yemen bureau chief for Al-Jazeera, which aired considerable citizen-generated footage. "This is an instance where revolutionary technological changes enabled actual revolutions."

## New media give traditional outlets the cover to tackle sensitive topics.

The convergence has given editors in traditional media the political cover to address topics that governments had long been able to keep out of view. "When [bloggers] raise certain issues, which then gain traction, it becomes more palatable if we then cover them," Khaled El-Sergany, then an editor of the Egyptian daily *Al-Dustur,* noted in a 2009 interview with CPJ. El-Sergany was already leveraging new media in a way that has come to fuller fruition today. *Al-Tahrir,* one of many new papers to emerge in Egypt since Mubarak's fall, carries some of the most popular and controversial postings from Facebook and Twitter daily. Elsewhere in its pages, many of the same topics are examined in depth.

Authorities have acknowledged that new media and citizen-generated content are permanent features of the media environment. Egypt's ruling Supreme Council of the Armed Forces posts its communiqués to the Egyptian people on its Facebook page and nowhere else. More insidious, authorities and their surrogates have established an online presence to intimidate and silence dissenting voices among citizens, bloggers, and professional journalists. The practice is most pervasive in Syria, Bahrain, and Saudi Arabia, CPJ research shows. Those who are perceived as anti-regime are regularly harassed, threatened, or worse. In Syria and Tunisia, security officials interrogated activists to gain their passwords to social networking sites such as Facebook, while some Internet traffic was apparently intercepted for the same purpose.

"In Syria, a large but undetermined number of people were detained simply for posting what the government regarded as subversive materials, but as the numbers mushroomed, the authorities have focused more and more on people posting news or details on upcoming protests," said Rami Nakhle, a Syrian blogger and activist who was forced into exile.

**A broader political discourse:** The disintegration of calcified political regimes in Tunisia, Egypt, and Libya has ushered in an era of new journalistic ventures. In a few short months, eight new television stations have emerged in Egypt along with a handful of fresh newspapers, including weeklies that have converted to a daily format. Libya, a country that was virtually devoid of independent media, has seen a burst of new entities, with more than 100 publications, 30 radio stations, seven television broadcasters, and several news websites, blogs, and active citizen-reporters. In Tunisia, dozens of newspaper licenses have been granted, according to the German-funded Tunisia Votes. A new regulatory body in Tunisia also approved requests for 12 radio and five television licenses, although the stations were not operational in late year because the prime minister's office hadn't signed off on the applications.

The emerging voices are "an indicator that the clock cannot be turned back—not just in politics but also in the news business," the analyst al-Zayyat said. "This diversification reflects the multitudes of opinions that exist in society … even when it mirrors messiness and political immaturity, which are also present in society. Media pluralism is a requisite for political pluralism."

The appearance of a prominent regime opponent such as Mohamed ElBaradei on state or private television, unthinkable in previous years, has become commonplace in Egypt. Critical political analysts, columnists, lawyers, intellectuals, trade unionists, and bloggers of every stripe have become fixtures on Egypt's political talk show circuit. Mosad Abu Fagr, an

Egyptian journalist, blogger, and novelist, could not get his work published in mainstream media before Mubarak's ouster and spent three years in detention. In 2011, Abu Fagr contributed regularly to the popular dailies *Al-Tahrir* and *Al-Badil*, published a novel, and advocated for the marginalized Bedouin community in Sinai.

The rising exercise of free expression was not contained to the handful of countries that underwent full-fledged uprisings; journalists are testing government tolerance for scrutiny in places such as Jordan, Mauritania, and Morocco. In Kuwait, news media assertively reported on a billion-dinar (US$3.6 billion) financial scandal involving members of parliament. Persistent editorial lines—in traditional and new media—forced the government to initiate an unprecedented inquiry and ultimately dislodge the prime minister, who is a member of the royal family, and his cabinet.

But regressive forces have much to lose from media diversity. In Tunisia, where private broadcast licensing lags, official media remain "largely off-limits to dissenting voices and in the grip of remnants of the deposed regime," said Fahem Boukadous, the last journalist to be released from prison there.

In Egypt, the new broadcasters were operating without licenses in late year, even though they submitted the necessary paperwork. That situation left outlets vulnerable to harassment and closure. One station director said authorities repeatedly told him that his license approval was imminent and that he should keep broadcasting. Yet police shut down that broadcaster, Al-Jazeera Mubasher Misr (a local affiliate of the Qatar-based broadcaster Al-Jazeera), twice in two weeks in what appeared to be retaliation for critical coverage.

In late year, as the military government faced off with citizens pushing for a swifter handover of power to civilians, Egyptian print and TV journalists were pressured to temper their editorial lines. The private television broadcasters ONTV and CBC were each taken off the air multiple times in December as they reported on the confrontations. "We are winning the fight for free expression, but there is plenty of resistance," said Abu Fagr, the blogger and novelist. "As a result, there's no knockout punch here, but we are winning on points."

**Evolving threats to journalists:** The region's revolutions have changed the nature of threats confronting journalists. Prolonged, politicized trials on issues such as defamation diminished in Egypt and Tunisia, while assaults and fatalities rose sharply in 2011. Imprisonments rose in Syria, where eight journalists were being held in late year, six without charge. "When you've got a revolution in full swing, regimes want fast results—courts won't do," said Al-Jazeera's Hashim. "Beatings, threats, and even murders become the norm in those circumstances."

Excluding Iraq, where a historic death toll tends to skew data on fatalities, 14 journalists and two media workers were killed in the Middle East and North Africa for work-related reasons in 2011. If Iraq data are set aside, that figure is the highest regional toll since 1995. In Libya, where CPJ recorded a single media fatality between 1992 and 2010, five journalists were killed in 2011. Syria and Tunisia both saw their first media fatality since CPJ began keeping detailed records in 1992. In Bahrain, two journalists died in custody from what the government called medical complications, although there were widespread allegations that the two had been tortured.

## *Facing an array of unpredictable new threats, from abduction to assault.*

The increase in deaths is the most disturbing of a diverse set of new threats to journalists. These include hundreds of instances of abduction, assault, confiscation, and destruction of equipment and footage, usually in an effort to suppress coverage of social unrest. By the end of the first quarter, CPJ had tracked more than 500 such attacks. The majority occurred in Tunisia, Egypt, and Libya during their respective revolutions. In Egypt alone, CPJ documented more than 100 attacks at the height of the media crackdown in the first few days of February. Assaults were also documented in Jordan, Morocco, Algeria, Iraq, Sudan, Mauritania, Saudi Arabia, Kuwait, and Lebanon.

Assaults continued to take place in Bahrain, Syria, and Yemen in late year amid confrontations between restive citizens and repressive regimes. In one tumultuous week in Egypt in November, CPJ recorded 35 cases of gunshot wounds, arbitrary detentions, physical and sexual assault, and abusive treatment in custody, including the withholding of medication.

In pre-revolutionary Egypt, journalists were more often subject to lengthy, contrived legal cases, mainly over defamation and *hisba*, a legal mechanism allowing government proxies to file claims as citizens concerned with the public interest. The Arabic Network for Human Rights Information, which provides legal representation to journalists, handled 220 such cases in 2010. In the first 10 months of 2011, there were only 39. "But in late year the number of politicized cases was rising again, as journalists started digging on some big corruption and mismanagement cases," said Rawda Ahmed, lead attorney in the network's legal unit.

For 23 years in Ben Ali's Tunisia, critical journalists were subjected to unfair trials and regularly imprisoned. But since Ben Ali's mid-January departure, only one Tunisian journalist has been taken to court in a defamation lawsuit apparently intended to silence dissent. The case was lodged not by the state or its proxies, but by a private plaintiff whom the defendant, Naji al-Khishnawi, editor of *Al-Shaab*, had named in an article about the failure to hold to account wealthy individuals with links to Ben Ali's regime.

The new threats are more unpredictable than traditional censorship, legal action, the withholding of advertising revenue, or other more customary methods. In Qaddafi's Libya or Hussein's Iraq, journalists knew what not to do to avoid the state's wrath. Today, journalists across the region have far less control over whether they become targets of harassment, physical assault, arbitrary detention, or worse.

**Legal and regulatory frameworks are changing:** Some government agencies in Egypt and Tunisia, long employed to suppress dissent in the media, have been dissolved or have undergone significant structural changes under sustained popular pressure. But uneasy with the pace, reach, and political implications of media liberalization, authorities have sought to reverse many of these gains.

In Egypt, the Ministry of Information was abolished in February, only to be reinstated in July. The abusive State Security Investigations Service (SSI), for decades a journalist's worst foe, was dissolved in March, but was immediately replaced with a similar security organ, the National Security Apparatus. Also in March, the ruling Supreme Council baldly attempted to censor editors, demanding that all news of the military be approved by the defense ministry before publication. Since then, journalists and commentators were repeatedly summoned for questioning after criticizing the military's performance on the air or in print. Bloggers Alaa Abd el-Fattah and Maikel Nabil Sanad were jailed in late year after criticizing the military. In September, the Supreme Council announced a return to the enforcement of the Mubarak-era Emergency Law, which allows civilians, including journalists, to be tried in state security courts.

A battery of laws continues to restrict media freedom in Egypt, the Egyptian journalist al-Zayyat said. "Unless those restrictive provisions— over 30 in the penal code alone—are addressed directly, we will continue to engage in window dressing, winning a victory here or there without addressing the core of the problem," he said. That sort of window dressing has taken place in Tunisia as well. The Tunisian Ministry of Information, long used to hamstring independent media, was dissolved within days of Ben Ali's fall in January. But the press department at the prime minister's office has effectively taken on the functions of the ministry, said Boukadous, the Tunisian journalist.

In Syria, the government announced in August that it had passed a new media law that would improve media freedom and end detention of journalists. But CPJ documented dozens of cases of local journalists who were held incommunicado and foreign journalists who were expelled before and after the passage of the new law. In Jordan, Morocco, Algeria, Iraq, and Mauritania—all countries experiencing protest movements—governments introduced some concessions while simultaneously tightening control in areas where they perceived themselves vulnerable.

...................................................

*Repressive agencies are dissolved only to be replaced by similar entities.*

...................................................

"Throughout much of the region, a repressive legal infrastructure continues to exist, but government's ability to enforce its will has in many cases weakened," Al-Jazeera's Hashim told CPJ. "So the authorities are sometimes compelled to adjust the rules, in part to give the appearance of having conceded something but also to deny critical journalists familiarity."

Trying to stave off growing protests, Jordan's King Abdullah approved modest constitutional reforms in September relating mostly to political parties and elections. At the same time, the lower house of parliament passed an anti-corruption bill that would have a chilling effect on investigative journalism by imposing high fines for publishing information on corruption. Similarly, Morocco passed by referendum constitutional reforms that marginally fulfilled popular demands for increased pluralism, but had little effect on media freedoms. Three weeks before the referendum, authorities sentenced outspoken editor Rachid Nini to a year in prison on antistate charges that CPJ found to be baseless.

In another effort to quell popular unrest, the Algerian government announced a package of proposed reforms that, among other things, would allow for private television and radio broadcasters, the creation of a committee to regulate the media in place of the justice ministry, and an end to prison terms for journalists convicted of defamation. But the measure, passed by parliament in December, also includes more than 30 vaguely worded articles that could be used to limit press freedom and punish critical reporting.

In Mauritania, after weeks of social unrest, the government in September lifted a prohibition against private broadcasters for the first time in the country's history, but erected steep financial and administrative barriers that many local journalists viewed as a continuation of the government's broadcast monopoly through other means. Parliament also approved a law eliminating prison terms for journalists convicted of insulting the president, foreign heads of state, or other diplomatic entities, replacing them with heavy monetary fines.

**Emerging media freedom groups:** The emergence of new voices extends to associations that aspire to represent journalists. A number of new or previously sidelined organizations have begun making themselves heard.

The National Syndicate of Tunisian Journalists, whose democratically elected board was decimated in a sustained campaign of intimidation by Ben Ali's regime in 2009, held recent elections that saw most of its previous leadership restored. The leading local press freedom group *Observatoire de la Liberté de la Presse, de L'Edition et de la Création*, founded in 2001 and almost immediately banned, was granted a license to operate shortly after Ben Ali's departure. The Tunisian Committee for the Protection of Journalists, established in 2008 and also immediately banned, was reconstituted in February and received a license to operate under the new name of the Tunisia Center for Press Freedom. It has since documented emerging threats to the press across the country.

In Egypt, where membership in the officially sanctioned journalists' syndicate has always been restricted to print journalists, several groups were working to establish alternative bodies to represent journalists in other media. In April, more than 30 local human rights groups, unions, research organizations, and a dozen of Egypt's most prominent press freedom advocates formed the National Coalition for Media Freedom, which seeks to improve working conditions for journalists, particularly through the reform of legislation long used to restrict coverage.

And in the tiny Gulf kingdom of Bahrain, critics say the officially sanctioned Bahraini Journalists Association has long been ineffectual. Although the association disputes the assertion, a new group has emerged to represent journalists inside Bahrain and in exile. Nada al-Wadi, a board member of the new, London-based Bahrain Press Association, told CPJ that the government-approved body "never represented the real concerns of working journalists." Al-Wadi's group is trying to change that. Its inaugural project was a 60-page report detailing hundreds of attacks on local and international media between February and September.

"The Bahrain Press Association is not pro- or anti-opposition," al-Wadi said. "It is pro-reporting."

*Mohamed Abdel Dayem is CPJ's program coordinator for the Middle East and North Africa. He is the author of the 2009 CPJ report, "Middle East bloggers: The street leads online."*

# Discarding Reform, Turkey Uses the Law to Repress

*By Robert Mahoney*

A critical journalist in Turkey these days needs a lawyer on standby. The press is laboring under a creaking judicial system and a panoply of antiquated and vague legislation that officials and politicians of every stripe find irresistible as a weapon against muckraking reporters and critical commentators.

After several years of legal and constitutional reform prompted by Turkey's application for European Union membership, moves to lighten the dead hand of the law on journalists are running out of steam. The EU, beset by economic woes and wary of further eastward expansion, has grown cool to the idea of embracing 75 million Turks. Prime Minister Recep Tayyip Erdoğan, buoyed by a landslide third-term election victory in June, is in no mood to be lectured by European officials on the human rights shortcomings of his administration. EU accession talks and, with it, Turkish law reform are treading water.

Besides, Erdoğan is presiding over a country with 9 percent annual economic growth and enhanced political clout in the region thanks to deft diplomatic maneuvering that put Ankara on the right side of the Arab uprisings in 2011. The United States seems wary of calling out Turkey on its human rights and press freedom record. Washington is comfortable with the narrative that Turkey, a NATO member and crucial U.S. ally in the region, is a progressive, secular democracy and a model of free speech compared with its neighbors Iran, Iraq, and Syria.

But for journalists, particularly Kurdish and leftist ones, progress in freedom of expression has not kept pace with political and economic advances. "Turkey is more open than before, but on press freedom we have more trouble," said Ruşen Çakır, a journalist for NTV and columnist in the daily *Vatan*. "It is really very contradictory. Western people also cannot understand what's happening in Turkey. On the one hand, Turkey is a kind of model to the Middle East; on the other hand, Turkey is bad news for freedom of the press," he said. "Turkey is really difficult to understand." Çakır was referring to the complex interplay of political, bureaucratic, and commercial interests that have polarized Turkish media and stifled much investigative reporting. These competing forces are underpinned by anachronistic laws and a sclerotic judicial system that are easily turned against the press.

...............................................

*The thousands of criminal cases against reporters have a devastating effect.*

...............................................

Journalists and press groups estimate there are 4,000 to 5,000 criminal cases currently open against reporters. The cases involve charges such as criminal defamation, influencing the outcome of a trial, and spreading terrorist propaganda. The bulk of these cases have not resulted in convictions historically, but the endless court proceedings and legal costs have had a severe chilling effect, according to reporters, media analysts, and lawyers interviewed by CPJ throughout 2011. Prosecutions have intensified since authorities in 2007 first detailed the "Ergenekon" conspiracy, an alleged nationalist military plot to overthrow the government. Journalists' sense of security nose-dived in March 2011 with the arrests of leading investigative reporters Ahmet Şık and Nedim Şener on Ergenekon-related charges, and then again in December with the government's roundup of more two dozen journalists on vague propaganda allegations.

Şık, who along with Şener, was still in pre-trial detention in late year, said he was arrested because he was writing a still-unpublished book, *The Imam's Army*, on the Gülen Islamic movement, which is close to the ruling Justice and Development Party (AKP). Erdoğan compared the book to a bomb. Şener is best-known for his work on the investigation into the murder of Turkish-Armenian journalist Hrant Dink, which has still not netted the masterminds of the crime.

Ergenekon comes against the backdrop of a shift in political and economic influence away from the staunchly secular and nationalist military to the AKP, a socially conservative movement rooted in Islam that was first elected in 2002. The legal system has become a battleground between the AKP and Kemalists, ultranationalists of the old order known as the "deep state," with journalists as collateral damage. Add to this a concentration of media ownership among conglomerates reluctant to jeopardize their vast non-media business interests by angering authorities, and journalists of all political persuasions feel exposed. The outcome in many cases is chronic self-censorship by reporters and commentators fearful of prosecution or losing their jobs.

"We oppose every kind of authoritarianism," said Markar Esenyan, news coordinator of the tiny independent daily *Taraf*, the first Turkish partner of WikiLeaks, the anti-secrecy organization. "That's why there are some 250 cases against the paper. The government and the military are against us." *Taraf*, often an outlier in the media scene, is in the mainstream in this regard. Nearly every newsroom in Istanbul has a clutch of reporters who are in and out of court every month. And prosecutors have a broad palette of laws to choose from.

"I can quote at least 40 articles in the Turkish penal code that are directly or indirectly limiting freedom of expression—and some of them are used in a terrible manner," said Orhan Cengiz, a lawyer and the head of the Human Rights Agenda Association. He laments what he sees as a decrease in political pressure by Brussels on the AKP administration to reform or repeal some of these laws. "The European Commission regularly published reports criticizing Turkey and made a kind of road map for further reforms. Unfortunately, for the past couple of years, we have been losing this EU momentum," he said. "It is a huge loss for Turkey. Both sides are tired. So many chapters [in the accession talks] are blocked. Between 2002 and 2005—even 2006—we had fantastic progress by this government because the EU used to exert pressure, but we don't have similar pressure right now."

*At least 40 articles in the penal code limit free expression, an expert says.*

After amendments to the Turkish Press Act were enacted in 2004, restrictions eased, at least for non-Kurdish journalists, in covering the role of the military in civilian life and the Kurdish independence struggle in southeast Turkey. But those gains were erased as new pressures arose for journalists reporting on the AKP and its allies. "The press freedom climate is like the Istanbul weather, always changing," said Nadire Mater, head of the independent news portal Bianet. "One day, there's an opening to the Kurds; the next, trials are started," she said, referring to the shift in the administration's attitude toward the independent press before and after Ergenekon.

Since Ergenekon and the investigations in 2009 into another anti-government plot known as Sledgehammer, reporters covering the two conspiracies have been hit with a series of prosecutions. Charges have been filed under Article 288 ("attempting to influence a trial") and Article 285 ("violation of confidentiality of an investigation") of the penal code. If they obeyed the letter of these laws, reporters covering police and court beats would be out of a job.

"In Article 288, the nature of the 'influence' is not defined, which allows judges to loosely interpret it," said Ash Tunç, associate professor of media studies at Istanbul Bilgi University. "Because of various punitive laws, the country remains a minefield for critical reporting and investigative journalism."

Legal landmines also include vague laws on criminal defamation, insult, and violation of privacy. And it's not just journalists in the crosshairs. "Since taking office in 2002, Tayyip Erdoğan used Article 8 of the penal code concerning crimes against dignity, and Article 125 on defamation, against stand-up comedians, political opponents, political cartoonists, and even a student theater group," Tunç said.

One of the most intimidating statutes, however, remains the 1991 Anti-Terrorism Act (Act 3713), which was prompted by the Kurdish rebellion that began several years earlier. Articles 6 and 7 of the law, the most frequently used against the media, outlaw the publication of statements by terrorist organizations, for example, and provide a one- to five-year prison term for making "propaganda" for such organizations. In 2010, the European Court of Human Rights in Strasbourg found that these provisions restricted freedom of expression and contravened Article 10 of the European Convention on Human Rights, to which Turkey is a signatory.

*An intimidating anti-terror law is used frequently against news media.*

Ankara, however, has a history of ignoring the court. This was highlighted in a July 2011 report by Thomas Hammarberg, human rights commissioner for the Council of Europe. While welcoming progress on some issues previously considered taboo, Hammarberg wrote that "the conditions underlying the very high number of judgments delivered for more than a decade by the European Court of Human Rights against Turkey in this field have not been effectively addressed to date by the Turkish authorities and continue to represent a constant, serious threat to freedom of expression in Turkey. The recent waves of arrests of journalists have particularly highlighted the reality of this risk."

The anti-terror law has been used repeatedly to close or suspend Kurdish publications and jail Kurdish journalists, most prominently Vedat Kurşun, editor-in-chief of Turkey's only Kurdish-language daily,

*Azadiya Welat*, who was sentenced to a total of 166 years in prison in 2010 on charges that included spreading propaganda. Kurdish journalists, particularly those based in the southeast, complain that critical reporting on the insurgency and the plight of ordinary Kurds is severely hampered by constant fear of prosecution and lack of access to Turkish civil and military officials. "The term 'propaganda' is not clearly defined," Bilgi University professor Tunç said of the Anti-Terrorism Act. "This code is randomly used against pro-Kurdish media outlets and journalists who investigate the Kurdish issue."

Turkish newspaper journalist and broadcaster Ertugrul Mavioglu, friend and collaborator of jailed journalist Şık, is among the latter group. Mavioglu is being prosecuted for propaganda because of a 2010 interview he conducted with Murat Karayilan, leader of the outlawed Kurdish Workers Party, or PKK. The journalist faces up to seven years in jail if convicted. Mavioglu faces an array of other charges as well. "When I write, I have a strong feeling that something may happen to me," he said, referring to legal sanctions. That type of chilling effect spread further and deeper across Turkey's press landscape in December when authorities detained at least 29 journalists on vague allegations they had conducted "propaganda" for a Kurdish group the government claimed was tied to the PKK. Despite international outcry, authorities provided no supporting evidence for the widespread crackdown.

Print and broadcasting are not the only victims of this restrictive legal regime. Prosecutors have begun targeting the Internet in recent years as

well, notably blocking YouTube from 2007 to 2010 for videos violating a long-standing law forbidding disrespect of Turkey's founder, Mustafa Kemal Atatürk. The blocking provisions were enacted in 2007 under Law 5651 that the government said was put in place to prevent child pornography and other criminal activity. However, many academics and journalists see the statute as the greatest threat to online freedom of expression in the country.

## An Internet filtering plan prompts tens of thousands to protest in Istanbul.

"The measures are used widely to block access to thousands of websites," said Yaman Akdeniz, author of a report on censorship for the Organization for Security and Co-operation in Europe. "Actual statistics are kept secret, but engelliweb.com estimates this number to be around 15,000. A considerable number of politically motivated websites are also blocked," he said. These include many Kurdish sites, journalists say.

Authorities went further in 2011, announcing plans to introduce mandatory content filtering by Internet service providers. The plan, which would have forced consumers to install software on their personal computers with one of four content-filter settings, galvanized the country's budding digital generation. Organizing themselves via social media, tens of thousands of protesters marched through Istanbul in May. The government backtracked a bit, settling on two content settings and, notably, making the filter optional for consumers. Still, ISPs are required to provide the filters, and the government sets the criteria for the filtering.

"Concerns remain for the system," warned Akdeniz. "It is mandatory for all ISPs to offer this [software] to users in Turkey, and any system maintained and run by a government agency will attract suspicion and criticism. Basically, we are still concerned, regardless of it being optional."

Blogger Erkan Saka thinks Law 5651 should be the prime concern. "We should focus more on the existing regulation," he said. "There are still access problems to various sites. The way they are restricted is the problem; it is very easy to restrict a website. That pattern continues even if there are no filters," he said. Cengiz, from the Human Rights Agenda Association, agrees. "A judge in any corner of the country can order a ban on an Internet site," he said.

Some press freedom advocates see Turkey's young people as a catalyst for reforming the restrictive legal landscape for media. Forty-five percent of the population is under 25.

"I am still hopeful for the digitally literate generation because the use of social media is on the rise," said Tunç, the professor. "It is not a perfect solution, but there is a hope in the blogosphere, for example, to bypass some of the oppressive laws and undertake independent publishing. The young Turkish generation is incredibly dynamic and active on the Internet, so now people are more aware of what's going on."

A number of journalists maintain blogs, but blogging in Turkey generally has been slow to take off, Saka noted. The real growth, he believes, has been in social media. (Turkey ranks among the leaders worldwide in Facebook use, according to the social network site.) "Most journalists have yet to tap the opportunities of new media," Saka said. "Social media are not yet filling in the gaps in investigation and coverage, but I'm optimistic that they will. Already that is how you hear about some of the news."

*Blogging is slow to take hold in Turkey, but social media use has exploded.*

Some reporters say they are beginning to use Twitter for newsgathering and dissemination. Several said that for the first time they ran a story in 2011 that was broken by "citizen journalists" on Twitter. News of the death of a man during clashes between police and anti-Erdoğan protesters during election campaigning in May in the northeastern city of Hopa came via Twitter because security forces blocked many mainstream journalists from entering the area.

But the hope that the new generation will push back against state control remains just that—a hope. "Lots of people are scared," said Akdeniz, "and therefore it remains to be seen whether people express themselves freely online." For that to happen, journalists believe, all of Turkish civil society, with EU and other international support, needs to push for reform of the legal system from root to branch. With two of the country's top journalists, Şık and Şener, behind bars and dozens of others in severe legal jeopardy because of that system, the urgency of the task is clear.

*Robert Mahoney is deputy director of the Committee to Protect Journalists. He has traveled to Turkey twice to do reporting for CPJ. He interviewed more than 20 media executives, journalists, academics, lawyers, and human rights defenders during a 2011 visit to the country.*

# Fear, Uncertainty Stalk
# Iranian Journalists in Exile

*By María Salazar-Ferro and Sheryl A. Mendez*

The days before Iran's June 2009 elections were euphoric, photographer Javad Moghimi Parsa remembers. In Tehran, the atmosphere was festive and the anticipation palpable. But the mood turned quickly as results were announced, giving the presidency back to Mahmoud Ahmadinejad. Thousands of people claiming fraud and demanding democracy crammed the streets and were met with brutal violence. Parsa covered the demonstrations in his time off from the semi-official Fars News agency. "This was the first time in my life I had seen so many people protesting together. I was in awe," he said. "So I followed them and took their pictures." Two weeks later, one of Parsa's photos appeared on the cover of *Time* magazine. Parsa, who had secretly sent images abroad, was warned by his boss that journalists filing material to foreign media would be considered spies. Terrified by the prospect of jail, the photographer fled Iran the next day.

Since June 2009, the Journalist Assistance program at the Committee to Protect Journalists has been in contact with 68 Iranian journalists who have fled their country. Many left in the months that immediately followed the 2009 protests. But as Iranian authorities have continued to aggressively silence dissent, maintaining a revolving prison door for critical journalists, the exodus of the Iranian media personnel has not slowed. Today, more than half of the Iranian journalists living in exile are under the age of 35. The bulk crossed over the Turkish or Iraqi borders, facing difficult paths to relocation. Thirty-five permanently resettled in Western countries, most having been granted political asylum. Many have financial worries, and nearly all expressed continuous fear of retaliation from Iran.

Journalists in Iran are required to register with the Ministry of Culture and Islamic Guidance. Those working for official or semi-official outlets are given specific instructions on what angle to give their news, and if they fail, they can be suspended for up to three months, according to CPJ interviews. The government's most frequently used weapon against the critical press until June 2009 had been the withholding of official subsidies, although journalists covering sensitive issues such as human rights sometimes did short prison stints. But the landscape changed with post-election demonstrations. In a full-scale effort to stifle criticism, authorities closed outlets, expelled foreign media, arrested dozens of journalists and media workers, ransacked homes, and seized property.

"When the arrest wave started, a lot of people who thought that if they kept quiet they would be spared were arrested," exiled political commentator Babak Dad said. "There was a list, and everyone on that list had to be taken in." By CPJ's count, more than 150 journalists have been detained at various times since then. Some have been released, even as authorities have made new arrests. Others have been sentenced in closed courts on vague antistate charges, drawing prison terms of up to 10 years. In jail, journalists are often kept in solitary confinement, denied family visits, and at times physically abused.

*Intimidation soars with more than 150 journalists detained at various times.*

Fearing this fate, Dad fled Iran in October 2009. He had worked as a journalist for two decades and had been an important figure in the country's burgeoning blogosphere. Dad also was a political commentator on the Persian service of the U.S. government-funded Voice of America; on the eve of the elections, he had warned listeners about the possibility of fraud. The next day, Dad received a call from a man claiming to have a package for him. Realizing authorities had him in their sights, Dad packed his two children and their dog into his car and sped out of Tehran. "This time next year," Dad told his children as they were leaving, "you could have a father you are proud of or a father who is dead from torture." For the next 120 days, Dad, the kids, and the dog slept at tourist campsites in northern Iran, changing locations every few days while Dad continued reporting. By the end of September, as more journalists were arrested and Dad felt his tail getting closer, the journalist used his last $20 to pay smugglers to lead them over the mountains into Iraq. The journey on horseback lasted four days.

Around that time, an arrest warrant was issued in Tehran for the young photojournalist Parsa for his collaboration with news media described as "enemy agencies." But Parsa had left Iran for Turkey in August. "Every step of the day I left was emotional because I knew it was the last time I would be in my country," Parsa said. At the airport, an Iranian immigration official questioned him intensely, asking about his destination, current job, and previous travel. "His questions were intimidating and I was petrified that I would never make it out," the journalist told CPJ. "Even when I was sitting in the airplane, ready to go, I was afraid that someone was going to come grab me."

More than half of the Iranian journalists who have left since June 2009 have done so secretly to avoid airports or border posts. Only a handful with long-standing connections to foreign media flew directly to Western countries with help from their employers. By late 2011, CPJ research shows, the 68 exiled journalists were spread among 18 countries worldwide. Their top hosts were France, Turkey, the United States, Germany, Norway, and Sweden. Twenty-eight had been granted asylum, and 14 were awaiting a final decision. The rest were registered refugees in transit countries.

*Sixty-eight exiled journalists now spread across 18 countries worldwide.*

Of the cases documented by CPJ, 35 journalists traveled through Turkey, where Iranians are not required to have entry visas. Turkish immigration laws grant government protection only to refugees from European or ex-Soviet countries, but a 1994 regulation allows non-Europeans to have temporary asylum-seeker status. For practical purposes, then, until non-European refugees are resettled to a third country, the U.N. High Commissioner for Refugees, or UNHCR, is their main source of protection. Iraqis and Iranians make up the two largest refugee populations in Turkey, according to the UNHCR.

Resettlement out of Turkey can be a long process. In some cases it can take the UNHCR up to three years to process applications, according to a 2010 report by the California-based organization OMID Advocates for Human Rights. Meanwhile, Turkish law requires refugees to register with local authorities in one of 30 cities where they must remain at all times. They are required to pay $227 in "stay" fees every six months, and are given minimal social and economic support. Failure to comply with Turkish law can result in prosecution, fines, imprisonment, or deportation.

"The time I was in Turkey was very difficult," said Parsa, who spent 16 months in the country before being relocated to Norway. "It was the toughest, most restricted, and frightening time of my life." Job opportunities are few, discrimination is common, and finding suitable housing is almost impossible, Parsa explained. Many of the journalists living in Turkey room together and pool their resources. CPJ has written letters to the UNHCR and other international bodies in support of 22 journalists, detailing their work and the persecution they endured. CPJ has also supported 16 with small grants to cover basic needs and travel expenses.

Tension among refugees in Turkey is common, often due to medical and psychological problems and uncertainty about the future, the OMID Advocates report states. Tensions are also fueled by widespread rumors about the resettlement process. In 2011, several journalists informed CPJ of schemes to speed resettlement through falsified letters from international organizations testifying to their vulnerability. The letters, the journalists said, are sold for up to $100 apiece outside the UNHCR offices in Ankara. (CPJ notified the UNHCR, which said it would investigate the claims.) But the most troubling rumors are about the presence of Iranian intelligence agents in Turkey, where they are said to harass, attack, and even snatch asylum-seekers. Two Iranian journalists exiled in Turkey confirmed having been directly approached by threatening, Farsi-speaking individuals.

Dad heard the same rumors in Iraq, where a much lower number of Iranian journalists have traveled. "One guy said people were abducted, put in cars, and taken back to Iran. Others were [said to be] killed in drive-by shootings," Dad recounted. Dad told CPJ that he had been followed on several occasions by individuals later identified by other refugees as Iranian agents. "They would wait outside the [UNHCR] offices, listening to what I was saying," Dad said. "So I tried to leave the country quickly for security reasons." Other refugees in Iraq also cite insecurity as their top concern.

Iraq is one of the countries with the highest numbers of internally displaced people in the world. As such, the relocation process for foreign refugees is often long and exhausting. Dad told CPJ that he visited the UNHCR offices in Arbil multiple times. "Each time, they would make me fill out another form and say they were understaffed and that I needed to come back later," Dad said. UNHCR did not respond to requests for comment.

So the journalist reached out to the French consulate in Arbil through a friend in Paris. With support from CPJ and other international organizations, Dad and his children were given emergency humanitarian visas and resettled to France within two months. Their dog, Nancy, was adopted by a local government official.

................................................

## For Iranians who fled to Iraq, a long and exhausting relocation process.

................................................

CPJ has documented 13 other cases of Iranian journalists who have been granted emergency visas, mostly to France and Germany. According to CPJ research, however, such visas are rare. In fact, most countries deny journalists and human rights defenders visas for fear that they will request political asylum, bringing political and budgetary headaches. "This is the problem with the refugee system generally. Conventions on human rights say people have the right to seek asylum, but international law doesn't have a lot to say about the practicalities of how to get there," Anwen Hughes, senior attorney for the refugee protection program at Human Rights First, told CPJ.

Fear among Iranian exiles is not restricted to Turkey and Iraq. Journalists who have been resettled or are living in Western countries also spoke to CPJ of indirect threats by the Iranian security apparatus. One journalist who has been granted asylum in Europe asked not to be identified for fear of retribution against his family in Iran. Another, Mohammad Kheirkhan, a photojournalist who lives in California, said his girlfriend in Iran was routinely harassed after he left the country. "At the beginning, they would ask her to go to court and ask her questions about what I was doing," Kheirkhan told CPJ. "Now, there are no more problems because I am not covering Iran anymore." Kheirkhan's brother also received threatening phone calls, the journalist told CPJ.

Kheirkhan is studying journalism but said that he tries to avoid reading news about Iran. "The thing is that even if you don't want to, you will see something on Facebook or somewhere, you will hear about your colleagues, journalists being detained, tortured." The photographer left Iran immediately after the elections and was never arrested. Yet he said that he often wakes up in a panic. "I dream about torture, that I am being lashed in public," he told CPJ.

## *A photographer avoids news of his homeland but still dreams of torture.*

The feelings of guilt expressed by Kheirkhan and other Iranian exiles is common among refugees, particularly journalists, according to Jack Saul, a psychologist and director of the International Trauma Studies Program at Columbia University. "They feel that they are abandoning their colleagues, and have a conflict around their professional responsibility and their personal safety," Saul told CPJ. The consequences of exile, he said, can at times be more severe than those of torture. Refugees often feel like they are still in a state of change. "Their trauma is not over as they continue to be in exile," he said.

For many of the journalists who have been resettled to the United States or Western Europe, the transition has not been easy. Only 14 said they have continued working in the profession, either with an international media outlet or with a Farsi-language, exile online publication. Most cannot make ends meet. Dad, who continues to blog and at times does commentary for VOA, does not get paid for his journalism. Instead, he relies on the small funds the French government provides him monthly. Photographer Ehsan Maleki, who is also in France, told CPJ that the government funds are so small that he is unable to pay his phone or Internet bills. "I escaped Iranian prisons," Maleki said, "but now I risk starving to death."

It is too early to know, Saul said, how the exiled journalists will fare. Dad, Parsa, and Kheirkhan said that by leaving Iran, they had made a decision to put safety above all else. Yet their decisions have been accompanied by ambivalence. Parsa said that fleeing was the only way to continue working as a journalist. For Kheirkhan, the decision was right only if he is able one day to return home.

*Maria Salazar-Ferro is coordinator of CPJ's Journalist Assistance program and its Global Campaign Against Impunity. Journalist Assistance Program Associate Sheryl A. Mendez is an editor and photojournalist who has worked in international hot spots such as Pakistan, Iran, Syria, Lebanon, and Iraq.*

# Bahrain

The government waged a brutal multifaceted crackdown against independent news media covering the country's months-long protest movement. Security forces subjected journalists to assaults, expulsions, detentions, politicized trials, prison terms, and lethal mistreatment in custody. Both international and local reporters were targeted: A journalist for the U.S. broadcaster ABC was beaten and his camera was confiscated in February; a photographer for the independent domestic daily *Al-Wasat* was beaten while covering a March protest. Authorities used live ammunition against protesters and reporters: *The New York Times* reported that two of its journalists came under helicopter fire in February. The Ministry of Information expelled CNN correspondent Mohammed Jamjoom over coverage of the unrest, and detained members of a CNN crew trying to interview human rights activist Nabeel Rajab. In June, a court convicted two critical, journalistic bloggers of a series of antistate charges and sentenced them to lengthy terms. Reports of torture and mistreatment of detainees were common: Two journalists, one a founder of *Al-Wasat*, died in government custody under circumstances authorities would not fully explain. *Al-Wasat*, the country's premier independent paper, was in the crosshairs throughout the year: Armed assailants stormed its printing facility in March; the Information Ministry briefly shut the paper in April; and the government filed criminal charges against three senior editors for "false news" the same month. CPJ honored *Al-Wasat* founder and editor Mansoor al-Jamri with its 2011 International Press Freedom Award.

KEY DEVELOPMENTS

» Press freedom conditions hit their worst point since Bahrain gained its independence in 1971.

» Two journalists die in state custody; widespread arrests, assaults, detentions are reported.

KEY DATA

## 19 Short-term detentions

Several international and local journalists were detained for days or weeks for their coverage of civil unrest, CPJ research shows.

## Detentions reflect a spring crackdown:

| | |
|---|---|
| 7 | Detained in March |
| 2 | Detained in April |
| 10 | Detained in May |

# 2 Killed in 2011

Zakariya Rashid Hassan al-Ashiri and Karim Fakhrawi were the first media fatalities CPJ recorded in Bahrain since the organization began keeping detailed data in 1992. Both died in government custody. Al-Ashiri, a critical blogger, died a week after his arrest on charges of disseminating false news. The government cited complications from sickle cell anemia, an assertion disputed by al-Ashiri's family. Fakhrawi, a founder of *Al-Wasat*, died in state custody three days later. The government pinned his death on kidney failure, but photographs published online showed a body identified as that of Fakhrawi with extensive cuts and bruises, CPJ research shows.

# 20 Expulsions, denials of entry

Intent on silencing international coverage of the unrest, authorities blocked numerous journalists from entering the country and expelled or deported others, CPJ research shows.

**A record of obstruction:**

17 Journalists denied entry. News outlets included the BBC, CNN, McClatchy Newspapers, and CBS

1 Journalist from CNN expelled

2 Journalists from *Al-Wasat* deported

# 92 Arrests, threats, harassment

Since civil unrest began on February 14, at least 92 local journalists endured arrests, threats, and harassment, according to the Bahrain Center for Human Rights.

**Breakdown of those targeted:**

46 Print journalists

22 Photographers

15 Internet reporters

9 Radio and television journalists

## Media fatalities in the region in 2011:

5 Iraq

5 Libya

**2 Bahrain**

2 Egypt

2 Syria

2 Yemen

1 Tunisia

# 1 Imprisoned on December 1, 2011

Online journalist Abduljalil Alsingace was serving a life sentence on antistate charges when CPJ conducted its annual prison census. A fellow online journalist, Ali Abdel Imam, was convicted in absentia on similar charges. In September, an appeals court upheld their sentences.

# Egypt

During the 18-day uprising that led to Hosni Mubarak's ouster, the government unleashed a systematic campaign to intimidate journalists and obstruct news coverage. Dozens of serious press freedom violations were recorded between January 25 and February 11, as police and government supporters assaulted journalists in the streets. One journalist was killed by sniper fire while covering the demonstrations. Authorities also detained scores of journalists, instituted a six-day Internet blackout, suspended mobile phone service, blocked satellite transmissions, revoked accreditations, erected bureaucratic obstacles for foreign reporters, confiscated equipment, and stormed newsrooms. After Mubarak's fall, the ruling Supreme Council of the Armed Forces showed its own hostility to critical news coverage. The council established a new censorship regime in March, telling editors they must obtain approval for coverage involving the armed forces. In July, the council reinstated the historically repressive Information Ministry; in September, it announced it would enforce the Mubarak-era Emergency Law that allows indefinite detention of civilians. Authorities raided broadcasters in September, October, and December, censored newspapers, and arrested critical bloggers. In October, a fatal confrontation between the military and civilians in front of the Television and Radio Union left dozens dead, including a journalist. The next month, at least 35 journalists were detained or assaulted while covering a week of demonstrations demanding the military hand over power to civilians. As the year ended, the first two rounds of parliamentary voting gave Islamist parties a significant lead over secular competitors.

KEY DEVELOPMENTS

» Local and foreign journalists are attacked, detained on a massive scale during popular uprising.

» Ruling military council continues restrictions, jails online journalists.

KEY DATA

160 **Attacks during uprising**
CPJ documented 160 attacks on journalists and news facilities over the 18-day popular uprising. Journalists were consistently targeted by plainclothes and uniformed agents of the government, CPJ research shows.

**Breakdown of attacks, from January 25 to February 11:**

70 Detentions

52 Assaults

28 Equipment seizures

10 Newsroom raids

## 2 Imprisoned on December 1, 2011

Two bloggers critical of the military were jailed in late year. Mikael Nabil Sanad was the first journalist to be detained in the post-Mubarak era, CPJ research shows. In December, an Egyptian court sentenced Sanad to two years in prison for "insulting the military" in writings that suggested the armed forces were a greater threat to Egyptians' freedom than Mubarak had been. Alaa Abd el-Fattah was charged in November with "inciting violence against the military" among other antistate counts after he criticized the military's actions in a deadly confrontation with Coptic Christian protesters.

**Imprisoned in Egypt on CPJ's annual census:**

2007    1

2008    1

2009    3

2010    1

2011    2

## 6 Days Internet disrupted

At the height of public demonstrations, Egypt tried to contain dissent by shutting down Internet access. Several other regional governments facing civil unrest tried this tactic as well, all with limited success. Historically, some Asian governments have also used Internet shutdowns to quell dissent.

## 2 Killed in 2011

Ahmad Mohamed Mahmoud, a journalist working for the newspaper *Al-Ta'awun*, was shot by a sniper on January 29 while filming violent confrontations between protesters and police. He died six days later. On October 9, Wael Mikhael, an Egyptian cameraman for the Coptic television broadcaster Al-Tareeq, was shot while filming violent clashes between Coptic Christian protesters and the military.

## 8.9 Million Facebook users

Egypt has the largest number of Facebook users in the Arab world, although penetration is greater in several regional countries, according to Facebook statistics. Journalists used social media extensively to disseminate information from Tahrir Square and other hot spots across the country.

**Regional use and rankings:**

**Egypt**: 8.9 million users
11% of the population

**Saudi Arabia**: 4.5 million
17% of the population

**Morocco**: 3.9 million
12% of the population

**Tunisia**: 2.74 million
26% of the population

**Algeria**: 2.72 million
7% of the population

**United Arab Emirates**: 2.6 million
57% of the population

# Iran

Two years after a contested presidential election, Tehran continued to use the mass imprisonment of journalists to silence dissent and quash critical news coverage. Imprisoned journalists suffered greatly amid the crowded and unsanitary conditions of notorious prisons such as Rajaee Shah and Evin. The health of many detainees severely deteriorated, while numerous others suffered abuse at the hands of prison guards. The detainees also faced a battery of punitive measures, from the denial of family visits to placement in solitary confinement. Authorities continued a practice of freeing some prisoners on furloughs while making new arrests. Six-figure bonds were often posted by the furloughed journalists who faced immense political pressure to falsely implicate their colleagues in crimes. While some large international news organizations maintained a presence in Tehran, their journalists could not move or report freely, particularly outside the capital. Politically sensitive topics such as the country's nuclear program or its plan to eliminate subsidies were largely off-limits to local and international reporters. The government also restricted adversarial reporting by using sophisticated technology to block websites, jamming satellite signals, and banning publications.

KEY DEVELOPMENTS

» Using imprisonment to silence critics, Iran is the world's worst jailer of journalists.

» CPJ names Iran one of the World's 10 Online Oppressors; authorities block millions of sites.

KEY DATA

## 21 Held in solitary confinement

Authorities routinely placed journalists in solitary confinement, often as a means of coercing false confessions. Of the imprisoned journalists on CPJ's census, about half have been put in solitary confinement at one point during their detention. Journalists also suffered from deteriorating health and abuse by prison guards, CPJ research shows.

**Detainees at risk:**

12 Suffered from poor health

14 Reported some form of abuse in prison

5 Denied family visits

4 Denied medical care

# 27.9 Million Internet users

World Bank data show the number of Internet users in Iran, a country of about 74 million, more than doubled from 2006 to 2009, the most recent year available. Iranian authorities maintain one of the world's toughest Internet censorship regimes, using sophisticated tactics and blocking millions of websites, including numerous news websites and social-networking sites such as Facebook and Twitter, CPJ research shows. Iranians often use proxy servers to overcome the obstacles. In a May report, CPJ named Iran one of the World's 10 Online Oppressors.

**CPJ's Online Oppressors:**

**Iran**

Belarus

Cuba

Ethiopia

Burma

China

Tunisia

Egypt

Syria

Russia

# 42 Imprisoned on December 1, 2011

Iran has sustained a widespread campaign against critical journalists since civil unrest erupted after the disputed June 2009 presidential election.

# 19.5 Years in prison

Among those being held in late 2011, blogger Hossein Derakhshan, who was detained in late 2008, was serving the longest documented sentence. In June, a Tehran appeals court upheld the 19½-year term on charges of "working with hostile governments," "propaganda against the state," and "insulting religious sanctities."

# 18 Forced into exile, 2010-11

Iran and Cuba topped the list of countries driving journalists into exile, according to CPJ research. Iran led the list for a second consecutive year; CPJ's 2009-10 survey found at least 29 Iranian editors, reporters, and photographers had fled into exile. The country's total exodus over the last decade is 66, behind only Ethiopia and Somalia, CPJ research shows.

**Top countries from which journalists fled in 2010-11:**

| | |
|---|---|
| Iran | 18 |
| Cuba | 18 |
| Ethiopia | 5 |
| Eritrea | 5 |
| DRC | 3 |
| Somalia | 3 |
| Pakistan | 3 |

# Iraq

Five journalists and a media worker were killed as Iraq maintained its position as one of the most dangerous countries for journalists. In August, the government adopted a law meant to offer journalists more protection, although its vague provisions did little initially to improve conditions. As demonstrations for economic and political reform spread with the Arab uprisings, journalists were consistently targeted for their coverage. Anti-riot police attacked, detained, and assaulted journalists covering protests. In their attempt to restrict coverage of the unrest, police raided news stations and press freedom groups, destroyed equipment, and arrested journalists. In Iraqi Kurdistan, authorities used aggression and intimidation to restrict journalists' coverage of violent clashes between security forces and protesters. Gunmen raided and destroyed equipment of an independent TV station and a radio station in Sulaymaniyah. Three journalists were fired upon in separate episodes in March, while two journalists were injured covering clashes in Sulaymaniyah in April. Prominent Iraqi Kurdish journalist Asos Hardi was badly beaten by an unidentified assailant.

KEY DEVELOPMENTS

» Nation remains among deadliest for journalists, with five killed in 2011.

» Central and Kurdish governments continue their crackdowns on critical journalists.

KEY DATA

## 5 Killed in 2011

Since 2003, 150 journalists have been killed for their work in Iraq, the highest number of fatalities in a single country in the world, CPJ research shows. Fifty-four media workers have been killed, and an additional 24 journalists were killed in circumstances that remain unclear.

The 2011 victims include Hadi al-Mahdi, a radio show host; Alwan al-Ghorabi, a cameraman; and correspondents Muammar Khadir

Abdelwahad, Sabah al-Bazi, and Mohamed al-Hamdani. Four of the 2011 victims were killed during insurgent attacks, reflecting the nation's continuing instability.

**Deaths in Iraq over time:**

| | |
|------|----|
| 2007 | 32 |
| 2008 | 11 |
| 2009 | 4 |
| 2010 | 5 |
| 2011 | 5 |

# 1st Impunity index ranking

Not a single conviction has been obtained in a journalist murder since 2003, according to CPJ research. With an impunity rate three times worse than that of any other nation, Iraq was ranked worst in the world for the fourth straight year, CPJ research shows. The index calculates unsolved journalist murders as a percentage of each country's population.

**World ranking on CPJ's Impunity Index:**

1. **Iraq**
2. Somalia
3. Philippines
4. Sri Lanka
5. Colombia

# 15,000 Syndicate members

The Iraqi Journalists' Syndicate, an independent association, counted more than 15,000 members by late 2011. The syndicate pressured the government to pass a Journalist Protection Law, which was adopted on August 9.

**New media laws in the region:**

**Saudi Arabia**: May 2011 measure set punishments for publishing material that contravenes Sharia law.

**Syria**: August 2011 legislation banned content said to harm national security.

**Algeria**: December 2011 legislation could punish critical reporting.

# 66 Attacks in 2011

Journalists were targeted with detentions, raids, assaults, injuries, and obstructions for their news coverage, CPJ research shows. CPJ recorded attacks through October 2011.

**Breakdown of attacks:**

26 Detentions

10 Assaults

8 Equipment seizures or destruction

6 Killed (including one media worker)

6 Injured

5 Raids

2 Obstructions

3 Drive-by shootings

# 5.6% Internet penetration

Iraq had one of the lowest Internet penetration rates in the region. Only Sudan and Mauritania had a smaller percentage of inhabitants on the Internet, according to the International Telecommunication Union.

**Regional ranking, from the lowest:**

1. Sudan
2. Mauritania
3. **Iraq**
4. Yemen
5. Libya

# Israel and the Occupied Palestinian Territory

Hamas forces in Gaza cracked down on journalists covering March demonstrations that called for Palestinian unity. Local journalists were attacked, media bureaus raided, and journalistic material confiscated. In April, three photographers were assaulted in the West Bank while covering skirmishes between Palestinians and Israeli settlers in a village south of Nablus. In May, an Israeli soldier shot and seriously wounded Palestinian photographer Mohammed Othman, who was covering clashes between the Israeli military and Palestinians near the Erez Crossing. New legal restrictions were introduced: In July, the Israeli parliament passed an "anti-boycott" law making it a civil offense to support any boycott, divestment, or sanction campaign aimed at Israel based on its Palestinian policies. Journalists could face legal action for even insinuating support of a boycott. Hamas, meanwhile, adopted a new requirement that international journalists obtain Interior Ministry permission before entering Gaza, news reports said. Israeli authorities were holding four Palestinian journalists without charge in late year; Hamas was imprisoning three others, also without charge.

KEY DEVELOPMENTS

» Hamas attacks press at Gaza protests; Israeli soldier shoots journalist at Erez Crossing.

» Israel passes restrictive "anti-boycott law" that will limit news and commentary.

KEY DATA

7 **Imprisoned on December 1, 2011**

Imprisonments reached the highest level in more than a decade, as both Israeli and Hamas authorities jailed journalists without charge.

**Imprisoned over time by either Hamas or Israeli authorities:**

|  | | |
|------|---|---|
| 2007 | 2 | (Both in Israeli custody) |
| 2008 | 4 | (One in Israeli custody; three in Hamas custody) |
| 2009 | 0 | |
| 2010 | 0 | |
| 2011 | 7 | (Four in Israeli custody; three in Hamas custody) |

## 7 Groups protesting anti-boycott law

In a move likely to restrict news coverage and commentary, the Israeli parliament passed an "anti-boycott" law in July, making it a civil offense to support any economic, cultural, or academic boycott of Israel, Israeli settlements, or Israeli institutions. Violators are subject to civil lawsuit and fines. The measure generated criticism from several domestic groups, the BBC reported.

## 5 Flotilla detentions

Israeli forces boarded two ships carrying aid bound for Gaza in November. Among the 27 detentions were journalists Hassan Ghani, a correspondent for Iran's Press TV; Lina Attallah, of *Al-Masry al-Youm*'s English edition; Jihan Hafiz, of Democracy Now; Casey Kauffmann of Al-Jazeera English; and Ayman al-Zubair of Al-Jazeera. Authorities confiscated equipment and footage. Israeli forces were heavily criticized in 2010 after they intercepted a Gaza-bound Turkish flotilla, killing nine passengers, injuring dozens, and arresting hundreds. News media were attacked and obstructed during the raids.

**The May 2010 flotilla raids:**

18 Journalists aboard the flotilla detained.

10 Countries represented by the detained journalists.

6 Journalists whose equipment was seized.

## 11 Assaulted by Hamas in March

Local and foreign journalists covering demonstrations in Gaza calling for political reconciliation between Palestinian factions were attacked on three separate days in March by Hamas security forces, CPJ research shows.

**Three days of anti-press violence:**

4 **journalists assaulted on March 16:**

- Ahmed Hethat, correspondent for the independent radio station Sawt al-Watan
- Mahmoud Abu Taha, presenter for Sawt al-Watan
- Akram Atallah, reporter for the West Bank-based daily *Al-Ayyam*
- Mohamed al-Baba, photographer for Agence France-Presse

2 **journalists assaulted on March 19:**

- Two unidentified Reuters staff members, one of whom was struck with an iron bar

5 **journalists assaulted on March 30:**

- Wissam Mohamed Yasin, correspondent for U.S. government-funded Al-Hurra
- Ayyad Talal Taha, reporter for Radio Watan
- Mohamad al-Hassoun, reporter for Radio Watan
- Mamdouh al-Sayyid, cameraman for Al-Arabiya
- Wajih al-Najjar, reporter for the Palestinian News Agency

# Jordan

Security forces tried to restrict coverage of the country's civil unrest by attacking journalists covering pro-reform protests, often confiscating or destroying their equipment. Authorities raided the office of a news website in April, destroying equipment and threatening staff members. The same month, Al-Jazeera received a series of threats that its offices and journalists would be attacked if the network did not tone down coverage of the protests; the network's Amman bureau chief said he had received death threats by telephone and social media. Other attacks included the hacking of a news website in February for refusing to take down a critical statement from a group of Jordanian tribesmen calling for political and economic reforms. In an Orwellian maneuver, the lower chamber of parliament passed a bill in September that was marketed as fighting corruption. In fact, some provisions would accomplish the opposite: They would impose heavy new fines against journalists who report on corruption without "solid facts." Facing heavy opposition from journalists, the upper chamber sent the bill to committee for further review. Despite a long list of press freedom abuses, Jordanian leaders escaped criticism from the United States, which sought to maintain close relations with the kingdom.

KEY DEVELOPMENTS

» Government forces, allies silence coverage through attacks, seizures, and threats.

» "Anti-corruption" legislation would restrict news coverage of corruption.

KEY DATA

**70** **Attacks on journalists**
Between February and July, a period of intense political unrest, CPJ recorded at least 70 direct attacks on journalists and news stations. Security forces assaulted journalists at protests, raided a news station, and threatened other journalists for their news coverage, CPJ research shows.

**Attacks between February and July:**

43 Assaults

23 Seizures or destruction of equipment

2 Threats

1 Office raid

1 Website hacked

# 16 Assaults at single protest

At a July demonstration in Amman, security forces beat 16 journalists wearing orange "press" vests, CPJ research shows. The vests, provided by the Public Security Directorate, were supposed to distinguish journalists from demonstrators and provide a greater level of safety. Jordan's royal court said it would cover the cost of medical treatment for the injured journalists.

**Of the injured journalists:**

2 Suffered broken bones

1 Underwent surgery

**The targeted journalists worked for a variety of organizations, including:**

Al-Jazeera

*The New York Times*

Agence France-Presse

# 52 Supporting Al-Jazeera

In April, 52 Jordanian journalists issued a statement expressing support for Al-Jazeera journalists threatened with attack for their coverage of the unrest.

**Another severe threat in April:**

**Six** unidentified men stormed the office of *Al-Muharrir*'s editor-in-chief, Jihad Abu Baidar, threatening to kill him and burn his offices if he did not withdraw an article about corruption, news reports said.

**One** *Al-Muharrir* employee was beaten by assailants, and one computer was destroyed.

# 60,000 Dinars in potential fines

On September 27, the chamber of deputies passed a measure billed as "anti-corruption" that would impose fines ranging from 30,000 to 60,000 dinars (US$42,300 to US$84,600) for public accusations of corruption "without solid facts." The legislation did not define what constitutes "solid facts." The upper house sent the bill to committee in late year. Other countries in the region adopted press legislation in 2011 that was portrayed as reform but actually imposed new penalties for critical reporting.

**Other restrictive regional measures:**

**Syria**: With a new law passed in August, journalists could face fines up to 1 million pounds (US$21,000) for vaguely defined violations such as coverage that harms "national unity and national security," according to CPJ research.

**Saudi Arabia**: With amendments adopted in May, first-time violators of the country's restrictive media law could face fines of 500,000 Saudi riyals (US$135,000), while second-time offenders could draw a 1 million riyal (US$270,000) fine and a potential ban on working, according to CPJ research.

# Libya

Journalists worked in extraordinarily dangerous conditions during the eight-month uprising that ended 42 years of rule by Muammar Qaddafi and led to his death. Five journalists were killed amid fierce fighting between rebels and loyalists. Qaddafi's regime unleashed a widespread campaign to silence foreign and local journalists, detaining dozens in abusive conditions. In February, Qaddafi invited reporters to the capital, Tripoli, only to restrict them to the Rixos Hotel, monitor their every move, and prevent them from reporting on anything other than the government line. In their efforts to block news coverage, authorities also jammed satellite signals, severed Internet service, cut off mobile phone networks and landlines, and attacked news facilities. While the crumbling regime was able to orchestrate coverage for a time in Tripoli, it failed to prevent the press from disseminating information about rebel advances in the rest of the country. Press freedom violations persisted after the Libyan rebel government, known as the National Transitional Council, or NTC, took power in August. One journalist was brutally assaulted in Benghazi that month, and the NTC placed one pro-Qaddafi journalist under house arrest.

KEY DEVELOPMENTS

» More than 100 anti-press attacks reported during the revolution.

» Qaddafi forces use mass detentions, obstruction in failed effort to silence coverage.

KEY DATA

## 101 Attacks on journalists, facilities

CPJ documented 101 attacks on journalists and news facilities during the eight-month revolution. Journalists were consistently targeted by government forces and subject to mass detentions, equipment confiscations, expulsions, and assaults, CPJ research shows.

50 Detentions

22 Expulsions

11 Assaults

8 Abuses in custody

5 Instances of equipment seizures or destruction

3 Other injuries

2 Attacks on news facilities

# 50 Detentions

Dozens of foreign and local journalists were detained during the eight-month conflict, several for extended periods. As the political unrest intensified between rebel forces and pro-Qaddafi militants, authorities stepped up intimidation of journalists, detaining them in abusive conditions, CPJ research shows.

# 5 Journalists killed

Libya was among the deadliest places for journalists in 2011. Five journalists were killed covering the conflict, CPJ research shows. The victims included Al-Jazeera cameraman Ali Hassan al-Jaber and Mohammed al-Nabbous of the online opposition broadcaster Libya Al-Hurra TV, both shot while covering unrest; acclaimed photojournalists Tim Hetherington and Chris Hondros, who were killed by a mortar round; and South African photographer Anton Hammerl, who was killed by government forces.

## Deadliest countries in 2011:

| | | |
|---|---|---|
| Pakistan | 7 | press fatalities |
| Libya | 5 | |
| Iraq | 5 | |
| Mexico | 3 | |

# 11 Missing for a time

During the height of the conflict, at least 11 local and international journalists were reported missing for varying periods, CPJ research shows. All were accounted for by late year.

## Those who went missing during the year:

### 7 Libyan journalists

Atef al-Atrash, freelance

Mohamed al-Sahim, freelance

Mohamed al-Amin, freelance

Idris al-Mismar, Arajin

Salma al-Shaab, Libyan Journalists Syndicate

Suad al-Turabouls, *Al-Jamahiriya*

Jalal al-Kawafi, freelance

### 4 International journalists

Ghaith Abdul-Ahad, *The Guardian*

Dave Clark, Agence France-Presse

Roberto Schmidy, Agence France-Presse

Joe Raedle, Getty Images

# 6 Months Internet disrupted

Initially shut down by authorities on February 19, Libya's Internet sustained disruptions until August 22. Other regional governments facing civil unrest tried this tactic as well, with limited success. Historically, some Asian governments have also used Internet shutdowns to quell dissent.

# Morocco

King Mohamed VI pledged a series of constitutional reforms in March after the region's wave of popular uprisings passed through the kingdom. But the reforms did not extend to opening up the press. Authorities took concerted measures to suppress coverage of mass protests in Casablanca's streets. During a March protest in the capital, Rabat, uniformed police assaulted several journalists covering its violent dispersal. The biggest and most controversial case in the kingdom was that of Rachid Nini, a prominent government critic, executive editor of the Moroccan daily *Al-Massae*, and owner of Al-Massae Media Group. He was detained in April and sentenced to one year in prison on charges of "denigrating judicial rulings" and "compromising the security and safety of the homeland and citizens."

KEY DEVELOPMENTS

» Police assault journalists covering pro-reform protests.

» Prominent journalist imprisoned after politicized trial; blogger also held.

KEY DATA

## 5 Assaulted at single March protest

On March 13, security forces used violent dispersal tactics to clamp down on protesters who took to the streets of Casablanca to call for government reforms and greater freedoms, CPJ research shows.

**Journalists from two papers were assaulted:**

3 from *Al-Ahdath al-Maghribia* (a private daily): Hanan Rahab, Owsi Mouh Lhasan, and Mohamed al-Adlani

2 from *Le Nouvel Observateur* (a French newsweekly): Ahmed Najim and Salah al-Maizi

## 49% Internet penetration

Morocco had the highest penetration of Internet users in North Africa, according to the International Telecommunication Union.

**An Internet leader in North Africa:**

| | |
|---|---|
| Morocco | **49%** |
| Tunisia | 36.8% |
| Egypt | 26.7% |
| Libya | 14% |
| Algeria | 12.5% |
| Mauritania | 3% |

## 7 Subjected to politicized charges

The Moroccan judiciary has frequently been used as a tool to silence the independent media. From 2009 to 2011, a number of newspapers were targeted in politicized criminal proceedings for their writings on taboo subjects such as the health of the king, the royal family, or government criticism, CPJ research shows.

**The targeted newspapers:**

2009    *Al-Jarida al-Oula, Al-Michaal, Le Journal Hebdomadaire,* and *Akhbar al-Youm*

2010    *Akhbar al-Youm, Le Journal*

2011    *Al-Massae*

## 2 Imprisoned on December 1, 2011

Nini often highlighted government corruption and criticized counterterrorism policies. The opinion piece that led to his arrest criticized Morocco's intelligence service and argued that it should be put under parliamentary oversight. In June, he was convicted and sentenced to a year in prison. Mohamed Dawas, a critical blogger, was also imprisoned in retaliation for his work. In September, he was sentenced to 19 months on trumped-up drug trafficking charges.

# 100,000
**Dirham fine for defamation**

Under Article 52 of the Press Law, journalists could face up to one year in jail and fines up to 100,000 dirhams (US$11,955) if convicted on defamation charges. Authorities have used this charge to silence independent media, CPJ research shows.

**Anti-press fines across the region:**

**Saudi Arabia**
1 million riyals (US$270,000) for any violations of the restrictive media law.

**Syria**
1 million pounds (US$21,000) for coverage that harms "national unity and national security."

**Jordan**
Under proposed legislation, 60,000 dinars (US$84,600) for reporting on corruption without "solid facts."

**Imprisoned in Morocco on CPJ's annual census:**

| | |
|---|---|
| 2007 | 0 |
| 2008 | 0 |
| 2009 | 1 |
| 2010 | 0 |
| 2011 | 2 |

# Saudi Arabia

Saudi authorities maintained a suffocating atmosphere of censorship as they further tightened the country's highly restrictive media law. In May, a royal decree amended five articles of the law, barring the publication of any material that contravenes Sharia law, impinges on state interests, promotes foreign interests, harms public order or national security, or enables criminal activity. In January, the Kingdom issued new regulations for online media that included several restrictive and vaguely worded provisions that grant the Ministry of Culture and Information sweeping powers to censor news outlets and sanction journalists. The government withdrew the accreditation of Riyadh-based Reuters correspondent Ulf Laessing in March, apparently angered by his coverage of a pro-reform protest. Reuters stood by the reporting. The same month, amid popular uprisings across the region, authorities banned three critical columnists working for the government-controlled daily *Al-Watan*. Authorities did not cite a reason, but all three had written about the region's political unrest. In late year, as demonstrations broke out in the kingdom's eastern province, authorities blocked local and international journalists from gaining access to the region. With a few exceptions, the demonstrations went uncovered.

KEY DEVELOPMENTS

» Vast repression grows more restrictive with media law amendments.

» Sensitive to unrest, government obstructs protest coverage.

KEY DATA

## 20 Minimum age

Article 5 of new online regulations issued in January requires operators of all news websites to obtain a license. Licenses are subject to several restrictive conditions: Saudi citizenship, a minimum age of 20 years, a high school degree, and "good conduct." The new regulations subject online media to the kingdom's highly repressive press law, CPJ research shows.

## 672,000 Requests to block websites

In July, the Communication and Information Technology Commission said Saudi officials and individuals had requested the government block a total of 672,000 websites in 2010. The commission characterized most as focused on pornography, gambling, and drugs, but CPJ research shows that authorities also blocked numerous human rights and news websites.

# 5th Worst nation for bloggers

CPJ has ranked Saudi Arabia among the 10 Worst Countries to Be a Blogger, based on the country's restrictive laws and the government's practice of blocking hundreds of thousands of websites.

## Global ranking on CPJ's Worst Blogging Nation survey:

1    Burma

2    Iran

3    Syria

4    Cuba

5    **Saudi Arabia**

6    Vietnam

7    Tunisia

8    China

9    Turkmenistan

10   Egypt

# 41% Internet penetration

Despite the heavy online censorship exercised by the government, Saudi Arabia has about 11.4 million Internet users, according to the International Telecommunication Union.

## Internet penetration in the Gulf region:

| UAE | 78% |
|---|---|
| Qatar | 69% |
| Bahrain | 55% |
| **Saudi Arabia** | **41%** |
| Kuwait | 38% |

# 1 million

## Fine in Saudi riyals

With the May amendments to the media law, first-time violators can face fines of 500,000 Saudi riyals (US$135,000), while second-time offenders could draw a 1 million riyal (US$270,000) fine and a potential ban on working, according to CPJ research. Syria also adopted a media law in 2011 that was portrayed as a reform but continued to impose punitive measures for critical reporting.

## Other regional measures, passed and pending:

**Syria:**
With a new law passed in August, journalists could face fines up to 1 million pounds (US$21,000) for vaguely defined violations such as coverage that harms "national unity and national security," according to CPJ research.

**Jordan:**
Under a bill passed by the lower house of parliament in September, journalists could face fines of up to 60,000 dinars (US$84,600) for publishing news about corruption "without solid facts," CPJ research shows. The proposal was pending in late year.

271

# Sudan

Sudan continued to impose extensive censorship by confiscating newspapers and shutting news outlets, and it maintained a hostile atmosphere through the frequent use of harassment and detention. Numerous press freedom violations were reported in the run-up to the January referendum that led to independence for South Sudan. On the eve of South Sudan's independence in July, the state-run National Council for Press and Publications announced the withdrawal of licenses for six newspapers partly owned by South Sudanese citizens that had run commentary critical of the Khartoum government. In September, the council ordered the suspension of another six sports-oriented publications for allegedly "inciting violence between teams." In June, authorities filed politicized criminal defamation charges against several journalists who covered the alleged rape and torture of a youth activist. After the end of the Muslim holy month of Ramadan, President Omar al-Bashir announced that he would pardon all imprisoned journalists. Jafaar al-Subki Ibrahim, a reporter for the private daily *Al-Sahafa* who had been held incommunicado and without charge since November 2010, was released after the announcement. But no formal pardon was ever issued, and four journalists were still in detention in late year. In September alone, the National Intelligence and Security Services blocked the distribution of four opposition newspapers without cause.

KEY DEVELOPMENTS

» Vast censorship practiced. Newspapers are confiscated, publishing licenses are pulled.

» Authorities charge, detain journalists to suppress human rights coverage.

KEY DATA

4 **Imprisoned on December 1, 2011**

Abdelrahman Adam Abdelrahman, Adam al-Nur Adam, and Zakaria Yacoub Eshag, all journalists with Netherlands-based Radio Dabanga, were being held on antistate charges. Dabanga is outlawed in Sudan because of its coverage of Darfur and human rights, highly sensitive topics for the government. The station uses shortwave frequencies to transmit its signal into Sudan. A fourth journalist, exiled Eritrean writer Jamal Osman Hamad, was also in custody.

**Imprisonments on CPJ's annual December 1 survey:**

| | |
|---|---|
| 2007 | 1 |
| 2008 | 0 |
| 2009 | 0 |
| 2010 | 3 |
| 2011 | 4 |

# $10,000
## Revenue lost from confiscations

*Al-Jarida*, an opposition newspaper, said it lost at least US$10,000 in revenue when its August 20, 21, and 22 editions were confiscated by authorities, according to the African Centre for Justice and Peace Studies.

## Two papers under fire:

4 **Confiscations**: *Al-Jarida* was confiscated a fourth time, in September, CPJ research shows.

5 **Seizures**: *Al-Midan*, a thrice-weekly opposition paper, was seized five times in September.

# 10 Charged for rape coverage

Charges were pending in late year against journalists who covered the alleged rape and torture of Safiya Ishag, a democracy youth activist detained after her participation in a January 30 demonstration, CPJ research shows. Some journalists faced multiple charges.

## Editors targeted:

7 Defamation complaints against *Ajras al-Huriya* Editor Abdullah Shaikh in connection with a piece headlined, "Rape ... under Sharia Law." Multiple state agencies filed duplicative claims.

6 Defamation complaints against Fayez al-Silaik, former editor of *Ajras al-Huriya*. Multiple state agencies filed duplicative claims.

# 0.86 Phone lines per 100 inhabitants

Sudan has the region's lowest rate of telecommunication access, which includes fixed telephone lines, Internet subscriptions, and Internet penetration, according to the International Telecommunication Union, or ITU. The rate illustrates the extreme difficulties journalists face in gathering and disseminating information.

## Regional ranking, from lowest, according to the ITU:

1 **Sudan**

2 Mauritania

3 Yemen

4 Iraq

5 Algeria

# 19 Newspaper confiscations

Sudanese authorities censored opposition newspapers by seizing their press runs, CPJ research shows. Seven publications were targeted, some on multiple occasions.

## Targeted newspapers:

*Al-Midan*

*Al-Jarida*

*Al-Sahafa*

*Akhbar al-Youm*

*Al-Ahdath*

*Ajras al-Huriya*

*Sawt Barout*

# Syria

The regime enforced an effective media blackout in March, banning international journalists from reporting or entering the country, and detaining local journalists who tried to cover protests seeking an end to Bashar al-Assad's rule. In a widespread campaign to silence media coverage, the government detained and assaulted journalists, expelled foreign journalists, and disabled mobile phones, landlines, electricity, and the Internet in cities where the protests broke out. The regime also extracted passwords of social media sites from journalists by using violence, and defaced social networking pages, while the pro-government online group Syrian Electronic Army hacked social media sites and posted pro-regime comments. In April, Al-Jazeera suspended its Damascus bureau after several of its journalists were harassed and received threats. Three days after the brutal assault of famed cartoonist Ali Ferzat in August, the government passed a new media law that "banned" the imprisonment of journalists and allowed for greater freedom of expression. It then followed up by jailing several journalists. In November, cameraman Ferzat Jarban was the first journalist to be killed in Syria in connection with his work since CPJ began keeping detailed records in 1992.

KEY DEVELOPMENTS

» Government imposes news blackout, censoring online reporting and hacking websites.

» Two cameramen are killed, the first journalist fatalities ever documented by CPJ in Syria.

KEY DATA

## 2 Killed in 2011

The victims were Ferzat Jarban and Basil al-Sayed, videographers who documented political unrest in highly restricted areas. Jarban was found dead in November, a day after being arrested in Al-Qasir. Al-Sayed was shot by security forces while filming in Homs in December.

### Media fatalities in the region in 2011:

| | |
|---|---|
| 5 | Iraq |
| 5 | Libya |
| 2 | Bahrain |
| 2 | Egypt |
| 2 | **Syria** |
| 2 | Yemen |
| 1 | Tunisia |

## 8 Imprisoned on December 1, 2011

The regime used mass detentions as a method to silence journalists' coverage of the revolution. CPJ identified at least eight journalists and bloggers imprisoned for their work. Due to the difficulty in obtaining information from Syria, the figure could be higher.

**Imprisoned in Syria on CPJ's annual census:**

| | |
|---|---|
| 2007 | 0 |
| 2008 | 0 |
| 2009 | 1 |
| 2010 | 2 |
| 2011 | 8 |

## 5,000 Civilians killed

The United Nations estimated about 5,000 people were killed in Syria after protests began in March. The regime responded to the civil unrest in brutal fashion, including a crackdown on media.

**Attacks against media during the uprising:**

27 Detentions

9 Expulsions

5 Interruptions of communications in the cities of Baniyas and Daraa

## 21 Age of jailed blogger

Syrian blogger Tal al-Mallohi was arrested in December 2009 at the age of 19. In February 2011, she was sentenced to five years in prison for violating Syria's state security laws. In a May 2011 report, CPJ named Syria one of the World's 10 Online Oppressors.

## 1 Million pound fine

Under a law adopted in August, journalists faced fines of up to 1 million pounds (US$21,000) for vaguely defined violations such as coverage that harms "national unity and national security," according to CPJ research. Syria was one of at least three governments that considered media laws in 2011 that were portrayed as reforms but imposed punitive measures for critical reporting.

**Other regional measures, passed and pending:**

**Saudi Arabia:**
With the May amendments to the media law, first-time violators could face fines of 500,000 Saudi riyals (US$135,000), while second-time offenders could draw a 1 million riyal (US$270,000) fine and a potential ban on working, according to CPJ research.

**Jordan:**
Under a bill passed by the lower house of parliament, journalists could face fines of up to 60,000 Jordanian dinars (US$84,600) for publishing news about corruption "without solid facts." The upper house sent the bill to committee in late year.

# Tunisia

The press enjoyed new freedom after Zine El Abidine Ben Ali was ousted in January amid widespread protests, although a photographer was killed covering the unrest. The release of veteran journalist Fahem Boukadous after several months in prison was welcome news for a press corps accustomed to continued harassment and detention during Ben Ali's 23-year reign. News media were able to report freely during parliamentary elections in October; no major press freedom violations were reported during the voting. But throughout the year journalists were still vulnerable to assault. In May, plainclothes police attacked several local and international journalists who were covering anti-government demonstrations. Licenses were issued to more than 100 new publications during the year, but some vestiges of censorship lingered. Hannibal TV, a station owned by a Ben Ali relative, was forced off the air for more than three hours in January.

KEY DEVELOPMENTS

» New government turns away from detentions, harassment.

» Press freedom surges after the fall of Ben Ali, but journalists still face attacks.

KEY DATA

## 1st Journalist killed

French photographer Lucas Mebrouk Dolega became the first journalist killed in Tunisia since 1992, when CPJ began compiling detailed records on journalist fatalities. He died from head injuries suffered while covering the January 14 protests that led to Ben Ali's ouster. As popular unrest spread, numerous journalist fatalities were reported throughout the region.

## 0 Imprisoned on December 1, 2011

Since the release of prominent journalist Boukadous on January 19, the new government has turned away from the use of detention to intimidate journalists. Under the Ben Ali regime, the government imprisoned journalists as a tool of repression, CPJ research shows.

**Tunisian journalists on CPJ's annual prison census:**

| 2007 | 2008 | 2009 | 2010 | 2011 |
|------|------|------|------|------|
| 2 | 0 | 2 | 1 | 0 |

# 26% Facebook penetration

Facebook played a pivotal role in galvanizing the public outrage that culminated in the ouster of Ben Ali. Authorities in the former regime were so concerned about the social media site that they stole the user names and passwords of independent journalists using Facebook to post news and images, CPJ research shows. With about 2.7 million users, Tunisia has the highest Facebook penetration in North Africa, based on the social media site's data and population statistics from the U.N. Population Fund.

## 1 Tunisia
**2.7 million users**
**26% of the population**

## 2 Morocco
3.9 million users
12% of the population

## 3 Egypt
8.9 million users
11% of the population

## 4 Algeria
2.7 million users
7% of the population

## 5 Libya
167,820 users
2.5% of the population

# 103 Publication licenses issued

Since January, the Ministry of Interior granted licenses to more than 100 publications, according to the German-funded Tunisia Votes, which aims to support professional journalism in Tunisia. The project was launched in collaboration with the Tunisian Center for the Freedom of Journalists.

**Breakdown by type:**

41   Weeklies

34   Monthlies

10   Dailies

7    Political party newspapers

11   Other

# 15 Journalists assaulted at May protest

On May 9, plainclothes police assaulted 15 local and international journalists and destroyed their cameras. The journalists were covering the largest anti-government demonstration since Ben Ali's ouster. The episode represented a major step backward for the new government.

**Those targeted included:**

3    Al-Jazeera journalists

1    Radio Kalima journalist

1    *La Presse* journalist

1    Associated Press journalist

# Yemen

A besieged government and its supporters retaliated fiercely against journalists covering the months of popular protests that sought an end to President Ali Abdullah Saleh's rule. Authorities detained local journalists, expelled international reporters, and confiscated newspapers in an effort to silence coverage, while government supporters and plainclothes agents assaulted media workers in the field. Two journalists covering anti-government protests were killed by gunfire, one by security forces who fired live ammunition to disperse a demonstration, the other by a sniper suspected to have been acting on behalf of the government. The government singled out Al-Jazeera in a months-long effort to silence its coverage. In March, plainclothes agents raided the station's Sana'a bureau, confiscating equipment. The raid followed the expulsion of two Al-Jazeera correspondents. Days later, authorities ordered Al-Jazeera's offices shut and its journalists stripped of accreditation. Other newsrooms were under direct fire. Armed men in civilian clothes tried to storm the offices of the independent daily *Al-Oula*, seriously wounding an editorial trainee, while military forces shelled the Yemeni satellite broadcaster Suhail TV, whose staff endured numerous other threats and detentions. In a rebuke to the regime, the 2011 Nobel Peace Prize was awarded to renowned Yemeni press freedom activist Tawakul Karman, chairwoman of Women Journalists Without Chains, along with two female African leaders.

KEY DEVELOPMENTS

» Government, allies wage violent campaign to suppress protest coverage.

» Two journalists fatally shot covering demonstrations; several newsrooms under siege.

KEY DATA

## 12,000 Newspaper copies seized

In May, security forces seized 12,000 copies of *Al-Oula*, an independent daily, and burned them at a military checkpoint. Authorities used newspaper seizures as a tactic to silence coverage of anti-government demonstrations.

**Other confiscations:**

**8,000** Copies of the independent weekly *Al-Yaqeen*

**3,000** Copies of the independent weekly *Al-Ahali*

**3,000** Copies of the independent weekly *Hadith al-Madina*

## 2 Killed in 2011

Jamal al-Sharaabi, a photojournalist for the independent weekly *Al-Masdar*, was shot by security forces dispersing demonstrations in March. Hassan al-Wadhaf, a cameraman for the Arabic Media Agency, died of injuries sustained when he was shot by a sniper at an anti-government protest in Sana'a.

## 37 Journalists assaulted

CPJ recorded numerous assaults against journalists covering anti-government demonstrations. Many journalists also saw their equipment confiscated or destroyed.

**Victims were from a variety of outlets:**

5 Al-Arabiya
5 BBC Arabic
5 Freelance
4 *Al-Oula* (local newspaper)
3 Suhail TV (local)
2 Al-Jazeera
2 *Al-Nidaa* (local independent weekly)
2 *Al-Thawra* (state-owned publication)
1 Agence France-Presse
1 Al-Alam TV (Iranian Arabic station)
1 *Al-Masdar* (local newspaper)
1 *The Guardian*
1 Qatar TV
1 *Al-Sahwa* (local news website)
1 Reuters
1 *Swiss Info*
1 European Pressphoto Agency

## 2 Imprisoned on December 1, 2011

In October, security forces arrested Abd al-Karim Thail, editor of the news website *3feb*, which focused on coverage of the country's unrest. No charges had been disclosed by late year. Abdulelah Hider Shaea, a frequent Al-Jazeera commentator and critic of the government's counterterrorist tactics, continued serving a five-year prison term on antistate charges. Antistate charges are commonly used against critical journalists worldwide.

## 8 Expelled in March

Several journalists were expelled for their coverage of the popular uprising. CPJ recorded eight expulsions between March 14 and 19, a period of particularly intense public protests:

**2 on March 13:** Reporter Patrick Symmes and photographer Marco Di Lauro, on assignment for *Outside*, a U.S.-based travel and adventure magazine

**4 on March 14:** Oliver Holmes, a contributor to *The Wall Street Journal* and *Time* magazine; Haley Sweetland Edwards, a contributor to the *Los Angeles Times*; Joshua Maricish, a photographer; and Portia Walker, a contributor to *The Washington Post*

**2 on March 19:** Al-Jazeera correspondents Ahmad Zeidan and Abdel Haq Sadah

# Middle East and North Africa Regional Data

**19**

Journalists
Killed in 2011

**144**

Journalists
In Exile 2001-11

**271**

Journalists Killed
Since 1992

**77**

Imprisoned on
December 1, 2011

**174**

Unsolved Journalist
Murders Since 1992

**5**

Missing as of
December 31, 2011

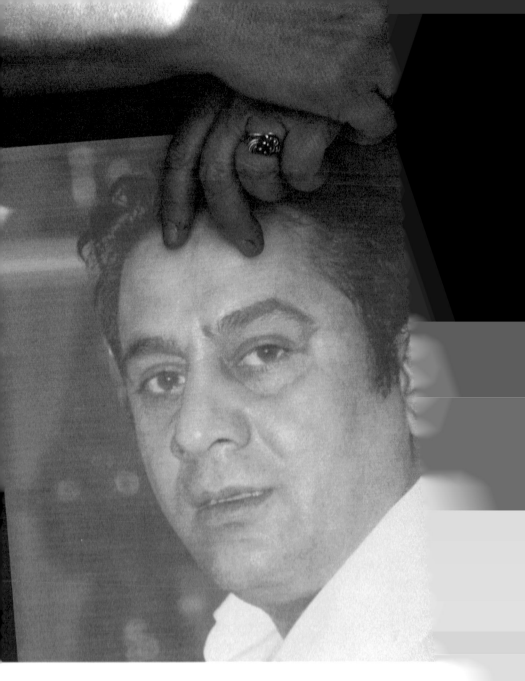

Journalists Kille

# Journalists Killed

PHOTO CREDITS

*Section break: A mourner holds a photo of slain Iraqi journalist Hadi al-Mahdi. (AFP/Ali Al Saadi)*

*Page 285: Photographer Tim Hetherington on assignment in Libya in March. Hetherington died on duty a month later. (Reuters/Finbarr O'Reilly)*

# Risks Shift as Coverage
# Of Political Unrest Proves Deadly

Pakistan remained the deadliest country for the press for a second year, while across the world coverage of political unrest proved unusually dangerous in 2011. CPJ's analysis found notable shifts from historical data: Targeted murders declined while deaths during dangerous assignments such as the coverage of street protests reached their highest level on record. Photographers and camera operators, often the most vulnerable during violent unrest, died at rates more than twice the historical average.

At least 46 journalists were killed around the world in direct relation to their work in 2011, with the seven deaths in Pakistan marking the heaviest losses in a single nation. Libya and Iraq, each with five fatalities, and Mexico, with three deaths, also ranked high worldwide for journalism-related fatalities. The global tally is consistent with the toll recorded in 2010, when 44 journalists died in connection with their work. CPJ is investigating another 35 deaths in 2011 to determine whether they were work-related.

CPJ's survey identified significant changes in the nature of journalist fatalities. Seventeen journalists died on dangerous assignments, many of them while covering the chaotic and violent confrontations between authorities and protesters during the uprisings that swept the Arab world. The victims included Hassan al-Wadhaf, a Yemeni cameraman shot by a sniper while covering anti-government protests in Sana'a, and Ahmad Mohamed Mahmoud, an Egyptian reporter gunned down while filming a protest in Cairo. "Journalists working in this environment are in no less danger than war correspondents covering an armed conflict," said Ahmed Tarek, a reporter for the Middle East News Agency who was assaulted by police while covering protests in Alexandria, Egypt. "The greatest danger journalists are facing today in post-revolution Arab countries is the targeting of journalists by political forces hostile to any-one who exposes them."

The 21 murders recorded in 2011 were the lowest total since 2002. Targeted murders—which historically account for nearly three-quarters of journalist deaths—constituted less than half of the 2011 toll. But murders were reported in both Russia and the Philippines, two countries long plagued by deadly, anti-press violence. In the southern Russian republic of Dagestan, an assassin waited outside the offices of the critical independent newspaper *Chernovik* and gunned down its founder, Gadzhimurad Kamalov. In the Philippines, CPJ documented the work-related murders of two radio commentators. One of them, Romeo Olea, was shot in the back while riding his motorcycle to work. CPJ is waging a Global Campaign Against Impunity that focuses particularly on those two countries.

Eight journalists died in combat situations in 2011, most of them during the Libyan revolution. The victims included the internationally acclaimed photojournalists Chris Hondros and Tim Hetherington, who were killed by a mortar round in the western city of Misurata, and Ali Hassan al-Jaber, a cameraman for Al-Jazeera who was shot outside Benghazi by forces loyal to Muammar Qaddafi. The Libyan conflict was "one of the truly televised revolutions," said James Foley, an American video journalist for *Global Post* who was detained there in April. "Everyone was using a camera—and a camera is much more recognizable."

Photojournalists suffered heavy losses in 2011. Photographers and camera operators constituted about 40 percent of the overall death toll, about double the proportion CPJ has documented since it began keeping detailed fatality records in 1992. Among those killed was Lucas Mebrouk Dolega, a photographer for European Pressphoto Agency who was struck by a tear gas canister fired by Tunisian security forces trying to quell a massive January protest that led to the ouster of President Zine El Abidine Ben Ali.

Nine online journalists were killed for their work during the year. Among the victims was Mexican reporter Maria Elizabeth Macías Castro, whose decapitated body was found near the city of Nuevo Laredo, along with a note saying she had been killed for reporting news on social media websites. Her murder was the first documented by CPJ worldwide that came in direct relation to journalism published on social media. The online death toll also included Mohammed al-Nabbous, founder of the website Libya Al-Hurra TV, who was killed while covering a battle in Benghazi. Al-Nabbous had been streaming live audio from the scene of the battle when his feed was suddenly interrupted by gunfire.

Internet journalists rarely appeared on CPJ's death toll before 2008. But since that time, as online journalists constitute an ever-greater proportion of the front-line reporting corps, the number of victims who worked online has increased steadily.

CPJ's analysis also found a high proportion of freelancers among the 2011 victims. One-third of the toll was composed of freelance journalists, more than twice the proportion that freelancers have constituted over time. Azerbaijani freelance reporter Rafiq Tagi died in November after being stabbed on a Baku street. He had been threatened over his critical coverage of both Islamist politics and government policies.

Anti-press violence continued at high levels in Pakistan, where 29 journalists have died in direct relation to their work in the past five years. The 2011 victims included Saleem Shahzad, a reporter for *Asia Times Online*, who was murdered after exposing links between Al-Qaeda and Pakistan's navy. Five of the seven fatalities in Pakistan were targeted murders, and all are unsolved. Long-term CPJ research shows Pakistan to be among the worst countries in the world in bringing the killers of journalists to justice. "The solution is simple and very difficult at the same time," said Pakistani reporter Umar Cheema, who was himself abducted and brutally assaulted in 2010. "The government should be taking it seriously and realize it is their duty to protect journalists. If a journalist is threatened, the culprit should be brought to justice. Even if in one case the culprits were brought to justice, that would be a clear message that the crime will not go unpunished."

The death toll in Libya, while high, was unsurprising given the armed revolt and overall level of violence. That Iraq, with five deaths, matched Libya's fatality rate illustrates the entrenched level of violence in that country. After record death tolls in the middle part of the last decade, fatalities in Iraq began dropping in 2008. But deaths have leveled out in recent

years as journalists continued to die in both targeted murders and insurgent attacks such as the March assault on a provincial government building in Tikrit that took the lives of reporters Sabah al-Bazi and Muammar Khadir Abdelwahad.

In Mexico, CPJ documented three deaths in direct relation to journalism and was investigating the killings of four other journalists. Mexican authorities appeared paralyzed in their efforts to combat pervasive anti-press violence; Congress continued to debate legislation in late year that would federalize crimes against free expression, taking the cases out of the hands of local officials who have been corrupted and cowed by criminal gangs. Mexican journalists continue to face a dark choice: Censor their own work or be at risk. Noel López Olguín, whose newspaper column "With a Lead Pen" took on drug trafficking and official corruption, was found in a clandestine grave in Veracruz state in May, two months after gunmen had abducted him.

Afghanistan and Somalia, two conflict-ridden countries with persistent levels of anti-press violence, each recorded fatalities in 2011. CPJ document-ed the deaths of two journalists and one media worker in Somalia, along with the killings of two journalists in Afghanistan. Two of the deaths, though a continent apart, bore similarities that illustrate the extreme danger of covering conflict. In Somalia, African Union troops fired on a humanitarian aid convoy, killing Malaysian cameraman Noramfaizul Mohd. The AU called the shooting accidental but released no details. In Afghanistan, a U.S. soldier shot Ahmad Omaid Khpalwak, a correspondent for Pajhwok Afghan News and the BBC, during an insurgent attack in Tarin Kot. The International Security Assistance Force in Afghanistan concluded that the soldier mistook Khpalwak's press card for a bomb trigger.

Two journalists died in Bahraini government custody. Karim Fakhrawi, a founder of the independent newspaper *Al-Wasat*, and Zakariya Rashid Hassan al-Ashiri, editor of a local news website in the village of Al-Dair, died within a week of each other in April. Although the government claimed the two died of natural causes, there were widespread allegations that abusive treatment led to their deaths. *Al-Wasat* co-founder Mansoor al-Jamri said the death of Fakhrawi was a message from the government to its critics: "This could happen to you, and no one will protect you, and no one can do anything for you."

Here are other trends and details that emerged in CPJ's analysis:

- The heaviest losses occurred in nations across the Middle East and North Africa, where CPJ documented 19 work-related fatalities in all. Thirteen work-related deaths were documented in Asia, eight in the Americas, four in Africa, and two in Europe and Central Asia.

- In two countries, Tunisia and Syria, CPJ recorded the first work-related deaths since it began compiling detailed data two decades ago. In Syria, freelance cameraman Ferzat Jarban was tortured and slain in Homs province after he had covered anti-government demonstrations. "The work of a reporter in Syria before and after the protests is much like working in a minefield," said Karim al-Afnan, a freelance journalist who was forced into exile in 2011. "The state views a journalist as a rival and their battle with journalists is one for survival."

- Five media support workers were killed worldwide. They include the Ivorian Marcel Legré, a printing press employee who was killed by supporters of Alassane Ouattara who at the time was locked in a presidential election dispute with incumbent Laurent Gbagbo. Legré's newspaper was seen as pro-Gbagbo.

- At least two journalists were reported missing during the year, both in Mexico. At least 11 journalists have been reported missing in Mexico over the past decade, by far the highest number worldwide. All are feared dead.

- Among murder victims, more than 70 percent had reported receiving threats in the weeks before they died. Long-term CPJ research shows that physical attacks are often preceded by phone or electronic threats.

- Other places with confirmed work-related fatalities were Brazil, Nigeria, Thailand, Panama, Peru, Dominican Republic, and Vietnam.

- Of the 35 deaths in which CPJ has yet to confirm a work-related motive, a large number, 20, are in the Americas. In much of the Americas, the web of crime and official corruption, combined with a lack of effective law enforcement, makes the determination of a motive exceedingly difficult.

CPJ began compiling detailed records on all journalist deaths in 1992. CPJ staff members independently investigate and verify the circumstances behind each death. CPJ considers a case work-related only when its staff is reasonably certain that a journalist was killed in direct reprisal for his or her work; in crossfire; or while carrying out a dangerous assignment.

If the motives in a killing are unclear, but it is possible that a journalist died in relation to his or her work, CPJ classifies the case as "unconfirmed" and continues to investigate. CPJ's list does not include journalists who died from illness or were killed in accidents—such as car or plane crashes—unless the crash was caused by hostile action. Other press organizations using different criteria cite higher numbers of deaths than CPJ.

*This report was compiled by CPJ staff with additional reporting by Kristin Jones and Dahlia El Zein.*

# 46 Journalists Killed: Motive Confirmed

## Afghanistan: 2

KILLED: JULY 28, 2011, IN TARIN KOT

### Ahmad Omaid Khpalwak, Pajhwok Afghan News, BBC

Khpalwak, 25, a BBC and Pajhwok Afghan News reporter, was among at least 22 people killed after gunmen and suicide bombers launched a combined attack on government buildings including the governor's office and police headquarters in Tarin Kot, capital of Uruzgan province, local and international news reports said.

The Taliban claimed responsibility for the series of explosions and subsequent gun battle with Afghan and NATO security forces, the reports said. News reports said Khpalwak was killed in crossfire after the initial bomb blasts.

Khpalwak was in the local branch office of state broadcaster Radio and Television of Afghanistan when the attack began, according to Danish Karokhel, the director of Pajhwok. Khpalwak, who had office space in the building, was filing his morning report at the time.

In a statement released on September 8, 2011, the International Security Assistance Force (ISAF) in Afghanistan said one of its soldiers had shot Khpalwak because he thought he was an armed insurgent reaching for a bomb under his vest. "He was unarmed; no weapon was found nearby. It appears all the rounds perceived as coming from him were instead fired by U.S. soldiers," the ISAF statement said. Investigators concluded troops may have mistaken a press card Khpalwak was holding up as identification for a bomb trigger.

The BBC reported that Khpalwak sent his brother two text messages shortly before his death. The first read: "I am hiding. Death has come." In the second, he wrote: "Pray for me if I die."

KILLED: SEPTEMBER 20, 2011, IN KABUL

## Farhad Taqaddosi, Press TV

Taqaddosi, a cameraman for Iran's Press TV, died in a Kabul hospital from injuries he suffered in the Taliban's September 13 attack on prominent international buildings in Kabul, the station reported.

In a well-orchestrated series of attacks, Taliban militants struck at the U.S. Embassy, NATO headquarters, and other buildings in central Kabul, news reports said. Seven civilians were killed and 15 wounded, news reports said. Taqaddosi was working at Press TV offices in central Kabul when the attack took place, the Iranian state outlet reported.

Taqaddosi was the 21st journalist to be killed in Afghanistan since the 2001 U.S. invasion, CPJ research shows. Fourteen, or two-thirds, of the fatalities were international journalists. Afghanistan is one of the few places in the world where this proportion exists, CPJ research shows. In most countries, even during times of war, local journalists are killed in far greater numbers than foreign journalists.

## Azerbaijan: 1

KILLED: NOVEMBER 23, 2011, IN BAKU

## Rafiq Tagi, freelance

Tagi, 61, a freelance reporter who contributed to the Azerbaijani service of the U.S. government-funded Radio Free Europe/Radio Liberty (RFE/RL) and a number of local news websites and newspapers, was known for his opposition to political Islam and his criticism of Azerbaijani authorities. He died in a Baku hospital, where he was being treated for stab wounds suffered in a November 19 attack.

In a November 21 interview conducted by RFE/RL at the hospital, the journalist described the attack and speculated on its motive. Tagi said he was returning to his Baku home, located near the main police headquarters, when he heard an unidentified man running behind him. The man ran up to Tagi and, without saying or taking anything, stabbed him seven times. Tagi underwent surgery for a damaged spleen.

In the interview, Tagi suggested the attack could have been related to an October article in which he criticized Iranian authorities for their theologically based policies and suppression of human rights. Tagi said Iranian clerics had issued a fatwa against him.

Tagi died in the hospital two days after giving the interview; initial reports said he had choked. A subsequent report by the Ministry of Health attributed the death to peritonitis. Colleagues found his death to be suspicious. According to local press reports and CPJ sources, Tagi was making a good recovery and his condition was considered stable at the time of his death. Doctors had checked on Tagi 10 minutes before he was found dead and found nothing of concern, the Azerbaijani division of PEN International reported. PEN said that visitors were concerned by lax security at the hospital given that Tagi had received death threats.

Tagi was imprisoned in May 2007 in connection with an article in the independent newspaper *Senet*, which asserted that Islam was hampering Azerbaijan's economic and political progress. At the time, Tagi was convicted of inciting religious hatred and sentenced to three years in prison. Tagi had received death threats from Islamists in Azerbaijan and neighboring Iran. CPJ spoke with his supporters in 2007, who expressed concern that Tagi was in danger.

A presidential spokesman said authorities were investigating the stabbing. The Iranian embassy in Azerbaijan denied official involvement in the attack, press reports said, although in a published statement the Iranian cleric Mohammed Fazel Lankarani welcomed Tagi's death as a "just sentence."

## Bahrain: 2

KILLED: APRIL 9, 2011, IN AL-DAIR

### Zakariya Rashid Hassan al-Ashiri, *Al-Dair*

Al-Ashiri, who moderated and wrote for a local news website in his home village of Al-Dair, died under mysterious circumstances while in government custody, regional and international news media reported.

Security forces had arrested al-Ashiri on April 2, charging him with disseminating false news and inciting hatred, the BBC reported. The site, named *Al-Dair* after the journalist's home village, was inaccessible inside Bahrain, local journalists said, but CPJ reviewed its contents and found no basis for the government's allegations. The arrest came amid sweeping civil unrest in Bahrain and a government crackdown on independent reporting.

Authorities claimed al-Ashiri died from complications of sickle-cell anemia, but the journalist's family told reporters that he did not suffer from that illness or any other ailment, news reports said.

Al-Ashiri was the first Bahraini journalist to die in direct relation to his work since CPJ started compiling detailed death records in 1992.

KILLED: APRIL 12, 2011, IN MANAMA

## Karim Fakhrawi, *Al-Wasat*

Fakhrawi, founder and board member of *Al-Wasat*, the country's premier independent daily, died in state custody a week after he was detained, according to news reports. Human rights defenders told CPJ that Fakhrawi had gone to a police station on April 5 to complain that authorities were about to bulldoze his house.

Bahrain's official news agency said on Twitter that Fakhrawi died of kidney failure. Photographs published online, however, showed a body identified as that of Fakhrawi with extensive cuts and bruises.

The journalist's arrest came amid sweeping civil unrest in Bahrain and a government crackdown on independent reporting. In early April, the government accused *Al-Wasat* of "deliberate news fabrication and falsification," said it would file criminal charges against three of the paper's senior editors, and deported two of its senior staffers.

Fakhrawi was one of numerous investors in *Al-Wasat*, local journalists told CPJ. He was also a book publisher, the owner of one of Bahrain's biggest bookstores, and a member of Al-Wefaq, Bahrain's chief opposition party.

Fakhrawi's death was the second media fatality in Bahrain in less than a week, both occurring in government detention facilities. In the two decades prior to that, no journalists had died in relation to their work in Bahrain, CPJ research shows.

## Brazil: 2

KILLED: JUNE 15, 2011, IN SERRA DO MEL

## Edinaldo Filgueira, *Jornal o Serrano*

Filgueira, 36, was shot six times by three unidentified men on a motorcycle as he left his office on the evening of June 15, local journalists said. He was founder and director of the local newspaper *Jornal o Serrano* and regional director of the ruling Workers' Party. He died at the scene.

On July 2, police arrested five suspects who they said belonged to a gang of contract killers. Police also seized several weapons and large quantities of ammunition in the arrests.

According to local press reports, Filgueira had received death threats after he published a poll criticizing the performance of the local government. Federal police chief Marcelo Mosele told CPJ that investigators were focusing on Filgueira's journalistic work as the motive for the crime.

KILLED: NOVEMBER 6, 2011, IN RIO DE JANEIRO

## Gelson Domingos da Silva, Bandeirantes

Domingos, 46, was shot and killed during a confrontation between state police and suspected drug traffickers in Rio de Janeiro, according to press reports. Domingos was a veteran cameraman for the national television network Bandeirantes.

Domingos had accompanied police on an early-morning raid at the favela, or shantytown, known as Antares, news reports said. Footage from Domingos' camera showed he was struck amid an intense exchange of fire between police and the suspects. Officials said the cameraman was struck by a shot to the chest fired from a high-powered assault rifle. Domingos was wearing a bullet-resistant vest, but it was not strong enough to withstand the blast, news reports said.

Four suspects were killed and nine arrested in the raid, which also netted weapons, drugs, and money, press reports said. No police fatalities were reported. Officials said they were trying to identify the individual who shot Domingos.

## Dominican Republic: 1

KILLED: AUGUST 2, 2011, NEAR LA ROMANA

## José Agustín Silvestre de los Santos, La Voz de la Verdad, Caña TV

The body of Silvestre, a magazine director and television host, was found on a highway outside La Romana with gunshot wounds to the head, neck, and abdomen. Silvestre, 59, had been seized by four men outside a La Romana hotel about an hour earlier, at 8 a.m., and forced into a Jeep, according to press reports.

On August 9 and 10, the attorney general's office and national police announced they had arrested five men who they said were involved in planning or carrying out the attack. Police seized several weapons, dozens of ammunition rounds, and 118,000 pesos (US$3,070). One suspect allegedly told investigators that the assailants had planned to abduct Silvestre and take him to the capital, Santo Domingo, but shot him when the journalist resisted. All five suspects were detained, as was a sixth man who was arrested later, press reports said.

Police alleged the attack was ordered by Matías Avelino Castro, also known as Joaquín Espinal Almeyda, a hotel owner and reputed drug trafficker. Authorities said they traced Avelino Castro's alleged involvement through a rental car that was used in the attack and leased through the suspect's girlfriend. The attorney general's office accused Avelino Castro of ordering the attack in retaliation for an article in the July issue of Silvestre's magazine, *La Voz de la Verdad* (Voice of the Truth). The story said a man named "Daniel," an alias used by the suspect, had been implicated in the recent murder of a local businessman and his driver, authorities said.

Silvestre, who hosted a Caña TV program of the same name as his magazine, had accused political figures and a priest of having involvement in drug trafficking and money laundering, press reports said. In May, a local prosecutor had filed a defamation complaint against Silvestre in connection with a television report that accused the official of having ties to drug traffickers. The journalist was jailed for several days until posting bail, according to news reports. The case was pending at the time of the murder, according to Elpidio Tolentino, a local official with the press group Colegio Dominicano de Periodistas, or CDP. Silvestre had told CDP that he had been followed by two cars that tried to intercept him on July 23.

In an August 9 press conference, prosecutor Frank Soto said witnesses had accused Silvestre of accepting money from drug traffickers on occasion for not publishing incriminating information or for running stories harmful to rivals, local press reports said. Tolentino said CDP challenged authorities to "more thoroughly investigate and to present any evidence they have supporting this claim. ... If this is true they must fully investigate it. If not, they must clean his reputation."

# Egypt: 2

KILLED: FEBRUARY 4, 2011, IN CAIRO

## Ahmad Mohamed Mahmoud, *Al-Ta'awun*

Mahmoud, a reporter for the newspaper *Al-Ta'awun*, was shot on January 29 as anti-government protests in Cairo turned violent. His wife, Inas Abdel-Alim, told Al-Jazeera that her husband had stepped on to his office balcony to record video of a confrontation between security forces and demonstrators on the street when security forces spotted him.

Abdel-Alim said that several witnesses told her a uniformed police captain yelled at Mahmoud to stop filming, but a sniper shot him in the head before he could react. "They meant to kill him. They aimed at his head with live ammunition," Abdel-Alim said on Al-Jazeera. "The perpetrator did this to him because he was filming what was happening. They didn't want us to cover the massacre that happened that day."

Mahmoud died after six days in a hospital in Cairo. His death was the first reported media fatality during the Egyptian uprising that started on January 25.

KILLED: OCTOBER 9, 2011, IN CAIRO

## Wael Mikhael, Al-Tareeq

Mikhael, an Egyptian cameraman for the Coptic television broadcaster Al-Tareeq, was shot while filming violent clashes between Coptic Christian protesters and the military in front of the headquarters of the Television and Radio Union, commonly referred to as Maspero, according to the broadcaster and other news reports.

Mikhael was shot in the head, the station said. The source of fire was not immediately clear, although news accounts reported that military forces had fired on protesters during the demonstrations. The cameraman was one of at least 25 people killed in the clashes, during which hundreds of others were injured, local and international news outlets reported. Mikhael is survived by a wife and three children.

# Iraq: 5

KILLED: FEBRUARY 24, 2011, IN RAMADI

## Mohamed al-Hamdani, Al-Itijah

Al-Hamdani, a correspondent for Al-Itijah satellite television in Al-Anbar province, was covering a religious celebration in a cultural center in Ramadi when a suicide bomber detonated explosives, news reports said. Ahmad Abd al-Salam, a correspondent for Al-Aan satellite TV station, and Ahmad al-Hayti, a radio reporter for Iraq Hurr, were injured in the attack, according to news reports.

Al-Hayti told his station that the celebration included a gathering of poets and writers reciting their work and had no security. Fourteen people were killed and 23 injured in the attack, according to news reports.

KILLED: MARCH 29, 2011, IN TIKRIT

# Muammar Khadir Abdelwahad, Al-Ayn

# Sabah al-Bazi, Al-Arabiya

Abdelwahad, 39, a correspondent for Al-Ayn news agency, and al-Bazi, 30, a correspondent for Al-Arabiya and contributor to Reuters and CNN, were killed when gunmen wearing military uniforms seized control of a provincial government building in Tikrit, capital of Saleheddin province.

The journalists were covering a provincial council meeting when the assailants—using car bombs, explosive vests, and grenades—mounted an assault on the government building in Tikrit, local and international news reported. At least 58 people were killed and nearly 100 were injured during the hours-long siege, according to news reports. Security forces regained control of the building after a fierce shootout, news reports said.

KILLED: JUNE 21, 2011, IN DIWANIYYA

# Alwan al-Ghorabi, Afaq

Al-Ghorabi, a cameraman for the Afaq satellite channel, died when a car bomb exploded in the city center, according to news reports. He was on assignment with numerous other journalists at the southern entrance of a Diwaniyya government compound when the bomb went off, local news reports said.

The journalists were about to accompany the provincial governor on a tour of a public works project, news reports said. More than 20 people were reported dead in the attack. No group immediately claimed responsibility.

Al-Ghorabi had worked for two years for Afaq, which was owned by Prime Minister Nouri al-Maliki's Dawa Party. He is survived by a wife and four children.

KILLED: SEPTEMBER 8, 2011, IN BAGHDAD

# Hadi al-Mahdi, freelance

Al-Mahdi, 45, a journalist, filmmaker, and playwright, was shot in his Baghdad home by assailants using pistols outfitted with silencers.

Al-Mahdi had hosted a thrice-weekly radio show, "To Whomever Listens," on independent Radio Demozy. The show covered social and political issues, including government corruption, bribery, and sectarianism. A Shiite, al-Mahdi had defended the rights of Sunnis.

On his Facebook page, al-Mahdi organized regular pro-democracy demonstrations and publicized threats he said he had received. Growing fearful for his safety, al-Mahdi had stepped down from the radio show about two months prior to his death, news reports said. Al-Mahdi had spent 18 years in exile, returning to Iraq in 2008. He is survived by his wife and three children.

## Ivory Coast: 1

KILLED: MAY 8, 2011, IN ABIDJAN

### Sylvain Gagnetau Lago, Radio Yopougon

The bullet-riddled body of Lago, 30, assistant editor-in-chief of Radio Yopougon, a community station, was found in a mass grave in Yopougon, the largest neighborhood in Abidjan and a stronghold of former president Laurent Gbagbo, according to the Ivorian Committee for the Protection of Journalists and CPJ sources.

Yopougon was a battleground between Gbagbo fighters and the Republican Forces of the Ivory Coast that had allied with presidential rival Alassane Ouattara during a five-month struggle for power following the disputed November 2010 election. The Republican Forces (known by the French acronym FRCI) ransacked Lago's station after seizing Yopougon in May, a month after ousting Gbagbo with the backing of French forces, the Ivorian journalist group said. Radio Yopougon was known for backing Gbagbo.

FRCI fighters publicly executed Lago and four other people accused of being Gbagbo militiamen on May 8, according to two eyewitnesses to the killing who spoke to CPJ on condition of anonymity for fear of reprisal. About 35 FRCI fighters aboard 4-by-4 trucks raided Lago's home that day and forced him and five other men to kneel on the street at gunpoint under interrogation, according to the witnesses whose accounts were broadly corroborated by local journalists. The fifth man managed to escape, but the fighters opened fire on Lago and four others before driving away, the witnesses said. When the fighters returned later to find the journalist still alive, they killed him, the witnesses said.

Local journalists told CPJ that Lago was known for his moderation. He had worked for both pro-Ouattara and pro-Gbagbo media outlets. A father of two, he was the secretary-general of the Organization of Professional Journalists of Ivory Coast.

CPJ has concluded that FRCI forces targeted Lago because of his public profile as a journalist with a media outlet whose management was favorable to Gbagbo. The Ouattara government made no arrests in the murder.

## Libya: 5

KILLED: MARCH 13, 2011, NEAR BENGHAZI

## Ali Hassan al-Jaber, Al-Jazeera

Cameraman al-Jaber was killed during the armed conflict between Libyan rebels and forces loyal to leader Muammar Qaddafi. He was shot during an ambush near the eastern city of Benghazi.

Al-Jaber was returning from covering an anti-Qaddafi demonstration in Suluq, southwest of Benghazi, when unidentified gunmen opened fire on a car carrying an Al-Jazeera crew, colleague Bayba Wald Amhadi reported. Al-Jaber, who was shot three times, was the first reported media casualty in the Libyan conflict. Al-Jazeera reporter Naser al-Hadar was injured during the attack.

Al-Jazeera reported that the bullets used in the attack, disintegrating frangible bullets, were the type of ammunition used by pro-Qaddafi forces.

Al-Jaber, 55, held a master's degree in cinematography from the Academy of Arts in Cairo, according to Al-Jazeera. He worked for Qatar Television for more than 20 years, as head of the film department. He was previously the director of the Qatar bureau of CNBC Arabiya, an Arabic-language financial and business information channel.

KILLED: MARCH 19, 2011, IN BENGHAZI

## Mohammed al-Nabbous, Libya Al-Hurra TV

An unknown gunman shot al-Nabbous, founder of the online opposition outlet Libya Al-Hurra TV, while he was covering a battle in Benghazi, according to news reports. He was the second journalist to be killed during the armed conflict between Libyan rebels and forces loyal to leader Muammar Qaddafi.

Al-Nabbous, 28, was streaming live audio from the scene of the battle when his feed was suddenly interrupted. Described as the face of citizen journalism in Libya, al-Nabbous established Libya Al-Hurra

TV to stream live feeds online and post commentary concerning the popular uprising. Al-Nabbous' broadcasts started on February 19, one month before he was killed.

## Anton Hammerl, freelance

Hammerl, a 41-year-old photographer of South African and Austrian descent, was shot and killed by government forces near Brega in eastern Libya on April 5. Three journalists traveling with him were detained by Libyan authorities until May 18 and announced Hammerl's death after they were released.

Hammerl, a married father of three, traveled to eastern Libya to cover the conflict as a freelancer. He was working on the front lines near Brega with three other foreign journalists—Clare Gillis, James Foley, and Manuel Varela (also known as Manu Brabo)—when they came under fire from government forces. Hammerl was shot in the abdomen, and Gillis, Foley, and Brabo were captured.

Gillis told *The Atlantic* magazine, "They took away our stuff, tied us up, threw us in the back of the truck. And we all looked down at Anton. ... I saw him not moving and in a pool of blood. Jim tried to talk to him—'Are you OK?'—and he didn't answer anymore."

For more than six weeks, the government alternately claimed that Hammerl was safe in custody or that he was not in government hands. Sources reported that the Libyan government had been in possession of Hammerl's passport, and thus was aware of his identity and his fate.

Under international humanitarian law applicable in the armed conflict in Libya, parties to a conflict have obligations regarding the missing and dead. Libya was obliged to take all feasible measures to account for persons reported missing as a result of fighting and provide family members with any information it had. Hammerl's family had repeatedly sought information about his whereabouts.

The Libyan government held Gillis, Foley, and Brabo until mid-May, when they were released in Tripoli, the capital. They traveled to Tunisia the following day, where they informed Hammerl's family of his death. International efforts were ultimately successful in gaining the release of the detained journalists, but the South African government appeared to have played no part. When South African

President Jacob Zuma visited Tripoli on April 10 and 11, he failed to bring up Hammerl's case, according to media reports.

The South African government reacted to the news of Hammerl's death by accusing the Libyan authorities of misinformation. "We kept getting reassured at the highest level that he was alive until his colleagues were released and shared the information," said Maite Nkoana-Mashabane, South Africa's international relations and cooperation minister.

Hammerl also held Austrian citizenship, and the Austrian government similarly criticized the Qaddafi regime. "We are very disappointed at the Libyan side that they had not conveyed the news," said Otto Ditz, Austria's ambassador to South Africa.

KILLED: APRIL 20, 2011, IN MISURATA

## Tim Hetherington, freelance

## Chris Hondros, Getty Images

Hetherington and Hondros, acclaimed international photographers who had worked in conflict zones all around the world, died in an explosion in the western city of Misurata. The *Los Angeles Times*, reporting from Misurata, a city that saw intense fighting between rebel and government forces, said the journalists had been working near the front lines of local militia. The blast was believed to have been caused by a mortar round, according to the *Times*, which cited doctors and colleagues.

Hetherington's death was reported soon after the explosion. Hondros was taken to a local medical center after suffering grave wounds. Getty Images, for which Hondros was working, disclosed his death in a message to CPJ late that day. Two other photographers were injured in the blast. News reports identified them as Guy Martin, a Briton working for the Panos photo agency, and Michael Brown, who was working for Corbis.

Hetherington, 40, a Briton, and U.S. journalist Sebastian Junger co-directed the 2010 Academy Award-nominated film "Restrepo," which documented the year they had embedded with the U.S. military in Afghanistan. Born in 1970, according to his online biography, Hetherington had won numerous awards, including a 2009 Alfred I. duPont Award for broadcast journalism.

Hondros, 41, an American, was a 2004 Pulitzer Prize finalist for his coverage of the unrest in Liberia. He had also worked in hot spots such as Kosovo, Sierra Leone, and Afghanistan, winning the Overseas

Press Club's Robert Capa Gold Medal in 2006 for his work in Iraq. His work appeared on the front page of the *Los Angeles Times* on the day of his death.

## Mexico: 3

KILLED: MARCH 2011, IN CHINAMECA

### Noel López Olguín, freelance

López, a columnist for the newspaper *La Verdad de Jáltipan* in the state of Veracruz, was kidnapped on March 8 by gunmen in two SUVs, local authorities told CPJ. On May 31, his body was found buried in a clandestine grave in the city of Chinameca, according to local news reports.

The discovery was made after the Mexican army arrested a reputed gang leader who gave a statement confessing to the killing, news reports said. According to a local investigator cited by The Associated Press, the journalist died from a blow to the head.

Family members told CPJ that López had a long career working as a columnist for *La Verdad de Jáltipan*, and also as a stringer and photographer for several papers in the state of Veracruz, including the weeklies *Noticias de Acayucan*, *El Horizonte*, and *Noticias de Veracruz*.

López wrote a column titled "Con pluma de plomo" (With a Lead Pen) in which he frequently and aggressively reported on local drug trafficking and official corruption, according to press reports. López identified drug kingpins by name, a practice that is generally off-limits in areas of Mexico where organized crime is prevalent.

Two weeks before he was seized, two *La Verdad de Jáltipan* executives were held captive for several hours, according to local press reports. Journalists in Jáltipan and the nearby town of Acayucan later limited their crime coverage, sources told CPJ.

Out of fear of reprisal, some media outlets distanced themselves from López after he was kidnapped, denying to CPJ that he'd ever worked for them or saying he'd only occasionally contributed a long time ago. But the head of the state Commission for the Defense of Journalists, Gerardo Perdomo, said López wrote regular stories and columns that sharply criticized local corruption.

KILLED: MARCH 25, 2011, IN MONTERREY

### Luis Emanuel Ruiz Carrillo, *La Prensa*

Ruiz, 21, a photographer with Monclova-based daily *La Prensa*, was found fatally shot in Monterrey, Nueva León state, early the morning of March 25, according to CPJ interviews and news accounts.

Ruiz had been abducted the previous night along with José Luis Cerda Meléndez, a Televisa-Monterrey entertainment show host, as the two were leaving the station's studios in a vehicle driven by Cerda's cousin, Juan Gómez Meléndez. According to press reports, unidentified armed men forced the three out of the vehicle and into a van.

Ruiz, Cerda, and Gómez were found with gunshot wounds to the head, local news reports said. Press reports said a graffiti message referencing a major drug cartel was found on a wall near Cerda's body. "Stop cooperating with the Zetas," it said. (In a strange twist, an armed individual seized Cerda's body in the midst of the police crime scene investigation and moved it to another location, the Spanish news agency EFE reported.)

Ruiz had traveled to Monterrey for a piece on Cerda, a one-time drug addict and street thug who had become a popular TV personality, *La Prensa*'s editorial director, Jesús Medina, told CPJ. "Luis was an incidental victim," he said.

Ruiz, who had just eight months on the job, was still in college and had won a state journalism award last year, Medina told CPJ. "There was so much ahead for him," he said. "He had a personal quality and a professional quality that made him stand out."

KILLED: SEPTEMBER 24, 2011, NEAR NUEVO LAREDO

## Maria Elizabeth Macías Castro, freelance

Macías' decapitated body was found on a road near the city of Nuevo Laredo, news reports said. A note found with the journalist's body said she had been killed for writing on social media websites and attributed the murder to a criminal group, news reports said. Her murder was the first ever documented by CPJ worldwide that was in direct relation to journalism published on social media.

Sources told CPJ that Macías, 39, reported the activities of criminal groups on Twitter and on the website Nuevo Laredo en vivo (Nuevo Laredo Live) under the pseudonym "La NenaDLaredo" (The girl from Laredo). The note found with her body identified the website and the pseudonym; headphones and a keyboard were placed next to her head. It was not immediately clear whether a particular story or Macías' uncensored reporting in general angered the killers. It was also unclear how the killers discovered her identity.

In northern Mexico, as in other parts of the country, organized crime groups have terrorized the local press into silence, leading citizens to begin reporting criminal activities on websites and social media, either anonymously or using pennames. Professional journalists told CPJ that they, too, reported stories under pseudonyms on social media websites that they couldn't cover under their own names through their traditional outlets. Facebook, Twitter, and other such websites were filling the void in covering crime and drug violence, CPJ research showed.

Sources told CPJ that Macías had reporting and administrative responsibilities for the local daily *Primera Hora*, although the newspaper would not confirm her employment status.

Mexican criminal groups began targeting social media users in 2011. On September 13, the bodies of two young people, who were not identified, were hung from a pedestrian overpass in Nuevo Laredo. Press accounts said notes left with the bodies warned against writing on websites.

## Nigeria: 1

KILLED: OCTOBER 22, 2011, IN MAIDUGURI

### Zakariya Isa, Nigeria Television Authority

Boko Haram, a militant Islamist group that seeks the imposition of Shariah law in the predominantly Muslim states of northern Nigeria, claimed responsibility for the murder of Isa, 41, a reporter and cameraman for the state-run Nigeria Television Authority, or NTA, in the northeastern state of Borno, according to local journalists and news reports.

About a month before the killing, Boko Haram had issued a statement saying it would attack media organizations for what it described as misrepresentations of its activities, according to press reports. Journalists told CPJ that Boko Haram perceived cameramen and photographers, particularly those working for state media, as potential spies.

In an emailed statement issued after the killing, Boko Haram spokesman Abul Qaqa said the militants killed Isa "because he was spying on us for Nigerian security authorities," according to Agence France-Presse. Local journalists and Nigerian authorities said the assertion was untrue, AFP reported.

# Pakistan: 7

## Wali Khan Babar, Geo TV

Babar, 28, was shot shortly after his story on gang violence aired on the country's most widely watched broadcaster, Geo TV. At least two assailants intercepted the journalist's car at 9:20 p.m. in Karachi's Liaquatabad area, shooting him four times in the head and once in the neck, Geo TV Managing Director Azhar Abbas told CPJ. Witnesses said one assailant spoke to Babar briefly before opening fire, Abbas said.

In April, police announced the arrests of five people and said additional suspects, including the mastermind, were still at large. Police said their initial investigations showed that Babar was killed for his reporting, news accounts said. Home Minister Rehman Malik said operatives of Muttahida Qaumi Movement, or MQM, were responsible for the killing, according to Abbas.

The MQM is Pakistan's third largest political party and considered its most influential secular political organization. Pakistani media reported that four witnesses to the killing had been shot and killed, as well as the brother of the police officer who was leading the investigation.

## Nasrullah Khan Afridi, Pakistan Television and *Mashreq*

Afridi, a reporter for Pakistan Television and the local *Mashreq* newspaper, was killed when his car blew up in the city of Peshawar, according to local and international news reports. An explosive device was detonated remotely shortly after he returned to the vehicle, which was parked in a densely populated shopping area, news reports said.

In a statement, the Pakistan Federal Union of Journalists (PFUJ) said Afridi, who was also the president of the Tribal Union of Journalists, was in Peshawar fleeing threats from militant groups. Mian Iftikhar Hussain, the information minister of Khyber Pakhtunkhwa province, called the death a targeted killing, according to PFUJ and Agence France-Presse, but he did not provide details. Khyber Pakhtunkhwa was formerly known as the North West Frontier Province.

Police said a warlord, Mangal Bagh, had threatened Afridi in Khyber,

AFP reported. In May 2006, CPJ reported that unidentified assailants had lobbed two hand grenades at Afridi's house in Bara, the main town of Khyber Agency in the Federally Administered Tribal Areas near the border with Afghanistan. Afridi had been the target of a death threat issued on a pirate radio station run by the Islamic militant organization Lashkar-e-Islam. The threat came after Afridi reported that authorities suspected Lashkar-e-Islam of being responsible for an attack in which a paramilitary soldier was injured. The journalist moved to Pakistan's capital, Islamabad, after the attack. He complained that local officials failed to provide security despite repeated requests. He subsequently moved to the wealthy Hayatabad township of Peshawar, where security was considered to be higher. But in mid-2007, grenades were lobbed at his Hayatabad home. No one was injured in the attack.

Afridi was popular, a senior figure in the tightly knit journalist community in the dangerous areas along the Afghan border. Hundreds of people, including colleagues, political leaders, and tribal elders, attended his memorial service. No arrests were made in the case.

KILLED: MAY 29 OR 30, 2011, IN MANDI BAHAUDDIN

## Saleem Shahzad, *Asia Times Online*

Shahzad, 40, vanished on May 29, after writing about alleged links between Al-Qaeda and Pakistan's navy. His body was found on May 31 near the town of Mandi Bahauddin, about 75 miles (120 kilometers) south of the capital, Islamabad. His friends said the body showed signs of torture around the face and neck. He had told colleagues that he had been receiving threats from intelligence officials in recent months.

Shahzad was reported missing after he failed to show up for a televised panel discussion in Islamabad. He was scheduled to discuss his recent article for *Asia Times Online* in which he reported that Al-Qaeda, having infiltrated the Pakistani navy, was behind a 17-hour siege at a naval base in Karachi on May 22. He said the attack came after authorities refused to release a group of naval officials suspected of being linked to militant groups. The attack, coming soon after the U.S. killing of Osama bin Laden on May 2, was deeply embarrassing to the Pakistani military. Earlier in May, three navy buses carrying recruits had been blown up via remote control devices in Karachi, the large port city where the navy is headquartered.

Shahzad's death also came a few days after the release of his book, *Inside the Taliban and Al-Qaeda*.

For months, the journalist had been telling friends that he had been warned by intelligence agents to stop reporting on sensitive security matters. In October 2010, Shahzad told Ali Dayan Hasan, a researcher for Human Rights Watch in Pakistan, that he had been threatened by a top official at a meeting at the headquarters of the Inter Services Intelligence Directorate in Rawalpindi.

Hasan said Shahzad sent him a note describing the meeting "in case something happens to me or my family in the future," Human Rights Watch reported. Hameed Haroon, president of the All Pakistan Newspapers Society and a former employer of Shahzad, said he had received a similar message at about the same time.

Shahzad was known for his courage and tenacity in reporting. He had started out as a beat reporter in the notoriously violent city of Karachi in the 1990s, but soon worked his way up to covering political, military, and security issues.

KILLED: JUNE 11, 2011, IN PESHAWAR

## Asfandyar Khan, *Akhbar-e-Khyber*

Khan, a reporter for the newspaper *Akhbar-e-Khyber*, died in a double bombing that took the lives of more than three dozen people. The first, small blast went off at a market, drawing a large crowd, including journalists such as Khan who were covering the story. A second, larger explosion, apparently a suicide bomb, went off after a crowd had grown.

Shafiullah Khan, 28, a trainee reporter at the daily *The News*, died six days later from extensive burn injuries suffered in the attack. Seven other journalists suffered minor injuries.

The attack took place near the city center, in an area where military facilities are concentrated and where many major Pakistani media organizations have their offices. Peshawar is the administrative center for the Federally Administered Tribal Areas and runs along the border with Afghanistan. With many insurgent groups based there, the city is notorious for its lack of security.

No group claimed responsibility for the bombings, and it was not clear if journalists or military personnel were the targets. Yousaf Ali, general secretary of the Khyber Union of Journalists, said Khan was in his early 30s and was survived by a sister.

Journalist Nasrullah Khan Afridi died in May 2011 when his car blew up in the same market. An explosive device was detonated remotely after he returned to his vehicle, which was parked in the densely populated shopping area.

KILLED: JUNE 17, 2011, IN WAH CANTONMENT

## Shafiullah Khan, *The News*

Khan, 28, a trainee reporter at the daily *The News*, died six days after suffering extensive burns in a June 11 double bombing in Peshawar that took the lives of more than three dozen people. The first, small blast went off at a market, drawing a large crowd, including journalists such as Khan who were covering the story. A second, larger explosion, apparently a suicide bomb, went off after a crowd had grown.

Khan, who also suffered shrapnel wounds to his right shoulder, died in a burn treatment center in Wah Cantonment, a military center near Rawalpindi, according to the Pakistan Press Foundation, a media support group.

Asfandyar Khan, a reporter for the newspaper *Akhbar-e-Khyber*, also died in the attack. Seven other journalists suffered minor injuries. The attack took place near the city center, in an area where military facilities are concentrated and where many major Pakistani media organizations have their offices. No group claimed responsibility for the bombings, and it was not clear if journalists or military personnel were the targets.

KILLED: OCTOBER 7, 2011, IN LAHORE

## Faisal Qureshi, *The London Post*

The body of Qureshi, 28, an editor for the political news website *The London Post*, was discovered at about 2 a.m. by his brother, Zahid, after family members found bloodstains outside the journalist's house, the Pakistani daily *The Express Tribune* reported. Police reports described Qureshi's body as showing signs of torture, with his throat slit, *The Express Tribune* said.

Another brother, Shahid, who lives in London, told CPJ that the killers had taken the journalist's laptop and telephone. Shahid Qureshi, who also wrote for *The London Post* website, told CPJ that he and his brother had received death threats from men who claimed they were from the Muttahida Qaumi Movement political party, or MQM. *The London Post* had run a series of stories on MQM leader Altan Hussain, describing his alleged flight to South Africa from England, where he was living in self-imposed exile.

The website was widely recognized as anti-MQM. MQM is Pakistan's third largest political party, and is considered the country's largest secular political party, with Karachi and the Sindh region as its power base.

## Javed Naseer Rind, *Daily Tawar*

Rind's body was found in Khuzdar on November 5, nearly two months after he had been abducted, according to news reports. The journalist had been shot multiple times in the head and chest, and his body showed numerous signs of torture, local news media reported. The killing appeared to have occurred shortly before the discovery.

An editor and columnist with the Urdu-language daily *Daily Tawar*, Rind had been kidnapped in his hometown of Hub in southern Baluchistan province on September 11. The *Daily Tawar* was known for its coverage of the many conflicts between rival groups and the government. Rind was also an active member of the separatist Baluch National Movement, news reports said.

The Baluchistan Union of Journalists condemned Rind's kidnapping and murder and demanded that the government put together a high-level committee to probe the attack. No group claimed responsibility for the killing.

## Panama: 1

## Darío Fernández Jaén, Radio Mi Favorita

Fernández, 62, was walking home with his son when an unidentified assailant approached and shot him twice, according to local news reports. He died at a local hospital. A politician with the Revolutionary Democratic Party and a former governor, Fernandez owned Radio Mi Favorita in the central province of Coclé.

Police were looking into reports that Fernández had received recent threats concerning the station's coverage of alleged irregularities in the allocation of local land titles, according to local news accounts. The station also reported allegations that officials had provided land to corporations close to the government.

A local government worker was arrested in November and charged with carrying out Fernández's murder. No evidence was immediately disclosed. A lawyer for the defendant said surveillance footage showed his client buying beer at a supermarket in Panama City, roughly two hours from Coclé, at the time of the shooting, news reports said.

# Peru: 1

KILLED: SEPTEMBER 8, 2011, IN CHIMBOTE

## Pedro Alfonso Flores Silva, Channel 6

Peruvian TV journalist Flores, 36, was riding home on his motorcycle on the Panamericana Norte Highway in the northwestern province of Casma when a hooded gunman in the back of a taxi shot him in the abdomen, local press reports said. The journalist managed to ride his motorcycle to a local hospital and was then transported to a hospital in Chimbote where he died.

Flores ran and hosted the Casma-based Channel 6 news program "Visión Agraria." His wife, Mercedes Cueva Abanto, told reporters that he had received anonymous death threats via text message for several months prior to his murder and that someone had vandalized his motorcycle. She said the threats apparently stemmed from corruption accusations Flores had made against Marco Rivero Huertas, mayor of Comandante Noel district. In an interview with Radio Santo Domingo, Isabel Flores, the journalist's sister, said her brother told her in the hospital before his death that he believed the mayor had ordered the killing.

Rivero told reporters he had once sued Flores for defamation but did not elaborate on the circumstances. He said he had nothing to do with the journalist's murder and that he was in "solidarity with the victim and his family," press reports said. Police arrested two suspects in the killing in September 2011, according to press reports.

# Philippines: 2

KILLED: JANUARY 24, 2011, IN PUERTO PRINCESA CITY

## Gerardo Ortega, DWAR

A gunman shot radio talk show host Ortega in the back of the head as the journalist was shopping in a Puerto Princesa City clothing store shortly after his morning broadcast, according to local and international news reports.

Police arrested a suspect near the scene with the help of witnesses, reports said. The suspect—named in local news reports as Marlon de Camata, but also known as Marvin Alcaraz—initially told police that the killing was robbery-related but later said that he and another man, Dennis Aranas, had a contract to kill Ortega for 150,000 pesos (US$3,370).

Police said they traced the murder weapon to a man named Romeo Seratubias, a former employee of a provincial governor who Ortega had accused of corruption, according to local news reports. Seratubias denied involvement in the shooting and said he had sold the gun, news reports said.

On January 26, Puerto Princesa City police filed charges against de Camata, Aranas, and Seratubias, along with two others accused of helping to prepare for the attack, according to the *Philippine Daily Inquirer.*

Ortega, 47, had received recent death threats from an unknown source, according to The Associated Press. The journalist had criticized local officials accused of corruption and had opposed provincial mining projects, news reports said.

KILLED: JUNE 13, 2011, IN IRIGA CITY

## Romeo Olea, DWEB

Olea, a radio commentator, was shot twice in the back while riding his motorcycle to work, according to news reports that quoted police sources.

Senior Police Superintendent Victor Deona told Agence France-Presse that the killing appeared to be work-related. Olea's wife, Raquel, said he had received recent death threats, AFP reported. She later told the *Philippine Daily Inquirer* that she had asked her husband to back away from the harsh commentaries featured on his daily show. "But he told me that if he stopped doing exposés, nobody else will do the job," she told the *Inquirer.*

Colleagues and supporters of Olea and Miguel Belen, a DWEB-FM broadcaster killed in July 2010, said the men had angered a political clan during the May 2010 local elections, the Philippine media reported. But Iriga City Mayor Madelaine Alfelor Gazmen warned reporters covering the killing not to rush to judgment about the motive or perpetrators. Although Olea had harshly criticized her administration, Gazmen condemned the shooting.

At Olea's burial, Camarines Sur Gov. Luis Raymund Villafuerte announced a 500,000 pesos (US$11,500) reward for anyone supplying information leading to the arrest of Olea's killers. Olea is survived by his wife and two children.

# Russia: 1

KILLED: DECEMBER 15, 2011, IN MAKHACHKALA

## Gadzhimurad Kamalov, *Chernovik*

A masked assailant apparently lying in wait fired 14 times as Kamalov, founder of the independent weekly *Chernovik*, was leaving work shortly before midnight. Kamalov, 46, who was also a contributing editor and writer, died en route to a local hospital. A *Chernovik* staffer who witnessed the murder through an office window told CPJ that the assailant fled the scene in a Lada Priora.

*Chernovik*, the most popular newspaper in Dagestan, was known for its independence and courageous coverage of government corruption, human rights abuses, and Islamic radicalism. From 2008 until 2011, *Chernovik* and five of its journalists, including then-editor and CPJ International Press Freedom Award winner Nadira Isayeva, were subjected to a politically motivated prosecution on trumped-up "extremism" charges stemming from the paper's critical coverage of regional police and the federal security service. The journalists were acquitted of the charges in May.

Biyakai Magomedov, editor of *Chernovik*, told CPJ that Kamalov had not disclosed recent threats. But a family member told the regional news website *Kavkazsky Uzel* that threats had been commonplace since the paper was launched in 2003. "Since the time *Chernovik* started publishing, there have been a number of threats, and he had foes," Khadzhimurad Radzhabov, a cousin and colleague of Kamalov, told *Kavkazsky Uzel*.

In recent television interviews, Kamalov had made critical comments about alleged regional government corruption. "Dagestan is sinking into idleness, into misguided scattering of federal money," *Kavkazsky Uzel* quoted Kamalov as saying in a February interview with the national television channel NTV. "You would not see a single Russian place with a bigger quantity of restaurants, banquet halls, saunas, casinos, and hookah parlors as Makhachkala."

Kamalov's name was among 16 included on a "death list" published anonymously and distributed in the form of a handout in Makhachkala in September 2009, according to Russian press reports. The handout, which named eight journalists among its targets, called for "destruction of the bandits and revenge for police officers and peaceful citizens."

# Somalia: 2

KILLED: SEPTEMBER 2, 2011, IN MOGADISHU

## Noramfaizul Mohd, Bernama TV

Mohd, 39, a veteran cameraman for the national Malaysian broadcaster Bernama TV, was struck by gunfire while covering a humanitarian aid mission in Mogadishu, Bernama TV said in a statement. Witnesses reported that African Union peacekeeping forces had fired on the Malaysian aid convoy, which was organized by the Putera 1Malaysia Club, as it was traveling to its base at the Mogadishu airport, news reports said.

Calling the shooting "deeply regrettable," the African Union Mission in Somalia (AMISOM) said it would undertake an investigation. On September 26, AMISOM announced that four AU soldiers from Burundi were responsible for the death and had been suspended.

In a three-paragraph statement, AMISOM characterized the killing as "accidental" but did not specify the soldiers' actions or describe their level of culpability. AMISOM said it "recommended" that Burundian authorities bring the four soldiers to trial "according to their country's military and judicial processes."

Mohd had covered earlier aid missions to Gaza and Pakistan, his father told Bernama TV. The journalist is survived by a wife and two sons. Aji Saregar, 27, a cameraman for Malaysia's TV3 who was also accompanying the convoy, was wounded in the right hand in the gunfire. Both journalists had planned to return to Malaysia the following day, Bernama TV reported.

KILLED: DECEMBER 18, 2011, IN MOGADISHU

## Abdisalan Sheikh Hassan, freelance

A gunman wearing a military uniform shot Hassan, 38, a freelance broadcast journalist, according to news accounts and CPJ interviews. Hassan was driving from the offices of HornCable TV to a press conference when the uniformed gunman intercepted his vehicle and opened fire, according to the station's director, Abdulle Haj Ali.

Hassan, shot in the head, died at a local hospital; a colleague riding in the car was unhurt. The shooting occurred around 4 p.m. in Mogadishu's central district of Hamar Jabar, local journalists told CPJ.

Hassan told colleagues that he had received several recent death threats via cell phone. Days before the shooting, Hassan had covered a tense session of the Transitional Federal Parliament during which violence broke out between supporters and opponents of Speaker Sharif Hassan Sheikh Adan, local journalists told CPJ.

Hassan contributed to HornCable TV and radio stations Hamar Radio and Voice of Democracy. Ali said Hassan was known for his courageous and balanced reporting. He was survived by a wife and four children.

# Syria: 2

KILLED: NOVEMBER 19 OR 20, 2011, IN AL-QASIR

## Ferzat Jarban, freelance

Jarban, a cameraman, was last seen being placed under arrest while he was filming an anti-government demonstration in the town of Al-Qasir on November 19, local press freedom groups reported, citing witnesses. He was found dead the next day in the middle of a main road in Al-Qasir, which is in the province of Homs. His body was mutilated and his eyes were gouged out, a member of the opposition Syrian revolutionary council in Homs told the London-based daily *Al-Sharq al-Awsat.* Al-Jazeera also reported the death, citing the revolutionary council as its source.

Jarban was the first journalist killed in Syria in connection to his work since CPJ started keeping detailed records in 1992. The freelance cameraman filmed demonstrations and the ensuing clashes with security forces in Homs and sent the footage to several Arabic news networks, *Al-Sharq al-Aswat* reported.

KILLED: DECEMBER 27, 2011, IN HOMS

## Basil al-Sayed, freelance

Al-Sayed, a videographer who documented clashes in Homs, died in an improvised hospital from a gunshot wound suffered five days earlier at a checkpoint in the Baba Amro neighborhood, according to news reports and a prominent activist interviewed by CPJ. Al-Sayed was shot in the head by security forces, news accounts said, citing local activists and relatives.

The 24-year-old regularly filmed unrest in Homs, including instances of security forces opening fire on demonstrators, Rami Jarrah, an exiled Syrian activist, told CPJ. Al-Sayed also interviewed Syrians about the political and economic implications of the country's turmoil. His footage appeared on the websites of citizen news organizations that published thousands of videos documenting the uprising. Jarrah said much of the footage from Baba Amro was taken by al-Sayed, who was known in Homs as "the revolution's journalist." With an effective ban on foreign journalists and with local media neutralized, international media relied heavily on footage shot by al-Sayed and other citizen journalists.

## Thailand: 1

KILLED: SEPTEMBER 24, 2011, IN YALA

### Phamon Phonphanit, *Sue Samut Atyakam*

Phamon, 61, a reporter with the Thai-language newspaper *Sue Samut Atyakam*, died at Yala Central Hospital from severe burns suffered while covering a series of timed bomb attacks in Sungai Khalok town, Narathiwat province, on September 16, according to news reports. At least six people died and more than 100 were injured by three car and motorcycle bomb explosions detonated at 20-minute intervals in a densely populated area of town, news reports said. A fourth bomb was found and defused by authorities, according to the reports.

No group took responsibility for the attack. Police detained two suspects who were allegedly identified by surveillance camera footage of the area where the bombs were detonated. Authorities said they planned to seek arrest warrants for additional suspects believed to be involved in the attacks, according to the reports.

Phamon's death came in the context of a Muslim separatist insurgency that started in January 2004 in Thailand's three southernmost provinces, Pattani, Narathiwat, and Yala. More than 4,800 people had been killed in violence associated with the insurgency. Chalee Boonsawat, a reporter with *Thai Rath*, the country's largest Thai-language newspaper, was killed on August 21, 2008, while covering another series of timed explosions in Sungai Kolok.

## Tunisia: 1

KILLED: JANUARY 17, 2011, IN TUNIS

### Lucas Mebrouk Dolega, European Pressphoto Agency

Dolega, 32, died from head injuries suffered while covering the massive January 14 protests that led to the ouster of President Zine El Abidine Ben Ali. The photographer was struck in the head by a tear gas canister fired by security forces, according to news reports. He died "carrying out his passion and his job," his family said in a statement announcing his death.

Dolega began working for the European Pressphoto Agency in 2006, covering assignments as varied as armed conflict, arts, culture, politics, and sports. He was dispatched to Tunisia to cover the burgeoning civil unrest, EPA Deputy Editor-in-Chief Frank Bengfort told CPJ.

On its website, EPA published a collection of works by Dolega, along with a remembrance of the photographer: "Lucas walked into our Paris office in April 2006. A young man who above all wanted to become a photojournalist, Lucas' passion was the image. He was driven by his need to cover major conflicts. He grew in those four years to become a thorough professional. And he did so with a total sense of decency. Based in Paris, he also covered politics, protests, and fashion in Europe. In 2008 he covered the situation in the Congo."

Dolega believed that "the closer, the better," EPA said. "His last pictures, transmitted by his colleagues after his injury, make us proud, as does his entire body of work."

## Vietnam: 1

KILLED: JANUARY 30, 2011, IN HO CHI MINH CITY

### Le Hoang Hung, *Nguoi Lao Dong*

Hung, 51, a reporter for the newspaper *Nguoi Lao Dong*, died in a Ho Chi Minh City hospital 10 days after an unknown assailant entered his house in Tan An town, dousing him with chemicals and setting him ablaze, according to local and international news reports. Hung, who was sleeping at the time of the attack, suffered severe burns to more than 20 percent of his body, according to news reports.

Some local media ran photographs showing the extent of the blaze. The bedroom walls were blackened with smoke and the furniture was charred. Hung's wife, Tran Thi Lieu, told reporters that the journalist had received threatening text messages that originated from unknown numbers prior to his death.

News reports said Hung had regularly covered official misconduct in the Mekong Delta region. BBC Southeast Asia correspondent Rachel Harvey said Hung was covering a case in which a local authority in the southern province of Long An was being sued for alleged illegal appropriation of land.

Police did not identify suspects in the case. Hung is survived by his wife and two daughters, 17 and 12.

# Yemen: 2

KILLED: MARCH 18, 2011, IN SANA'A

## Jamal al-Sharaabi, *Al-Masdar*

Al-Sharaabi, a photojournalist for the independent weekly *Al-Masdar*, was one of at least 44 civilians killed when government security forces opened fire on a peaceful demonstration in a square outside the main gate of Sana'a University, according to news reports.

Al-Sharaabi was shot in the face. The 35-year-old father of four was the first confirmed media fatality in the political unrest that began in Yemen in January.

KILLED: SEPTEMBER 24, 2011, IN SANA'A

## Hassan al-Wadhaf, Arabic Media Agency

Al-Wadhaf, a Yemeni cameraman for the Arabic Media Agency, was shot twice in the face by a sniper while covering an anti-government protest in Sana'a on September 19, news reports said. He managed to film the shooting and was taken to the hospital in the immediate aftermath, but died five days later from his injuries.

The fatal shots were fired by an unidentified rooftop sniper, whose affiliation could not be verified. Snipers firing into crowds of anti-government demonstrators shot numerous other people in previous days, according to international news reports.

The Arabic Media Agency, a production company, provided reports for the Saudi-based satellite news channel Al-Ekhbariya, the U.S. government-funded Al-Hurra, and the Iraqi state outlet Al-Iraqiya, among others.

# Media Workers Killed

# 5 Media Workers Killed

## Ivory Coast: 1

KILLED: FEBRUARY 28, 2011, IN KOUMASSI

### Marcel Legré, La Refondation

A mob armed with machetes dragged Legré, a printing press employee for the media group La Refondation, from his home in Koumassi and hacked him to death, according to local journalists and news reports. The assailants were believed to be supporters of Alassane Ouattara, the opposition party leader who was locked in a protracted electoral dispute at the time with incumbent Laurent Gbagbo. (Ouattara was sworn in as president in May 2011.)

Legré's affiliation with La Refondation, publisher of the daily newspaper *Notre Voie*, which backed Gbagbo, was the likely motive, news reports said. Koumassi, an Abidjan suburb, was home to many Ouattara supporters.

## Libya: 1

KILLED: MARCH 15, 2011, IN AJDABIYA

### Mohamed Shaglouf, freelance

Shaglouf, a driver working for four *New York Times* journalists in Libya, was killed by fighters loyal to Libyan leader Muammar Qaddafi at a checkpoint in Ajdabiya, the *Times* told CPJ, citing an account from the driver's brother.

Pro-Qaddafi forces seized *Times* journalists Anthony Shadid, Stephen Farrell, Lynsey Addario, and Tyler Hicks at the checkpoint, holding them captive for six days. The *Times* journalists lost sight of Shaglouf after their capture. Shaglouf's body had not been recovered by late 2011, according to his brother.

# Mexico: 1

KILLED: FEBRUARY 9, 2011, IN TORREÓN

## Rodolfo Ochoa Moreno, Grupo Multimedios Laguna

Ochoa, 27, an engineer for Grupo Multimedios Laguna, was killed by gunmen who burst into the media group's transmission facilities on February 9. The group stole and destroyed equipment, and shot Ochoa as he was calling the police, said Juan Carlos Zuñiga, a TV host with Grupo Multimedios.

Heriberto Gallegos, manager of the nearby Radiorama Laguna, said the men also stormed his station's transmission facilities and damaged its equipment. He said the attack was intended to generate panic among the public in Torreón, a large city in north-central Mexico and a battleground for two competing crime gangs.

"Both of them want to show their power. Both of them want to show the government cannot control them, and the people must do what they say," Gallegos said.

Zuñiga said Grupo Multimedios Laguna had not covered organized crime out of fear of reprisal from the cartels.

# Somalia: 1

KILLED: AUGUST 4, 2011, IN MOGADISHU

## Farah Hassan Sahal, Radio Simba

Hassan, 45, a logistics manager and driver for Radio Simba, died after being shot three times outside the station's office in the volatile Bakara Market area of Mogadishu, local journalists told CPJ.

The shooting came during intense fighting between Al-Shabaab insurgents and government-allied African Union troops, local reports said.

Hassan's colleagues said the shots came from the direction of the AU forces. He is survived by a wife and five children, Radio Simba Director Abdullahi Ali Farah told CPJ.

# Yemen: 1

KILLED: OCTOBER 22, 2011, IN SANA'A

## Fuad al-Shamri, Al-Saeeda TV

Al-Shamri, chief financial officer of Al-Saeeda TV, was killed by sniper fire while trying to escape the station's headquarters during heavy fighting, local news outlets and the Yemeni Journalists Syndicate reported. The station's offices were shelled amid clashes between pro- and anti-government forces, although it was not clear whether the building had been directly targeted.

Another employee, Mohamed Abd al-Ghani Dabwan, was hospitalized with serious injuries after being caught in the crossfire, news reports said.

# Journalists Killed:
# Motive Unconfirmed

# 35 Journalists Killed:
# Motive Unconfirmed

## Bolivia: 1

KILLED: APRIL 20, 2011, IN LA PAZ

### David Niño de Guzmán, Agencia de Noticias Fides

Niño de Guzmán, 42, news director for the La Paz-based Agencia de Noticias Fides, was found dead on April 21, the victim of an explosive device, after being reported missing two days earlier.

Niño de Guzmán's body was discovered around midday in La Paz's Retamanis neighborhood near the Orkojahuira River, news reports said. A forensic report said the explosive device had destroyed the journalist's abdomen, according to press reports.

News reports, citing police, said the death occurred sometime early on April 20. La Fuerza Especial de Lucha Contra el Crimen, the special investigative unit of the Bolivian police, was investigating several theories for the journalist's death, news reports said.

Julieta Tovar, a reporter for Agencia de Noticias Fides, told CPJ she was not aware of any threats against Niño de Guzmán. Police said none of the journalist's belongings had been stolen, news reports said.

During his 16 years as a journalist, Niño de Guzmán worked for several top news dailies, including *La Razón* and *El Diario*, and for Cadena A television. He joined Agencia de Noticias Fides, a Jesuit-affiliated agency, as a reporter in 2006 and became news director in March 2010. In a statement, five Bolivian press organizations called on authorities to investigate Niño de Guzmán's death, adding that a journalism-related motive should not be ruled out, *Los Tiempos* reported.

# Brazil: 4

KILLED: APRIL 9, 2011, IN VITÓRIA DE SANTO ANTÃO

## Luciano Leitão Pedrosa, TV Vitória and Radio Metropolitana FM

Television and radio journalist Pedrosa was shot at a restaurant in Vitória de Santo Antão in northeastern Pernambuco state, according to press reports.

An assailant fired multiple shots after entering the restaurant at about 9 p.m., the Recife-based *Diario de Pernambuco* reported. Pedrosa, struck once in the head, was pronounced dead at the scene. The unidentified gunman fled on a motorcycle driven by another individual who had been waiting outside, press reports said.

Pedrosa, 46, had hosted a program on TV Vitória, "Ação e Cidadania" (Action and Citizenship), for seven years, and had reported for the FM radio station Metropolitana. According to press reports, Pedrosa was known for his critical coverage of criminals and municipal authorities. The Pernambuco daily *Jornal do Commercio* reported that the journalist had received threats, but had not complained to authorities. The paper did not specify the nature of the threats.

Police told reporters that the gunman had declared it was a robbery, but work-related motives had not been ruled out given the critical nature of Pedrosa's reporting. Pedrosa was a harsh critic of the local municipal government, *Diario de Pernambuco* reported.

KILLED: MAY 3, 2011, IN RIO CLARO

## Valério Nascimento, *Panorama Geral*

Brazilian newspaper owner and journalist Nascimento was shot in the head and chest outside the doorway to his home in Rio Claro, Rio de Janeiro state, news reports said.

Police did not disclose a motive for the killing, although investigators told *O Globo* that the latest issue of *Panorama Geral* had cited alleged irregularities in the mayor's office in the neighboring town of Bananal. The paper had also criticized the management of Bananal's public services, including sewage treatment, public parks, and health clinics, according to press reports. Nascimento, who was also active in area politics, served as president of his local residents' association and had twice run for alderman.

*Panorama Geral* had published only four editions, according to local news reports.

## Auro Ida, freelance

Veteran political reporter Ida, 53, was in a car with a female companion in late evening when an unidentified man approached on a bicycle. The assailant ordered the woman out of the vehicle and shot Ida several times, press reports said. The journalist had served as the city government's communications secretary, was a founder of the news site *Midianews,* and wrote an opinion column for the news website *Olhar Direto.*

Police initially said they were investigating the murder as a crime of passion, press reports said. After members of Congress asked that police elaborate on that claim, a judge ruled on August 11 that the investigation be carried out in secret, press reports said. In an interview on the day of the ruling, Antônio Carlos Garcia, head of the local homicide unit, said police had not ruled out any lines of investigation.

Laura Petraglia, a reporter for *Olhar Direto,* told CPJ that at the time of his death, Ida had been investigating a story concerning local political corruption. The president of the state legislative assembly, José Riva, said that Ida had recently told him he was receiving threats but did not elaborate on their nature. The local journalists union asked that federal police take on the case because local authorities weren't paying sufficient attention to a professional motive, *Diario de Cuiabá* reported.

## Valderlei Canuto Leandro, Radio Frontera

Canuto, 32, a radio journalist who hosted the show "Sinal Verde" (Green Signal), was shot at least eight times by unidentified assailants on a motorcycle in the city of Tabatinga, in the state of Amazonas, local press reports said. He had been returning from a local marketplace a block away from his home, his brother Alderli Canuto told CPJ.

Canuto was known for his criticism of local authorities, according to *Blog Da Floresta,* a local news blog. In May, Canuto had filed a complaint with the prosecutor's office alleging that Tabatinga Mayor Samuel Benerguy had threatened him concerning his coverage of alleged corruption, local press reports said.

In a September 9 article posted on *Blog Da Floresta,* Benerguy said he had no involvement in Canuto's killing and had never threatened the journalist. The mayor told *Blog Da Floresta* that he was saddened by Canuto's death and wanted the crime to be solved.

Sávio Pinzon, police chief in the state's capital, Manaus, told CPJ that authorities were looking into the journalist's work as a possible motive.

## China: 1

KILLED: SEPTEMBER 19, 2011, IN LUOYANG

### Li Xiang, Luoyang TV

Unidentified assailants fatally stabbed Li, 30, at least 10 times early in the morning, news reports said. Police told reporters that the journalist's laptop, camera, and wallet were stolen during the assault.

News accounts reported that Li may have been targeted for his coverage of a recent food scandal involving the recycling of waste oil into cooking oil. Police had arrested 32 people and confiscated 100 tons of the carcinogenic product known as "gutter oil" from Henan and two other provinces, according to Agence France-Presse. In his last microblog post, Li highlighted a discrepancy between the illegal oil manufacturing reported in Henan and the findings of local food safety officials who had denied the existence of such illicit production, news reports said.

Police arrested two suspects on September 21. Local news reports said the motive was robbery, although a police spokesperson told AFP the case was still under investigation.

## Colombia: 1

KILLED: JUNE 30, 2011, IN ARBOLETES

### Luis Eduardo Gómez, freelance

An unidentified assailant shot Gómez, 70, as he returned home with his wife, and then fled on a motorcycle, news reports said.

Gómez, a freelance journalist and a government witness in an investigation into links between politicians and paramilitary groups, had reported on local corruption in the Urabá region of Antioquia, according to the Colombian press freedom group Foundation for Press Freedom. Most recently, he had written about tourism and the environment for the local newspapers *El Heraldo de Urabá* and *Urabá al día*, among others. The newspaper *El Colombiano* said the journalist had not received any threats prior to his death.

Gómez was also participating as a witness in the attorney general's investigation into links between politicians and illegal right-wing paramilitary groups, a case commonly known as the "parapolitics" scandal. Another witness in the case was killed a few days before the journalist's death, and investigators said other witnesses had disappeared, press reports said.

Gómez was also investigating the unsolved murder of his son two years earlier, the daily *El Espectador* said.

Until 2006, the violent Urabá region of Antioquia province had been controlled for many years by the paramilitary group United Self-Defense Forces of Colombia, press reports said. Colombian provincial journalists, working in areas where paramilitaries and other illegal armed groups had been prevalent, faced severe challenges in reporting on the organizations' activities, CPJ research shows.

## Democratic Republic of the Congo: 1

KILLED: JUNE 22, 2011, IN KIRUMBA

### Witness-Patchelly Kambale Musonia, freelance

The body of Musonia, 32, host of a daily talk show on community station Radio Communautaire de Lubero Sud, was found early in the morning in Kirumba, a city in North Kivu province. He had been shot by unidentified gunmen as he walked home from his office at Congo Chine Télécoms, where he worked as a local communications officer, according to local journalists and the local press freedom group Journaliste En Danger.

Station director Jean Maliro told CPJ that witnesses who claimed they heard gunshots around 7:30 p.m. reported that the gunmen seemed to have been waiting for the journalist.

Musonia, the father of a 7-month-old, was the host of a news review show titled "Wake Up Kirumba," Maliro said. In his last program, Musonia had discussed with a local civil society leader the recent arrests of a dozen people accused of trafficking military weapons, Maliro said.

# El Salvador: 1

KILLED: APRIL 25, 2011, IN ILOPANGO

## Alfredo Antonio Hurtado, Canal 33

Hurtado, 39, was commuting to his job as night cameraman for Canal 33's "Teleprensa" news program at around 7 p.m. when two men boarded the San Salvador-bound bus and shot him multiple times in the chest and head, according to local press reports and CPJ interviews.

The assailants, believed to be gang members, fled into a neighborhood known for gang activity. News reports citing police said that none of the journalist's possessions were taken and that no suspects had been apprehended.

Police were investigating several possible motives for the killing, news reports said. Narciso Castillo, director of Canal 33, told CPJ that Hurtado's journalistic work had not been ruled out, citing his coverage of gang violence. Hurtado, who was also an editor, had worked with "Teleprensa" for two years, Castillo said.

# Guatemala: 1

KILLED: MAY 18 OR 19, 2011, IN NUEVA CONCEPCIÓN

## Yensi Roberto Ordoñez Galdámez, Channel 14

The body of Ordoñez, a television reporter and teacher, was discovered on May 19 in a black vehicle parked outside the primary school where he taught, press reports said. He had knife wounds in the neck and chest, according to the rescue workers who found him.

News reports said authorities had been tipped off by an anonymous call. Family members quoted by the Guatemala City-based daily *Prensa Libre* said Ordoñez had left his home the previous night and did not return.

Ordoñez was a news reporter on Channel 14, a local cable station, according to news reports. *Prensa Libre* quoted the station's director, Roberto Santizo, as saying that Ordoñez had received threats in relation to his reporting. The journalist and teacher had also hosted children's and music programs on Channel 14, local press reports said.

Family members said Ordoñez was being extorted, press reports said, although the nature of the extortion was not clear.

# Honduras: 4

KILLED: MAY 11, 2011, IN SAN PEDRO SULA

## Héctor Francisco Medina Polanco, Omega Visión

Provincial television journalist Medina was shot around 7:30 p.m. on May 10 outside his home in Morazán in the northern department of Yoro. He died the next day from related complications at a municipal hospital in San Pedro Sula.

The journalist, who produced and hosted the "TV9" news program for the local cable company Omega Visión, was on his motorcycle returning home from work when he was shot in the arm and the back by two unidentified assailants on a motorcycle who had been following him, according to CPJ interviews and press reports.

According to the Tegucigalpa-based *El Heraldo*, Medina had reported on corruption in the local mayor's office and on regional land disputes. The journalist's brother, Carlos, told CPJ that Medina had been threatened several times in the previous six months. *El Heraldo* said the journalist had reported threats to the local authorities.

Medina also worked for a government education project, his brother said.

KILLED: MAY 19, 2011, IN DANLÍ

## Luis Ernesto Mendoza Cerrato, Channel 24

At least three hooded assailants armed with AK-47s shot television station owner Mendoza, 39, as he arrived at Channel 24 broadcast facilities at about 7 a.m., according to press reports.

Mendoza, who was shot multiple times, was pronounced dead at the scene. Police said they believed it was a contract killing but did not provide any details. In addition to owning Channel 24, Mendoza had investments in real estate and in the coffee and agricultural industries.

KILLED: JULY 14, 2011, IN LEMPIRA

## Nery Geremías Orellana, Radio Joconguera and Radio Progreso

Journalist and political activist Orellana, 26, was shot in the head by unknown assailants while he was riding his motorcycle to work. He was found on the road between the towns of San Lorenzo and Candelaria and taken to a nearby Salvadoran hospital, where he later died.

Orellana was manager of the local radio station Radio Joconguera and correspondent for the Christian-oriented station Radio Progreso. He was also an active member of the National Front of Popular Resistance, or FNRP, an organization that supported the ousted President Manuel Zelaya.

Although Radio Joconguera was primarily devoted to music, Orellana regularly alloted airtime to the FNRP, local news reports said. He also coordinated a news program for the station that denounced local corruption, according to a colleague, the Rev. José Amílcar.

Amílcar told CPJ that he and Orellana had received anonymous death threats via text message and had been heckled on the street.

KILLED: DECEMBER 6, 2011, IN TEGUCIGALPA

## Luz Marina Paz Villalobos, Cadena Hondureña de Noticias

Unidentified gunmen fired at least 37 times at Paz, who was in a car near her home, The Associated Press reported. The journalist and her cousin, Delmer Osmar Canales Gutiérrez, who worked as her driver, were both killed. Paz was testing a car she was considering buying from an army colonel, Marco Tulio Leiva, press reports said.

Paz, 38, was the host of the morning news program "3 en la noticia" (Three on the News) on Cadena Hondureña de Noticias (Honduran News Network). She had also worked for Radio Globo, a radio station known for criticizing the 2009 coup that ousted Manuel Zelaya, news reports said.

Authorities said they were investigating several potential motives for the attack. Héctor Iván Mejía, a spokesman for the Ministry of Security, told reporters that investigators were looking into the background of Canales and were considering the possibility of a carjacking. Mejía said the journalist's work was also being considered as a possible motive.

Officials were looking into reports that the journalist had received threats related to her refusal to cooperate with criminals trying to extort money from a small business she ran.

# India: 2

KILLED: FEBRUARY 22, 2011, NEAR RAIPUR

## Umesh Rajput, Nai Dunia

Two masked gunmen on motorcycles fatally shot Rajput, 32, a reporter with the Hindi-language daily *Nai Dunia* (New World), outside his residence near Raipur district in Chhattisgarh state, according to local news reports.

The motive in the attack was unclear. Rajput's family said a health worker had threatened the journalist two weeks before the shooting in relation to a story about a patient who had developed an infection, local news reports said. The reports also said police found a note near his body that contained a work-related death threat. The English-language daily *Indian Express* said police were skeptical of the note, saying it may have been a diversionary tactic by Maoist insurgents. Insurgent groups, government security forces, and state-supported vigilantes have clashed in recent years in the state.

KILLED: JUNE 11, 2011, IN POWAI

## Jyotirmoy Dey, *Midday*

Multiple men on motorcycles fired several shots at Dey as he drove past them on his own motorcycle in Powai, a suburb of Mumbai. The journalist died at the scene from five bullet wounds to the head and chest, his colleagues at *Midday* told CPJ. Dey, special investigations editor for *Midday*, was known for his hard-hitting coverage of Mumbai's crime world.

Police in Mumbai arrested seven suspects on June 27, according to local and international news reports. Investigators believed reputed crime boss Chhota Rajan ordered the killing, police told reporters at a press conference. The motive for the killing was not immediately clear, police said, although colleagues told reporters they believed Dey had been targeted for his reporting.

Dey had covered crime in Mumbai for 22 years and had written two books, *Zero Dial: The Dangerous World of Informers* and *Khallas*.

# Iraq: 2

KILLED: FEBRUARY 17, 2011, IN MOSUL

## Hilal al-Ahmadi, freelance

Freelance journalist al-Ahmadi, 57, was gunned down in front of his home in eastern Mosul as he left for work, according to news reports. Colleagues told the local press freedom group Journalistic Freedoms Observatory and local media that al-Ahmadi was a well-known writer in Mosul and that much of his writing, which appeared in a number of publications, focused on financial and administrative corruption.

KILLED: APRIL 8, 2011, IN BAGHDAD

## Taha Hameed, Al-Massar TV

Hameed, director of the satellite news channel Al-Massar TV, was killed in southern Baghdad, CNN reported. Hameed was traveling with human rights activist Abed Farhan Thiyab when unknown gunmen fired on their car, killing them both. Al-Massar TV was affiliated with Prime Minister Nouri al-Maliki's Dawa party.

## Mexico: 4

KILLED: JUNE 20, 2011, IN VERACRUZ

## Miguel Ángel López Velasco, *Notiver*
## Misael López Solana, *Notiver*

Miguel Ángel López Velasco, 55, a prominent columnist with the Veracruz daily *Notiver*, his wife, Agustina Solano de López, and their son Misael López Solana, 21, a *Notiver* photographer, were killed by unidentified assailants who broke into their home around 5:30 a.m., the newspaper reported.

Miguel López, a former deputy editor with *Notiver*, wrote a column under the pseudonym Milo Vela that addressed politics, security issues, and general interest topics. He was also the editor of the newspaper's police section, press reports said. Journalists told CPJ the murders could have been retaliation for a recent column about local drug trafficking. Mourning the death of the López family members, *Notiver* did not publish an edition on June 21, the Mexico City-based daily *La Jornada* reported.

Veracruz Gov. Javier Duarte de Ochoa visited the offices of *Notiver* and gave a statement to reporters. "Today in a cowardly act, an act that harms all society—because it is not an attack against a medium of communication, it is not even an attack against a professional group, it is an attack against society as a whole, against Veracruz society—they killed our friend Miguel Ángel López Velasco," Duarte said. He promised a full investigation, the Mexico City-based daily *Milenio* said.

Three days after the murders, Veracruz State Attorney General Reynaldo Escobar Pérez announced that investigators had identified the mastermind as Juan Carlos Carranza Saavedra, known as "El Ñaca," the Mexico City daily-based *El Universal* reported. In a press conference, Escobar said he wouldn't disclose details of the case, including possible motives, because it might obstruct the investigation, press reports said. The attorney general said the state was offering a reward of more than US$250,000 for information on the case.

KILLED: JULY 2011, IN VERACRUZ

## Yolanda Ordaz de la Cruz, *Notiver*

The decapitated body of veteran police beat reporter Ordaz was found at 4 a.m. on July 26, two days after she was seized by armed men as she left her home. The body was found near the offices of the newspaper *Imagen*.

In a press conference, state prosecutor Reynaldo Escobar Pérez said Ordaz's murder was not linked to her work and that the evidence indicated her killers were members of organized crime. He also suggested the journalist might have had ties to organized crime. *Notiver* immediately called for the prosecutor's resignation in an editorial, saying, "We strongly reject this accusation and designate it as unfair, irresponsible, and stupid."

Authorities appeared to take a broader view of the investigation in their subsequent statements. A spokeswoman for the prosecutor's office, Magda Zayas, told CPJ the journalist's work was being considered as a possible motive.

On August 5, Veracruz Gov. Javier Duarte de Ochoa said authorities were pursuing multiple lines of investigation. He said investigators found an identification card belonging to Ordaz among the possessions of two unidentified criminal suspects killed in a military operation earlier that week, press reports said. Mexico's Human Rights Commission said it would investigate Ordaz's killing, The Associated Press said.

A note found with Ordaz's body seemed to connect her murder to the killing in June of well-known columnist Miguel Angel López Velasco, the spokeswoman Zayas said. She said the note, signed "Carranza," said: "Friends can also betray you." Reporters in Veracruz told CPJ that the gruesome killing and the placement of the body near a newspaper appeared to be an ominous message meant for the press.

KILLED: AUGUST 24 OR 25, 2011, IN CULIACÁN

## Humberto Millán Salazar, *A Discusión* and Radio Fórmula

Millán's body was found in a field in the state of Sinaloa on the outskirts of the state capital, Culiacán, with a gunshot wound to the head. He had been abducted a day earlier by men in two SUVs who intercepted him on his way to work.

Millán was the host of a show on Radio Fórmula and ran and wrote a column for the news website *A Discusión*. The violent Sinaloa cartel was dominant in the area, but local journalists said it was more likely that the journalist was murdered because of his coverage of local politics. Berzahi Osuna Enciso, a colleague at the radio station, told CPJ that Millán's killers would likely be found among his political enemies.

On September 2, Millán's family members submitted a CD to authorities that they said the journalist had left in a safe with instructions to publicize if anything happened to him, local press reports said. Investigators did not disclose the contents of the CD.

## Pakistan: 4

KILLED: JANUARY 3, 2011, IN PIDARAK

## Ilyas Nizzar, *Darwanth*

Nizzar's body was found with multiple gunshot wounds along a dirt road in Pidarak, Baluchistan province, six days after he was reported missing, local news reports said.

Alongside Nizzar's body was that of Qambar Chakar, a Baluch Students Organization leader who had disappeared from his home in Turbat on November 27, 2010. A general assignment reporter for the newsmagazine *Darwanth*, Nizzar was also considered a prominent activist, according to some local news reports.

KILLED: FEBRUARY 18, 2011, IN TURBAT

## Abdost Rind, freelance

Rind, a 27-year-old part-time reporter for the *Daily Eagle*, an Urdu-language newspaper, was shot four times before his assailants escaped on a motorcycle in the Turbat area of Baluchistan province.

He died immediately, local news reports said. The Pakistan Federal Union of Journalists reported that Rind's family believed his killing was directly related to his work as a journalist.

Rind was also an activist in the Baluch separatist movement, which seeks greater independence for the vast region and an ultimate break from Pakistani rule. Government military and intelligence operations frequently target activists, and many Baluch journalists straddle the line between political activism and journalism.

KILLED: APRIL 2, 2011, IN KARACHI

## Zaman Ibrahim, *Daily Extra News*

Ibrahim was riding his motorcycle when two motorcyclists shot him in the head, according to Pakistani news reports. The journalist had worked for several small Urdu-language papers. He also was involved with a local group called the People's Aman Committee, the ruling Pakistan Peoples Party's militant counterpoint to the armed militias of the opposition Muttahida Qaumi Movement and Awami National Party. The groups are known for their violent tactics.

Ibrahim, 40, had two children. Although he had worked for several different newspapers for several years, his most recent job was at the *Daily Extra News*. Police told reporters investigating the shooting that they believed he was killed over an internal party dispute.

KILLED: AUGUST 14, 2011, IN KHUZDAR

## Muneer Shakir, freelance

Shakir, who wrote for the *Online News Network* and was a correspondent for the Baluch television station Sabzbaat, was shot repeatedly by two men on a motorcycle shortly after midday as he headed home from the press club in Khuzdar, the district capital in the center of Baluchistan, according to the Human Rights Commission of Pakistan. He died at Khuzdar's District Headquarters Hospital.

Shakir's colleagues in the Baluchistan Union of Journalists said the 30-year-old reporter had been working on and off as a journalist for about eight years, and they did not know of any threats directed at him. But representatives of the Pakistan Press Foundation, a media support group, told CPJ that Shakir had also been an activist with Baluch separatist organizations and said that was the probable reason he was targeted. Pakistani military and intelligence operations frequently target activists, and many Baluch journalists straddle the line between political activism and journalism.

## Paraguay: 1

KILLED: MARCH 3, 2011, IN YTAKYRY

### Merardo Alejandro Romero Chávez, La Voz de Ytakyry

Armed men shot Romero, 49, in his home in front of his children, according to press reports. Romero was the host of a political talk show on the community radio station La Voz de Ytakyry and was a member of the local Esperanza Colorada political party.

In the days after the murder, Romero's widow, Gloria Torres, told reporters that her husband had said that three members of a rival political party would be responsible if anything happened to him: Miguel Angel Soria, former mayor of Ytakyry; José Valenzuela, Soria's chief political adviser; and Hugo Barreto, the mayor. Soria, a powerful figure in local politics, told reporters that neither he nor Valenzuela had anything to do with the murder and that he hoped authorities would solve the crime. All three men denied the accusations to authorities.

Romero had accused Soria of corruption, news reports said. At the time, Soria was a candidate for a senior position in the Honor Colorado political party, news reports said.

The journalist's wife said Romero had received multiple death threats by phone and text message, the most recent coming two weeks before the murder. Authorities allegedly tracked the phone threats to Valenzuela and determined that he had offered the gunmen US$2,000 to commit the murder, press reports said.

Authorities arrested three men in September and October 2011, and charged them with planning and carrying out the murder, news reports said. Investigators said they connected the suspects to Valenzuela and charged him with being the mastermind. Valenzuela's whereabouts were not immediately known, however, and he was considered a fugitive. Investigators said they were investigating Romero's political activity and his journalism as possible motives.

# Peru: 2

KILLED: MAY 3, 2011, IN VIRÚ

## Julio Castillo Narváez, Ollantay Radio

Castillo, a provincial radio host, was shot at least six times as he was having lunch at a local restaurant in the northern city of Virú, local press reports said.

Castillo, who hosted a news show on Ollantay Radio, was known for his criticism of local authorities, the regional press group Instituto Prensa y Sociedad (IPYS) said in a statement. News media reported that Castillo had received repeated death threats via phone.

Ollantay Radio was vandalized after Castillo had reported on a local politician, prompting its staff to seek police protection, IPYS said. The request was not granted.

KILLED: SEPTEMBER 14, 2011, IN PUEBLO NUEVO

## José Oquendo Reyes, Radio Alas Peruanas and BTV Canal 45

Oquendo was shot five times at close range by unidentified men on a motorcycle outside his home in Pueblo Nuevo in the southern region of Chincha, local news reports said. He was the host of the news program "Sin Fronteras," which aired on Radio Alas Peruanas and television station BTV Canal 45.

Oquendo was known for his investigative pieces, Luz Córdova Pecho, president of the local press group Asociación Nacional de Periodistas in Chincha, told CPJ. The journalist's wife, Marina Juárez, told CPJ that he had not received any recent threats.

# Philippines: 3

KILLED: MARCH 24, 2011, IN MALABON CITY

## Maria Len Flores Somera, DZME

An unidentified gunman shot Somera, host of a public affairs program, before fleeing the scene in a Jeep, according to The Associated Press. Somera, a 44-year-old mother of three, died on the way to a local hospital from a gunshot wound to the head.

Police Chief Nicanor Bartolome said investigators were looking into a land dispute involving Somera. She was the president of a local housing association and discussed her work with the group on the air. Agence France-Presse, citing a statement from DZME, said the journalist's radio broadcasts covered the conditions of disadvantaged people in the Philippines. She also frequently criticized officials for failing to provide adequate public services, Reuters reported.

KILLED: AUGUST 22, 2011, IN E.B. MAGALONA

## Niel Jimena, DYRI-RMN

Two gunmen shot Jimena, 42, five times while he was on a motorcycle near his home in the Negros Island town of E.B. Magalona, according to local and international news reports. He died before arriving at a local hospital, news reports said.

Jimena broadcast political commentary on DYRI-RMN in nearby Iloilo City, leasing airtime under a common practice known as block-timing. He also hosted the twice-weekly radio program "Judge," which was known for its criticisms of the mayor and other local elected officials. The National Union of Journalists of the Philippines said Jimena appeared to have received threats from a politician he criticized on air before his death.

On September 12, police filed a murder complaint against two "professional assassins" in connection with the killing. Negros Occidental Senior Superintendent Allan Guisihan declined to identify the two, saying they were still being sought. Guisihan said witnesses had identified the assailants, who were also on a motorcycle. "They were not wearing masks when the gunmen shot the victim in a lighted area," he told the *Philippine Daily Inquirer*.

Several newspapers reported that the journalist was widely believed to be an informant for the Philippine Drug Enforcement Agency. "We are not ruling out that he might have been killed because of his work as a broadcaster, but our investigation points more to the drug angle," Guisihan said.

KILLED: OCTOBER 14, 2011, IN LIANGA

## Roy Bagtikan Gallego, freelance

Gallego, a radio commentator and tribal activist, was gunned down in southern Surigao del Sur province just days before he was scheduled to launch a new radio program. Provincial police said they had reached no conclusions on the motive and had not identified any suspects, local news reports said.

Gallego was on his motorcycle when he was shot several times by assailants on motorcycles in Lianga town, according to local news reports and the National Union of Journalists of the Philippines. The reports said Gallego was due to start a new block-time program on 92.7 Smile FM San Francisco. In 2010, he had hosted a similar program on DXSF San Francisco Radio.

Block-timing is a common practice in the Philippines in which broadcasters lease airtime from a radio station and typically solicit their own advertising. A number of block-time commentators have been killed in the Philippines, according to CPJ research. Gallego, a tribal leader of the Manobo tribe, was a critic of local mining practices and was politically active in the region.

## Sierra Leone: 1

KILLED: JUNE 12, 2011, NEAR GRAFTON

### Ibrahim Foday, *The Exclusive*

Foday, 38, a reporter for the private daily *The Exclusive*, died from a stab wound suffered during violent clashes over a disputed 10-acre plot between the neighboring villages of Kossoh and Grafton, about 15 miles (25 kilometers) southeast of the capital, Freetown, according to the Sierra Leone Association of Journalists.

Police said they arrested two suspects, Victor Haffner, a Kossoh community leader, and a police constable, Musa Samura. A third suspect, Haffner's driver, was being sought, local journalists said.

*The Exclusive* said Foday was targeted as both a journalist, for taking photographs during the clashes, and as a perceived party to the dispute because of his role as a Grafton youth leader. Potential witnesses could be deterred from speaking out because of the presence of a police barracks in the area and the influence of the Kossoh leader, according to local journalist Emma Black, who covered the murder for Sky Radio.

Six people were injured over the course of three days of clashes, according to *Exclusive* Publisher Sheik Sesay, who said Foday had written four stories about the land dispute and had not reported any threats. Foday was the father of two, according to local journalists.

## Uganda: 1

KILLED: DECEMBER 1, 2011, NEAR KAMPALA

### Charles Ingabire, *Inyenyeri News*

Ingabire, 32, an exiled Rwandan journalist and founder of the online *Inyenyeri News*, was shot twice in the lower abdomen by multiple assailants while outside a bar in the suburbs of Uganda's capital, Kampala, according to local journalists and news reports. The shooting occurred about 2 a.m.

In 2008, Ingabire launched the *Inyenyeri News* website from Kampala. He previously lived in Kigali, Rwanda's capital, working as a reporter for the now-banned independent weekly *Umoco* and running a company that granted small loans to local businesses. In 2007, he left Kigali for Kampala and worked as a correspondent for the Rwandan weekly *Umuvugizi*.

The journalist had been targeted before. In October 2011, unknown assailants attacked Ingabire, demanding he shutter his website, news reports said. *Inyenyeri News* was highly critical of the Rwandan government and extensively covered the Rwandan military, often publishing interviews with exiled Rwandan soldiers.

Ingabire is survived by his wife and five-month-old daughter.

## Venezuela: 1

KILLED: MAY 17, 2011, IN LA VICTORIA

### Wilfred Iván Ojeda, *El Clarín*

Ojeda, 56, a political columnist with the daily *El Clarín* and a longtime activist with the opposition Democratic Action Party, was found in a vacant lot, shot in the head, gagged, hooded, and with his hands tied, according to local investigators.

The journalist's vehicle was found 15 miles (25 kilometers) from the scene. The daily *El Nacional* said Ojeda was driving the previous afternoon when his vehicle was intercepted by unidentified assailants. His belongings did not appear to have been taken, the police said.

Local journalists said Ojeda's columns focused on local politics. Venezuelan prosecutors said they were considering the victim's journalism as a possible motive, local press reports said.

Journalists in Prison

# Journalists in Prison

PHOTO CREDITS

*Section break: Israeli soldiers detain a Palestinian cameraman in the West Bank village of Nabi Saleh. (Reuters/Mohamad Torokman)*

*Page 343: In Istanbul, demonstrators decry imprisonment of journalists. (AFP/Mustafa Ozer)*

# Journalist Imprisonments Jump Worldwide, and Iran Is Worst

The number of journalists imprisoned worldwide shot up more than 20 percent to its highest level since the mid-1990s, an increase driven largely by widespread jailings across the Middle East and North Africa. In its annual census of imprisoned journalists, CPJ identified 179 writers, editors, and photojournalists behind bars on December 1, an increase of 34 over its 2010 tally.

Iran was the world's worst jailer, with 42 journalists behind bars, as authorities kept up a campaign of anti-press intimidation that began after the country's disputed presidential election more than two years ago. Eritrea, China, Burma, Vietnam, Syria, and Turkey also ranked among the world's worst.

CPJ's census found stark differences among regions. For the first time since CPJ began compiling annual prison surveys in 1990, not a single journalist in the Americas was in jail for work-related reasons on December 1. Imprisonments also continued a gradual decline in Europe and Central Asia, where only eight journalists were jailed, the lowest regional tally in six years. But those improvements were swamped by large-scale jailings across the Middle East and North Africa, where governments were holding 77 journalists behind bars, a figure that accounted for nearly 45 percent of the worldwide total. Asian and African nations also accounted for dozens of imprisonments.

While Iran's 2009 post-election crackdown marked the beginning of widespread press imprisonments there, authorities maintained a revolving cell door since that time, freeing some detainees on furloughs even as they made new arrests. Journalists freed on furloughs often posted six-figure bonds and endured enormous political pressure to keep silent or turn on their colleagues. "The volume of arrests, interrogations, and people out on bail is enormous," said Omid Memarian, an exiled Iranian journalist. "The effect is that many journalists know they should not touch critical subjects.

It really affects the way they cover the news because they are under constant fear and intimidation." Among the 2011 detainees was Iranian editor Mohammad Davari, a CPJ International Press Freedom Award winner whose website exposed the abuse and rape of inmates at the now-closed Kahrizak Detention Center. More than half of the Iranian detainees were being held on antistate charges similar to those lodged against Davari.

Antistate charges such as treason, subversion, or acting against national interests were the most common allegations brought against journalists worldwide. At least 79 journalists were being held on such charges, CPJ's survey found.

..................................................

## An alarming rise in the number held without charge or due process.

..................................................

But the 2011 census also found an alarming rise in the number of journalists held without charge or due process. Sixty-five journalists, accounting for more than a third of those in prison worldwide, were being held without any publicly disclosed charge, many of them in secret prisons without access to lawyers or family members. In some instances, governments such as those in Eritrea, Syria, and Gambia have denied the very existence of these jailed journalists. Reports of mistreatment and torture are common in these cases in which authorities operate without accountability and in contravention of international norms. Unconfirmed reports have identified at least six of these journalists as having died of mistreatment in custody. CPJ continues to list these detainees as it investigates the cases.

Imprisoning journalists without charge was practiced most commonly by the government of Eritrea, the world's second worst jailer of the press with 28 behind bars. Although many have been jailed for a decade, not a single Eritrean detainee has ever been publicly charged with a crime. Those jailed included the Swedish-Eritrean editor Dawit Isaac, who has been held since the government shuttered the country's independent press in 2001. Despite rising pressure from the European Parliament, Eritrean President Isaias Afewerki has made only vague assertions that Isaac made "a big mistake."

In a number of countries, authorities targeted journalists covering marginalized ethnic groups. Nowhere was this more evident than in China, where the government ruthlessly cracked down on editors and writers who sought to give voice to the nation's Tibetan and Uighur minority groups. Seventeen of the 27 journalists jailed in China covered oppressed ethnic groups. (Most of the others were online writers expressing dissident political views.) The detainees included Dokru Tsultrim, a monk whose news journal covered Tibetan affairs and who wrote critically about government policies toward Tibetans. Others may languish in China's prison without coming to the notice of news organizations or advocacy groups. "We know so few of the names of people who have been detained or imprisoned for political crimes," said John Kamm, chairman of the Dui Hua Foundation, a group that advocates for Chinese political prisoners.

Despite being widely credited for their reform plans, Burma's new civilian government leaders did little to change the severely repressive practices of their military predecessors. Authorities were jailing at least 12 journalists by December 1, a figure consistent with tallies over the past decade and one exceedingly high given the country's size. The world's fourth worst jailer of the press, the Burmese government was holding people such as Hla Hla Win, an undercover reporter for the exile-run Democratic Voice of Burma. She was arrested in 2009 while trying to report a piece marking the second anniversary of the Saffron Revolution, a series of monk-led demonstrations that was violently put down by government troops. "After politicians, journalists are the second main target," said Zin Linn, an exiled Burmese journalist and vice president of the Thailand-based Burma Media Association. That hasn't changed with the new government, he added. "I'm not expecting them to be released very quickly."

An ongoing crackdown against online reporting and commentary made Vietnam the world's fifth worst jailer. All nine of the Vietnamese journalists behind bars on December 1 were bloggers who covered politically sensitive

topics or the affairs of religious minorities. Among the detainees was Pham Minh Hoang, a blogger who wrote about official corruption, environmental degradation, and perceived government foreign policy failures.

Worldwide, 86 journalists whose work appeared primarily online were in jail on December 1, constituting nearly half of the census. The proportion is consistent with those seen in CPJ's previous two surveys, which had followed several years of significant increases in the numbers of imprisoned online journalists. Print journalists constituted the second largest professional group, with 51 jailed worldwide. The other detainees were from radio, television, and documentary filmmaking.

The number of journalists jailed in the Middle East and North Africa jumped by about 50 percent over the previous year. The increase came not only in nations such as Syria, where a repressive regime was jailing eight journalists in a desperate bid to retain power by suppressing independent reporting. Imprisonments were also reported in the stable democracy of Turkey, which was holding eight journalists when CPJ conducted its survey. While stepping up their past practice of imprisoning Kurdish editors and writers, authorities also began targeting mainstream journalists engaged in investigative reporting. The detainees in Turkey included Ahmet Şık and Nedim Şener, both prominent authors and newspaper journalists who critically probed government shortcomings. "After the imprisonment of these two journalists, it's more threatening for all journalists," said Erkan Saka, a political blogger and lecturer at Istanbul Bilgi University. "There is more self-censorship."

## Ethiopia uses a terror law to criminalize coverage of opposition groups.

Although the vast majority of detainees were local journalists being held by their own governments, eight international journalists were among those on CPJ's 2011 census. They included two Swedes, Johan Persson and Martin Schibbye, who were detained in Ethiopia while covering the activities of a separatist group. Seven journalists in all were being held in Ethiopia, five of them on vague and unsubstantiated terror charges. Despite international criticism, Ethiopia aggressively expanded the use of its antiterror law to criminalize news coverage of opposition groups. "It shows the government has no fear," said Kassahun Yilma, an Ethiopian journalist who fled the country in 2009 when confronted with the prospect of imprisonment. Any critical Ethiopian reporter ends up facing the same dilemma, he said. "Should we stay at home and go to jail for nothing, or flee?"

CPJ confirmed the deaths of two journalists in Bahraini government custody. Karim Fakhrawi, a founder of the country's leading independent newspaper *Al-Wasat*, and Zakariya Rashid Hassan al-Ashiri, editor of a local news website in his village of Al-Dair, died in Bahraini prisons within a week of each other in April. The government claimed the two died of natural causes, despite widespread allegations that abusive treatment led to their deaths.

Here are other trends and details that emerged in CPJ's analysis:

- The worldwide total was at its highest point since 1996, when CPJ recorded 185 journalists behind bars, a figure driven by Turkey's suppression of ethnic Kurdish journalists. The increase over the 2010 tally was the biggest single-year jump in a decade.

- At least 78 freelance journalists were in prison worldwide, constituting about 45 percent of the census, a proportion consistent with those seen in the previous two surveys. Freelance journalists can be vulnerable to imprisonment because they often do not have the legal and monetary support that news organizations can provide to staffers.

- Antistate charges were the most common charge used to jail journalists. Violations of censorship rules, the second most common charge, were applied in 14 cases.

- In 11 cases, governments used a variety of charges unrelated to journalism to retaliate against critical writers, editors, and photojournalists. Such charges ranged from drug possession to tax evasion. In the cases included in this census, CPJ determined that the charges were most likely lodged in reprisal for the journalist's work.

- Charges of criminal defamation, reporting "false" news, and engaging in ethnic or religious "insult" constituted the other charges filed against journalists in the census.

- For the first time in more than a decade, China did not lead or jointly lead the list of countries jailing journalists. That it was supplanted in 2011 was a reflection of the high numbers in Iran rather than a significant drop in China. The total of 27 journalists jailed in China on December 1 was consistent with figures documented over the past several years.

- For the first time since 1996, no Cuban journalists appeared on CPJ's census. The Cuban government was holding as many as 29 journalists in 2003, following a massive crackdown on dissent. The last of those detainees was freed in April 2011. Although no Cuban journalist was jailed on December 1, CPJ research shows that authorities continued to detain reporters and editors on a short-term basis as a form of harassment.

- In 2011, CPJ advocacy led to the early release of at least 65 imprisoned journalists worldwide. Among those freed were two CPJ International Press Freedom Award winners: Cuban writer Héctor Maseda Gutiérrez and Azerbaijani editor Eynulla Fatullayev.

- Two other CPJ awardees, Shi Tao in China and Davari in Iran, remained in jail on December 1. Shi was serving a 10-year prison term in China for divulging a propaganda department order that was retroactively declared a state secret.

CPJ believes that journalists should not be imprisoned for doing their jobs. The organization has sent letters expressing its serious concerns to each country that has imprisoned a journalist.

CPJ's list is a snapshot of those incarcerated at midnight on December 1, 2011. It does not include the many journalists imprisoned and released throughout the year; accounts of those cases can be found at cpj.org. Journalists remain on CPJ's list until the organization determines with reasonable certainty that they have been released or have died in custody.

Journalists who either disappear or are abducted by nonstate entities such as criminal gangs or militant groups are not included on the prison census. Their cases are classified as "missing" or "abducted."

*This analysis was compiled by CPJ staff with reporting by Kristin Jones.*

# 179 Journalists Imprisoned
# On December 1, 2011

## Azerbaijan: 1

IMPRISONED: OCTOBER 28, 2011

### Avaz Zeynally, *Khural*

Authorities in Baku arrested Zeynally on bribery and extortion charges stemming from a complaint filed by Gyular Akhmedova, a member of parliament. Akhmedova alleged that the editor had tried to extort 10,000 manat (US$12,700) from her in an August encounter, news reports said. A Nasimi District Court judge ordered that Zeynally be held in pretrial detention for three months, the independent Caucasus news website *Kavkazsky Uzel* reported. He faced up to 12 years in prison if convicted.

Zeynally denied the charges and described a much different encounter with Akhmedova. In September, Zeynally reported in *Khural* that Akhmedova had offered him money in exchange for his paper's loyalty to authorities. He said he had refused the offer.

Emin Huseynov, director of the Baku-based Institute for Reporters' Freedom and Safety, told CPJ that Zeynally's paper had criticized President Ilham Aliyev's repressive policies toward independent journalists and opposition activists. Before his arrest, Zeynally had published two commentaries in *Khural* that were especially critical of the administration. In the first, the editor disparaged comments made by Aliyev in a mid-October Al-Jazeera interview that painted a glowing picture of the country's development. In the second commentary, Zeynally accused the government of retaliatory prosecution against his newspaper, Huseynov told CPJ.

On October 19, the same day Akhmedova filed her complaint, court officers in Baku raided *Khural*'s newsroom and confiscated all of its reporting equipment. The raid stemmed from a 2010 defamation lawsuit filed by two presidential administration officials over a story alleging corruption. Court officers said Zeynally had failed to pay 15,000 manat (US$19,000) in damages that a Baku court had imposed in the case earlier in 2011, *Kavkazsky Uzel* reported. *Khural*'s website continued

347

to operate, but the print edition ceased following Zeynally's imprisonment and the police raid.

## Bahrain: 1

IMPRISONED: MARCH 17, 2011

### Abduljalil Alsingace, freelance

Alsingace, a journalistic blogger and human rights defender, was among a number of high-profile government critics arrested in March as the government renewed its crackdown on dissent.

In June, he was sentenced to life imprisonment for "plotting to topple the monarchy." In all, 21 bloggers, human rights activists, and members of the political opposition were found guilty on similar charges and handed lengthy sentences. (Ali Abdel Imam, another journalistic blogger, was sentenced to 15 years in prison but was in hiding in late year.)

On his blog, *Al-Faseela* (Sapling), Alsingace wrote critically about human rights violations, sectarian discrimination, and repression of the political opposition. He also monitored human rights for the Shiite-dominated opposition Haq Movement for Civil Liberties and Democracy.

Alsingace had been arrested on antistate conspiracy charges in August 2010 as part of widespread reprisals against political dissidents. He was released in February 2011 as part of a government effort to appease a then-nascent protest movement.

## Burma: 12

IMPRISONED: FEBRUARY 2004

### Ne Min (Win Shwe), freelance

Ne Min, a lawyer and a former stringer for the BBC, was sentenced to 15 years in prison on May 7, 2004. He was charged with illegally passing information to "anti-government" organizations operating in border areas, according to the Assistance Association for Political Prisoners in Burma, a prisoner aid group based in Thailand.

It was the second time that Burma's military government had imprisoned the well-known journalist, also known as Win Shwe, on charges related to disseminating information to news sources outside Burma. In 1989, a military tribunal sentenced Ne Min to 14 years of hard labor for "spreading false news and rumors to the BBC to fan further disturbances in the country" and "possession of documents including anti-government literature, which he planned to send to the BBC," according to official radio reports. He served nine years at Rangoon's Insein Prison before being released in 1998.

Exiled Burmese journalists told CPJ that Ne Min had provided news to political groups and exile-run news publications before his second arrest in February 2004.

IMPRISONED: NOVEMBER 27, 2007

## Win Maw, Democratic Voice of Burma

Military intelligence agents arrested Win Maw, an undercover reporter for the Democratic Voice of Burma, an Oslo-based Burmese exile news organization, in a Rangoon tea shop shortly after he had visited an Internet café. He is serving a 17-year jail sentence on various charges related to his news reporting.

Authorities accused him of acting as the "mastermind" of DVB's in-country news coverage of the 2007 Saffron Revolution, a series of Buddhist monk-led protests against the government that was put down by lethal military force, according to DVB.

The front man for the well-known pop band Shwe Thanzin (Golden Melody), Win Maw started reporting for DVB in 2003, a year after he was released from a seven-year prison sentence for composing pro-democracy songs, according to DVB. His video reports often focused on the activities of opposition groups, including the 88 Generation Students group.

After being arrested in November 2007, Win Maw was sentenced in closed-court proceedings on November 11, 2008, to seven years in prison for penal code violations stemming from the possession of video and recording equipment, and the Immigration Act violations related to crossing the Burmese border without a valid passport.

In March 2009, he was sentenced to an additional 10 years for violations of the Electronics Act after police raided his house while he was in detention and uncovered a computer disk with information destined for DVB, the news organizations said. The charges also related to his sending letters to DVB from an Internet café. The 11 months he spent in prison awaiting trial were not counted toward his sentence, according to the Canadian human rights group Centre for Law and Democracy.

Win Maw was being held at the remote Thandwe Prison in Arakan state, nearly 600 miles from his Rangoon-based family. Family members said police had tortured him during interrogations and denied him adequate medical attention after breaking his nose, according to DVB.

Win Maw received the 2010 Kenji Nagai Memorial Award, an honor bestowed on Burmese journalists in memory of the Japanese photojournalist shot and killed by Burmese troops while covering the 2007 Saffron Revolution. The award was created by APF, a Japanese video news agency, and the Burma Media Association, an exile-run press freedom group.

IMPRISONED: JANUARY 29, 2008

## Nay Phone Latt (Nay Myo Kyaw), freelance

Nay Phone Latt, also known as Nay Myo Kyaw, wrote a blog and owned three Internet cafés in Rangoon. He was arrested under the 1950 Emergency Provision Act on national security-related charges, according to news reports. His blog posts provided breaking news updates on the military's crackdown on the 2007 Saffron Revolution, and the reports were cited by a number of international news outlets, including the BBC. He also served as a youth member of the opposition National League for Democracy party, according to Reuters.

In July 2008, a court formally charged Nay Phone Latt with causing public offense and violating video and electronic laws when he posted caricatures of ruling generals on his blog, Reuters reported.

During closed judicial proceedings at Insein Prison on November 10, 2008, Nay Phone Latt was sentenced to 20 years and six months in prison, according to the Burma Media Association, a press freedom advocacy group, and news reports. He was transferred from Insein to Pa-an Prison in Karen state in late 2008, news reports said. The Rangoon Divisional Court later reduced the prison sentence to 12 years on appeal.

In 2010, he was honored with the prestigious PEN/Barbara Goldsmith Freedom to Write Award for his creative and courageous blog postings. At the New York ceremony honoring him, chairwoman Tina Brown read a statement that Nay Phone Latt managed to dispatch from prison: "This award is dedicated to all writing hands which are tightly restricted by the unfairness and are strongly eager for the freedom to write, all over the world."

IMPRISONED: JUNE 13, 2008

## Thant Zin Aung, freelance

Thant Zin Aung, an independent video journalist from Rangoon, was arrested as he was about to board a flight to Thailand with video footage showing the destruction caused by Cyclone Nargis, according to the Assistance Association for Political Prisoners in Burma. He was tried alongside journalists Maung Thura and Zaw Thet Htwe.

The trial, conducted inside Insein Prison, led to prison sentences in November 2008 that totaled 18 years. The sentence was reduced to 10 years on appeal. In 2011, Thant Zin Aung was being held in Pa-an Prison in the eastern state of Karen.

Thant Zin Aung was sentenced under the Television and Video Law, which prohibits copying or distributing video that is not approved by government censors, and the Electronics Act, which sets broad prohibitions against using technology for perceived "antistate" reasons.

IMPRISONED: JUNE 13, 2008

## Zaw Thet Htwe, freelance

Police arrested Rangoon-based freelance journalist Zaw Thet Htwe in the town of Minbu, where he was visiting his mother, Agence France-Presse reported. The sportswriter had been working with comedian-blogger Maung Thura in delivering aid to victims of Cyclone Nargis and videotaping the relief effort.

The journalist, who formerly edited the popular sports newspaper *First Eleven*, was indicted in a closed tribunal on August 7, 2008, and tried along with Maung Thura and two activists, AFP reported. The group faced multiple charges, including violating the Video and Electronics acts, disrupting public order, and engaging in unlawful association, news reports said. The Electronics Act allows for harsh prison sentences for anyone who uses electronic media to send information outside the country without government approval.

The Thailand-based Assistance Association for Political Prisoners in Burma said police officials confiscated a computer and cell phone during a raid on Zaw Thet Htwe's Rangoon home.

In November 2008, Zaw Thet Htwe was sentenced to a total of 19 years in prison, according to the exile-run Mizzima news agency. The Rangoon Divisional Court later reduced the term to 11 years, Mizzima reported. The journalist was serving his sentence in Taunggyi Prison in Shan state, nearly 400 miles from his home and family. Maung Thura, who was sentenced to 35 years in prison, was freed in an October 2011 amnesty of political prisoners.

Zaw Thet Htwe had been arrested before, in 2003, and given the death sentence for plotting to overthrow the government, news reports said. The sentence was later commuted to three years in prison, according to the exile-run news website *The Irrawaddy*. AFP reported that his 2003 arrest was related to a story about a misappropriated sports grant.

IMPRISONED: JUNE 18, 2009

## Zaw Tun (Win Oo), freelance

Zaw Tun, a freelance journalist and former chief reporter for the magazine *The News Watch*, was sentenced to two years' imprisonment after being arrested in June 2009, according to the Assistance Association for Political Prisoners in Burma. At Bahan Township Court, he was charged with obstructing a public servant.

A security officer found Zaw Tun, also known as Win Oo, near the home of the opposition leader Aung San Suu Kyi, who was then under house arrest. The officer arrested the journalist for purportedly responding impolitely to questions. In 2011, Zaw Tun was being held in Insein Prison.

IMPRISONED: JUNE 26, 2009

## Ngwe Soe Lin (Tun Kyaw), Democratic Voice of Burma

Ngwe Soe Lin, an undercover video journalist with the Democratic Voice of Burma (DVB), was arrested after leaving an Internet café in the Tamwe Township of Rangoon, according to DVB. Before the journalist's conviction, DVB had publicly referred to him only as "T."

Ngwe Soe Lin was one of two cameramen who took video footage of children orphaned by the 2008 Cyclone Nargis disaster for a documentary titled, "Orphans of the Burmese Cyclone." The film was recognized with a Rory Peck Award for best documentary in November 2009. DVB said that another video journalist, identified only as "Zoro," went into hiding after Ngwe Soe Lin's arrest.

On January 27, 2010, a special military court attached to Rangoon's Insein Prison sentenced Ngwe Soe Lin, also known as Tun Kyaw, to 13 years in prison for sending video footage outside of the country to DVB in violation of the Electronics Act, and for attending a 2008 DVB training session in Thailand in violation of the Immigration Act, according to DVB.

The trial was closed to the public and no court documents of his conviction have been released, according to the Canada-based human rights group Centre for Law and Democracy. In 2011, Ngwe Soe Lin was being held in Lashio Prison.

IMPRISONED: SEPTEMBER 11, 2009

## Hla Hla Win, Democratic Voice of Burma

## Myint Naing, freelance

Hla Hla Win, an undercover reporter with the Democratic Voice of Burma (DVB), was arrested while on a reporting assignment in Pakokku Township, Magwe Division, where she had conducted interviews with Buddhist monks in a local monastery. Her assistant, Myint Naing, was also arrested, according to the independent Asian Human Rights Commission.

Hla Hla Win was working on a story for the second anniversary of the 2007 Saffron Revolution, in which Buddhist monk-led protests were put down by lethal military force, according to her DVB editors. In October 2009, a Pakokku Township court sentenced Hla Hla Win and Myint Naing to seven years in prison each on charges of using an illegally imported motorcycle in violation of the Import/Export Act, and not registering as guests in Pakokku in violation of the Cities Act.

After being interrogated in prison, Hla Hla Win was sentenced to an additional 20 years in prison on December 30, 2009, on charges of violating the Television and Video Act and Electronics Act. Myint Naing was sentenced to an additional 25 years under the Electronics Act, the Asian Human Rights Commission said. The act allows for harsh prison sentences for anyone who uses electronic media to send information outside the country without government approval.

Hla Hla Win first joined DVB as an undercover reporter in December 2008. According to her editors, she played an active role in covering issues considered sensitive to the government, including local reaction to the controversial 2009 trial of opposition leader Aung San Suu Kyi, a Nobel Peace Prize laureate.

The Assistance Association for Political Prisoners in Burma said that Hla Hla Win was not provided legal representation during the trial. The court refused to hear her appeal in April 2010, and her family members publicly disowned her because of her activities, the association said. She has been transferred to Katha Prison, which the Canadian human rights group Centre for Law and Democracy characterized as a labor prison.

In 2010, Hla Hla Win received the Kenji Nagai Memorial Award, an honor bestowed on Burmese journalists in memory of the Japanese photojournalist shot and killed by Burmese troops while covering the 2007 Saffron Revolution. The award was created by APF, a Japanese video news agency, and the Burma Media Association, an exile-run press freedom group.

An initial report that the media assistant Myint Naing was among those released in an October 2011 government amnesty proved not to be true.

IMPRISONED: OCTOBER 14, 2009

## Nyi Nyi Tun, *Kandarawaddy*

A court attached to Rangoon's Insein Prison sentenced Nyi Nyi Tun, editor of the *Kandarawaddy*, a news journal based in Karenni state, to 13 years in prison in October 2010, a year after his initial detention.

The court found Nyi Nyi Tun guilty of several antistate crimes, including violations of the Unlawful Association, Immigration, and Wireless acts, according to Mizzima, a Burmese exile-run news agency, and the Asian Human Rights Commission.

Nyi Nyi Tun was initially detained on terrorism charges in October 2009, according to the Assistance Association for Political Prisoners in Burma, a Thailand-based advocacy organization. Authorities originally tried to connect him to a series of bomb blasts in Rangoon, but apparently dropped the allegations.

Nyi Nyi Tun told his family members that he had been tortured during his interrogation, Mizzima reported. The reported torture lasted for six days and included sodomy and repeated kicks to the head and face, according to the assistance association. Nyi Nyi Tun suffers from partial paralysis. He was among a group of 15 prisoners who staged a hunger strike in October 2011 to protest their continued detention.

After his arrest in 2009, Burmese authorities shut down *Kandarawaddy*, a local-language journal that operated out of the Kayah special region near the country's eastern border, according to the Burma Media Association, a press freedom advocacy group.

IMPRISONED: APRIL 15, 2010

## Sithu Zeya, Democratic Voice of Burma

Sithu Zeya, a video journalist with the Democratic Voice of Burma (DVB), was arrested while covering a grenade attack that left 10 dead and hundreds injured during the annual Buddhist New Year water festival in Rangoon, according to DVB. He was sentenced on two separate occasions to a total of 18 years in prison for his reporting activities.

On December 21, 2010, he was sentenced to eight years in prison under the Immigration and Unlawful Association acts on charges of illegally crossing the border and having ties to DVB.

DVB editors said Sithu Zeya was near the crowded area where the blast occurred and started filming the aftermath as authorities began to arrive on the scene. Authorities seized his laptop computer, video camera, and MP3 player, according to DVB. A police official, Khin Yi, said at a May 6, 2010, press conference that Sithu Zeya had been arrested for taking video footage of the attack.

On September 14, 2011, he was sentenced to an additional 10 years in prison under the Electronics Act. A Rangoon court ruled that his online activities threatened to "damage the tranquility and unity in the government," according to international press reports.

His mother, Yee Yee Tint, told DVB after a prison visit in May 2010 that the journalist had been denied food and that the beatings he suffered during police interrogations had left him with a constant ringing in his ear. The Canada-based Centre for Law and Democracy said he was tortured in a variety of ways, including beatings on the soles of his feet, being hung upside down, and being forced to maintain stress positions.

DVB Deputy Editor Khin Maung Win told CPJ that Sithu Zeya had been forced to reveal under torture that his father, Maung Maung Zeya, also served as an undercover DVB reporter. (Maung Maung Zeya was arrested two days later.) The Assistance Association for Political Prisoners in Burma reported that Sithu Zeya was placed in an isolation cell in January 2011 for failing to comply with prison regulations. He was taken out of the isolation cell every 15 minutes and forced to repeatedly squat and crawl as punishment, the assistance association said.

Both of his convictions were based solely on his forced confessions, without any independent corroborating evidence, the Centre for Law and Democracy said.

IMPRISONED: APRIL 17, 2010

## Maung Maung Zeya (Thargyi Zeya)

Democratic Voice of Burma

Maung Maung Zeya, an undercover reporter with the Democratic Voice of Burma (DVB), was taken into custody two days after his son and fellow DVB journalist, Sithu Zeya, was arrested for filming the aftermath of a fatal bomb attack during a Buddhist New Year celebration, according to DVB. At the time of his arrest, authorities confiscated many of his personal belongings, claiming they were tools for illegal activities bought with funds supplied by illegal outside organizations, according to the Canada-based Centre for Law and Democracy.

Maung Maung Zeya, also known as Thargyi Zeya, was sentenced on February 6, 2011, to 13 years under the Unlawful Association Act, Electronics Transactions Law, and Immigration Act. He was being held in 2011 in remote Hsipaw Prison, away from his son in Insein Prison and his Rangoon-based family, according to the Assistance Association for Political Prisoners in Burma.

Maung Maung Zeya was first detained and interrogated at the Bahan Township police station in Rangoon and transferred on June 14, 2010, to Insein Prison. Maung Maung Zeya told a legal adviser that he was drugged during the initial days of his detention, according to the Centre for Law and Democracy.

DVB editors said Maung Maung Zeya was a senior member of its undercover team in Burma and was responsible for operational management, including assigning stories to other DVB journalists. DVB Deputy Editor Khin Maung Win told CPJ that authorities had offered to free Maung Maung Zeya if he divulged the names of other undercover DVB reporters.

## Burundi: 1

IMPRISONED: NOVEMBER 28, 2011

### Hassan Ruvakiki, Radio Bonesha

National Intelligence Service agents arrested Ruvakiki, a reporter for the private broadcaster Radio Bonesha, as he covered a press conference in the capital, Bujumbura, during the Summit of Heads of States of the East African Community, according to local journalists.

Ruvakiki was held without access to legal counsel for two days before intelligence service spokesman Télésphore Bigiriman confirmed his arrest in an interview with Agence France-Presse, according to news reports. The journalist was interrogated about alleged interactions with the head of a rebel group, he told AFP. The arrest came amid a government clampdown on coverage of the group.

Radio Publique Africaine, another independent station, had recently aired an interview with Pierre Claver Kabirigi, a former police officer who claimed to head the newly formed rebel group Front for the Restoration of Democracy–Abanyagihugu, according to news reports. Other independent news outlets picked up the interview, prompting the government-controlled media regulatory agency to issue a directive forbidding coverage that "can undermine the security of the population," according to news reports.

On November 30, a judge charged Ruvakiki with "participating in acts of terrorism," according to news reports. Local journalists told CPJ they believed the charges against Ruvakiki were intended to intimidate critical news media. Ruvakiki was also a local correspondent for the Swahili service of the French government-funded Radio France Internationale.

## China: 27

IMPRISONED: SEPTEMBER 13, 2003

### Huang Jinqiu (Qing Shuijun, Huang Jin), freelance

Huang, a columnist for the U.S.-based website *Boxun News*, was arrested in Jiangsu province, and his family was not notified of his arrest for more than three months. On September 27, 2004, the Changzhou Intermediate People's Court sentenced him to 12 years in prison on charges of "subversion of state authority," along with four years' deprivation of political rights. The sentence was unusually harsh and appeared linked to his intention to form an opposition party.

Huang worked as a writer and editor in his native Shandong province, as well as in Guangdong province, before leaving China in 2000 to study journalism at the Central Academy of Art in Malaysia. While he was overseas, he began writing political commentary for *Boxun News* under the penname Qing Shuijun. He also wrote articles on arts and entertainment under the name Huang Jin. Huang's writings reportedly caught the attention of the government in 2001. He told a friend that authorities had contacted his family to warn them about his writings, according to *Boxun News*.

In January 2003, Huang wrote in his online column that he intended to form a new opposition party, the China Patriot Democracy Party. When he returned to China in August 2003, he eluded public security agents just long enough to visit his family in Shandong province. In the last article he posted on *Boxun News*, titled "Me and My Public Security Friends," he described being followed and harassed by security agents.

Huang's appeal was rejected in December 2004. He was given a 22-month sentence reduction in July 2007, according to the U.S.-based prisoner advocacy group Dui Hua Foundation. The journalist, who suffered from arthritis, was serving his term in Pukou Prison in Jiangsu province. *Boxun News* reported in 2010 that he had been refused a request for bail on medical grounds.

IMPRISONED: DECEMBER 13, 2003

## Kong Youping, freelance

Kong, an essayist and poet, was arrested in Anshan, Liaoning province. A former trade union official, he had written online articles that supported democratic reforms, appealed for the release of then-imprisoned Internet writer Liu Di, and called for a reversal of the government's "counterrevolutionary" ruling on the pro-democracy demonstrations of 1989.

Kong's essays included an appeal to democracy activists in China that stated, "In order to work well for democracy, we need a well-organized, strong, powerful, and effective organization. Otherwise, a mainland democracy movement will accomplish nothing." Several of his articles and poems were posted on the *Minzhu Luntan* (Democracy Forum) website.

In 1998, Kong served time in prison after he became a member of the Liaoning province branch of the China Democracy Party (CDP), an opposition party. In 2004, he was tried on subversion charges along with co-defendant Ning Xianhua, who was accused of being vice chairman of the CDP branch in Liaoning, according to the U.S.-based advocacy organization Human Rights in China and court documents obtained by the U.S.-based Dui Hua Foundation. On September 16, 2004, the Shenyang Intermediate People's Court sentenced Kong to 15 years in prison, plus four years' deprivation of political rights. His sentence was reduced to 10 years on appeal, according to the Independent Chinese PEN Center.

Kong suffered from hypertension and was imprisoned in the city of Lingyuan, far from his family. The group reported that his eyesight was deteriorating. Ning, who received a 12-year sentence, was released ahead of schedule on December 15, 2010, according to Radio Free Asia.

IMPRISONED: NOVEMBER 24, 2004

## Shi Tao, freelance

Shi, former editorial director of the Changsha-based newspaper *Dangdai Shang Bao* (Contemporary Trade News), was detained near his home in Taiyuan, Shanxi province, in November 2004.

He was formally charged with "providing state secrets to foreigners" by sending an email on his Yahoo account to the U.S.-based editor of the website *Minzhu Luntan* (Democracy Forum). In the email, sent anonymously in April 2004, Shi transmitted notes from the local propaganda department's recent instructions to his newspaper. The directives prescribed coverage of the outlawed Falun Gong and the anniversary of the military crackdown on demonstrators at Tiananmen Square. The National Administration for the Protection of State Secrets retroactively certified the contents of the e-mail as classified, the official Xinhua News Agency reported.

On April 27, 2005, the Changsha Intermediate People's Court found Shi guilty and sentenced him to a 10-year prison term. In June of that year, the Hunan Province High People's Court rejected his appeal without granting a hearing.

Court documents in the case revealed that Yahoo had supplied information to Chinese authorities that helped them identify Shi as the sender of the email. Yahoo's participation in the identification of Shi and other jailed dissidents raised questions about the role that international Internet companies play in the repression of online speech in China and elsewhere.

In November 2005, CPJ honored Shi with its annual International Press Freedom Award for his courage in defending the ideals of free expression. In November 2007, members of the U.S. House Committee on Foreign Affairs rebuked Yahoo executives for their role in the case and for wrongly testifying in earlier hearings that the company did not know the Chinese government's intentions when it sought Shi's account information.

Yahoo, Google, and Microsoft later joined with human rights organizations, academics, and investors to form the Global Network Initiative, which adopted a set of principles to protect online privacy and free expression in October 2008.

Human Rights Watch awarded Shi a Hellman/Hammett grant for persecuted writers in October 2009.

IMPRISONED: DECEMBER 3, 2004

## Zheng Yichun, freelance

Zheng, a former professor, was a regular contributor to overseas news websites, including the U.S.-based *Epoch Times*, which is affiliated with the banned religious movement Falun Gong. He wrote a series of editorials that directly criticized the Communist Party and its control of the media.

Because of police warnings, Zheng's family remained silent about his detention in Yingkou, Liaoning province, until state media reported that he had been arrested on suspicion of inciting subversion. Zheng was initially tried by the Yingkou Intermediate People's Court on April 26, 2005. No verdict was announced and, on July 21, he was tried again on the same charges. As in the April 26 trial, proceedings lasted just three hours. Though officially "open" to the public, the courtroom was closed to all observers except close family members and government officials. Zheng's supporters and a journalist were prevented from entering, according to a local source.

Prosecutors cited dozens of articles written by the journalist and listed the titles of several essays in which he called for political reform, increased capitalism in China, and an end to the practice of imprisoning writers. On September 20, 2005, the court sentenced Zheng to seven years in prison, to be followed by three years' deprivation of political rights.

Sources familiar with the case believe that Zheng's harsh sentence may be linked to Chinese leaders' objections to the *Epoch Times* series "Nine Commentaries on the Communist Party," which called the Chinese Communist Party an "evil cult" with a "history of killings" and predicted its demise.

Zheng is diabetic, and his health declined after his imprisonment. After his first appeal was rejected, he intended to pursue an appeal in a higher court, but his defense lawyer, Gao Zhisheng, was himself imprisoned in August 2006. Zheng's family was unable to find another lawyer willing to take the case.

In summer 2008, prison authorities at Jinzhou Prison in Liaoning informed Zheng's family that he had suffered a brain hemorrhage and received urgent treatment in prison. However, no lawyer would agree to represent Zheng in an appeal for medical parole, according to Zheng Xiaochun, the journalist's brother, who spoke with CPJ by telephone.

IMPRISONED: DECEMBER 23, 2005

## Yang Tongyan (Yang Tianshui), freelance

Yang, commonly known by his penname, Yang Tianshui, was detained along with a friend in Nanjing, eastern China. He was tried on charges of "subverting state authority," and on May 17, 2006, the Zhenjiang Intermediate People's Court sentenced him to 12 years in prison.

Yang was a well-known writer and member of the Independent Chinese PEN Center. He was a frequent contributor to U.S.-based websites banned in China, including *Boxun News* and *Epoch Times*. He often wrote critically about the ruling Communist Party, and he advocated for the release of jailed Internet writers.

According to the verdict in Yang's case, which was translated into English by the U.S.-based Dui Hua Foundation, the harsh sentence against him was related to a fictitious online election, established by overseas Chinese citizens, for a "democratic Chinese transitional government." His colleagues say that without his prior knowledge, he was elected to the leadership of the fictional government. He later wrote an article in *Epoch Times* in support of the model.

Prosecutors also accused Yang of transferring money from overseas to Wang Wenjiang, who had been convicted of endangering state security. Yang's defense lawyer argued that this money was humanitarian assistance to the family of a jailed dissident and should not have constituted a criminal act.

Believing that the proceedings were fundamentally unjust, Yang did not appeal. He had already spent 10 years in prison for his opposition to the military crackdown on demonstrators at Tiananmen Square in 1989.

In June 2008, Shandong provincial authorities refused to renew the law license of Yang's lawyer, press freedom advocate Li Jianqiang. In 2008, the PEN American Center announced that Yang was a recipient of the PEN/Barbara Goldsmith Freedom to Write Award.

IMPRISONED: JUNE 25, 2007

## Qi Chonghuai, freelance

Qi and a colleague, Ma Shiping, criticized a local official in Shandong province in an article published June 8, 2007, on the website of the U.S.-based *Epoch Times*, according to Qi's lawyer, Li Xiongbing. On June 14, the two posted photographs on Xinhua news agency's anti-corruption Web forum showing a luxurious government building in the city of Tengzhou.

Police in Tengzhou detained Ma on June 16 on charges of carrying a false press card. Qi, a journalist of 13 years, was arrested in his home in Jinan, the provincial capital, more than a week later, and charged with fraud and extortion, Li said. Qi was convicted and sentenced to four years in prison on May 13, 2008.

Qi was accused of taking money from local officials while reporting several stories, a charge he denied. The people from whom he was accused of extorting money were local officials threatened by his reporting, Li said. Qi told his lawyer and his wife, Jiao Xia, that police beat him during questioning on August 13, 2007, and again during a break in his trial. Qi was being held in Tengzhou Prison, a four-hour trip from his family's home, which limited visits.

Ma, a freelance photographer, was sentenced in late 2007 to one and a half years in prison. He was released in 2009, according to Jiao Xia.

Qi was scheduled for release in 2011. In May, local authorities informed Qi that the court had received new evidence against him. On June 9, less than three weeks before the end of his term, a Shandong provincial court sentenced him to another eight years in jail, according to the New York-based advocacy group Human Rights in China and Radio Free Asia.

Human Rights in China, citing an online article by defense lawyer Li Xiaoyuan, said the court tried Qi on a new count of stealing advertising revenue from a former employer, *China Security Produce News*. The journalist's supporters speculated that the new charge came in reprisal for Qi's statements to his jailers that he would continue reporting after his release, according to *The New York Times*.

IMPRISONED: MARCH 26, 2008

## Dhondup Wangchen, Filming for Tibet

Police in Tongde, Qinghai province, arrested Wangchen, a Tibetan documentary filmmaker, shortly after he sent footage filmed in Tibet to colleagues, according to the production company, Filming for Tibet. A 25-minute film titled "Jigdrel" (Leaving Fear Behind) was produced from the tapes. Wangchen's assistant, Jigme Gyatso, was also arrested, once in March 2008 and again in March 2009, after speaking out about his treatment in prison, Filming for Tibet said.

Filming for Tibet was founded in Switzerland by Gyaljong Tsetrin, a relative of Wangchen, who left Tibet in 2002 but maintained contact with people there. Tsetrin told CPJ that he had spoken to Wangchen on March 25, 2008, but that he had lost contact after that. He learned of the detention only later, after speaking by telephone with relatives.

Filming for the documentary was completed shortly before peaceful protests against Chinese rule of Tibet deteriorated into riots in Lhasa and in Tibetan areas of China in March 2008. The filmmakers had gone to Tibet to ask ordinary people about their lives under Chinese rule in the run-up to the Olympics.

The arrests were first publicized when the documentary was screened in August 2008 before a small group of foreign reporters in a hotel room in Beijing on August 6. A second screening was interrupted by hotel management, according to Reuters.

Officials in Xining, Qinghai province, charged the filmmaker with inciting separatism and replaced the Tibetan's own lawyer with a government appointee in July 2009, according to international reports.

On December 28, 2009, the Xining Intermediate People's Court in Qinghai sentenced Wangchen to six years' imprisonment on subversion charges, according to a statement issued by his family.

Wangchen was born in Qinghai but moved to Lhasa as a young man, according to his published biography. He had recently relocated with his wife, Lhamo Tso, and four children to Dharamsala, India, before returning to Tibet to begin filming, according to a report published in October 2008 by the *South China Morning Post*. Lhamo Tso told Radio Netherlands Worldwide in 2011 that her husband was working extremely long hours in prison and had contracted hepatitis B.

Tsetrin told CPJ that Wangchen's assistant, Gyatso, was arrested on March 23, 2008. Gyatso, released on October 15, 2008, later described having been brutally beaten by interrogators during his seven months in detention, according to Filming for Tibet. The Dharamsala-based Tibetan Center for Human Rights and Democracy reported that Gyatso was rearrested in March 2009 and released the next month.

IMPRISONED: DECEMBER 8, 2008

## Liu Xiaobo, freelance

Liu, a longtime advocate for political reform and the 2010 Nobel Peace Prize laureate, was imprisoned for "inciting subversion" through his writing.

Liu was an author of Charter 08, a document promoting universal values, human rights, and democratic reform in China, and was among its 300 original signatories. He was detained in Beijing shortly before the charter was officially released, according to international news reports.

Liu was formally charged with subversion in June 2009, and he was tried in the Beijing Number 1 Intermediate Court in December of that year. Diplomats from the United States, United Kingdom, Canada, and Sweden were denied access to the trial, the BBC reported. On December 25, 2009, the court convicted Liu of "inciting subversion" and sentenced him to 11 years in prison and two years' deprivation of political rights.

The verdict cited several articles Liu had posted on overseas websites, including the BBC's Chinese-language site and the U.S.-based websites *Epoch Times* and *Observe China*, all of which had criticized Communist Party rule. Six articles were named—including pieces headlined, "So the Chinese people only deserve 'one-party participatory democracy?'" and "Changing the regime by changing society"—as evidence that Liu had incited subversion. Liu's income was generated by his writing, his wife told the court.

The court verdict cited Liu's authorship and distribution of Charter 08 as further evidence of subversion. The Beijing Municipal High People's Court upheld the verdict in February 2010.

In October 2010, the Nobel Prize Committee awarded Liu its 2010 Peace Prize "for his long and nonviolent struggle for fundamental human rights in China." His wife, Liu Xia, was kept under tight surveillance following the award, according to international news reports.

Liu was allowed to attend a memorial service for his father in September 2011, international news reports said.

IMPRISONED: FEBRUARY 26, 2009

## Kunchok Tsephel Gopey Tsang, *Chomei*

Public security officials arrested Kunchok Tsephel, an online writer, in Gannan, a Tibetan Autonomous Prefecture in the south of Gansu province, according to Tibetan rights groups. Kunchok Tsephel ran the Tibetan cultural issues website *Chomei*, according to the Dharamsala-based Tibetan Centre for Human Rights and Democracy. Kate Saunders, U.K. communications director for the International Campaign for Tibet, told CPJ by telephone from New Delhi that she learned of his arrest from two sources.

The detention appeared to be part of a wave of arrests of writers and intellectuals in advance of the 50th anniversary of the March 1959 uprising preceding the Dalai Lama's departure from Tibet. The 2008 anniversary had provoked ethnic rioting in Tibetan areas, and foreign reporters were barred from the region.

In November 2009, a Gannan court sentenced Kunchok Tsephel to 15 years in prison for disclosing state secrets, according to The Associated Press.

IMPRISONED: MARCH 17, 2009

## Kunga Tsayang (Gang-Nyi), freelance

The Public Security Bureau arrested Kunga Tsayang during a late-night raid, according to the Dharamsala-based Tibetan Centre for Human Rights and Democracy, which said it had received the information from several sources.

An environmental activist and photographer who also wrote online articles under the penname Gang-Nyi (Sun of Snowland), Tsayang maintained his own website titled *Zindris* (Jottings) and contributed to others. He wrote several essays on politics in Tibet, including "Who Is the Real Instigator of Protests?" according to the New York-based advocacy group Students for a Free Tibet.

Kunga Tsayang was convicted of revealing state secrets and sentenced in November 2010 to five years in prison, according to the center. Sentencing was imposed during a closed-court proceeding in the Tibetan area of Gannan, Gansu province.

A number of Tibetans, including journalists, were arrested around the March 10 anniversary of the failed uprising in 1959 that prompted the Dalai Lama's departure from Tibet. Security measures were heightened in the region in the aftermath of ethnic rioting in March 2008.

IMPRISONED: MARCH 28, 2009

## Tan Zuoren, freelance

Tan, an environmentalist and activist, had been investigating the deaths of schoolchildren killed in the May 2008 earthquake in Sichuan province when he was detained in Chengdu. Tan, believing that shoddy school construction contributed to the high death toll, had intended to publish the results of his investigation ahead of the first anniversary of the earthquake, according to international news reports.

His supporters believe Tan was detained because of his investigation, although the formal charges did not cite his earthquake reporting. Instead, he was charged with "inciting subversion" for writings posted on overseas websites that criticized the military crackdown on demonstrators at Tiananmen Square on June 4, 1989.

In particular, authorities cited "1989: A Witness to the Final Beauty," a firsthand account of the Tiananmen crackdown published on overseas websites in 2007, according to court documents. Several witnesses, including the prominent artist Ai Weiwei, were detained and blocked from testifying on Tan's behalf at his August 2009 trial.

On February 9, 2010, Tan was convicted and sentenced to five years in prison, according to international news reports. On June 9, 2010, the Sichuan Provincial High People's Court rejected his appeal. Tan's wife, Wang Qinghua, told reporters in Hong Kong and overseas that he had contracted gout and was not receiving sufficient medical attention.

IMPRISONED: JULY 2009

## Memetjan Abdulla, freelance

Abdulla, editor of the state-run China National Radio's Uighur service, was detained in July 2009 for allegedly instigating ethnic rioting in the Xinjiang Uighur Autonomous Region through postings on the Uighur-language website *Salkin*, which he managed in his spare time, according to international news reports. A court in the regional capital, Urumqi, sentenced him to life imprisonment on April 1, 2010, the reports said. The exact charges against Abdulla were not disclosed.

The U.S. government-funded Radio Free Asia reported on the sentence in December 2010, citing an unnamed witness at the trial. Abdulla was targeted for talking to foreign journalists in Beijing about the riots, and translating articles on the *Salkin* website, RFA reported. The Germany-based World Uyghur Congress confirmed the sentence with sources in the region, according to *The New York Times.*

IMPRISONED: JULY 2009

## Tursunjan Hezim, *Orkhun*

Details of Hezim's arrest following 2009 ethnic unrest in northwestern Xinjiang Uighur Autonomous Region first emerged in March 2011. Police in Xinjiang detained foreign journalists and severely restricted Internet access for several months after rioting broke out on July 5, 2009, in Urumqi, the regional capital, between groups of Han Chinese and the predominantly Muslim Uighur minority.

The U.S. government-funded Radio Free Asia (RFA), citing an anonymous source, reported that a court in the region's far western district of Aksu had sentenced Hezim along with other journalists and dissidents in July 2010. Several other Uighur website managers received heavy prison terms for posting articles and discussions about the previous year's violence, according to CPJ research.

Hezim edited a well-known Uighur website, *Orkhun.* U.S.-based Uighur scholar Erkin Sidick told CPJ that the editor's whereabouts had been unknown from the time of the rioting until news of the conviction surfaced in 2011. Hezim was sentenced to seven years in prison on unknown charges in a trial closed to observers, according to Sidick, who had learned the news by telephone from his native Aksu, and RFA. Chinese authorities frequently restrict information on sensitive trials, particularly those involving ethnic minorities, according to CPJ research.

IMPRISONED: JULY OR AUGUST 2009

## Gulmire Imin, freelance

Imin was one of several administrators of Uighur-language Web forums who were arrested after July 2009 riots in Urumqi, in Xinjiang Uighur Autonomous Region. In August 2010, Imin was sentenced to life in prison on charges of separatism, leaking state secrets, and organizing an illegal demonstration, a witness to her trial told the U.S. government-funded broadcaster Radio Free Asia.

Imin held a local government post in Urumqi. As a sidelight, she contributed poetry and short stories to the cultural website *Salkin*, and had been invited to help moderate the site in late spring 2009, her husband, Behtiyar Omer, told CPJ.

Authorities accused Imin of being an organizer of major demonstrations on July 5, 2009, and of using the Uighur-language website to distribute information about the event, RFA reported. Imin had been critical of the government in her online writings, readers of the website told RFA. The website was shut down after the July riots and its contents were deleted.

She was also accused of leaking state secrets by phone to her husband, who lives in Norway. Her husband told CPJ that he had called her on July 5 only to be sure she was safe.

The riots, which began as a protest of the death of Uighur migrant workers in Guangdong province, turned violent and resulted in the deaths of 200 people, according to the official Chinese government count. Chinese authorities shut down the Internet in Xinjiang for months after the riots as hundreds of protesters were arrested, according to international human rights organizations and local and international media reports.

IMPRISONED: JULY OR AUGUST 2009

## Nijat Azat, *Shabnam*

## Nureli, *Salkin*

Authorities imprisoned Nureli, who goes by one name, and Azat in an apparent crackdown on Uighur-language website managers. Azat was sentenced to 10 years and Nureli three years on charges of endangering state security, according to international news reports. The precise dates of their arrests and convictions were not clear.

Their sites, which have been shut down by the government, had run news articles and discussion groups concerning Uighur issues. *The*

*New York Times* cited friends and family members of the men who said they were prosecuted because they had failed to respond quickly enough when they were ordered to delete content that discussed the difficulties of life in Xinjiang. Their whereabouts were unknown in late 2011.

IMPRISONED: AUGUST 7, 2009

## Dilixiati Paerhati, *Diyarim*

Paerhati, who edited the popular Uighur-language website *Diyarim*, was one of several online forum administrators arrested after ethnic violence in Urumqi in July 2009. Paerhati was sentenced to a five-year prison term in July 2010 on charges of endangering state security, according to international news reports.

He was detained and interrogated about riots in the Xinjiang Uighur Autonomous Region on July 24, 2009, but released without charge after eight days. Agents seized Paerhati from his apartment again on August 7, 2009, although the government issued no formal notice of arrest, his U.K.-based brother, Dilimulati, told Amnesty International. News reports, citing his brother, said Paerhati was prosecuted for failing to comply with an official order to delete anti-government comments on the website.

IMPRISONED: OCTOBER 1, 2009

## Gheyrat Niyaz (Hailaite Niyazi), *Uighurbiz*

Security officials arrested website manager Niyaz, sometimes referred to as Hailaite Niyazi, in his home in the regional capital, Urumqi, according to international news reports. He was convicted under sweeping charges of "endangering state security" and sentenced to 15 years in prison.

According to international media reports, Niyaz was punished because of an August 2, 2009, interview with *Yazhou Zhoukan* (Asia Weekly), a Chinese-language magazine based in Hong Kong. In the interview, Niyaz said authorities had not taken steps to prevent violence in the July 2009 ethnic unrest that broke out in China's far-western Xinjiang Uighur Autonomous Region.

Niyaz, who once worked for the state newspapers *Xinjiang Legal News* and *Xinjiang Economic Daily*, also managed and edited the website *Uighurbiz* until June 2009. A statement posted on the website quoted Niyaz's wife as saying that while he did give interviews to foreign media, he had no malicious intentions.

Authorities blamed local and international Uighur sites for fueling the violence between Uighurs and Han Chinese in the predominantly Muslim Xinjiang region. *Uighurbiz* founder Ilham Tohti was questioned about the contents of the site and detained for more than six weeks, according to international news reports.

IMPRISONED: APRIL 6, 2010

## Tashi Rabten, freelance

Public security officials detained Tashi Rabten for publishing a banned magazine and a collection of articles, according to *Phayul*, a pro-Tibetan independence news website based in New Delhi.

Tashi Rabten, a student at Northwest Minorities University in Lanzhou, Gansu province, edited the magazine *Shar Dungri* (Eastern Snow Mountain) in the aftermath of ethnic rioting in Tibet in March 2008. The magazine was banned by local authorities, according to the International Campaign for Tibet. The journalist later self-published a collection of articles titled *Written in Blood*, saying in the introduction that "after an especially intense year of the usual soul-destroying events, something had to be said," the campaign reported.

The book and the magazine discussed democracy and recent anti-China protests; the book was banned after he had distributed 400 copies, according to the U.S. government-funded Radio Free Asia (RFA). Tashi Rabten had already been detained once before, in 2009, according to international Tibetan rights groups and RFA.

A court in Aba prefecture, a predominantly Tibetan area of Sichuan province, sentenced him to four years in prison in a closed-door trial on June 2, 2011, according to RFA and the International Campaign for Tibet. RFA cited a family member saying he had been charged with separatism, although CPJ could not independently confirm the charge.

IMPRISONED: MAY 24, 2010

## Dokru Tsultrim (Zhuori Cicheng), freelance

A monk at Ngaba Gomang Monastery in western Sichuan province, Dokru Tsultrim was detained in April 2009 for alleged anti-government writings and articles in support of the Dalai Lama, according to the Dharamsala-based Tibetan Centre for Human Rights and Democracy and the International Campaign for Tibet. Released after a month in custody, he was detained again in May 2010, according to the Dharamsala-based *Tibet Post International*. No formal charges or trial proceedings were disclosed.

At the time of his 2010 arrest, security officials raided his room at the monastery, confiscated documents, and demanded his laptop, a relative told *The Tibet Post International*. He and a friend had planned to publish the writings of Tibetan youths detailing an April 2010 earthquake in Qinghai province, the relative said.

Dokru Tsultrim, originally from Qinghai province, which is on the Tibetan plateau, also managed a private Tibetan journal, *Khawai Tsesok* (Life of Snow), which ceased publication after his 2009 arrest, the center said. "Zhuori Cicheng" is the Chinese transliteration of his name, according to Tashi Choephel Jamatsang at the center, who provided CPJ with details by email.

IMPRISONED: JUNE 28, 2010

## Liu Xianbin, freelance

A court in western Sichuan province sentenced Liu Xianbin to 10 years in prison on charges of inciting subversion through articles published on overseas websites between April 2009 and February 2010, according to international news reports. One was titled "Constitutional Democracy for China: Escaping Eastern Autocracy," according to the BBC.

The sentence was unusually harsh; inciting subversion normally carries a maximum five-year penalty, international news reports said. Liu also signed Liu Xiaobo's pro-democracy Charter 08 petition. (Liu Xiaobo, who won the 2010 Nobel Peace Prize for his actions, is serving an 11-year term on the same charge.)

Police detained Liu Xianbin on June 28, 2010, according to the Washington-based prisoner rights group Laogai Foundation. His sentencing in 2011 came during a crackdown on bloggers and activists who sought to organize demonstrations inspired by uprisings in the Middle East and North Africa, according to CPJ research.

Liu spent more than two years in prison for involvement in the 1989 anti-government protests in Tiananmen Square. He later served 10 years of a 13-year prison sentence handed down in 1999 after he had founded a branch of the China Democracy Party, according to *The New York Times*.

IMPRISONED: JUNE AND JULY 2010

## Buddha, freelance

## Jangtse Donkho (Nyen, Rongke), freelance

## Kalsang Jinpa (Garmi), freelance

The three men, contributors to the banned Tibetan-language magazine *Shar Dungri* (Eastern Snow Mountain), were detained in Aba, a Tibetan area in southwestern Sichuan province, the U.S. government-funded Radio Free Asia (RFA) reported.

Jangtse Donkho, an author and editor who wrote under the penname Nyen, meaning "Wild One," was detained on June 21, 2010, RFA reported. The name on his official ID is Rongke, according to the International Campaign for Tibet. Many Tibetans use only one name.

Buddha, a practicing physician, was detained on June 26 at the hospital where he worked in the town of Aba. Kalsang Jinpa, who wrote under the penname Garmi, meaning "Blacksmith," was detained on June 19, RFA reported, citing local sources.

On October 21, 2010, they were tried together in the Aba Intermediate Court on charges of inciting separatism that were based on articles they had written in the aftermath of the March 2008 ethnic rioting. RFA, citing an unnamed source in Tibet, reported that the court later sentenced Jangtse Donkho and Buddha to four years' imprisonment apiece and Kalsang Jinpa to three years. In January 2011, the broadcaster reported the three had been placed at the Mian Yang jail near the Sichuan capital, Chengdu, where they were subjected to hard labor.

*Shar Dungri* was a collection of essays published in July 2008 and distributed in western China before authorities banned the publication, according to the advocacy group International Campaign for Tibet, which translated the journal. The writers assailed Chinese human rights abuses against Tibetans, lamented a history of repression, and questioned official media accounts of the March 2008 unrest.

Buddha's essay, "Hindsight and Reflection," was presented as part of the prosecution, RFA reported. According to a translation of the essay by the International Campaign for Tibet, Buddha wrote: "If development means even the slightest difference between today's standards and the living conditions of half a century ago, why the disparity between the pace of construction and progress in Tibet and in mainland China?"

The editor of *Shar Dungri*, Tashi Rabten, was also jailed in 2010.

IMPRISONED: OCTOBER 1, 2010

## Jolep Dawa, *Durab Kyi Nga*

A court in Aba in southwestern Sichuan province sentenced Jolep Dawa, a Tibetan writer and editor, to three years in prison in October 2011, according to U.S. government-funded Radio Free Asia and the India-based Tibetan Centre for Human Rights and Democracy.

He had been held in detention without trial since October 1, 2010, the organizations said. The exact date of the sentencing was not reported, and the charges against the writer were not disclosed. Jolep Dawa, who is also a teacher, edited a monthly Tibetan-language magazine, *Durab Kyi Nga*, according to the broadcaster and the rights group.

IMPRISONED: FEBRUARY 20, 2011

## Chen Wei, freelance

Police in Suining city, Sichuan, detained Chen among the dozens of lawyers, writers, and activists jailed nationwide following anonymous online calls for a nonviolent "Jasmine Revolution" in China, according to international news reports. The Hong Kong-based Chinese Human Rights Defenders reported that Chen was formally charged on March 28 with inciting subversion of state power.

Chen's lawyer, Zheng Jianwei, made repeated attempts to visit him but was not allowed access until September 8, according to the rights group and the U.S. government-funded broadcaster Radio Free Asia. RFA reported that police had selected four pro-democracy articles Chen had written for overseas websites as the basis for criminal prosecution. In December, a court in Suining sentenced Chen to nine years in prison on charges of "inciting subversion," a term viewed as unusually harsh.

One other writer detained following the "Jasmine Revolution," Ran Yunfei, was also indicted on subversion charges but was released in August. He and several others remained under restrictive residential surveillance, according to CPJ research. Chinese Human Rights Defenders reported that at least two other activists remained in criminal detention for transmitting information online related to the protests. Chen's case, however, was the only one linked in public reports to independent journalistic writing.

Chen, a student protester during the 1989 Tiananmen Square incident, had been imprisoned twice before for democracy activism, according to Chinese Human Rights Defenders.

IMPRISONED: OCTOBER 19, 2011

## Choepa Lugyal (Meycheh), freelance

Security officials detained Choepa Lugyal, a publishing house employee who wrote online under the name Meycheh, at his home in Gansu province on October 19, according to the Beijing-based Tibetan commentator Woeser and the Tibetan Centre for Human Rights and Democracy, which is based in India. Choepa Lugyal wrote several print and online articles, including pieces for the Tibetan magazine *Shar Dungri*, according to the center.

Chinese authorities banned *Shar Dungri*, which was published in the aftermath of 2008 ethnic unrest between Tibetans and Han Chinese, and jailed several contributors, including Buddha, Jangtse Donkho, and Kalsang Jinpa. Editor Tashi Rabten was sentenced in July 2011 to four years in prison on charges described by family members as separatism-related.

## Egypt: 2

IMPRISONED: MARCH 28, 2011

### Maikel Nabil Sanad, freelance

Police arrested Sanad, a political blogger and activist, after he wrote an article criticizing the military's performance and lack of transparency before and after the ouster of Hosni Mubarak, according to news accounts. Sanad, who maintained his own blog, *Ibn Ra*, also described being tortured by the military during a previous detention.

On April 10, a military court in Cairo sentenced Sanad to three years in prison for "insulting the military," defense lawyer Ali Atef told CPJ. After Sanad appealed and was granted a retrial, a court sentenced him in December to two years on the same charge.

Sanad waged a hunger strike in August to protest his continued imprisonment and mistreatment by military prison guards, his brother, Marc, told CPJ.

IMPRISONED: OCTOBER 30, 2011

### Alaa Abd el-Fattah, freelance

Military prosecutors summoned Abd el-Fattah, a prominent journalistic blogger, for questioning in connection with his critical coverage of the October 9 clashes between troops and Coptic Christian protesters that resulted in the deaths of at least 25 people, including journalist Wael Mikhael.

Abd el-Fattah, a critic of Egypt's practice of subjecting civilians to military proceedings, objected to questioning by the military and demanded that any case against him be handled by civilian authorities. In response, the military prosecutor ordered he be detained for 15 days pending investigation, according to news reports. The same day, the prosecutor filed a series of antistate charges against him, including "inciting violence against the military." His case was transferred to a civilian court in late November.

Abd el-Fattah and his wife and fellow blogger, Manal, had been critical of the military regime in articles posted to their blog, *Manalaa*. Abd El-Fattah also wrote an October 20 opinion piece in the independent daily *Al-Shorouk* in which he criticized the military's investigation of the clashes with Coptic Christians, saying it could not conduct an impartial investigation into its own activities. The article detailed his view of the October 9 clashes and the two ensuing days he spent at the morgue, encouraging victims' families to demand autopsy reports.

In 2006, Abd el-Fattah was detained for 45 days without charge after writing in support of reformist judges and better election monitoring.

## Eritrea: 28

IMPRISONED: SEPTEMBER 2001

**Said Abdelkader**, *Admas*

**Yusuf Mohamed Ali**, *Tsigenay*

**Amanuel Asrat**, *Zemen*

**Temesken Ghebreyesus**, *Keste Debena*

**Mattewos Habteab**, *Meqaleh*

**Dawit Habtemichael**, *Meqaleh*

**Medhanie Haile**, *Keste Debena*

**Seyoum Tsehaye**, freelance

More than 10 years after imprisoning leading editors of Eritrea's once-vibrant independent press and permanently banning their publications to silence growing criticism of President Isaias Afewerki, Eritrean authorities had yet to account for the whereabouts, health, or legal status of the journalists, some of whom may have died in secret detention.

The journalists were arrested without charge after the government suddenly announced on September 18, 2001, that it was closing the country's independent newspapers. The papers had reported on divisions within the ruling Party for Democracy and Justice (PFDJ) and advocated for full implementation of the country's constitution. A dozen top officials and PFDJ reformers, whose pro-democracy statements had been covered by the independent newspapers, were also arrested.

Authorities initially held the journalists at a police station in the capital,

Asmara, where they began a hunger strike on March 31, 2002, and smuggled a message out of jail demanding due process. The government responded by transferring them to secret locations without ever bringing them before a court or publicly registering charges.

Over the years, Eritrean officials have offered vague and inconsistent explanations for the arrests—from nebulous antistate conspiracies involving foreign intelligence to accusations of skirting military service or violating press regulations. Officials at times have even denied that the journalists existed. Meanwhile, shreds of often unverifiable, second- or third-hand information smuggled out of the country by people fleeing into exile have suggested the deaths of as many as five journalists in custody.

In February 2007, CPJ established that one detainee, Fesshaye "Joshua" Yohannes, a co-founder of *Setit* and a 2002 recipient of CPJ's International Press Freedom Award, had died in custody at the age of 47. Addressing reports of Yohannes' death in an interview with the U.S. government-funded broadcaster Voice of America, Eritrean presidential spokesman Yemane Gebremeskel declared: "In the first place, I don't know the person you're talking about."

CPJ is seeking corroboration of three reports suggesting the deaths of up to four other detained journalists. An unbylined report on the Ethiopian pro-government website *Aigaforum* in August 2006 quoted 14 purported guards from Eiraeiro Prison as citing the deaths of prisoners whose names closely resembled Yusuf Mohamed Ali, Medhanie Haile, and Said Abdelkader. The details could not be independently confirmed, although CPJ sources considered it to be generally credible. In 2009, the London-based Eritrean opposition news site *Assena* posted purportedly leaked death certificates of Yohannes, Ali, Haile, and Abdelkader. CPJ could not verify the authenticity of the documents. In 2010, Eritrean defector Eyob Habtemariam, who claimed to have been a prison guard, told the Ethiopian government-sponsored Radio Wegahta that Habteab had died along with the four others.

CPJ continues to seek confirmation of the reported deaths. It lists the journalists on the 2011 prison census as a means of holding the government accountable for their fates. Relatives of the journalists also told CPJ that they maintain hope their loved ones are still alive.

Several CPJ sources say most of the journalists were being held in a secret prison camp called Eiraeiro, near the village of Gahtelay, and in a military prison, Adi Abeito, based in the capital, Asmara. Eritrean government officials in Asmara referred CPJ's inquiries to the Eritrean Embassy in Washington. The embassy did not respond to CPJ's requests for information.

IMPRISONED: SEPTEMBER 23, 2001

## Dawit Isaac, *Setit*

Eritrea's imprisonment of Isaac, a co-founder of *Setit* with dual Eritrean and Swedish citizenship, has drawn considerable international attention, particularly in 2011 on the 10th anniversary of his arrest.

Isaac has been held incommunicado except for brief contact with his family in 2005. Asked about Isaac's crime in a May 2009 interview with Swedish freelance journalist Donald Boström, Eritrean President Isaias Afewerki declared, "I don't know," but said the journalist had made "a big mistake," without elaborating. In April 2010, Eyob Bahta Habtemariam, an Eritrean defector who claimed to have been a guard at two prisons northeast of Asmara, said Isaac was in poor health, according to media reports. In August 2010, Yemane Gebreab, a senior presidential adviser, declared in an interview with Swedish daily *Aftonbladet* that Isaac was held for "very serious crimes regarding Eritrea's national security and survival as an independent state."

In July 2011, Isaac's brother Esayas and three jurists—Jesús Alcalá, Prisca Orsonneau, and Percy Bratt—filed a writ of habeas corpus with Eritrea's Supreme Court. The writ calls for information on the journalist's whereabouts and a review of his detention.

On September 16 in Strasbourg, the European Parliament signaled a break from quiet diplomacy to secure Isaac's release to public confrontation when it passed a strongly worded resolution calling for the immediate and unconditional release of Isaac and other prisoners of conscience "who have been jailed simply for exercising their right to freedom of expression."

On the day marking the 10th anniversary of Isaac's imprisonment, Nobel Prize laureates Mario Vargas Llosa and Herta Müller, as well as John Ralston Saul, president of PEN International, signed a statement calling on Sweden and the European Union to take a tougher approach toward Eritrea to secure Isaac's release. In October, the World Association of Newspapers and News Publishers awarded Isaac its 50th anniversary Golden Pen of Freedom.

IMPRISONED: FEBRUARY 15, 2002

## Hamid Mohammed Said, Eri-TV

During a July 2002 fact-finding mission to the capital, Asmara, a CPJ delegation confirmed that Eritrean authorities had arrested three state media reporters in February 2002 as part of the government's mass crackdown on the press, which began in September 2001. Reporters

Saadia Ahmed and Saleh Aljezeeri were released, according to CPJ sources.

Sources told CPJ they believed Eri-TV reporter Said was still being held in an undisclosed location. The government has refused to respond to numerous inquiries from CPJ and other international organizations seeking information about the journalist's whereabouts, health, and legal status.

IMPRISONED: FEBRUARY 19, 2009

**Esmail Abd-el-Kader**, Radio Bana

**Ghirmai Abraham**, Radio Bana

**Issak Abraham**, Radio Bana

**Mohammed Dafla**, Radio Bana

**Araya Defoch**, Radio Bana

**Simon Elias**, Radio Bana

**Yirgalem Fesseha**, Radio Bana

**Biniam Ghirmay**, Radio Bana

**Mulubruhan Habtegebriel**, Radio Bana

**Bereket Misguina**, Radio Bana

**Mohammed Said Mohammed**, Radio Bana

**Meles Nguse**, Radio Bana

A U.S. diplomatic cable released by WikiLeaks in November 2010 identified February 19, 2009, as the date Eritrean security forces raided the Education Ministry-sponsored station Radio Bana and arrested its entire staff.

The cable, by then-U.S. Ambassador Ronald McMullen and dated February 23, 2009, attributes the information to the deputy head of mission of the British Embassy in Asmara in connection with the detention of a British national who volunteered at the station. According to the cable, the volunteer reported being taken by security forces with the Radio Bana staff to an unknown location six miles (10 kilometers) north of Asmara and later separated from them. The volunteer was not interrogated and was released the next day. According to the cable, some staff members were released as well.

At least 12 journalists working for Radio Bana have been held incommunicado since, according to several CPJ sources. The reasons for the detentions are unclear, but CPJ sources say the journalists were either accused of providing technical assistance to two opposition radio stations broadcasting into the country from Ethiopia, or of taking part in a meeting in which detained journalist Meles Nguse spoke against the government. Their close collaboration with two British nationals on the production of educational programs may have also led to their arrests, according to the same sources.

Ghirmai Abraham had been producer of an arts program with government-controlled state radio Dimtsi Hafash, and Issak Abraham had produced a Sunday entertainment show on the same station. Issak Abraham and Habtegebriel, a reporter with state daily *Hadas Eritrea*, had co-authored a book of comedy. Misguina (also a film director and scriptwriter), Nguse (also a poet), and Fesseha (a poet as well) were columnists for *Hadas Eritrea*.

In 2011, based on new information obtained from recently escaped journalists, CPJ identified at least six imprisoned Radio Bana journalists that were previously not listed in the organization's annual census. They are Mohammed, deputy director of the station, presenters Abd-el-Kader and Defoch, and producers Ghirmay, Elias, and Dafla.

None of the detainees' whereabouts, health, or legal status had been disclosed by late year.

IMPRISONED: JANUARY OR FEBRUARY 2009

## Habtemariam Negassi, Eri-TV

Negassi, a veteran cameraman and head of the English desk at the government-controlled broadcaster Eri-TV, was arrested around the same time as journalists from Radio Bana, according to CPJ sources. The reason for the arrest was unknown; no charges were publicly filed.

Eritrean authorities typically refuse to disclose even the most basic information about detainees, but CPJ continues to gather details from journalists who recently escaped the country. While the government's motivation in imprisoning journalists is unknown in most cases, CPJ's research has found that state media journalists work in a climate of intimidation, retaliation, and absolute control.

The Information Ministry employs some 100 journalists, many of them conscripts of the country's mandatory national service, and hundreds of support staff, according to journalists in exile. Over the years, CPJ has documented a broad pattern in which Information Minister Ali Abdu has arbitrarily imprisoned journalists he suspects of being sources for diaspora news websites or of attempting to leave the country to escape the oppressive conditions. In this context of extreme repression, CPJ considers journalists attempting to escape the country or in contact with third parties abroad as struggling for press freedom.

IMPRISONED: FEBRUARY AND MARCH 2011

## Nebiel Edris, Dimtsi Hafash

## Eyob Kessete, Dimtsi Hafash

## Tesfalidet Mebrahtu, Dimtsi Hafash, Eri-TV

## Mohamed Osman, Dimtsi Hafash

## Ahmed Usman, Dimtsi Hafash

The government did not disclose why it arrested Kessete, a reporter for the Amharic-language service of government-controlled radio Dimtsi Hafash, but CPJ sources believe he was suspected of helping people escape the country.

Authorities had previously detained Kessete in early 2009 after he attempted to flee Eritrea himself. His family acted as his guarantor at that time, and he was released. His private website and email were searched by the government during the 2009 arrest, according to CPJ sources. His current location is unknown.

Authorities arrested Edris of the Arabic service of government-controlled Dimtsi Hafash, Usman of the Tigre service, and Osman of the Bilen-language service in February, according to CPJ sources. The reasons for the arrests were not disclosed.

Authorities imprisoned Mebrahtu, a prominent sports journalist with state-run radio Dimtsi Hafash and television Eri-TV, on suspicion of attempting to flee the country, according to CPJ sources. Mebrahtu is reportedly detained in either Mai Serwa or Adi Abeto prison.

While it is very difficult to obtain details from Eritrea, CPJ continues to gather information on the imprisoned from journalists who have recently escaped the country. The government's motivation in imprisoning journalists is unknown in most cases, but CPJ's research has found an environment in which state media journalists are under the absolute control of Information Minister Ali Abdu.

The ministry employs some 100 journalists, many of them conscripts under the country's mandatory national service, and hundreds of support staff, according to journalists in exile. Former state media journalists told CPJ they worked under the close scrutiny and direction of Abdu and his censors, with no editorial freedom. "You're given directives as to how you write. We had to inform Ali Abdu each time we want to interview someone, and we cannot proceed until he approves," said one former senior journalist, who spoke on condition of anonymity in order to protect relatives still in Eritrea.

Over the years, CPJ has documented a broad pattern of intimidation in which Abdu has arbitrarily imprisoned journalists he suspects of being sources for opposition diaspora news websites or of attempting to leave the country to escape the oppressive conditions. For example, television presenter Paulos Kidane was among several journalists imprisoned in 2006 on suspicion of communicating with opposition websites abroad; he later died while attempting to flee the country. In this context of extreme repression, CPJ considers journalists attempting to escape the country or in contact with third parties abroad as struggling for press freedom.

## Ethiopia: 7

IMPRISONED: DECEMBER 2006

### Saleh Idris Gama, Eri-TV
### Tesfalidet Kidane Tesfazghi, Eri-TV

In 2011, the government of Prime Minister Meles Zenawi publicly addressed the detentions of Gama and Tesfazghi after years in which they refused to disclose information about the journalists' whereabouts, legal status, or health. The two journalists from Eritrea's state broadcaster Eri-TV were arrested in late 2006 at the Kenya-Somalia border during Ethiopia's invasion of southern Somalia.

The Ethiopian Foreign Ministry first disclosed the detention of Tesfazghi, a producer, and Gama, a cameraman, in April 2007, and presented them on state television as part of a group of 41 captured terrorism suspects, according to CPJ research. Though Eritrea often conscripted journalists into military service, the video did not present any evidence linking the journalists to military activity. The ministry pledged to subject some of the suspects to military trials, but did not identify them by name.

In a February 2011 interview with CPJ, Ethiopian Foreign Ministry spokesman Dina Mufti denied the journalists were in Ethiopian custody. "We don't have two journalists in prison or detention here. We don't know their whereabouts and I have no idea where they are," he told CPJ. "In Ethiopia, we have freedom of press. It is simply malicious propaganda put forth by the Eritrean guys."

However, in a September 2011 press conference with exiled Eritrean journalists in Addis Ababa, Zenawi declared that Gama and Tesfazghi would be freed if investigations determined they were not involved in any espionage activities, according to news reports and journalists who participated in the press conference. The whereabouts of the journalists were unknown.

IMPRISONED: JUNE 19, 2011

## Woubshet Taye, *Awramba Times*

Police arrested Taye, deputy editor of the leading independent newspaper *Awramba Times*, after raiding his home in the capital, Addis Ababa, and confiscating documents, cameras, CDs, and selected copies of the newspaper, according to local journalists.

Shortly after Taye's arrest, government spokesman Shimelis Kemal denied that Taye or any other journalist was in custody. "We have a law prohibiting pretrial detention of journalists. No arrest could be initiated on account of content," he told CPJ. A week later, however, Kemal announced that Taye was among nine people arrested on suspicion of planning terrorist attacks on infrastructure, telecommunications, and power lines in the country, with the support of an unnamed international terrorist group and Ethiopia's neighbor, Eritrea, according to news reports.

Authorities took Taye to the Maekelawi Federal Detention Center where he was held without charge for 81 days under a far-reaching anti-terrorism law, according to CPJ research.

On September 6, Taye was charged with terrorism without the presence of his lawyer, according to local journalists. CPJ believes the charges against Taye are false, politically motivated, and perpetuate a long and documented pattern of harassment over his critical coverage.

In November 2005, as a senior reporter with the now-banned private weekly *Hadar*, Taye was detained for a week in a crackdown on dissent and critical coverage of the government's brutal response to protests over disputed elections, according to local journalists. In May 2010, a regulatory official threatened Taye, accusing him of "inciting and misguiding the public" over an editorial that raised questions about the lack of public enthusiasm for parliamentary elections in which the ruling party swept 99.6 percent of the seats, according to news reports. Prior to his arrest, Taye had written a column criticizing what he saw as the ruling party's methods of weakening and dividing the media and the opposition, Taye's editor, Dawit Kebede, told CPJ.

Taye was being held at Kality Prison in Addis Ababa in late year.

## Reeyot Alemu, freelance

Ethiopian security forces arrested Alemu, known for critical columns in the leading independent weekly *Feteh*, at an Addis Ababa high school where she taught English, according to news reports. Authorities raided Alemu's home and seized documents and other materials before taking her into custody at the Maekelawi Federal Detention Center.

A week after Alemu's arrest, Ethiopian government spokesman Shimelis Kemal announced that the journalist was among nine people arrested on suspicion of planning terrorist attacks on infrastructure, telecommunications, and power lines in the country, with the support of an unnamed international terrorist group and Ethiopia's neighbor, Eritrea, according to news reports

Alemu was held without charge for 79 days under a far-reaching anti-terrorism law, and was charged on September 6 with terrorism, without the presence of her lawyer, according to local journalists.

CPJ believes the charges against Alemu are baseless and a reprisal for her critical coverage. In the last column before her arrest, Alemu criticized the ruling party's alleged methods of coercion and compared Prime Minister Meles Zenawi to the late Libyan leader Muammar Qaddafi, according to local journalists. Her newspaper has also faced government persecution for its coverage. Since its inception in 2008, authorities have questioned *Feteh* editor Temesghen Desalegn twice and filed 41 lawsuits against him, according to local journalists.

Alemu was being held at Kality Prison in Addis Ababa in late year.

## Johan Persson, freelance

## Martin Schibbye, freelance

Ethiopian security forces detained Persson and Schibbye, freelancers with the Sweden-based photo agency Kontinent, in a shootout with rebels of the separatist Ogaden National Liberation Front, or ONLF. The journalists, who were slightly injured in the crossfire, had embedded with ONLF fighters after crossing into Ethiopia from neighboring Somalia.

The ONLF has been waging a low-level insurgency since 1984 in Ethiopia's Somali-speaking, oil-rich Ogaden region; the Ethiopian government has banned independent media access to the area amid allegations of human rights abuses. The Ethiopian Parliament formally designated the ONLF a terrorist entity in May 2011 under a far-reaching anti-terrorism law. Under the law, journalists reporting statements or activities by terror-designated entities risk up to 20 years in prison if the government deems their coverage favorable to the groups.

Shortly after Persson and Schibbye's arrests, Ethiopia's government-controlled public broadcaster ERTA showed a video montage posted on the pro-government Ogaden website *Cakaara News*, presenting the journalists as accomplices to terrorists, according to CPJ research. Part of the footage appeared to have been shot by the journalists themselves, including clips showing them taking photos and interviewing people in refugee camps, and Persson handling an assault rifle. Other clips were shot by authorities after the arrests. "We came to the Ogaden region to do interviews with the ONLF," Schibbye is heard saying, speaking under instructions while in custody.

Using a provision of the anti-terrorism law, which allows for extended detention without charge, Ethiopian public prosecutors held Persson and Schibbye without charge for 68 days, according to CPJ research. On September 6, Persson and Schibbye were taken to court and charged with terrorism, without the presence of their lawyers, Swedish Foreign Ministry spokesman Anders Jörle told CPJ.

In an October interview with Norwegian newspaper *Aftenposten*, Ethiopian Prime Minister Meles Zenawi said the journalists "are, at the very least, messenger boys of a terrorist organization. They are not journalists." He referenced the government-produced video released in July, saying, "We have video clippings of this journalist training with the rebels." CPJ condemned the statements as predetermining the outcome of the journalists' trial.

In October, Persson and Schibbye pleaded not guilty to charges of involvement in terrorist activities but acknowledged entering the country illegally, according to news reports. They were convicted on both charges in December and sentenced to 11 years in prison apiece.

Persson had done work for Kontinent for five years, covering dangerous assignments across the globe, including the conflict in the Democratic Republic of Congo, according to colleague Jacob Zocherman. Schibbye, an experienced reporter, had written, among other things, a series of reports on human trafficking in Asia, Zocherman said.

Persson and Schibbye were being held at Kality Prison in Addis Ababa.

IMPRISONED: SEPTEMBER 9, 2011

## Eskinder Nega, freelance

Ethiopian security forces arrested Nega, a prominent journalist, government critic, and dissident blogger, on accusations of involvement in a vague terrorism plot. Nega was taken to the Maekelawi Federal Detention Center and held under a provision of the anti-terrorism law that allows for extended detention without charge.

Shortly after Nega's arrest, the ruling Ethiopian People's Revolutionary Democratic Front-controlled state television portrayed the journalist and four others arrested as "spies for foreign forces" and accused them of having links with the banned opposition movement Ginbot 7, which the Ethiopian government formally designated as a terrorist entity. In an interview with Agence France-Presse, government spokesman Shimelis Kemal accused the detainees of plotting "a series of terrorist acts that would likely wreak havoc."

In November, a judge charged Nega with providing support to Ginbot 7, according to local journalists. Five exiled Ethiopian journalists were charged in absentia.

CPJ believes the charges against Nega are baseless and fall into a long and well-documented pattern of persecution of the journalist over his critical coverage of the government. In February, police arrested Nega as he exited a cybercafé; a deputy police commissioner threatened to jail him over his online columns comparing the uprising in Egypt with Ethiopia's 2005 pro-democracy protests, according to news reports. Nega's coverage of the government's brutal repression of those protests had previously landed him in jail for 17 months on antistate charges. After his release, authorities banned his newspaper and denied him a license to start a new publication, while pursuing hefty fines against him, according to CPJ research.

Nega was being held at Kality Prison in Addis Ababa.

## Gambia: 1

IMPRISONED: JULY 7, 2006

## "Chief" Ebrima Manneh, Daily Observer

In 2011, the government's justice minister publicly acknowledged knowing the condition of "Chief" Ebrima Manneh, a reporter with the pro-government *Daily Observer* who disappeared in state custody after his 2006 arrest by two plainclothes officers of the National Intelligence Agency. The reason for the arrest remained unclear, although some colleagues believe it was linked to his attempt to republish a BBC article critical of President Yahya Jammeh.

Sketchy and conflicting details about Manneh's whereabouts, health, and legal status have emerged over the years. Eyewitnesses reported seeing him in government custody in December 2006 and in July 2007, according to CPJ research. Agence France-Presse quoted an unnamed police official in 2009 as saying that Manneh had been spotted at Mile 2 Prison in 2008. But the official also speculated that Manneh was no longer alive, AFP reported.

In October 2011, Justice Minister Edward Gomez said in an interview with the local newspaper *Daily News* that Manneh was alive. "Chief Ebrima Manneh is alive, and we will talk about this case later," Gomez told AFP in a subsequent interview. His comments contrasted with a series of government denials and obfuscations.

In a nationally televised meeting with local media representatives in March 2011, President Jammeh described Manneh as having died while denying any government involvement in the journalist's fate. "Let me make it very clear that the government has nothing to do with the death of Chief Manneh," he said. In July, national police spokesman Yorro Mballow told CPJ that police had no information about Manneh. In September, Vice President Isatou Njie-Saidy told CPJ that the government did not arrest Manneh and that she had no knowledge of his whereabouts.

The Gambia has resisted international appeals to free Manneh by, among others, six U.S. senators, UNESCO, and the Court of Justice of the Economic Community of West African States.

## India: 2

IMPRISONED: JANUARY 2, 2011

### Sudhir Dhawale, *Vidrohi*

Dhawale, a Mumbai-based activist and journalist, wrote about human rights violations against Dalits in the Marathi-language *Vidrohi*, a monthly he founded and edited.

Police arrested Dhawale in the Wardha district of Maharashtra state, where he had traveled to attend a Dalit meeting, and charged him with sedition and involvement with a terrorist group under the Unlawful Activities (Prevention) Act, according to local and international news reports. They said a Maoist insurgent in custody had accused him of involvement in the banned organization's war against the state in central tribal areas of India, according to *The Wall Street Journal.* Police also searched Dhawale's home the following day, seizing books and a computer, the news reports said.

Dhawale's supporters said he was detained because he was a critic of a state-supported, anti-Maoist militia active in Chhattisgarh state, a center of the civil violence between Maoists and the state. In a documentary on the case, Darshana Dhawale, the journalist's wife, said police had accused her husband of supporting the Maoists in his writings. The makers of the film—titled "Sudhir Dhawale: Dissent = Sedition?"—also interviewed Anand Teltumbde of the Mumbai-based Committee for the Protection of Democratic Rights, who said Dhawale's publication covered the Maoists but did not support them.

On January 20, police accused him of hanging Maoist posters in an unrelated case in Gondia district in December 2010. Authorities filed a new charge of waging war against the state, which carries a potential death penalty under the Indian penal code. His wife says he was in Mumbai, not Gondia, in December, according to local news reports. Dhawale was refused bail, and a trial date had yet to be scheduled as of late year.

IMPRISONED: SEPTEMBER 10, 2011

## Lingaram Kodopi, freelance

Police said they arrested Kodopi in a public market in Dantewada district accepting a bribe from a representative of a steel company wanting to operate in a Maoist insurgent-controlled area, local news reports said. The journalist denied the charge and said that police had targeted him since he refused to work for them under a program to recruit tribal youths to defeat the insurgents, the New Delhi-based newsmagazine *Tehelka* reported.

Police accused Kodopi of being a "Maoist associate." He was charged with antistate activities under the Unlawful Activities (Prevention) Act, the Chhattisgarh Public Security Act, and the Indian penal code, *Tehelka* reported. He had not been brought to trial by late year, and the total penalty he faced was not clear.

Local human rights activists and journalists said authorities wanted to prevent Kodopi, 25, from publicizing the role of police in recent violence in the state. In April, the journalist documented the destruction of houses during an anti-Maoist police operation in three Dantewada district villages and "recorded on video precise narrations of police atrocities," *Tehelka* reported. Himanshu Kumar, a local human rights activist, told the *Indian Express* that Kodopi had evidence of government involvement in burning down three villages.

Kodopi told journalists he had fled police harassment in 2010 to study journalism and work as a freelancer in New Delhi, the *Indian Express* reported. While he was there, police back in Dantewada accused him of being a senior Maoist commander and masterminding an attack against a politician in Chhattisgarh. Kodopi denied the accusations in a press conference in Delhi, the *Indian Express* said, and he was not taken into custody at the time.

Police in Dantewada would not explain whether Kodopi was believed to be a low-level Maoist "associate," as alleged in the 2011 case, or a senior commander, as they said in 2010. "We are still ascertaining his role," District Police Superintendent Ankit Garg told *Tehelka*.

## Iran: 42

IMPRISONED: JANUARY 25, 2007

### Adnan Hassanpour, *Aso*

Security agents seized Hassanpour, former editor of the now-defunct Kurdish-Persian weekly *Aso*, in his hometown of Marivan, Kurdistan province, according to news reports.

In July 2007, a Revolutionary Court convicted Hassanpour on anti-state charges and sentenced him to death. After a series of appeals and reversals, he was sentenced in May 2010 to 15 years in prison, defense lawyer Saleh Nikbakht told the Reporters and Human Rights Activists News Agency.

The government's case against Hassanpour amounted to a series of assertions by security agents, defense attorney Sirvan Hosmandi told CPJ in 2008. Hassanpour's sister, Lily, told CPJ that she believed his critical writings were behind the charges.

IMPRISONED: JULY 1, 2007

### Mohammad Seddigh Kaboudvand, *Payam-e-Mardom*

Plainclothes security officials arrested journalist and human rights activist Kaboudvand at his Tehran office, according to Amnesty

International and CPJ sources. He was being held at Evin Prison in Tehran.

Authorities accused Kaboudvand, head of the Human Rights Organization of Kurdistan and managing editor of the weekly *Payam-e-Mardom*, of acting against national security and engaging in propaganda against the state, according to his organization's website. A Revolutionary Court in Tehran sentenced him to 11 years in prison.

Kaboudvand, 48, was reported in ill health in 2011, but authorities refused requests for medical furlough, his wife, Farinaz Baghban Hassani, told the reformist news website *Jonbesh-e-Rah-e-Sabz*.

Based on their visits and consultation with a prison physician, family members believe Kaboudvand may have suffered a stroke while in custody, according to news accounts. Human Rights House of Iran reported in July 2010 that Kaboudvand suffered severe dizziness, disruption of his speech and vision, and disorders in his limb movements. At times, the journalist has been denied family visits and telephone calls with relatives, his wife told *Jonbesh-e-Rah-e-Sabz*.

The opposition website *Daneshjoo News* reported that Kaboudvand sent an October 6, 2011, letter to the U.N. special rapporteur for human rights in Iran, describing violations of human rights in prison.

IMPRISONED: OCTOBER 8, 2008

## Mojtaba Lotfi, freelance

A clergyman and blogger, Lotfi was arrested by security forces on a warrant issued by the religious Clergy Court in Qom. Authorities accused him of publishing the views of Ayatollah Hossein-Ali Montazeri, the now-deceased cleric who had criticized President Mahmoud Ahmadinejad's positions.

Authorities did not specify articles or publications in which the views were supposedly cited. In November 2009, Lotfi was convicted of several charges, including spreading antistate information, and sentenced to four years in prison followed by a period of exile, according to online reports.

In July 2010, the Human Rights House of Iran reported that Lotfi had been transferred to the remote village of Ashtian for 10 years of enforced internal exile. Lotfi, an Iran-Iraq War veteran who was exposed to chemical agents, suffers from a respiratory illness which has worsened during his confinement, the reformist news website *Norooz News* reported.

IMPRISONED: NOVEMBER 2008

## Hossein Derakhshan, freelance

On December 30, 2008, a judiciary spokesman confirmed at a press conference in Tehran that Derakhshan, a well-known Iranian-Canadian blogger, had been detained since November 2008 in connection with comments he allegedly made about a key cleric, according to local and international news reports. The exact date of Derakhshan's arrest is unknown, but word of his detention was first reported on November 17, 2008, by *Jahan News*, a website close to the Iranian intelligence service. The site claimed Derakhshan had confessed to "spying for Israel" during the preliminary interrogation.

Known as the "Blogfather" for his pioneering online work, Derakhshan started blogging after the September 11 terrorist attacks on the United States. A former writer for reformist news-papers, he also contributed opinion pieces to *The Guardian* of London and *The New York Times.* The journalist, who lived in Canada during most of the decade prior to his detention, returned to Tehran a few weeks before his detention, *The Washington Post* reported. In November 2009, the BBC Persian service reported that Derakhshan's family had sought information about his whereabouts and the charges he faced, and expressed concern about having very limited contact with him.

In September 2010, the government announced that Derakhshan had been sentenced to 19 and a half years in prison, along with a five-year ban on "membership in political parties and activities in the media," according to the International Campaign for Human Rights in Iran and other sources. Derakhshan has spent much of his imprisonment in solitary confinement at Evin Prison, according to multiple sources. The International Campaign for Human Rights in Iran, citing a source close to the journalist's family, said Derakhshan had been beaten and coerced into making false confessions about having ties to U.S. and Israeli intelligence services.

IMPRISONED: JUNE 2009

## Ahmad Zaid-Abadi, freelance

Zaid-Abadi, who wrote a weekly column for *Rooz Online*, a Farsi- and English-language reformist news website, was arrested in Tehran, according to news reports. Zaid-Abadi had also been a sup-porter of the defeated 2009 presidential candidate Mehdi Karroubi and had served as director of the politically active Organization of University Alumni of the Islamic Republic of Iran.

On November 23, 2009, Zaid-Abadi was sentenced to six years in prison, five years of internal exile in Khorasan province, and a "lifetime deprivation of any political activity" including "interviews, speeches, and analysis of events, whether in written or oral form," according to the Persian service of the German public broadcaster Deutsche Welle. An appeals court upheld the sentence on January 2, according to *Advar News*.

In February 2010, Zaid-Abadi and fellow journalist Massoud Bastani were transferred to Rajaee Shahr Prison, a facility known for housing people convicted of drug-related crimes. Zaid-Abadi's wife, Mahdieh Mohammadi, said prison conditions were crowded and unsanitary, the International Campaign for Human Rights in Iran reported. She said she feared malnutrition and the spread of disease. In August 2011, Zaid-Abadi was granted a 48-hour furlough after posting bail of $500,000, the U.S. government-funded Radio Farda reported.

IMPRISONED: JUNE 14, 2009

## Kayvan Samimi, *Nameh*

Samimi, manager of the now-defunct monthly *Nameh*, was serving a six-year prison sentence along with a 15-year ban on "political, social, and cultural activities," the *Aftab News* website reported.

Initially held at Evin Prison, Samimi was subjected to mistreatment. In February 2010, he was transferred to solitary confinement after objecting to poor prison conditions, according to Free Iranian Journalists, a website devoted to documenting cases of jailed reporters and editors. He and 14 other prisoners later went on a 16-day hunger strike to protest abuse at the prison. In November 2010, Samimi was transferred to Rajaee Shah Prison in Karaj, which houses violent criminals, according to news reports. In May 2011, he and several other political prisoners waged a hunger strike to protest mistreatment there, reformist news websites reported.

In August 2011, the reformist news website *Jonbesh-e-Rah-e-Sabz* reported that Samimi was in poor health and suffered from liver problems. Prison authorities refused medical leave for treatment outside the prison, the news site reported.

IMPRISONED: JUNE 19, 2009

## Bahman Ahmadi Amouee, freelance

Amouee, a contributor to reformist newspapers such as *Mihan*, *Hamshahri*, *Jame'e*, *Khordad*, *Norooz*, and *Sharq*, and the author of an eponymous blog, was arrested with his wife, Zhila Bani-Yaghoub, according to news reports. Bani-Yaghoub, editor-in-chief of the *Iranian Women's Club*, a news website focusing on women's rights, was released on bail in August 2009, according to the BBC Persian service.

In January 2010, Amouee was sentenced to 34 lashes, along with seven years and four months in prison. In March of the same year, an appeals court reduced the sentence to five years in prison, according to *Rooz Online*.

Amouee was being held in Evin Prison, according to news reports, with part of his term served in solitary confinement. In July 2010, Amouee and 14 other prisoners staged a 16-day hunger strike to protest mistreatment at Evin Prison. Prison officials punished them by denying family visits for a month, *Jonbesh-e-Rah-e-Sabz* reported.

IMPRISONED: JULY 3, 2009

## Issa Saharkhiz, freelance

Saharkhiz, a columnist for the reformist news websites *Rooz Online* and *Norooz* and a founding member of the Association of Iranian Journalists, was arrested while traveling in northern Iran, the association said in a statement. His lawyer said his client was charged with "participation in riots," "encouraging others to participate in riots," and "insulting the supreme leader," according to *Rooz Online*.

Saharkhiz was sentenced to three years in prison, a five-year ban on political and journalistic activities, and a one-year ban on foreign travel, the reformist news website *Jonbesh-e-Rah-e-Sabz* reported in September 2010. In an interview with Radio Zamaneh, Mehdi Saharkhiz said his father would not appeal the court's decision. "He said that all sentencing is made under [Ayatollah Ali] Khamenei's direct supervision and the judiciary has nothing to do with it. Therefore, neither the lower court nor the appeals court is official in any way, and they are only for show."

Saharkhiz has had a long career in journalism. He worked for 15 years for IRNA, Iran's official news agency, and ran its New York office for part of that time. He returned to Iran in 1997 to work in Mohammad Khatami's Ministry of Islamic Guidance, in charge of domestic publications. Journalist Ahmad Bourghani and Saharkhiz came to be known as the architects of a period of relative freedom for the press in Iran. But as the regime took a more conservative bent, Saharkhiz was forced to leave the ministry and was eventually banned from government service. He founded a reformist newspaper, *Akhbar-e-Eghtesad*, and monthly magazine, *Aftab*, both of which were eventually banned. He wrote articles directly critical of Khamenei, Iran's supreme leader.

During his imprisonment, which began at Evin Prison, Saharkhiz was subjected to constant pressure, including being kept in a prison yard overnight in freezing temperatures without shoes or socks, according to *Rooz Online*.

Saharkhiz's son, Mehdi, told the BBC Persian service that the journalist had waged a hunger strike in October 2011. Mehdi Saharkhiz expressed concern about his father's well-being, telling the BBC that the journalist suffered from blood pressure, spine, and neck problems.

IMPRISONED: JULY 5, 2009

## Massoud Bastani, *Farhikhtegan* and *Jomhoriyat*

Bastani, a journalist for the reformist newspaper *Farhikhtegan* and *Jomhoriyat*, a news website affiliated with the defeated 2009 presidential candidate Mir-Hossein Mousavi, was arrested when he went to a Tehran court seeking information about his wife, journalist Mahsa Amrabadi, according to local news reports. Amrabadi, arrested with two other journalists in June 2009, was released the next month.

Bastani was among more than 100 opposition figures and journalists who faced a mass, televised judicial proceeding in August 2009 on vague antistate accusations, according to news reports. On October 20, 2009, the news site *Norooz* reported that a court had sentenced Bastani to six years in prison for "propagating against the regime and congregating and mutinying to create anarchy."

Bastani was being held at Rajaee Shahr Prison, a facility reserved for hardened criminals, along with fellow journalist Ahmad Zaid-Abadi, according to the reformist daily *Etemad*. In July 2010, Bastani's family told reporters that he had suffered an infection in his jaw that had gone untreated in prison, the Human Rights House of Iran reported.

Authorities restricted Bastani's family visits to once every two weeks. His wife, Mahsa Amrabadi, was found guilty in October 2010 on antistate charges related to "interviews and journalistic reports," Human Rights House reported. She was sentenced to one year in prison, although she was not immediately taken into custody, the reformist news website *Jonbesh-e-Rah-e-Sabz* reported.

IMPRISONED: JULY 12, 2009

## Saeed Matin-Pour, freelance

Matin-Pour, a journalist who wrote for his own blog and for the newspapers *Yar Pag* and *Mouj Bidari* in western Azerbaijan province, was first arrested in May 2007. Released on bail, he was rearrested in July 2009 amid the government's massive crackdown on dissidents and the press.

A Revolutionary Court in Tehran convicted Matin-Pour of having "relations with foreigners" and "propagating against the regime," according to local news reports. He was sentenced to an eight-year prison term.

Matin-Pour's wife, Atieh Taheri, told the Human Rights Activists News Agency that the journalist's health had deteriorated in Evin Prison and that officials had denied him proper medical care, according to news reports. Matin-Pour spent much of his imprisonment in solitary confinement amid abusive treatment, leading to heart and respiratory problems, reformist news websites reported.

IMPRISONED: SEPTEMBER 5, 2009

## Mohammad Davari, *Saham News*

Davari, editor-in-chief of *Saham News*, a website affiliated with the defeated 2009 presidential candidate Mehdi Karroubi, was charged with several antistate counts, including "propagating against the regime," and "disrupting national security." The charges stemmed from Davari's reporting on widespread complaints of abuse and rape of inmates at Kahrizak Detention Center. The detention center was closed in July 2009 after *Saham News* and others documented the pervasive abuse.

In May 2010, Davari was sentenced to five years in prison, according to the website of Reporters and Human Rights Activists of Iran. His family said he was being held at Tehran's Evin Prison.

Davari was tortured and coerced into making false statements against Karroubi, along with false statements recanting his Kahrizak Detention Center reports, according to an April 6 report by Reporters and Human Rights Activists. When Davari complained about poor prison conditions, officials placed him in solitary confinement and denied him family visits, according to news reports.

In mid-2011, Davari was sentenced to an additional year in prison, allegedly for his participation in teacher protests in 2006, reformist news websites reported in July. In recognition of his exemplary journalism, CPJ honored Davari with its International Press Freedom Award in November 2010.

IMPRISONED: SEPTEMBER 16, 2009

## Mehdi Mahmoudian, freelance

Mahmoudian, a political journalist and blogger, was serving a five-year prison term on charges of "mutiny against the regime" for his role in documenting complaints of rape and abuse of detainees at the Kahrizak Detention Center, reformist news websites reported.

The detention center was closed in July 2009 after Mahmoudian and others documented the pervasive abuse. Mahmoudian also worked with journalist Emadeddin Baghi at the Center for the Defense of Prisoners' Rights.

Held at Rajaee Shahr Prison, Mahmoudian was in poor health and suffering from kidney ailments, according to the German public news organization Deutsche Welle. Mahmoudian's mother, Fatemeh Alvandi, told the International Campaign for Human Rights in Iran in April 2011 that her son developed epilepsy while in prison and was in dire physical and psychological condition. Mahmoudian was hospitalized in October 2011 but returned to prison the next month, according to reformist news websites.

IMPRISONED: DECEMBER 13, 2009

## Seyed Hossein Ronaghi Maleki (Babak Khorramdin), freelance

Ronaghi Maleki, writing under the name Babak Khorramdin, discussed politics in a series of critical blogs that were eventually blocked by the government. He was also a founder of the anti-censorship group Iran Proxy, which was launched in 2003.

In October 2010, a Revolutionary Court sentenced Ronaghi Maleki to 15 years in prison on antistate conspiracy charges, the reformist news website *Jonbesh-e-Rah-e-Sabz* reported. The first year of his term was served largely in solitary confinement, defense lawyer Mohammad Ali Dadkhah told the International Campaign for Human Rights in Iran.

Ronaghi Maleki's family said the journalist was in poor health and had severe kidney problems that were going untreated, according to the campaign. In May 2011, Ronaghi Maleki was transferred to a hospital in hand and ankle cuffs, where he underwent kidney surgery, the campaign reported. He was hospitalized in custody again in October 2011, when he underwent additional kidney surgery, the Human Rights House of Iran reported.

IMPRISONED: FEBRUARY 9, 2010

## Ali Malihi, freelance

Malihi, a contributor to the reformist publications *Etemad*, *Irandokht*, *Shahrvand-e-Emruz*, and *Mehrnameh*, was charged with several anti-state counts, including "mutiny against the regime" and "insulting the president." Malihi was sentenced to a four-year prison term, which an appeals court upheld in September 2010, according to the Committee of Human Rights Reporters. Malihi was also a leader of the politically active Iranian Students Association.

The reformist news site *Jonbesh-e-Rah-e-Sabz* and others published a February 2010 petition signed by 250 civil society activists demanding Malihi's release and stating that he was a nonpartisan journalist. In a March 2010 letter to Tehran's prosecutor, Malihi's father said the journalist had endured severe beatings while being held at Evin Prison, according to the reformist site *Advar News*.

IMPRISONED: FEBRUARY 25, 2010

## Hengameh Shahidi, *Etemad-e-Melli*

In November 2009, a Revolutionary Court sentenced Shahidi to six years and three months in prison on several antistate charges, including "propagating against the regime," according to the International Campaign for Human Rights in Iran. The verdict was upheld in February 2010, and Shahidi was taken into custody the next day, according to the Committee of Human Rights Reporters.

Shahidi wrote extensively about Iranian and international politics, human rights, and women's rights. A reformist who also worked for Mehdi Karroubi's 2009 presidential campaign, she had written many articles condemning the practice of stoning.

A fellow prisoner severely beat Shahidi in May 2010 as prison authorities stood by, prompting relatives to have deep concerns about her well-being, the reformist website *Kalame* reported. Shahidi was granted a short medical leave in June 2011, after which she was returned to prison, according to the International Campaign for Human Rights in Iran.

IMPRISONED: MARCH 3, 2010

## Abolfazl Abedini Nasr, *Bahar Ahvaz*

Abedini, who wrote about labor issues for the provincial weekly, was arrested in Ahvaz and transferred to Evin Prison in Tehran, according to the website of Reporters and Human Rights Activists.

An Ahvaz court sentenced Abedini to 11 years in prison on antistate charges that included having "contact with enemy states," the reformist news website *Jonbesh-e-Rah-e-Sabz* reported in April 2011. Abedini was not represented by a lawyer at trial. When Abedini appealed, a Khuzestan provincial appellate court would not allow a defense lawyer to present arguments, the reformist website *Kalame* reported. The appeals court upheld the verdict.

In September 2010, Human Rights House in Iran reported that Abedini had been beaten at Ahvaz Prison. He was transferred to Tehran's Evin Prison later that same month, the group reported. On May 4, 2011, a Revolutionary Court judge sentenced Abedini to an additional year in prison on the charge of "propagating against the regime," Human Rights House reported. The basis for the additional charge was not disclosed.

IMPRISONED: JULY 27, 2010

## Siamak Ghaderi, freelance

Ghaderi was arrested in connection with entries he posted on his blog, *IRNA-ye maa*, or Our IRNA, a reference to the Islamic Republic's official news agency. In the entries, he wrote about street protests and other developments after the contested 2009 presidential election, according to the reformist news website *Jonbesh-e-Rah-e-Sabz*.

In January 2011, Ghaderi was sentenced to four years in prison and 60 lashes on charges of "propagating against the regime," "creating public anxiety," and "spreading falsehoods," according to the BBC's Persian service.

Ghaderi was an editor and reporter for IRNA for 18 years until he was dismissed for writing about the 2009 election on his blog, *Jonbesh-e-Rah-e-Sabz* said. Pro-government news websites, among them *Rasekhoon* and *Haghighat News*, called him a "seditionist" who was arrested for "immoral" acts. Ghaderi's blog was repeatedly blocked by authorities before he was detained, *Jonbesh-e-Rah-e-Sabz* reported.

Among the entries that authorities found objectionable was a piece in which Ghaderi interviewed several Iranian homosexuals. The article was an apparent reaction to President Mahmoud Ahmadinejad's public assertion that "there are no homosexuals in Iran." The lashes in his sentence were for "cooperating with homosexuals," the BBC reported. The reformist news website *Kaleme* reported in July 2011 that Ghaderi was being held at Evin Prison.

IMPRISONED: SEPTEMBER 12, 2010

## Mohammad Reza Pourshajari (Siamak Mehr), freelance

Pourshajari, a journalistic blogger who wrote under the penname Siamak Mehr, was arrested at his home in Karaj, outside Tehran, according to news and human rights websites. In his blog *Gozaresh be Khaak-e-Iran* (Reports to the Soil of Iran), Pourshajari was critical of Iran's theological state.

In an open letter dated December 2010, published by the Human Rights and Democracy Activists of Iran, Pourshajari described his arrest and subsequent detention. He said intelligence agents confiscated a computer hard drive, satellite receiver, and numerous documents. Pourshajari was taken to Rajaee Shahr Prison, where interrogators tortured him and subjected him to a mock execution, he wrote. Pourshajari said he was not allowed visitors, phone calls, or access to a lawyer.

In December 2010, Pourshajari was sentenced to three years in prison on charges of "propagating against the regime" and "insulting the supreme leader," Human Rights Activists for Democracy in Iran reported. In October 2011, Pourshajari was transferred to Ghezel Hessar Prison, where hardened criminals are confined, the group said.

Pourshajari was due to be tried in December 2011 on an additional count of "insulting sanctities," a charge that could bring the death penalty, according to news accounts. The basis for the new charge was not disclosed.

IMPRISONED: OCTOBER 28, 2010

## Arash Honarvar Shojaei, freelance

Nearly a year after Shojaei was first jailed, a special clerical court sentenced the blogger and cleric to four years in prison and 50 lashes on October 2, 2011, on multiple charges of "acting against national security," "espionage," and "cooperation with foreign embassies," the reformist news outlet Radio Zamaneh reported.

Shojaei was author of the book, *Madar-e-Shari'at*, about the dissident cleric, Ayatollah Mohammad Kazem Shariatmadari, according to Radio Zamaneh. Shariatmadari had opposed the principle of *velayat-e faqih*, which seeks to convey unlimited power to the supreme leader.

Shojaei was being held at Evin Prison, where he endured torture and several months of solitary confinement, according to Human Rights House of Iran and Radio Zamaneh. He was suffering from the effects of epilepsy, Radio Zamaneh said.

IMPRISONED: MARCH 2, 2011

## Fereydoun Seydi Rad, freelance

Seydi Rad, a journalistic blogger, was arrested in Arak in March, although his detention was not disclosed for several months, according to news accounts. His sister, Faranak Seydi, told the reformist news website *Jonbesh-e-Rah-e-Sabz* that family members had maintained silence because they feared further reprisals. The Committee of Human Rights Reporters said Seydi Rad spent 43 days in solitary confinement under interrogation.

In August, a Revolutionary Court in Tehran sentenced Seydi Rad to one year in prison for "propagating against the regime" in his blog, *Arak Green Revolution*. Seydi Rad wrote about the pro-democracy movement, student protests, and labor strikes in the city of Arak.

The court also sentenced him to two years in prison for taking part in a 2010 protest and attending the 2009 funeral of Ayatollah Hossein-Ali Montazeri, the cleric who had criticized President Mahmoud Ahmadinejad's positions.

Faranak Seydi told *Jonbesh-e-Rah-e- Sabz* that his family had only been able to visit him in person twice, and their other weekly visits had been through a booth.

IMPRISONED: JULY 2011

## Mehrdad Sarjoui, *Iran News*

Sarjoui, who covered international news for the English-language daily *Iran News* and other publications, was arrested at his home and transferred to the Intelligence Ministry's Ward 209 at Evin Prison, the BBC Persian service reported. The reformist news website *Kaleme* reported that he was being held in Evin Prison.

No formal charges had been disclosed by late year. Sarjoui had previously worked in the international relations department of the government's Strategic Research Center, according to the U.S. government-funded Radio Free Europe/Radio Liberty. Staff members for the research agency have access to politically sensitive material, which has placed them under intense scrutiny by government security agents.

IMPRISONED: JULY 27, 2011

## Ali Dini Torkamani, freelance

Torkamani, an economist and author of several books, was arrested after writing articles critical of government policies for a number of publications, particularly the energy trade journal *Danesh-e-Naft*, according to news accounts. He also gave interviews to the U.S. government-funded Radio Farda and other media outlets in which he criticized government plans to eliminate consumer subsidies.

Torkamani and some other analysts had argued that the plan, supported by President Mahmoud Ahmadinejad, was insufficiently researched. He had also participated in an academic debate that challenged the plan. Authorities had not disclosed formal charges or Torkamani's whereabouts by late year.

IMPRISONED: JULY 31, 2011

## Kouhyar Goudarzi, Committee of Human Rights Reporters

Goudarzi, a veteran journalist for the Committee of Human Rights Reporters who had completed a one-year prison term in December 2010, was seized by suspected government agents in July 2011 and taken to an undisclosed location, the reformist news website *Kaleme* reported. By October, *Kaleme* reported, Goudarzi was being held by the Intelligence Ministry.

Numerous journalists working for the Committee of Human Rights Reporters have been detained for varying periods of time since 2009 in connection with their reporting on human rights abuses. The human rights committee said judicial authorities have sought to link the organization to external political parties.

Authorities also targeted Goudarzi's family and friends. His mother, Parvin Mokhtare, was being held in a prison in Kerman in late year on charges of "insulting the supreme leader" and "giving interviews to foreign media" concerning government harassment of the journalist, *Jonbesh-e-Rah-e-Sabz* reported. Two of Goudarzi's friends were briefly detained and later took their own lives, according to news accounts.

The Committee of Human Rights Reporters said Goudarzi was being held in Evin Prison, where he has been denied contact with family members.

IMPRISONED: JULY 31, 2011

## Saeed Jalalifar, Committee of Human Rights Reporters

Jalalifar, who had reported on child labor and political prisoner issues for the committee, was first arrested in December 2009. He was free on bail for more than a year before being summoned back to Evin Prison in July 2011, the BBC Persian service reported.

The opposition website *Pars Daily News* reported that Jalalifar was then sentenced to three years in prison on charges of "assembly and collusion against the regime."

Numerous journalists working for the committee have been detained for varying periods of time since 2009 in connection with their work in exposing human rights violations and government malfeasance.

IMPRISONED: AUGUST 26, 2011

## Morteza Moradpour, *Yazligh*

Moradpour, who wrote for *Yazligh*, a children's magazine, was serving a three-year prison term on charges of "propagating against the Islamic Republic of Iran," "mutiny," and "illegal congregation," according to the Committee of Human Rights Reporters.

Moradpour was first arrested in 2009 along with several family members during a protest over Azeri-language rights in Tabriz in northwestern Azerbaijan province, according to the committee. Two issues of *Yazligh* were used as evidence in the trial against him, the news website *Bizim Tabriz* reported. Moradpour's attorney said the charges were politically motivated, the news website *Tabriz Sesi* reported. The Committee of Human Rights Reporters said pressure on members of Azeri civil society had increased as the government attempted to marginalize the ethnic minority.

The journalist was jailed at the Tabriz Information Office Detention Center before being transferred to Tabriz Central Prison, where he spent nearly two months in solitary confinement.

On November 10, 2009, Moradpour was sentenced to three years in prison, Azeri news websites reported. He was released on the equivalent of US$50,000 bail in late 2010, according to *Baybak*, a local Azeri news website. (The practice of releasing convicted inmates on bail or furlough is common in Iranian jurisprudence.)

Moradpour was rearrested based on the original conviction on August 26, 2011, after taking part in protests related to the environmental degradation of Lake Orumiyeh in northwestern Iran, reformist news websites reported.

IMPRISONED: SEPTEMBER 2011

## Hadi Ahmadi, Iranian Students News Agency

Security forces in Karaj arrested Ahmadi in mid-September, according to Aftab News Agency and the pro-opposition Radio Koocheh. An economics reporter, Ahmadi had worked for the semi-official Iranian

Students News Agency, or ISNA, since 2006.

Ahmadi contacted his family by telephone after his arrest, but said he did not know the basis for his arrest, the Human Rights House of Iran reported. No formal charges were immediately disclosed.

The state-supported ISNA is run largely by Iranian university students. Originally established to publish news from Iranian universities, it now covers a variety of national and international topics. Four other ISNA journalists were jailed in October 2011.

IMPRISONED: SEPTEMBER 5, 2011

Omid Behroozi, *Majzooban-e-Noor*

Reza Entessari, *Majzooban-e-Noor*

Amir Eslami, *Majzooban-e-Noor*

Afshin Karampour, *Majzooban-e-Noor*

Hamid Moradi, *Majzooban-e-Noor*

Farshid Yadollahi, *Majzooban-e-Noor*

Authorities arrested at least 30 members of the religious minority Gonabadi Dervishes following a confrontation with plainclothes agents in the town of Kavar in Fars province, a spokesman for the group told the International Campaign for Human Rights in Iran. Among the detainees were a number of journalists for *Majzooban-e-Noor*, a website that reported news about the group, the International Campaign and the reformist news website *Rooz Online* reported.

Six of the website staffers were among those who remained in prison when CPJ conducted its annual census on December 1, 2011. In a September 12 article, *Majzooban-e-Noor* said agents had targeted the journalists in an effort to silence news coverage about the group.

The detainees were initially placed in solitary confinement and were not allowed to telephone their families for three weeks. In subsequent calls to relatives, the detainees said they were being held at Intelligence Ministry Ward 209 at Evin Prison, the reformist website *Kaleme* reported.

IMPRISONED: SEPTEMBER 18, 2011

Amir Ali Allamehzadeh, Iranian Labor News Agency

Plainclothes police arrested Allamehzadeh, an international affairs reporter for Iranian Labor News Agency, or ILNA, at his father's home in Tehran, the International Campaign for Human Rights in Iran and

*Jonbesh-e-Rah-e-Sabz* reported.

No formal charges were immediately disclosed, although the warrant was authorized by an investigative judge presiding in the Government Employees and Media Court, indicating that the charges would be work-related. Security agents searched the family's home in October, seizing several undisclosed items.

Allamehzadeh was being held in late year in a security ward at Evin Prison overseen by Revolution Guards, according to human rights websites. In a visit with his father, a distraught Allamehzadeh said he could not talk about conditions in prison, *Jonbesh-e-Rah-e-Sabz* reported.

IMPRISONED: SEPTEMBER 18, 2011

## Mojtaba Mir Tahmaseb, freelance

Tahmaseb was among five filmmakers arrested just as the BBC Persian service aired a critical documentary on Supreme Leader Ayatollah Ali Khamenei, according to news accounts. Although the others were released, the Intelligence Ministry issued a statement accusing Tahmaseb of serious crimes, including "fulfilling the needs of the intelligence service of Britain," "providing propaganda for psychological war for Iran's enemies," and "money laundering." The filmmaker was being held at Evin Prison in late year, Radio France Internationale reported.

It was not clear why the government initially targeted the group of filmmakers. The BBC reported that the five filmmakers were not involved in the production of the Khamenei documentary.

Tahmaseb had directed the 2011 documentary, "This Is Not a Film," which depicted the detention of another director, Ja'far Panahi. Prior to his arrest, on September 5, Tahmaseb was taken off a flight to Europe, and his passport was confiscated, the BBC Persian service reported. His wife traveled in his place to present "This Is Not a Film" at a variety of film festivals.

IMPRISONED: OCTOBER 1, 2011

## Saeed Nazari, Iranian Students News Agency
## Ali Nezamolmolki, Iranian Students News Agency

IMPRISONED: OCTOBER 5, 2011

## Farzad Sadri, Iranian Students News Agency

Authorities arrested the three journalists in the southern city of Shiraz and placed them in an intelligence agency detention center, the Human Rights Activists News Agency and the reformist news website *Kaleme* reported. No formal charges were immediately disclosed.

Agents also seized a number of undisclosed items from the home of Sadri, a regional editor for the news agency, *Kaleme* reported. The state-supported Iranian Students News Agency, or ISNA, is run largely by Iranian university students. Originally established to publish news from Iranian universities, it now covers a variety of national and international topics. Another ISNA journalist, Hadi Ahmadi, was jailed in September 2011.

ISNA did not issue a public response to the arrests.

IMPRISONED: NOVEMBER 11, 2011

## Raed al-Majed, freelance

## Adel al-Yahya, Al-Adalah

Al-Yahya, a presenter for the private Kuwaiti television station Al-Adalah, and al-Majed, a freelance cameraman, were detained in the southern city of Abadan on charges of espionage and entering the country illegally, according to news reports.

Kuwaiti newspapers said the journalists intended to produce a report about Kuwaitis who married Iranian citizens. The Kuwaiti Bar Association said the two journalists had received permits from Iranian authorities prior to traveling to the country, according to Iranian news reports.

IMPRISONED: NOVEMBER 13, 2011

## Hassan Fathi, *Ettelaat*

Security forces arrested Fathi, editor of the Iranian daily *Ettelaat*, at his home in Tehran, the BBC Persian service reported. His wife told the BBC that security forces confiscated Fathi's laptop and satellite receiver.

The semi-official Fars news agency said Fathi was arrested after reporting for the BBC Persian service on an explosion at an ammunition depot that killed 17 Revolutionary Guards. Fars alleged that Fathi was a contributor to the banned BBC Persian service and accused him of "spreading lies and disrupting public minds." Iran bans cooperation with foreign news agencies.

In a statement, the BBC Persian service said Fathi was interviewed as an independent analyst and did not work for the organization. The broadcaster said it had no office or journalists working in Iran. Fathi's whereabouts and legal status were not immediately disclosed.

IMPRISONED: NOVEMBER 14, 2011

## Rojin Mohammadi, freelance

Mohammadi, an Iranian medical student and political blogger based in Manila, was arrested when she arrived at Tehran's international airport on a flight from Istanbul, according to news accounts. She was free on bail for several days before being summoned back to Evin Prison in late November, according to the Committee of Human Rights Reporters.

Security agents confiscated her laptop computer and other belongings. The committee, citing unnamed sources, said Mohammadi was placed in solitary confinement at Evin Prison. A judge based at the prison charged her with "assembly and collusion with the intent to disrupt state security," "propagating against the regime," and "human rights activities."

IMPRISONED: NOVEMBER 18, 2011

## Davood Khodakarami, *Bayram Monthly*

Khodakarami, a journalist for the Azeri-language *Bayram Monthly*, was detained in the northwestern province of Zanjan, according to news reports. He had gone to a Zanjan bus terminal to ship copies of his publication to the city of Tabriz. Khodakarami was being held at Zanjan's intelligence office; no charges were immediately disclosed.

*Bayram Monthly* is the only publication in the city of Zanjan that covers cultural and social issues. According to opposition website *Iran Global*, security forces had gone to Khodakarami's home several times since August, threatening his family and searching the premises and confiscating his computer and personal items.

# Israel and the Occupied Palestinian Territory: 7

IMPRISONED: MAY 8, 2011

## Walid Khalid Harb, *Falastin*

Israeli authorities arrested Harb, director of the Hamas-affiliated *Falastin*, at his home in the northern West Bank town of Isskaka, the newspaper reported. An Israeli military court ordered that Harb be held in administrative detention. He was jailed at Nafha Prison in the Negev desert in late year, according to his employer.

Under administrative detention procedures, authorities may hold detainees for six months without charge or trial and then extend the detention an unlimited number of times. No formal charges were brought by late year.

Authorities had arrested Harb before, in May 2007, CPJ research shows. His attorney, Tamar Pelleg, told CPJ at the time that she believed his work at *Falastin* played a role in that detention.

IMPRISONED: JUNE 28, 2011

## Nawaf al-Amer, Al-Quds

Al-Amer, satellite program coordinator for London-based Al-Quds television, was arrested by Israeli authorities at his home in the town of Kufr Khalil, near Nablus. Al-Amer had previously worked for the London-based, pan-Arab daily *Al-Quds al-Arabi*.

An Israeli military court ordered that al-Amer be held in administrative detention for six months. Under administrative detention procedures, authorities may hold detainees for six months without charge or trial and then extend the detention an unlimited number of times. On October 26, Israeli authorities informed al-Amer's wife that the detention had been extended for another four months, local press freedom groups reported. No explanation was given for the extension, and no formal charges had been lodged by late year.

Al-Amer was working on a book detailing mistreatment of Palestinians being held in Israeli jails, his son wrote in an online article published prior to the arrest.

IMPRISONED: AUGUST 21, 2011

## Amer Abu Arafa, Shihab News Agency

Israeli authorities arrested Abu Arafa, a correspondent for the Gaza-based Shihab News Agency, at his home in Hebron, the news outlet reported. An Israeli military court ordered that Abu Arafa be held at the Ofer administrative detention center for six months, Shihab said.

Under administrative detention procedures, authorities may hold detainees for six months without charge or trial and then extend the detention an unlimited number of times. His family told Shihab that authorities had accused the journalist of being a "security threat," although no formal charges had been filed by late year.

The news agency, based in the Gaza Strip, pursues an editorial line that is critical of Israel and the Palestinian Authority, CPJ research shows. Abu Arafa covered news in Hebron and the surrounding area for the agency, Shihab told CPJ. Shortly before his arrest, Abu Arafa wrote a story about the arrests of 120 Hamas members by Israeli authorities in Hebron, Shihab told CPJ.

Abu Arafa was arrested before, in May 2010, by Palestinian security forces, CPJ research shows. His father told Shihab that his son was taken from their home by the Palestinian Intelligence Services for reasons linked to his work. Two months later, a Palestinian court sentenced Abu Arafa to three months in prison and a fine of 500 Jordanian dinars (US$700) after finding him guilty of "resisting the policies of the authorities" in connection with his reporting, Shihab told CPJ at the time.

IMPRISONED: NOVEMBER 14, 2011

## Raed al-Sharif, Radio Marah

Al-Sharif, a journalist for the independent Hebron-based Radio Marah, was arrested after Israeli military forces raided his home in the southern West Bank town, according to news reports. He was ordered held in administrative detention. Under administrative detention procedures, authorities may hold detainees for six months without charge or trial and then extend the detention an unlimited number of times.

An Israeli army spokeswoman said al-Sharif was arrested for "suspected involvement in terrorist activity," according to the independent Bethlehem-based Ma'an News Agency. The Palestinian Journalists Syndicate said in a statement that al-Sharif's arrest was an attempt by Israeli authorities to censor an independent journalist. No charges had been disclosed as of late year.

Local press freedom groups said al-Sharif had been detained for a short period in October 2010.

IMPRISONED: NOVEMBER 22, 2011

## Ziyad Awad, Aswar Press Agency

Hamas security forces arrested Awad, a photojournalist for the Aswar Press Agency, at his home in Gaza, the agency and other local news outlets reported. Agents confiscated his computer and other equipment, and placed him in a jail run by the internal security directorate, according to news reports.

No charges were immediately disclosed. Authorities said the detention was "security-related" but did not elaborate, Aswar said in a statement. The news agency noted that the arrest took place the same week Hamas authorities had detained or interrogated a number of other journalists. Aswar, which is critical of the Gaza-based Hamas government, said the detention was reprisal for its coverage.

IMPRISONED: NOVEMBER 22, 2011

## Mahmoud al-Barbar, freelance

Hamas forces arrested al-Barbar, a journalistic blogger, at his Gaza home and confiscated his computer and mobile phone, according to regional news reports. He was being held in a jail run by the internal security directorate, the Palestinian Journalists Syndicate said.

On his blog, *Mahmoud Gaza*, and in articles contributed to Arabic news websites, al-Barbar was critical of Hamas policies and what he perceived to be the government's lack of democratic principles. He has also appeared on television news programs to comment on what he saw as a lack of youth participation in the political process.

No charges were immediately disclosed. The arrest came amid a flurry of interrogations and detentions of journalists in Gaza.

IMPRISONED: NOVEMBER 24, 2011

## Hani al-Agha, Al-Nahar News Agency

Al-Agha, editor-in-chief of the Gaza-based Al-Nahar News Agency, was arrested by Hamas security forces at the Rafah Crossing as he was returning from a trip to Egypt, according to Al-Nahar and regional news reports. Three days later, security forces raided his home and confiscated his computer along with other work-related documents, the news agency said in a statement.

The journalist was being held in a jail run by the internal security directorate. Hamas authorities did not disclose charges against the journalist, saying only that it was "security-related," according to local news outlets. In its statement, Al-Nahar said the arrest was reprisal for the agency's critical coverage of the Hamas government. A number of other Gaza-based journalists were interrogated or detained in late November.

# Ivory Coast: 4

IMPRISONED: JULY 21, 2011

## Hermann Aboa, Radiodiffusion Télévision Ivoirienne

Aboa, a television presenter with state broadcaster Radiodiffusion Télévision Ivoirienne (RTI), was arrested on antistate charges in connection with his role as moderator of a partisan political show when the station was controlled by former President Laurent Gbagbo.

From November 2010 to February 2011, Aboa was one of four moderators of the show "Raison d'État" (National Interest), which exclusively featured guests favorable to then-President Gbagbo, according to CPJ research. Gbagbo was locked in a five-month power struggle with rival Alassane Ouattara, whose U.N.-certified victory in the November 2010 presidential elections was challenged by Gbagbo until French-backed Ouattara forces ousted him in April.

Ivorian investigating magistrate Mamadou Koné charged Aboa with antistate crimes, including endangering state security and public order, participation in an insurrection, and incitement to ethnic hatred, according to news reports and local journalists. Less than a week after the arrest, Ouattara declared in a press conference at U.N. headquarters that Aboa's program was "really calling on hate, hatred," and inciting "people to kill each other." He compared Aboa's program to Radio Mille Collines, a Rwandan government-sponsored station that directed killings during the 1994 genocide in that country. Ouattara also accused the journalist of accepting money from Gbagbo "to buy arms, to distribute arms to mercenaries."

Based on footage of Aboa's program, CPJ determined that the accusations regarding Aboa's performance as a journalist were baseless. Authorities did not disclose any evidence to support the arms-smuggling accusations, and local journalists question the allegations. He was the only one of four program moderators to be prosecuted.

Aboa fled the country in April following Gbagbo's fall, but he returned in June in response to Ouattara's call for exiles to come home after the conflict had ended, according to CPJ research.

In interviews with CPJ in October, Ivorian State Prosecutor Koffi Simplice said Aboa was in preventive detention pending completion of an investigating magistrate's probe. He said such investigations could last as long as five years. Aboa was being held in Abidjan's MACA Prison, according to local journalists. In November, authorities denied Aboa's petition for release on bail, according to news reports. No date for a trial had been set by late year.

IMPRISONED: NOVEMBER 24, 2011

## César Etou, *Notre Voie*
## Didier Dépry, *Notre Voie*
## Boga Sivori, *Notre Voie*

Public Prosecutor Simplice Kouadio ordered the arrests of Editor Etou, copy editor Dépry, and political desk chief Sivori following the publication of columns critical of the government, according to local journalists and news reports. The daily *Notre Voie* is known as favoring former leader Laurent Gbagbo.

Authorities interrogated the journalists over a critical November 21 column concerning the government's reported acquisition of Mercedes Class E vehicles for members of the cabinet, defense lawyer Serge Essouo told CPJ. The journalists were also questioned about a November 24 column that criticized the government's dismissive reaction to a *Notre Voie* report regarding currency valuation.

Police detained the trio without formal charge beyond the 48-hour constitutional limit on pretrial detention and in contravention of Ivory Coast's 2004 Press Law, which bans the detention of journalists for press matters, according to local journalists and CPJ research. On November 29, a judge charged the journalists under the penal code with "incitement to theft, looting and destruction of private property via a press channel," Essouo told CPJ.

The three were being held in Abidjan's MACA Prison, according to local journalists.

## Kazakhstan: 1

IMPRISONED: JANUARY 7, 2009

## Ramazan Yesergepov, *Alma-Ata Info*

Two months after Yesergepov published explosive internal memos from the KNB, the Kazakh security service, authorities arrested the editor at an Almaty hospital, where he was undergoing treatment for a heart condition, according to CPJ interviews and news accounts. Yesergepov was transported to a detention facility in the southern city of Taraz.

The KNB memos, published in Yesergepov's newspaper, *Alma-Ata Info*, showed high-ranking agents conspiring to influence a prosecutor and a judge in a tax-evasion case. Yesergepov also wrote a commentary on the contents of the memos. The KNB retroactively declared the memos classified and charged Yesergepov with "collecting state secrets." Authorities tried him behind closed doors, denied him a lawyer of his choosing, and barred access to his own case file.

In August 2009, a Taraz City Court judge sentenced Yesergepov to three years in prison. Raushan Yesergepova, the journalist's wife, told CPJ that the state-appointed defense lawyer did not attend Yesergepov's final hearing. Subsequent appeals—which Yesergepov prepared himself—were denied, as were appeals for early release and transfer to a lower-security facility.

During a June 2010 fact-finding mission to Almaty, CPJ Europe and Central Asia Program Coordinator Nina Ognianova tried to visit Yesergepov in prison. Kazakh authorities initially approved the visit, but officials with the local penitentiary service revoked the approval on the day Ognianova traveled to the prison colony in Taraz.

A CPJ delegation advocated on behalf of Yesergepov in an October 2010 meeting with Kazakh Ambassador Kairat Abdrakhmanov, chairman of the permanent council of the Organization for Security and Co-operation in Europe. In the meeting, at OSCE headquarters in Vienna, Ognianova and CPJ Senior Adviser Jean-Paul Marthoz detailed violations of Yesergepov's rights to a fair trial.

In January 2011, authorities denied Yesergepov's appeal for early release, saying he "did not show signs of improved behavior," news reports said. The reports quoted authorities as saying Yesergepov violated prison rules by turning on the lights in his cell when he needed to take medication at night.

## Kyrgyzstan: 1

IMPRISONED: JUNE 15, 2010

### Azimjon Askarov, freelance

Askarov, a contributor to the independent news website *Voice of Freedom* and director of the local human rights group Vozdukh (Air), was serving a life term on a series of fabricated charges that included incitement to ethnic hatred and complicity in the murder of a police officer.

Authorities in the southern Jalal-Abad region arrested Askarov after a violent confrontation between police and villagers in Bazar-Korgon. One police officer was killed in the conflict. The episode took place amid deadly ethnic clashes between Kyrgyz and Uzbek residents, which engulfed all of southern Kyrgyzstan in June 2010. The clashes left hundreds dead, and forced up to a half-million people to flee their homes. According to press reports and CPJ sources, Askarov was reporting on violence, destruction, looting, and human rights abuses in Bazar-Korgon at the time.

CPJ research shows that Askarov was imprisoned in retaliation for his journalism and human rights work. Before his arrest, Askarov had reported allegations that regional police had fabricated criminal cases against innocent people and had tortured detainees in custody. As a result of Askarov's work, several senior law enforcement officials had been dismissed from their posts, according to *Voice of Freedom* and CPJ sources.

Regional prosecutors initially charged Askarov, 61, with organizing the riots, but later expanded his indictment to include complicity in the murder of a police officer, possession of ammunition and extremist literature, and attempted kidnapping, regional press reports said. Askarov denied the charges and said he had not been present at the scene. In June 2011, Askarov told the independent news website *Fergana News* that he came to the scene of the killing only after his neighbors alerted him to the events. During his trial, Askarov said, neighbors wanted to testify on his behalf, but regional police and prosecutors threatened them into silence.

Askarov, held by the same department whose officer was killed in Bazar-Korgon, was beaten by police while in custody, defense lawyer Nurbek Toktakunov told CPJ. Toktakunov said he himself was attacked by relatives of the deceased officer. Authorities did not investigate the reports, according to CPJ research.

On September 15, 2010, Judge Nurgazy Alimbayev pronounced Askarov guilty on all charges and sentenced him to life in prison. Toktakunov said the prosecution had failed to produce any evidence or witness testimony that implicated Askarov.

## Libya: 1

IMPRISONED: AUGUST 21, 2011

### Hala al-Misrati, Al-Libiya

Al-Misrati, an anchor for the daily news show "Libya Today" on state-aligned Al-Libiya television, was being held under house arrest, news reports said. Rebel forces detained her after seizing Tripoli and storming the station, which was launched in 2009 by Saif al-Islam, a son of the late leader Muammar Qaddafi.

Al-Misrati was known for her staunch support of Qaddafi's regime during the popular uprising that began in Libya in February. In an August 21 broadcast, aired as rebel forces were advancing on the capital, she was shown brandishing an automatic weapon and saying that she was ready to die for Qaddafi.

The London-based daily *Al-Sharq al-Wasat* quoted al-Misrati as saying that she was compelled to take a hard-line in support of the Qaddafi government. She told the paper that rebel forces had treated her well.

## Morocco: 2

IMPRISONED: APRIL 28, 2011

### Rachid Nini, *Al-Massae*

Nini, executive editor of the Moroccan daily *Al-Massae*, was arrested following the publication of several articles criticizing perceived abuses in the country's counterterrorism efforts. In May, a Casablanca court refused to release the prominent journalist on bail. His lawyers argued that their client was being improperly prosecuted under the penal code, which provides harsher penalties than the press code, according to news reports.

In June, he was sentenced to one year in prison for "denigrating judicial rulings" and "compromising the security and safety of the homeland and citizens." Nini was being held at Okacha Prison in Casablanca in late year, according to *Al-Massae*.

Long known as an outspoken government critic, Nini had also denounced official corruption, called for increased political freedom, and sought the annulment of Morocco's anti-terrorism law.

IMPRISONED: SEPTEMBER 5, 2011

### Mohamed al-Dawas, freelance

Authorities arrested al-Dawas, a critical journalist who wrote for the blog *Al-Fnidaq Online*, in the northern city of Fnidaq, according to news reports. On September 22, a court in Tetouan sentenced the blogger to a 19-month prison sentence on drug trafficking charges and a fine of 20,000 dirhams (US$2,472), defense lawyer Abdel al-Sadiq al-Bushtawy told CPJ.

Al-Bushtawy said his client denied the drug trafficking allegations, which the defense considered retaliation for al-Dawas' critical writing. *Al-Fnidaq Online* features the work of several journalists who write about local government corruption. A report by the French news outlet France 24 quoted several local journalists as saying they, too, believed the arrest to be retaliation for al-Dawas' critical writing.

Al-Bushtawy told CPJ that the defense team was not given an adequate opportunity to present its case. In protest, the defense team withdrew from what it deemed unfair proceedings, and the court tried al-Dawas without counsel. An appeal was pending in late year.

## Rwanda: 2

IMPRISONED: JULY 8, 2010

### Agnès Uwimana, *Umurabyo*
### Saidati Mukakibibi, *Umurabyo*

Authorities arrested Uwimana, founder and chief editor of the independent vernacular weekly *Umurabyo*, and its deputy editor, Mukakibibi, in July 2010, defense lawyer Nsabayezu Evariste told CPJ. By February 2011, Kigali's High Court sentenced Uwimana and Mukakibibi to 17 and seven years, respectively, on charges of incitement to violence, genocide denial, and insulting the head of state in connection with several opinion pieces published in mid-2010, according to news reports. The publication closed after their arrest.

Although the publication was considered sometimes sensational, local journalists told CPJ, *Umurabyo* raised questions about a number of sensitive topics, including the July 2010 murder of journalist Jean-Léonard Rugambage, the fallout between President Paul Kagame and two now-exiled military leaders, growing divisions within the Rwandan army, and the need for justice for ethnic Hutus killed in the 1994 genocide.

Both single mothers and the sole breadwinners in their families, the two journalists filed appeals with the Supreme Court. Uwimana and Mukakibibi were being held at Central Prison in the capital, Kigali.

# Sudan: 4

IMPRISONED: OCTOBER 30, 2010

**Abdelrahman Adam Abdelrahman**, Radio Dabanga
**Adam al-Nur Adam**, Radio Dabanga
**Zakaria Yacoub Eshag**, Radio Dabanga

The Sudanese National Intelligence and Security Services arrested several journalists and human rights activists during a raid on the shared Khartoum offices of Radio Dabanga and the Human Rights and Advocacy Network for Democracy, according to local and international news reports.

Abdelrahman, the station's Sudan director, and reporters al-Nur and Eshag remained in custody in late year, according to local journalists. Although the station is outlawed in Sudan because of its coverage of Darfur and human rights, it is based in the Netherlands and uses shortwave frequencies to transmit its signal into Sudan.

The three journalists were being held on antistate charges stemming from their reporting on the humanitarian situation in Darfur, the station reported. The journalists were also accused of threatening national peace and security, espionage against the state, and undermining the constitutional system, Dabanga said on its website.

The defendants, all of whom were being held at Khartoum's Kober Prison, went on trial in July 2011, at which time they denied all charges against them. Their trial was pending in late year.

IMPRISONED: OCTOBER 24, 2011

**Jamal Osman Hamad**, freelance

Security forces in Khartoum arrested Hamad, an exiled Eritrean journalist, according to Sudanese human rights groups and exiled Eritrean journalists. Authorities did not immediately disclose Hamad's whereabouts or legal status.

Hamad is a veteran journalist who had been living in Sudan for several years and writing for the Eritrean opposition news website *Adoulis*. His articles have been critical of Eritrean government policies.

# Syria: 8

IMPRISONED: DECEMBER 27, 2009

## Tal al-Mallohi, freelance

Al-Mallohi, a journalistic blogger, was detained in December 2009 after she was summoned for questioning by security officials, according to local rights groups. In February 2011, she was sentenced by a state security court to five years in prison on a fabricated charge of "disclosing information to a foreign country that must remain a secret for national safety."

The private newspaper *Al-Watan* said in October 2010 that al-Mallohi was suspected of spying for the United States. But lawyers allowed into the closed-court session said the judge "did not give evidence or details as to why she was convicted," the BBC reported. The U.S. State Department condemned the trial, saying in a statement that the allegations of espionage were baseless.

Al-Mallohi's blog was devoted to Palestinian rights and was critical of Israeli policies. It also discussed the frustrations of Arab citizens with their governments and what she perceived to be the stagnation of the Arab world. Al-Mallohi's case gained widespread attention in the Arab blogosphere, on social media websites, and with human rights activists worldwide.

IMPRISONED: JULY 20, 2011

## Mohamed-Jamal al-Tahan, *Tishreen*

Two security agents arrested the veteran journalist al-Tahan at his home in Aleppo, according to news reports and human rights groups. An editor for the state-owned daily *Tishreen*, al-Tahan also contributed to several Arabic newspapers. He had written in support of the country's popular uprising, regional news media reported.

Al-Tahan's whereabouts, well-being, and legal status were unknown in late year. In November, regional news media said they had received unconfirmed but credible reports that al-Tahan may have died in detention. CPJ could not independently corroborate those reports.

IMPRISONED: AUGUST 19, 2011

## Tariq Saeed Balsha, freelance

Balsha, a freelance cameraman, was arrested in the coastal city of

Latakia three days after he covered an episode in which government troops opened fire at Al-Raml Palestinian refugee camp, according to local press freedom groups.

Balsha's footage of demonstrations and authorities' efforts to quash the unrest have been posted to a number of websites, including the Shaam News Network, a loose-knit citizen news organization that has published thousands of videos documenting the popular uprising in Syria. Shaam's footage has been used by international news organizations such as Al-Jazeera and the BBC.

In November, the Syrian Center for Media and Freedom of Expression reported that Balsha was being held at Latakia Central Prison. No charges had been disclosed by late year.

IMPRISONED: AUGUST 22, 2011

## Adel Walid Kharsa, freelance

Security forces arrested Kharsa in connection with his coverage of protests in Hama, according to human rights organizations. Kharsa's whereabouts, well-being, and legal status were unknown in late year, but Amnesty International said it was concerned he may have been tortured in detention.

Kharsa had been living in the United Arab Emirates until June, when he decided to move back to his hometown of Hama to report on the country's popular uprising. Amnesty International said Kharsa had tried working anonymously in his reporting for international news outlets, but his identity became known to Syrian intelligence officers.

IMPRISONED: SEPTEMBER 3, 2011

## Amer Matar, freelance

Security forces in Damascus arrested Matar, a contributor to the pan-Arab daily *Al-Hayat*, according to local news outlets and CPJ interviews. Authorities did not disclose any formal charges or trial proceedings by late year.

Matar had covered protests in Damascus and was himself politically active, calling for peaceful anti-regime demonstrations on his Facebook page. He had previously been detained for more than two weeks in April 2011.

IMPRISONED: OCTOBER 14, 2011

## Jihad Jamal, freelance

Jamal was arrested at a Damascus café along with Sean McAllister, a British reporter working for Channel 4. McAllister was released six days later, Channel 4 reported. McAllister said he last saw Jamal blindfolded and on his knees in an interrogation room in an unmarked building in central Damascus.

Jamal, a contributor to local news websites, also aggregated news stories for dissemination to international outlets, McAllister told CPJ. He had been arrested twice before in 2011, in March and August, the latter detention lasting for 60 days, McAllister said.

IMPRISONED: OCTOBER 24, 2011

## Hussein Ghrer, freelance

Security forces arrested the prominent blogger Ghrer and brought him to a central Damascus prison, according to the Syrian Center for Media and Freedom of Expression and several journalists. Ghrer appeared before a magistrate on November 20, when he was charged with "weakening national sentiments," "forming an association without a permit," and "inciting demonstrations," according to the Syrian Center. He was transferred to the central prison in Adra, about 25 miles (40 kilometers) from Damascus.

Days before he was detained, Ghrer wrote on his blog: "Silence doesn't serve us after today. We don't want a country where we get imprisoned for uttering a word. We want a country that embraces and welcomes words." His blog featured stories about other detained bloggers in Syria, the country's popular uprising, and Israel's occupation of Palestinian and Syrian territories, among other topics.

The Syrian Center said Ghrer suffers from coronary disease and high blood pressure and requires daily medications.

IMPRISONED: NOVEMBER 18, 2011

## Alaa al-Khodr, Syrian Arab News Agency

Security forces detained al-Khodr, local director for the official Syrian Arab News Agency in the eastern city of Deir al-Zour, according to news reports. On the day of his arrest, al-Khodr had resigned from his post to protest "the regime's human rights violations against civilians," Agence France-Presse reported. At a demonstration that day, he wore a sign on his chest that read "I am a Syrian journalist" and a sticker on his mouth to signify the regime's brutal repression.

The Syrian news agency has disputed reports of al-Khodr's arrest and the circumstances of his resignation. Al-Khodr's whereabouts, well-being, and legal status were unknown in late year.

# Thailand: 1

IMPRISONED: APRIL 30, 2011

## Somyot Prueksakasemsuk, *Voice of Taksin*

Somyot was arrested on April 30 at a Thai border checkpoint at Aranyaprathet province while attempting to cross into neighboring Cambodia. Agence France-Presse reported that police first issued a warrant for his arrest on April 12. He was held without bail in a Bangkok detention center for 84 days, the maximum period allowable under Thai criminal law, before formal *lèse majesté* charges were filed against him on July 26.

The charges stemmed from two articles deemed critical of Thai monarch Bhumibol Adulyadej that were published in the now-defunct *Voice of Taksin*, a highly partisan newsmagazine affiliated with the United Front for Democracy Against Dictatorship street protest group. (The magazine had been accused in the past of running articles that incited UDD followers to violence.)

Somyot, a labor activist and political protest leader, was founder and editor of the controversial publication. According to local media reports, he refused to reveal the identity of the author who wrote the contested articles in February and March 2010, both of which were published under the pseudonym Jit Polachan, according to local news reports.

On November 1, a criminal court refused a bail application submitted by Somyot's lawyer. He faced a possible prison term of 30 years. *Lèse majesté* charges in Thailand carry a maximum of 15-year jail terms and have been abused for political purposes by both sides of Thailand's protracted political conflict. His trial began in late year.

# Turkey: 8

IMPRISONED: JANUARY 30, 2009

## Vedat Kurşun, *Azadiya Welat*

Kurşun, former editor-in-chief of *Azadiya Welat*, Turkey's sole Kurdish-language daily, was arrested at Istanbul's Ataturk Airport, according to the press freedom group Bia. He was charged under the country's Anti-Terror Law with spreading propaganda for the banned Kurdistan Workers Party, or PKK, in the paper's 2007 and 2008 coverage.

In May 2010, Kurşun was sentenced to 166 years and six months in prison on 103 counts of spreading "propaganda on behalf of the terrorist organization" and "committing crimes on behalf of the organization," according to Dogan News Agency. In 2010, the Journalists Association of Turkey honored Kurşun with its Press Freedom Award.

In a special supplement titled "Arrested Newspaper," written by jailed journalists and distributed by several dailies in July 2011, Kurşun wrote that "my file has no other evidence in it but newspapers." He also faulted the official translation of his work, saying it was done by someone not fluent in Kurdish.

IMPRISONED: MARCH 29, 2009

## Barış Açıkel, *Devrim Yolunda İşçi Köylü*

Açıkel, news editor for the now-inactive daily *Devrim Yolunda İşçi Köylü* (Worker Peasant on the Path to Revolution), was sentenced to 12 years in prison on charges of propagandizing for the Workers' and Peasants' Liberation Army of Turkey, according to Justice Ministry records. The government has labeled the organization a terrorist group because it has targeted counterterrorist operatives for attack. The paper, which focused on workers' rights and labor news, was an official organ of the group.

In a July statement, Açıkel said he had actually been sentenced to a 13-year prison term and a fine of 78,000 Turkish lira (US$44,735).

In a July 2011 supplement titled "Arrested Newspaper," written by jailed journalists and distributed by several dailies, Açıkel described intense official harassment prior to his sentencing. He wrote that prosecutors had opened separate criminal cases for each new issue of his newspaper, a situation that led to multiple hearings on a daily basis. CPJ research shows that Turkish authorities often file repetitive and duplicative charges against critical journalists as a means of harassment.

IMPRISONED: APRIL 14, 2009

## Ahmet Birsin, Gün TV

Birsin, general manager of a regional pro-Kurdish television news station in southeastern Turkey, faced trial in late year for assisting an offshoot of the banned Kurdistan Workers Party (PKK), attending PKK events, possessing PKK documents, and assisting the PKK in its press work, according to Justice Ministry documents. His lawyer, Fuat Coşacak, told CPJ that the charges were retaliatory and without basis.

Birsin described his arrest in a May 2009 letter published in the daily *Gündem*. He said police came to his office on the night of April 13, searched the building and confiscated archival material, computer hard drives, laptops, cameras, and other broadcast equipment.

Birsin was imprisoned for 14 months before an indictment was issued against him.

IMPRISONED: JANUARY 5, 2010

## Bedri Adanir, *Hawar* and Aram

Adanir, owner of the pro-Kurdish publishing house Aram and editor-in-chief of the daily *Hawar*, faced trial in late year on charges of spreading propaganda for the banned Kurdistan Workers Party, or PKK, in books and the articles published by his company, Justice Ministry records show.

Adanir, who was being held in Diyarbakir Prison, was rebuffed in his requests to be released on bail while his case was pending. The charges could bring 50 years in prison.

Adanir already served a 15-month prison sentence, imposed in 2009, on similar propaganda charges, the state Anatolian Agency reported. Those charges stemmed from a book published by Aram and written by PKK leader Abdullah Ocalan, titled *Kültür-Sanat Devrimi Üzerine* (On the Revolution of Culture and Art), according to Bia, a Turkish press freedom group.

IMPRISONED: JUNE 20, 2010

## Hamdiye Çiftçi, Dicle News Agency

Çiftçi, a reporter for the pro-Kurdish Dicle News Agency, which closely follows Kurdish issues in the southeastern province of Hakkari, faced trial in late year on charges of attending demonstrations organized by Koma Civakên Kurdistan, an offshoot of the banned Kurdistan Workers Party, according to Justice Ministry documents. Handwritten notes about the Koma Civakên Kurdistan and Kurdistan Workers Party were found in her home, the government said.

In a July 2011 newspaper supplement written by jailed journalists and distributed by several dailies, Çiftçi wrote that merely being a Kurdish journalist had made her a terrorist collaborator. Her lawyer, Fahri Timur, told CPJ that evidence brought against his client was directly linked to her work: "Her doing her job at a political rally, for example, is portrayed as an endorsement of its political content." He said the handwritten notes reflected what any journalist would compile while covering a meeting or rally.

IMPRISONED: JULY 22, 2010

## Ozan Kilinc, *Azadiya Welat*

Kilinc, editor-in-chief of the Kurdish daily *Azadiya Welat*, Turkey's sole Kurdish-language daily, was charged under the country's Anti-Terror Law with spreading propaganda for the banned Kurdistan Workers Party, or PKK.

A criminal court in Diyarbakir sentenced the journalist to 21 years in prison, the BBC reported. *Yuksekova Haber*, a local news website, said Kilinc was being held at Diyarbakir Prison. Verdat Kurşun, a predecessor in the paper's top editorial post, was also in prison when CPJ conducted its annual census on December 1.

IMPRISONED: MARCH 6, 2011

## Nedim Şener, *Posta*

Şener, a columnist for the daily *Posta* and author of two books detailing the 2007 assassination of journalist Hrant Dink, went on trial in late year on charges of aiding the Ergenekon conspiracy, an alleged nationalist military plot to overthrow the government.

Şener said he believes the charges were retaliation for his work on the Dink murder. Ongoing trials of defendants in the Dink murder are widely viewed as insufficient because they involve only the accused gunman and other low-level participants. Evidence presented by Şener and other journalists points to police and national intelligence officials being neglectful, if not complicit, in the murder.

IMPRISONED: MARCH 6, 2011

## Ahmet Şık, freelance

Şık, a prominent reporter who had written for the dailies *Cumhuriyet* and *Radikal* and the weekly *Nokta*, went on trial in late year on charges of aiding the Ergenekon conspiracy, an alleged nationalist military plot to overthrow the government.

Şık, co-author of a 2010 book on Ergenekon, had been known throughout his career for his critical writings about the "deep state," the purported secular, nationalist forces operating within the army, security agencies, and government ministries. Before being arrested, Şık was writing a new book with the working title, *The Imam's Army*, which was to allege the existence of a shadowy organization operating within police and other government agencies and said to be populated by members of the Sufi Muslim religious community known as Fettullah Gülen.

A draft of the new book was deleted from the computers of his publishing house and that of a colleague during police raids, *Hürriyet Daily News* reported. The interrogations of Şık focused almost exclusively on the unfinished book, according to the paper. The government's indictment, which appeared months after the arrest, focused on Şık's journalistic activities, especially in regard to the book, the local press freedom group Bia said.

"Criticizing the government and drawing attention to the dangerous network of people in the police and judiciary who are members of the Gülen community is enough in today's Turkey to become an Ergenekon suspect," Şık told CPJ from prison through his lawyer, Tora Pekin.

## Uzbekistan: 5

IMPRISONED: MARCH 15, 1999

## Muhammad Bekjanov, *Erk*
## Yusuf Ruzimuradov, *Erk*

Bekjanov, editor of the opposition newspaper *Erk*, and Ruzimuradov, a reporter for the paper, continued to serve lengthy prison terms in Uzbekistan. Regional press reports said Bekjanov was serving his term at a penal colony outside Kasan in southwestern Uzbekistan, while Ruzimuradov was being held at a penal colony outside Navoi in central Uzbekistan.

Bekjanov and Ruzimuradov were detained in Ukraine—where they had lived in exile and produced their newspaper—and were extradited at the request of Uzbek authorities. Six months after their arrest, a Tashkent court sentenced Bekjanov to 14 years in prison and Ruzimuradov to a 15-year term on charges of publishing and distributing a banned newspaper. Both reporters were also convicted of participating in a banned political protest and attempting to overthrow the regime.

According to CPJ sources and news reports, both men were tortured before their trial started. After the verdict was announced in November 1999, the two were jailed in high-security penal colonies for individuals convicted of serious crimes.

In a 2003 interview conducted at a prison hospital where he was being treated for tuberculosis, Bekjanov described being beaten and tortured in prison. He suffered a broken leg and hearing loss as a result, according to The Associated Press and the London-based Institute for War and Peace Reporting.

Bekjanov's wife, Nina Bekjanova, visited him in 2006 in prison, and told the independent news website *Uznews* that the journalist had lost most of his teeth due to repeated beatings. Exiled Uzbek journalists, local human rights workers, and other CPJ sources in the region said they had unsuccessfully tried to obtain updated information about the well-being of the journalists. Officials at the Uzbekistan Embassy in Washington did not respond to CPJ's October 2011 request seeking information about the well-being of the two reporters.

IMPRISONED: JULY 24, 2002

## Gayrat Mehliboyev, freelance

Mehliboyev, a contributor to the state-owned weekly *Hurriyat*, was being held in a penal colony in the central city of Zarafshan. He was arrested in the capital, Tashkent, while reporting on a rally held in support of the banned Islamist group Hizb ut-Tahrir.

In February 2003, seven months after his arrest, a court in Tashkent convicted Mehliboyev of anti-constitutional activities, participating in extremist religious organizations, and inciting religious hatred. He was sentenced to seven years in prison, a term that an appeals court reduced by six months.

Prosecutors introduced a 2001 *Hurriyat* article as evidence of his alleged crimes. In the article, Mehliboyev argued that instead of building a Western-style democracy in Uzbekistan, authorities should consider introducing religious rule. Prosecutors insisted in court that his arguments reflected the ideas of Hizb ut-Tahrir. At trial, Mehliboyev repeatedly said he was assaulted by guards at the pretrial facility where he was being held, local and international human rights groups reported at the time.

Mehliboyev was later sentenced to an additional prison term. In September 2006, the Tashkent regional court sentenced him to six more years on extremism charges, the independent news website *Uznews* reported. Prison authorities claimed the journalist advocated Hizb ut-Tahrir ideas to other inmates and kept religious writings in his cell. Mehliboyev denied the accusations; he said he had kept only private notes detailing mistreatment in prison.

Officials at the Uzbekistan Embassy in Washington did not respond to CPJ's October 2011 request seeking updated information about Mehliboyev's status and well-being.

IMPRISONED: JUNE 7, 2008

## Salidzhon Abdurakhmanov, *Uznews*

Abdurakhmanov, 61, a reporter for the independent news website *Uznews*, was being held at a penal colony outside the southern city of Karshi after he was convicted in a politicized prosecution on charges of possessing drugs with intent to sell. CPJ has determined the charges were fabricated.

Authorities in Nukus, in Uzbekistan's Karakalpakstan Autonomous Republic, detained Abdurakhmanov after traffic officers stopped his car and claimed they found four ounces (114 grams) of marijuana and less than a quarter ounce (about five grams) of opium in his trunk, *Uznews* reported. Abdurakhmanov denied possessing the drugs, and said police had planted them in retaliation for his reporting on corruption in the agency. Police questioned Abdurakhmanov extensively about his journalism, searched his home, and confiscated his personal computer, CPJ sources said.

The prosecution was marked by irregularities. Investigators failed to maintain chain of custody for the seized drugs, and they did not present fingerprints or other evidence that Abdurakhmanov ever handled the material, defense lawyer Rustam Tulyaganov told CPJ. Ignoring the lack of evidence, a court in Nukus convicted the journalist in October 2008 and sentenced him to 10 years in prison. Higher courts denied his appeals.

Abdurakhmanov had reported on corruption in regional law enforcement agencies, including the traffic police, for *Uznews*. He also contributed to the U.S. government-funded broadcasters Radio Free Europe/Radio Liberty and Voice of America, and the London-based Institute for War and Peace Reporting.

In September 2011, authorities rebuffed Abdurakhmanov's application for amnesty, citing alleged violations of penal colony rules, according to *Uznews*. Ilhom Nematov, Uzbekistan's ambassador to the United States, did not respond to CPJ's October 2011 request for information on Abdurakhmanov's well-being.

IMPRISONED: FEBRUARY 22, 2009

## Dilmurod Saiid, freelance

Saiid was serving a prison term of 12 and a half years on fabricated charges of extortion and forgery. Authorities arrested Saiid in his hometown, Tashkent, and placed him in detention in the central city of Samarkand after a local woman accused him of extorting US$10,000 from a local businessman. The accuser soon withdrew the accusation, saying she had been coerced, but authorities refused to release the journalist, according to Saiid's lawyer, Ruhiddin Komilov.

In March 2009, Samarkand prosecutors said new witnesses had come forward to accuse Saiid of extortion, the independent regional news website *Fergana News* reported. Prosecutors also said several local farmers had accused Saiid of using their signatures to create fraudulent court papers. At Saiid's trial, *Fergana News* reported, the farmers publicly recanted and said prosecutors had pressured them to testify against the journalist.

Komilov told CPJ that authorities failed to notify him of court hearing dates. In July 2009, a Tailak District Court judge sentenced the journalist in a closed proceeding without Komilov, Saiid's family, or the press in attendance. Saiid was being held in a high-security penal colony outside the city of Navoi in central Uzbekistan.

Saiid was imprisoned in retaliation for his journalism, CPJ's analysis found. Before his imprisonment, Saiid had reported on official abuses against farmers for the independent regional news website *Voice of Freedom* as well as for a number of local publications. As a member of the Tashkent-based human rights group Ezgulik, Saiid had also helped local farmers defend their rights in regional courts, local sources told CPJ.

In November 2009, the journalist's wife and 6-year-old daughter were killed in a car accident while on their way to visit him in prison, regional press reports said. Ezgulik appealed for Saiid's release on humanitarian grounds, but the appeal was denied. In September 2011, authorities rejected Saiid's application for amnesty, citing alleged violations of penal colony rules, *Uznews* reported.

Officials at the Uzbekistan Embassy in Washington did not respond to CPJ's October 2011 request seeking updated information about Saiid's well-being.

## Vietnam: 9

IMPRISONED: APRIL 19, 2008

### Nguyen Van Hai (Nguyen Hoang Hai), freelance

Hai was arrested and held without charge for five months, according to news reports. A closed court convicted him of tax evasion on

September 10, 2008.

Hai, who also goes by the name Nguyen Hoang Hai, was an outspoken commentator on his political blog *Dieu Cay* (The Peasant's Pipe). He was sentenced to two and a half years in prison for failing to pay 10 years of taxes on the part of a building he had rented to an optical shop. International news reports quoted his lawyer as saying the taxes should have been paid by the tenant, according to the rental agreement.

Several of Hai's blog entries had touched on politically sensitive issues. He had reported on national protests against China, which disputed Vietnam's claim to sovereignty over the nearby Spratly and Paracel islands. He also called for demonstrations against the Beijing Olympic torch relay, which was to pass through Ho Chi Minh City, according to the website of Viet Tan, an exiled pro-democracy organization.

In April 2009, Hai was transferred to the southern Cai Tau Prison, several hours from his home in Ho Chi Minh City, and was denied family visits, according to Viet Tan and international human rights groups. He was scheduled for release after serving his sentence on October 20, 2010, but authorities continued to detain him on the grounds that he was still under investigation.

According to the Free Journalists Network of Vietnam, his family filed 12 different formal requests, petitions, and appeals for visitation in 2011, none of which the authorities acknowledged. Canadian Embassy officials were also refused permission to visit Hai in prison, according to the network.

IMPRISONED: SEPTEMBER 13, 2008

## Pham Thanh Nghien, freelance

A Haiphong city court sentenced online writer Nghien on January 29, 2010, to four years in prison and three years of house arrest on charges of spreading antistate propaganda. She was first arrested when more than 20 police officers raided her home on September 13, 2008, during a government crackdown on dissidents. She was originally charged with staging a protest at her home, erecting banners protesting government policy in a maritime dispute involving China, and posting the images on the Internet.

State prosecutors dropped those initial charges and instead singled out an online article Nghien had written for foreign media in which she criticized public officials for siphoning off compensation funds intended for survivors of fishermen killed by Chinese maritime patrols in 2007, according to international news reports.

Nghien was also accused of criticizing the government in interviews with Western media outlets, including the U.S. government-funded Radio Free Asia. Her half-day trial was closed to foreign media and diplomats, news reports said. She was held in solitary confinement until her sentencing in January 2010.

On July 4, 2008, before her arrest, Nghien was severely beaten by four plainclothes police officers who threatened her and her family if she continued her outspoken criticism of government policies, according to Front Line, a human rights group. Nghien wrote several online articles in promotion of human rights, democracy, and better treatment of landless peasants, according to international news reports. She was being held at Thanh Liet Detention Center in Hanoi.

IMPRISONED: AUGUST 13, 2010

## Pham Minh Hoang (Phan Kien Quoc), freelance

Hoang, a university mathematics professor and political blogger associated with the exiled Viet Tan pro-democracy party, was first arrested in Ho Chi Minh City and charged under Article 79 of the penal code for activities aimed at overthrowing the government.

On August 10, 2011, Ho Chi Minh City's People's Court sentenced him to three years in prison and another three years of house arrest for "activities aimed at overthrowing the government," according to local and international news reports. The prison term was later reduced on appeal to 17 months, according to Viet Tan.

The national security-related charges referred to 33 articles written under Hoang's penname, Phan Kien Quoc, according to news reports. The entries focused on corruption, environmental degradation, and perceived government failures to protect the country's territorial sovereignty from Chinese intervention, according to Viet Tan. The journalist was also convicted on charges of having membership in Viet Tan.

The courts ruled that the year Hoang spent in pre-trial detention at the Ministry of Public Security's Detainment Center in Saigon District 1 would count against his sentence.

IMPRISONED: OCTOBER 18, 2010

## Phan Thanh Hai (Anh Ba Saigon), freelance

Hai, a political blogger who wrote under the penname Anh Ba Saigon, was first taken into custody on a provisional four-month detention while authorities conducted further investigation. He was held without formal charge throughout 2011.

Police raided his Ho Chi Minh City home, seizing computers, documents, and articles he had downloaded from the Internet, Agence France-Presse reported. According to his wife, Nguyen Thi Lien, police said they had evidence that he had written and published "false information" on his blog.

Hai's blog often touched on issues considered sensitive by the Vietnamese authorities, including a scandal at state-run shipbuilder Vinashin, maritime and territorial disputes with China, and a controversial Chinese-supported bauxite mining project in the country's Central Highlands.

On April 23, 2011, his wife and three children were allowed to visit him at Ho Chi Minh City's Phan Dang Luu Detention Center but were not permitted to give him needed medications, according to a BBC report. No trial date had been set when CPJ completed its prison census on December 1, 2011.

IMPRISONED: MARCH 26, 2011

## Lu Van Bay (Tran Bao Viet), freelance

Bay, also known as Tran Bao Viet, was arrested after police raided his house and confiscated his computers and copies of his published articles, according to news reports. On August 22, 2011, he was sentenced by a court in southern Kien Giang province to four years in prison and three years of house arrest on charges of "conducting propaganda against the state," a penal code offense.

The court's judgment cited 10 articles Bay posted on overseas websites—including *Dam Chin Viet* (Vietnamese Birds), *Do Thoa* (Dialogue), and *To Quoc* (Fatherland)—that were critical of Vietnam's one-party system and called for multi-party democracy.

IMPRISONED: JULY 30, 2011

## Dang Xuan Dieu, freelance

## Ho Duc Hoa, freelance

Dieu and Hoa, religious activists and contributors to the news website *Vietnam Redemptorist News*, were detained on July 30 at Tan Son Nhat airport in Ho Chi Minh City. *Vietnam Redemptorist News*, an online publication run by the Congregation of the Most Holy Redeemer, reports on the plight of the country's persecuted Catholic minority.

Dieu and Hoa were detained on unspecified charges under Article

79 of the penal code, which outlines penalties for activities aimed at overthrowing the government. Under Vietnamese law, the maximum penalties for violations are life imprisonment or capital punishment. The two were both also accused of membership in the outlawed, exile-run Viet Tan party.

Dieu and Hoa were both being held at Hanoi's B14 Detention Center, according to Viet Tan.

IMPRISONED: AUGUST 3, 2011

## Paulus Le Van Son, freelance

Son, a blogger and contributor to the news websites *Vietnam Redemptorist News* and *Bao Khong Le* (Newspaper Without Lanes), was arrested in front of his home in the capital, Hanoi. News reports, citing an eyewitness, said police knocked him from his motorcycle to the ground, grabbed his arms and legs, and threw him into a waiting police vehicle.

He was detained on unspecified charges under Article 79 of the penal code, which outlines penalties for activities aimed at overthrowing the government. Under Vietnamese law, the maximum penalties for violations are life imprisonment or capital punishment. Son was also accused of membership in the outlawed, exile-run Viet Tan party.

*Vietnam Redemptorist News*, an online publication run by the Congregation of the Most Holy Redeemer, reports on the plight of the country's persecuted Catholic minority. *Bao Khong Le* focuses on issues such as corruption and sovereignty conflicts with China. In the months before his arrest, Son posted a number of sensitive entries to his own blog, addressing anti-China protests and territorial disputes with China.

Son had been briefly detained earlier, in April 2011, when he attempted to attend a court hearing for pro-democracy dissident Cu Huy Ha Vu. Son's personal blog covered sensitive political and social issues, including anti-China demonstrations, government harassment of prominent pro-democracy and Catholic Church activists, and violence in schools.

Son was being held at Hanoi's B14 Detention Center, according to news reports.

IMPRISONED: AUGUST 7, 2011

## Nguyen Van Duyet, freelance

Duyet, a contributor to the news website *Vietnam Redemptorist News* and president of the Association of Catholic Workers, was detained in Vinh city, Nghe An province. *Vietnam Redemptorist News*, an online publication run by the Congregation of the Most Holy Redeemer, reports on the plight of the country's persecuted Catholic minority.

He was detained under Article 79 of the penal code, which outlines penalties for activities aimed at overthrowing the government. Under Vietnamese law, the maximum penalties for violations are life imprisonment or capital punishment. Duyet was also accused of membership in the outlawed, exile-run Viet Tan party.

He was being held at Hanoi's B14 Detention Center, Viet Tan reported.

# Yemen: 2

IMPRISONED: AUGUST 16, 2010

## Abdulelah Hider Shaea, freelance

Shaea, a freelance journalist and a frequent commentator on Al-Jazeera, was sentenced in January 2011 to five years in prison for "belonging to an illegal armed organization" and "recruiting young people, including foreigners, to the organization by communicating with them via the Internet."

In February, after social unrest erupted in Yemen, President Ali Abdullah Saleh pardoned Shaea among other prisoners, according to local news reports. In a phone call to Saleh, however, U.S. President Barack Obama expressed concern that Shaea should not be released, according to a White House statement that did not elaborate on the reasons.

In a 2010 interview with CPJ, Shaea said that government interrogations had focused on his reporting and that agents had directed him to stop working on counterterrorism topics.

Shaea, known for his coverage of extremist groups such as Al-Qaeda, was critical of Yemen's counterterrorism policies. Using his tribal affiliation to gain access, he conducted several interviews with senior members of Al-Qaeda in the Arabian Peninsula. In December 2009, Shaea interviewed the U.S.-born militant Anwar Awlaki for ABC News. Awlaki was killed in a September 2011 U.S. drone attack.

IMPRISONED: OCTOBER 14, 2011

## Abd al-Karim Thail, *3feb*

Security forces arrested Thail, editor-in-chief of the news website *3feb*, as he was leaving his Sana'a home, according to the Yemeni Journalists Syndicate and local news reports. His brother, Bassam, and a friend, Hamir al-Muqbeeli, were detained with him, according to news accounts.

No charges had been disclosed in late year. The journalists syndicate said it formed a committee to monitor the cases of Thail and another detained journalist, Abdulelah Hider Shaea. The website *3feb* published news about the country's popular uprising. The site was only sporadically accessible in late year.

# CPJ International Press Freedom Awards

Since 1991, CPJ has honored journalists from around the world with its annual International Press Freedom Awards. Recipients have shown extraordinary courage in the face of great risk, standing up to tyrants and documenting events in dark corners of the world. Here are excerpts from the acceptance speeches given by the 2011 awardees in November. Our story on page 10 describes their work.

## Javier Arturo Valdez Cárdenas, Mexico

"I dedicate this award to the brave journalists, and to the children and youths who are living a slow death. I have preferred to give a face and a name to the victims, to create a portrait of this sad and desolate panorama, these leaps and bounds and shortcuts toward the apocalypse, instead of counting deaths and reducing them to numbers."

GETTY IMAGES

# Natalya Radina, Belarus

"All of Belarus today is a big prison. And this prison has continued to exist for 17 years, in part because of foreign indifference. Today we witness how dictatorships around the world are being toppled. We have the power to destroy the prison in the heart of Europe as well. Please do not forget about Belarus. My country's 10 million people are counting on you."

# Umar Cheema, Pakistan

"Like me, Pakistan is reinventing itself. The ongoing crises of various natures have altered the map of power centers. A vocal media, an assertive judiciary, and a vibrant civil society are harbingers of a promising Pakistan. The forces of repression hit back in frustration. We have lost many colleagues in a culture of impunity. Nevertheless, there is no let-up in our resilience."

GETTY IMAGES

# Mansoor al-Jamri, Bahrain

"It is a great honor for me to be with you here in New York to receive the International Press Freedom Award 2011, and while I am with you I am thinking of my country, which has joined the Arab Spring since the beginning of this year. But unlike other countries in the region, Bahrain is located in the oil-rich Gulf region, and what is happening in this small country proves the universality of human rights and democracy."

GETTY IMAGES

433

# International Press Freedom Award Recipients 1991-2010

**1991**
Byron Barrera, *La Época*, Guatemala
Bill Foley and Cary Vaughan, United States
Tatyana Mitkova, TSN, former Soviet Union
Pius Njawe, *Le Messager*, Cameroon
IMPRISONED:
Wang Juntao and Chen Ziming, *Economics Weekly*, China

**1992**
Muhammad al-Saqr, *Al-Qabas*, Kuwait
Sony Esteus, Radio Tropic FM, Haiti
David Kaplan, ABC News, United States
Gwendolyn Lister, *The Namibian*, Namibia
Thepchai Yong, *The Nation*, Thailand

**1993**
Omar Belhouchet, *El Watan*, Algeria
Nosa Igiebor, *Tell*, Nigeria
Veran Matic, Radio B92, Yugoslavia
Ricardo Uceda, *Sí*, Peru
IMPRISONED:
Doan Viet Hoat, *Freedom Forum*, Vietnam

**1994**
Iqbal Athas, *The Sunday Leader*, Sri Lanka
Daisy Li Yuet-wah, Hong Kong Journalists Association, Hong Kong
Aziz Nesin, *Aydinlik*, Turkey
In memory of staff journalists, *Navidi Vakhsh*, Tajikistan
IMPRISONED:
Yndamiro Restano, freelance, Cuba

**1995**
Veronica Guerin, *Sunday Independent*, Ireland
Yevgeny Kiselyov, NTV, Russia
Fred M'membe, *The Post*, Zambia
José Rubén Zamora Marroquín, *Siglo Veintiuno*, Guatemala
IMPRISONED:
Ahmad Taufik, Alliance of Independent Journalists, Indonesia

1996
J. Jesús Blancornelas, *Zeta*, Mexico
Yusuf Jameel, *Asian Age*, India
Daoud Kuttab, Internews Middle East, Palestinian Authority Territories
IMPRISONED:
Ocak Isik Yurtcu, *Ozgur Gundem*, Turkey

1997
Ying Chan, *Yazhou Zhoukan*, United States
Shieh Chung-liang, *Yazhou Zhoukan*, Taiwan
Victor Ivancic, *Feral Tribune*, Croatia
Yelena Masyuk, NTV, Russia
Freedom Neruda, *La Voie*, Ivory Coast
IMPRISONED:
Christine Anyanwu, *The Sunday Magazine*, Nigeria

1998
Grémah Boucar, Radio Anfani, Niger
Gustavo Gorriti, *La Prensa*, Panama
Goenawan Mohamad, *Tempo*, Indonesia
Pavel Sheremet, ORT, *Belorusskaya Delovaya Gazeta*, Belarus
IMPRISONED:
Ruth Simon, Agence France-Presse, Eritrea

1999
María Cristina Caballero, *Semana*, Colombia
Baton Haxhiu, *Koha Ditore*, Kosovo
Jugnu Mohsin and Najam Sethi, *The Friday Times*, Pakistan
IMPRISONED:
Jesús Joel Diáz Hernández, Cooperativa Avileña de Periodistas
    Independientes, Cuba

2000
Steven Gan, *Malaysiakini*, Malaysia
Zeljko Kopanja, *Nezavine Novine*, Bosnia-Herzegovina
Modeste Mutinga, *Le Potentiel*, Democratic Republic of Congo
IMPRISONED:
Mashallah Shamsolvaezin, *Asr-e-Azadegan* and *Neshat*, Iran

2001
Mazen Dana, Reuters, West Bank
Geoff Nyarota, *The Daily News*, Zimbabwe
Horacio Verbitsky, freelance, Argentina
IMPRISONED:
Jiang Weiping, *Qianshao*, China

2002
Ignacio Gómez, "Noticias Uno," Colombia
Irina Petrushova, *Respublika*, Kazakhstan
Tipu Sultan, freelance, Bangladesh
IMPRISONED:
Fesshaye Yohannes, *Setit*, Eritrea

2003
Abdul Samay Hamed, Afghanistan
Aboubakr Jamaï, *Le Journal Hebdomadaire* and *Assahifa al-Ousbouiya*,
    Morocco
Musa Muradov, *Groznensky Rabochy*, Russia
IMPRISONED:
Manuel Vázquez Portal, Grupo de Trabajo Decoro, Cuba

2004
Alexis Sinduhije, Radio Publique Africaine, Burundi
Svetlana Kalinkina, *Belorusskaya Delovaya Gazeta*, Belarus
In memory of Paul Klebnikov, *Forbes Russia*, Russia
IMPRISONED:
Aung Pwint and Thaung Tun, freelance, Burma

2005
Galima Bukharbaeva, Institute for War and Peace Reporting, Uzbekistan
Beatrice Mtetwa, media and human rights lawyer, Zimbabwe
Lúcio Flávio Pinto, *Jornal Pessoal*, Brazil
IMPRISONED:
Shi Tao, freelance, China

2006
Jamal Amer, *Al-Wasat*, Yemen
In memory of Atwar Bahjat, Al-Arabiya, Iraq
Madi Ceesay, *The Independent*, Gambia
Jesús Abad Colorado, freelance, Colombia

2007
Mazhar Abbas, ARY One World Television, Pakistan
Gao Qinrong, China
Dmitry Muratov, *Novaya Gazeta*, Russia
Adela Navarro Bello, *Zeta*, Mexico

2008
Bilal Hussein, The Associated Press, Iraq
Danish Karokhel and Farida Nekzad, Pajhwok Afghan News, Afghanistan

Andrew Mwenda, *The Independent*, Uganda
IMPRISONED:
Héctor Maseda Gutiérrez, Grupo de Trabajo Decoro, Cuba

2009
Mustafa Haji Abdinur, Radio Simba and Agence France-Presse, Somalia
Naziha Réjiba, *Kalima*, Tunisia
IMPRISONED:
Eynulla Fatullayev, *Realny Azerbaijan*, Azerbaijan
J.S. Tissainayagam, *OutreachSL* and the *Sunday Times*, Sri Lanka

2010
Nadira Isayeva, *Chernovik*, Russia
Dawit Kebede, *Awramba Times*, Ethiopia
Laureano Márquez, *Tal Cual*, Venezuela
IMPRISONED:
Mohammad Davari, *Saham News*, Iran

# CPJ Burton Benjamin Memorial Award

Since 1991, CPJ has given the Burton Benjamin Memorial Award to an individual in recognition of a lifetime of distinguished achievement in service of press freedom. The award honors Burton Benjamin, the CBS News senior producer and former CPJ chairman who died in 1988. In November 2011, CPJ honored Dan Rather. Here is an excerpt from his acceptance speech.

## Dan Rather, United States

"Tonight, if I can convince you of anything, it is to buck the current system. Remember anew that you are a public servant and your business is protecting the public from harm—even if those doing harm also pay your salary. To quote Ed Murrow, there is a great and perhaps decisive battle to be fought against ignorance, intolerance, and indifference. This weapon of television could be useful. And wouldn't it be great if our country could get used to that."

GETTY IMAGES

# Burton Benjamin Memorial Award Recipients 1991-2010

1991
Walter Cronkite
CBS News

1992
Katharine Graham
*The Washington Post* Company

1993
Ted Turner
CNN

1994
George Soros
Open Society Institute

1995
Benjamin C. Bradlee
*The Washington Post*

1996
Arthur Ochs Sulzberger
*The New York Times*

1997
Ted Koppel
ABC News

1998
Brian Lamb
C-SPAN

1999
Don Hewitt
CBS News

2000
Otis Chandler
Times Mirror Company

2001
Joseph Lelyveld
*The New York Times*

2002
Daniel Pearl
*The Wall Street Journal*

2003
John F. Burns
*The New York Times*

2004
John S. Carroll
*Los Angeles Times*

2005
Peter Jennings
ABC News

2006
Hodding Carter III

2007
Tom Brokaw
NBC News

2008
Beatrice Mtetwa

2009
Anthony Lewis

2010
Aryeh Neier
Open Society Institute

# CPJ at a Glance

## How did CPJ get started?

A group of U.S. foreign correspondents created CPJ in response to the often brutal treatment of their local colleagues by authoritarian governments and other enemies of independent journalism.

## Who runs CPJ?

CPJ has a staff of 27 at its New York headquarters, including area specialists for each major world region. CPJ has a San Francisco-based Internet advocacy coordinator, representatives in Europe, and consultants stationed around the world. A board of prominent journalists directs CPJ's activities.

## How is CPJ funded?

CPJ is funded solely by contributions from individuals, corporations, and foundations. CPJ does not accept government funding.

## Why is press freedom important?

Without a free press, few other human rights are attainable. A strong press freedom environment encourages the growth of a robust society, which leads to stable, sustainable democracies and healthy social, political, and economic development. CPJ works in more than 120 countries, many of which suffer under repressive regimes, debilitating civil war, or other problems that harm press freedom and democracy.

## How does CPJ protect journalists?

By publicly revealing abuses against the press and by acting on behalf of imprisoned and threatened journalists, CPJ effectively warns journalists and news organizations where attacks on press freedom are occurring.

CPJ organizes vigorous public protests and works through diplomatic channels to effect change. CPJ issues news alerts, protest letters, and in-depth special reports; publishes press freedom commentary daily on the CPJ Blog; and produces *Attacks on the Press*, a comprehensive annual survey of international press freedom.

## Where does CPJ get its information?

CPJ has full-time program coordinators monitoring the press in Africa, the Americas, Asia, Europe and Central Asia, and the Middle East and North Africa. It also has an Internet advocacy coordinator addressing threats to online expression. The coordinators track developments through their own independent research, fact-finding missions, and firsthand contacts in the field, including reports from other journalists. CPJ shares information on breaking cases with other press freedom organizations through the International Freedom of Expression Exchange, a global electronic network.

## When would a journalist call upon CPJ?

*In an emergency.* Using local and foreign contacts, CPJ intervenes whenever local and foreign correspondents are in trouble. CPJ notifies news organizations, government officials, and human rights organizations immediately of press freedom violations.

*When traveling on assignment.* CPJ advises journalists covering dangerous assignments.

*When covering the news.* Attacks against the press are news, and they often serve as the first signal of a crackdown on all freedoms. CPJ is uniquely situated to provide journalists with information and insight into press conditions around the world.

# How to Report an Attack on the Press

CPJ needs accurate, detailed information in order to document abuses of press freedom and help journalists in trouble. CPJ corroborates the information and takes appropriate action on behalf of the journalists and news organizations involved.

## What to report:

### Journalists who are:

- Arrested
- Assaulted
- Censored
- Denied credentials
- Harassed
- Kidnapped
- Killed
- Missing
- Threatened
- Wounded
- Wrongfully expelled
- Wrongfully sued for libel or defamation

### News organizations that are:

- Attacked, raided, or illegally searched
- Censored
- Closed by force
- Subject to confiscation of editions or jamming of transmissions
- Subject to vandalism or destruction
- Wrongfully sued for libel or defamation

# Contact information

Call collect if necessary.

## Africa:

(212) 465-9344, x117
Email: africa@cpj.org
Twitter: @africamedia_CPJ

## Americas:

(212) 465-9344, x120 and x146
E-mail: americas@cpj.org
Facebook: @cpjenespanol

## Asia:

(212) 465-9344, x140 and x115
Email: asia@cpj.org
Facebook: @cpjasia

## Europe and Central Asia:

(212) 465-9344, x101 and x106
Email: europe@cpj.org

## Middle East and North Africa:

(212) 465-9344, x103
Email: mideast@cpj.org
Facebook: @cpjinarabic

## Worldwide:

(212) 465-1004
Email: info@cpj.org
Twitter: @pressfreedom
Facebook: @committeetoprotectjournalists

# CPJ Staff

**EXECUTIVE DIRECTOR**
Joel Simon

**DEPUTY DIRECTOR**
Robert Mahoney

**EDITORIAL DIRECTOR**
Bill Sweeney

**DIRECTOR OF DEVELOPMENT AND OUTREACH**
John D. Weis

**ADVOCACY AND COMMUNICATIONS DIRECTOR**
Gypsy Guillén Kaiser

**DIRECTOR OF FINANCE AND ADMINISTRATION**
Lade Kadejo

**SENIOR PROGRAM OFFICER**
Kavita Menon

**SENIOR EDITOR**
Elana Beiser

**DEPUTY EDITOR FOR INNOVATION**
Kamal Singh Masuta

**DEPUTY EDITOR FOR NEWS**
Shazdeh Omari

**SENIOR ADVISER FOR JOURNALIST SECURITY**
Frank Smyth

ADVOCACY AND COMMUNICATIONS ASSOCIATE
Magnus Ag

COORDINATOR, IMPUNITY CAMPAIGN AND
JOURNALIST ASSISTANCE PROGRAM
María Salazar-Ferro

JOURNALIST ASSISTANCE PROGRAM ASSOCIATE
Sheryl A. Mendez

IMPUNITY CAMPAIGN CONSULTANT
Elisabeth Witchel

SENIOR EUROPEAN CONSULTANT
Jean-Paul Marthoz

EUROPEAN CONSULTANT
Borja Bergareche

EXECUTIVE ASSISTANT AND BOARD LIAISON
Gregory Fay

PROGRAM ASSISTANT
Alice Forbes Spear

## Advocacy Programs

AFRICA ADVOCACY COORDINATOR
Mohamed Keita

EAST AFRICA CONSULTANT
Tom Rhodes

AMERICAS SENIOR PROGRAM COORDINATOR
Carlos Lauría

AMERICAN RESEARCH ASSOCIATE
Sara Rafsky

MEXICO REPRESENTATIVE
Mike O'Connor

ANDES CORRESPONDENT
John Otis

ASIA PROGRAM COORDINATOR
Bob Dietz

ASIA SENIOR RESEARCH ASSOCIATE
Madeline Earp

SENIOR SOUTHEAST ASIA REPRESENTATIVE
Shawn W. Crispin

EAST ASIA AND INTERNET CONSULTANT
Sky Canaves

EUROPE AND CENTRAL ASIA PROGRAM COORDINATOR
Nina Ognianova

EUROPE AND CENTRAL ASIA RESEARCH ASSOCIATE
Muzaffar Suleymanov

MOSCOW CORRESPONDENT
Elena Milashina

INTERNET ADVOCACY COORDINATOR
Danny O'Brien

MIDDLE EAST AND NORTH AFRICA COORDINATOR
Mohamed Abdel Dayem

MIDDLE EAST AND NORTH AFRICA RESEARCH ASSOCIATE
Dahlia El-Zein

TURKEY CONSULTANT
Özgür Öğret

# Spotlight on Giving

The John S. and James L. Knight Foundation has been a long-time supporter of CPJ's work to defend individual journalists and uphold media freedom worldwide. Thanks to crucial assistance from the Knight Foundation, CPJ has built a Global Campaign Against Impunity to ensure that the killers of journalists do not get away with murder. CPJ research shows that more than 70 percent of journalists killed worldwide are targeted for assassination. Their killers are rarely brought to justice.

CPJ's Global Campaign Against Impunity is transforming the legal landscape and strengthening press freedom. In 2007, CPJ launched pilot projects to end impunity for journalist murders in Russia and the Philippines, two countries that have routinely allowed attacks against the press to go unchecked. Our advocacy has put the issue of impunity on the political agendas in both countries and drawn international attention to the crises.

CPJ began the next phase of the impunity project at our 2011 International Press Freedom Awards dinner, which brought together hundreds of prominent journalists and business leaders. We highlighted the progress we have made so far in the fight against impunity and announced a new challenge grant from the Knight Foundation to support innovative campaigning. CPJ announced that Knight, which has supported the impunity project since its inception, had offered to match, dollar-for-dollar, any additional funds raised at the dinner.

The impunity appeal, which was made by NBC News anchor Brian Williams, yielded nearly $90,000 in individual contributions, many from first-time donors. Knight Foundation President Alberto Ibargüen was so impressed by the response that he pledged on the spot to double the matching gift. CPJ will use these Knight funds, together with individual contributions, to raise the visibility of our campaign against impunity and experiment with social media tools to promote greater engagement. CPJ is grateful that the Knight Foundation has played such a significant role in shaping our legacy through contributions to core support, special projects, and endowment.

# Contributors

The Committee to Protect Journalists is extremely grateful to the foundations, corporations, and individuals whose generosity made our press freedom work possible. The following contributed $10,000 or more in 2011. A more complete list of CPJ supporters will be reproduced in our annual report.

Adessium Foundation
Advance Publications
Alcoa
Allen & Company
Franz and Marcia Allina
Christiane Amanpour
American Express Company
Americas Business Council Foundation
AOL Huffington Post Media Group
Argus Media Inc. / Petroleum Argus
The Associated Press
Barclays Capital
The Neil Barsky and Joan S. Davidson
   Foundation
Best Buy Co., Inc.
Mary Billard and Barry Cooper
Molly C. Bingham
The Morton K. & Jane Blaustein
   Foundation, Inc.
Bloomberg
Boies, Schiller & Flexner LLP
Katherine and David Bradley
Brunswick Group LLC
Carnegie Corporation of New York
CBS News
Connie Chung and Maury Povich
Citigroup
CNBC, Inc.

CNN
Columbia University
Comcast Corporation
Condé Nast Publications Inc.
Credit Suisse
Crowell & Moring LLP
Debevoise & Plimpton
Deluxe Entertainment
   Services Group
Disney-ABC Television Group
The Dow Chemical Company
Dow Jones Company
Dow Jones Foundation
ESPN
David Evans
*Financial Times*
Firebird Management LLC
Flora Family Foundation
The Ford Foundation
Ford Motor Company
Fox News
Gensler
Getty Images
The Goldhirsh Foundation
Goldman Sachs & Co.
Google, Inc.
Ian Hague
Sharon Held

HSBC Bank USA N.A.
Gwen Ifill
Larry Jinks
Joan & James Shapiro Foundation
John S. & James L. Knight
   Foundation
Michael Katz Foundation of the
   Jewish Communal Fund
Jonathan Klein
David and Esther Laventhol
The Leon Levy Foundation
Steve and Amy Lipin
Lippincott
MacAndrews and Forbes
   Holdings Inc.
Holly and John Madigan
The Marc Haas Foundation
Robert R. McCormick Foundation
Mediavest
Microsoft
Morgan Stanley
NBC News
NBCUniversal
The New York Times Company
*The New Yorker*
Samuel I. Newhouse Foundation Inc.
News Corporation
The Nielsen Company
The Oak Foundation
Omidyar Network Fund Inc.

Open Society Foundations
The Nicholas B. Ottaway
   Foundation
The Overbrook Foundation
Norman Pearlstine
Providence Equity Partners LLC
Prudential Financial
Dan and Jean Rather
RLM Finsbury
Diane Sawyer
Showtime
Harry Smith
Sony Corporation of America
St. Petersburg Times Fund
Paul E. Steiger
Structure Tone
The Thiel Foundation
Thomson Reuters
Time Inc.
Time Warner Inc.
Turner Broadcasting System, Inc.
UBS AG
Katrina van den Heuvel
Viacom
United Airlines
The Wall Street Journal
The Washington Post Company
Weil, Gotshal & Manges LLP
Brian Williams
Anonymous (3)

# In-Kind Contributions

CPJ's work is made possible in part through the in-kind services provided by the following organizations:

Agence France-Presse
The Associated Press
Bloomberg
Debevoise & Plimpton LLP

Factiva
Getty Images
NBCUniversal
Thomson Reuters

United Airlines is the preferred airline of the Committee to Protect Journalists.

# Index by Country

CPJ    Committee to Protect Journalists